S0-BNJ-556

32361

Eyewitness Accounts of the American Revolution

Memoirs of the American Revolution as Relating to the State of South Carolina

John Drayton

The New York Times & Arno Press

Reprinted from a copy in the
Columbia University Libraries

*

Copyright © 1969 by Arno Press, Inc.
All Rights Reserved

*

Library of Congress Catalog Card No. 77-76244

*

Manufactured in the United States of America

MEMOIRS

OF THE

AMERICAN REVOLUTION,

FAC ... TER ELYSIUM ... NOBIS

WILLIAM HENRY DRAYTON

Engraved by Wright & Smith.
Charleston SoCa

MEMOIRS

OF THE

AMERICAN REVOLUTION,

FROM ITS COMMENCEMENT TO THE YEAR 1776, INCLUSIVE;

AS RELATING TO

THE STATE OF SOUTH-CAROLINA:

AND OCCASIONALLY REFERING

TO THE STATES OF

NORTH-CAROLINA AND GEORGIA.

BY JOHN DRAYTON, L.L.D.

AUTHOR OF "A VIEW OF SOUTH-CAROLINA" AND A MEMBER OF THE ROYAL
SOCIETY OF SCIENCES OF GOTTINGEN.

———————————————— the Prince who intrigues with foreigners
against his People, does it, at the peril of his Crown.—*Dalrymple's Memoirs.*

———— revocate animos, moestumque timorem
Mittite: forsan et hæc olim meminisse juvabit.
Æn. I. v. 206, 207.

IN TWO VOLUMES.

VOL I.

CHARLESTON:
PRINTED BY A. E. MILLER, 120, BROAD-STREET.

1821.

District of South-Carolina, to wit:

✥◯◯◯◯✥
◯   ◯
◯ SEAL. ◯
◯   ◯
✥◯◯◯◯✥

BE IT REMEMBERED, that on the fifteenth day of May, Anno Domini, one thousand eight hundred and twenty-one, and in the forty-fifth year of the Independence of the United States of America, the Honorable John Drayton, District Judge of the United States of America for South-Carolina District, deposited in this office the title of a book, the right whereof he claims as author and proprietor, in the words following, to wit:

"Memoirs of the American Revolution, from its commencement to the year 1776, inclusive; as relating to the State of South-Carolina; and occasionally refering to the States of North-Carolina and Georgia. By John Drayton, L.L. D. Author of "A View of South-Carolina," and a Member of the Royal Society of Sciences of Gottingen. —— the Prince who intrigues with foreigners against his people, does it, at the peril of his crown.—*Dalrymple's Memoirs.* ——revocate animos, moestumque timorem Mittite: forsan et hæc olim meminisse juvabit. *Æn. I. v.* 206, 207. In two Volumes."

In conformity with the act of Congress of the United States, entitled "An act for the Encouragement of Learning, by securing the Copies of maps, charts, and books, to the authors and proprietors of such copies, during the times therein mentioned," and also to the act entitled "An act supplementary to an act, entitled, 'An act for the encouragement of learning, by securing the copies of maps, charts, and books, to the authors and proprietors of such copies, during the times therein mentioned,' and extending the benefits thereof to the arts of designing, engraving and etching historical and other prints."

JAMES JERVEY,
Clerk of the District of South-Carolina.

TO

THE HONORABLE, THE SENATE,

AND

THE HONORABLE THE HOUSE OF REPRESENTATIVES

OF

SOUTH-CAROLINA:

GENTLEMEN,

WHEN a Legislature so respectable, as that, of which you are the component parts, thought fit to encourage the publication of the following pages, and to extend towards them your beneficent patronage; I did not farther weigh the cost, or the responsibility: but immediately determined on placing the same, into the hands of the printer, with all possible dispatch. For, as they treat of matters intimately connected, with the liberties we enjoy, and the interests over which you preside: it became peculiarly obligatory on me, to present them to your consideration, at as early a moment, as opportunities would permit.

You will find therein, many revolutionary matters brought into view, which occasioned much anxiety at the periods when they happened; and, which a lapse of time had nearly obliterated from the tablets of memory. The patriots of those days, with one or two exceptions, have left the scenes of life, for happier destinies; but, their actions have thrown a radiance behind them, which will serve to direct the course of the Statesmen and the youth, who are ardent to tread in the honorable and useful steps of their progenitors. To many of you, Gentlemen, I would appeal, as to the truth of this assertion; in the exciting feelings you experience, when recollecting the virtues of your fathers or relations—whose names, adorn the pages of these Memoirs. And when you reflect, that when they are no more, you are obeying the calls of your country, and are urging your course in the same road to fame, along which they have passed—your breasts will warm, to deeds of honour and celebrity; and your actions will tend, towards your country's glory.

That you have already deserved the public approbation, your actions at your last and former Sessions will prove; by the many laws you have made, for the dissemination of knowledge—the establishment of schools throughout the State—the support and protection of your State College—the surveying the various districts of the State, and thence producing a beautiful and authentic map of the whole—the opening of internal navigation—the amelioration of the public roads, and the passes across the mountains—and the remunerations which you have given, to the war-worn soldier—and to the widow—and to the orphan: where their hus-

band's, their father's, or their relation's services, were freely given, and their blood was shed, for the liberty which is now enjoyed.

To a Legislature, which has done, and will continue to perform these exalted acts, I now beg leave, to present the product of my labours—to its patronage, I respectfully offer the Memoirs, which I have written. And, if having marked any periods in their proper character—or, having brought forward men, or measures, into public notice, that otherwise might have passed away unobserved and forgotten, I have employed my time for the public good —I shall flatter myself, it has been usefully employed, as I trust it ever has been, in supporting the honour and the independence, of my native country.

With profound respect,

Gentlemen,

I subscribe myself,

Your most obliged,

And grateful

Fellow-Citizen,

JOHN DRAYTON.

PREFACE.

———

W HEN my father, William Henry Drayton, died at Philadelphia in September 1779, he left many valuable papers in manuscript; some of them were original, but most of them were copies from Congressional documents, which during the year 1779 he had prepared, as necessary for a history of the American Revolution, in which, he was about to engage. The Gentleman (a member of Congress) who managed his affairs at Philadelphia after his decease, did not think it proper these papers should fall into the hands of his family; as containing, many secrets of State: and they were consequently destroyed. Some few, however, escaped this general ruin; accompanied by a book, in which Mr. Drayton had written several passages on various subjects, to be incorporated into his contemplated history, as they might apply; and these, came into my hands.

Beside these papers, when he departed from this State in March 1778, on his delegation to Congress, he left a manuscript in two volumes, written by himself; from the latter end of the year 1773, to near the close of that of 1776; as well grounded on his own knowledge of passing events, as of that derived from the many high and important official stations he filled, in a series of public services—also, a variety of original letters, among which were some, from the Earl of Dartmouth, one of the King of England's principal Secretaries of State, to the provincial Governors of North-Carolina, South-Carolina, and Georgia—and from Sir James Wright, Governor of Georgia, to General Gage, and Admiral Graves—Council of Safety's, and Secret Committee's papers—and other documents, supporting the narration in his manuscript—all of which, have remained in the possession of his family, unseen by any one.

As these books and papers contain matters relating to the early part of the American Revolution in the Southern Colonies of the Union, which have not been published in any histories hitherto written, I have been induced to submit them to the public, under the form of Memoirs; that being the only mode which would permit me to use my father's manuscripts and papers, with any satisfaction to myself. For his manuscript volumes, being written hastily as events occurred; were collections of facts, neither sufficiently digested for history, nor distributed into that order, which, had he lived, would have been done, before presentation to the public eye. They were besides, more calculated for a general history of the American Revolution; and were not sufficiently connected, to have appeared as proceeding from his pen. For these reasons, I determined they never should appear, but under my control, through my hands, and in my own language, except some parts which are in my father's words: being of opinion, that if I took on myself to give them publicity, I alone should be answerable for any faults of the composition. And I hope this explanation will be received, as an apology to those of my friends, who, placing a high value on original and authentic manuscripts, have wished I should publish them without alteration or defalcation; as thereby giving a better insight of the feelings and transactions of the times, to which they relate, than could be conveyed by any narration which was not contemporaneous. As to publishing them without alteration or defalcation, I could not allow myself to be the means of spreading before the public manuscripts written in haste; where many blanks occurred, which it was not in my power to supply, with the matter intended. And as to the narration not being contemporaneous, I was generally with my father, until the last year of his life; when I was placed at Princetown in the Jerseys, under the care of Dr. Witherspoon, then President of the College, and a Member of the Continental Congress: and although my youth cannot permit me to consider myself as contemporaneous— yet, during that time, I knew many of the characters who are mentioned in this work; and often attending my father on public occasions, I remember many things, which, otherwise, it could not be supposed, opportunities permitted me to know, or my youth to recollect: and I even entered into the public feelings, as to some of them. This will enable me to connect or explain, some parts of the narrative—to add to it, from the papers in my hands, which he had not used—and, to present a work, which I hope will be a tolerable picture of dangers, which have been overcome; and of times, which are past. From all these sources of information, I have entered on the arduous and delicate task, of writing these Memoirs; and in doing so, I consider my father's manuscripts, as the basis on which they rest; and the accompanying papers, as proving and illustrating the accounts which are related.

As I began this work with a determination, of stating nothing, but what I either knew, or believed, to be true; and as in so doing, I was conscious my relation would, in some cases, run counter to what had been published by others; I thought it adviseable to follow Sir John Dalrymple's mode of proving and illustrating the chapters, by immediately connecting with each one, the documents relating to the same: and I trust in being so engrafted into the work, they will, not only form one of its most valuable recommendations— but, will justify me in the views I have taken, of men and of measures. It has been my practice, not to trust to printed books; but to procure access to authentic manuscripts, or to papers printed by authority: and this I have done, where opportunities permitted—or, where individuals were willing to impart the information they possessed ; and I have generally quoted from the books or papers in my possession. I have found myself under difficulties, in writing the eighteenth chapter of these Memoirs ; as the manuscripts which had been my guide, did not treat of the matters contained therein ; and, as the Journals of the Privy Council for the year 1776, have not aided me ; although many and particular inquiries have been made for the same. both at public offices, and of the heirs of John Rutledge, and of Rawlins Lowndes, both of whom were at the head of affairs during the early part of our revolution : the first, with the title of President and Commander in Chief—and the latter, with that of Governor and Commander in Chief. I had, however, a few papers, which with other assistances, enabled me to write the same. And among the latter, I cannot forbear mentioning the name of John S. Cogdell, late Comptroller-General of this State : to whose friendly and particular researches in the office of the Clerk of the House of Representatives at Columbia, I am indebted, for the only account I have been able to give, of the authority, by which, the Great Seal of this State, was contrived and made.

I am also indebted, to Col. Thomas Roper, for the votes of Assembly, printed by the order of that House, respecting the transactions of our first American Congress, which took place at New-York in October 1765 ; and for those printed by its order, after the Stamp-Act had been passed by the King and Parliament of Great Britain.

To Col. Daniel Stevens, for the account which I have given of the proceedings of the people, after the stamped paper, had arrived in the port of Charlestown.

To John Champneys, for the manuscript Journals of the Commons-House of Assembly of this then province, from the 2d day of August 1774, to the 15th day of September 1775, inclusive.

To Thomas Winstanley, for the manuscript Journals of the Provincial Council, for the years 1774, and 1775.

To Elias Horry, Intendant of Charleston, for the Printed Extracts of the Provincial Congress of South-Carolina, for the year 1776.

To Benjamin Elliott, for the Orderly Book of Barnard Elliott, while he was Captain in the second regiment of Infantry, and Major in the regiment of Artillery.

To James Nicholson, for Captain Mason's Orderly Book, while he was in the second regiment of Infantry.

And to various other gentlemen, who were so polite as to aid me, with information they possessed, or with papers, of public authority ; among whom, the liberal assistance of Patrick Duncan entitles him to particular thanks.

b

The portrait at the beginning of this book, is engraved from an engraving done in France, of a picture drawn in India ink by Mons. De Simitiere at Philadelphia, about the latter end of the year 1778, or the beginning of the year 1779; which, with many other likenesses by the same artist, of Members of Congress, and public officers, were sent to Europe to be engraved; and after the peace of 1783, many of these engravings were exported to the United States for sale.

The Sullivan's Island Map, and plan of the Fort thereon, was made, partly from one drawn by Lieut. Col. James, of the Royal Regiment of Artillery; who was the British Engineer on board of the Thunder Bomb vessel, which discharged the shells against the fort on the 28th of June; and partly, with the assistance of Captains Richard Bohun Baker, and Henry Gray, who were Lieutenants in the second regiment of Infantry, and assisted in fighting the cannon of the fort at Sullivan's Island, on the said 28th day of June.

The Map respecting Colonel Williamson's expedition against the Cherokees, was made from a manuscript draft of the same, found among my father's papers; and which was corrected, by refering to the maps of Melish's Military Atlas: and that part of it, which is within the bounds of South-Carolina, containing almost the whole of Pendleton District, and a small part of Greeneville District, was drawn and corrected, by reference to the late boundary map between South-Carolina and North-Carolina, in the Secretary's office; and to the map of Pendleton District, in the possession of Major Wilson, Engineer of this State.

The Map respecting Ninety-Six Court-House and Gaol, and the encampments connected therewith, was made from the District Maps of Abbeville and Edgefield in the hands of Major Wilson; the Court-House, Gaol, Spring and encampments, were located agreeably to the manuscript of William Henry Drayton, aided by surveys caused to be made by Mr. James Nicholson for that purpose.

I have been told by some, that although the persons whose names are mentioned in the following pages, be generally dead; yet, every thing said of them therein, may not be agreeable to their descendants; and therefore, as few names as possible, should be brought into public view. In this, I am sensible I tread on tender ground; as every writer must do, who treats of parties, and of revolutions; and, objections made on this ground, are the prices which we must all pay, for the liberty we now enjoy. Yet, I trust I shall stand excused to the public, and to the many descendants of honorable men, who now hold, and enjoy the confidence of their fellow citizens, both in private and in public life, when they consider, that if I have treated of their ancestors, I have also done so of mine—and in both cases, I have given to the best of my power and opportunities, a faithful relation of their translations, from British subjects, to American citizens—so, as to introduce them to the knowledge of men, from the first commencement of opposition, to that vigorous conduct, which, casting a radiance around them, rewarded them with the admiration of their fellow citizens, and with high offices of honour and confidence. To have suppressed their names, would have been to have suppressed a course of anxious and arduous services, which entitled them to the thanks of a grateful people. Besides, I professed to treat of particulars; and I could not give just ideas of the public opinion, during the various stages of the American Revolution, or, of oppositions arising in our public councils, unless the names of those leaders who took part therein were mentioned. It is their names, as men of standing in society, and in whom the people trusted, that stamp authenticity and value on the accounts of those periods—it is for that purpose, they have been introduced; and, I hope in having done so, it has been done respectfully. As to those, who took active and prominent parts, in support of the British Administration in opposition to the American Revolution, their names have already been given to the public, by public authority, and by writers, in terms suitable to their conduct. And when their actions are treated of, I have done nothing more, than the Memoirs required; and to which, they had subjected themselves, by the parts which they took in favour of Royalty and taxation, against Republicanism and liberty. Yet, in these cases, I hope I have done it discreetly; and I trust it may be so received, among their descendants; many of whom, are now respectable members of the community, enjoying the public confidence—and being ready with their lives and fortunes, to defend American liberty, and our happy constitution.

It has been suggested to me by others, the work would be unnecessarily increased, by speaking of local matters; of themselves little important, as tending to American independence. From persons, who are more ready to object to the actions of others, than to bring forth any labours or merits of their own, this might have a discouraging effect; as supposing, it might be the opinion of the community. But, I believe the public opinion to be too liberal, to entertain ideas of this kind; or, to wish, that authentic information should be withholden, which the want of papers, and documents, has hitherto, kept from publicity. Besides, occurrences, however trivial, are interesting to the inhabitants of those parts of the State, where they happened; they are also, connected with characters; and in spreading them to public view, we promote the best ends of history—the knowledge of men—and the knowledge of measures.

Under such impressions, I have written these Memoirs; hoping thereby, to arrest from oblivion matters connected with the American Revolution, and of importance to this State; which otherwise, would have been totally lost. And if in doing so, I have met the public expectation; or, have in any manner answered the object of their wishes; I shall consider myself happy in having undertaken the task: which, the protection of Providence, and the assistance of my friends, have enabled me in such manner to perform. On the 14th of August 1819, I commenced writing the Memoirs; but was frequently interrupted by the official duties I had to fulfil, and the various calls otherwise made upon my time. Notwithstanding which, seventeen chapters were completed in 1820; and the work was put to the press on the 5th of February 1821: the same being written and copied over in my own hand writing, during that time.

In presenting it thus hastily composed, I fear it is offered, labouring under some errors, and many imperfections; but I trust to the liberality of a generous public, and an impartial criticism: which, while they notice faults with tenderness, will duly appreciate the motive which led to the publication—that of gleaning a few flowers, remaining after a rich harvest; which may assist in embellishing the memories of our Statesmen—or, be added to that garland of honour, which is already placed on the altar of American Liberty.

THE AUTHOR.

South-Carolina, Charleston, July 21st, 1821.

BIOGRAPHICAL SKETCH

OF

WILLIAM HENRY DRAYTON.

———

WILLIAM HENRY DRAYTON was born in South-Carolina, at Drayton-Hall on Ashley River, in September 1742. He was the eldest son of John Drayton, whose father Thomas Drayton was a descendant of the Drayton family of Northamptonshire in England; and who came to South-Carolina, from the Island of Barbadoes, in the year 1671, with Sir John Yeamans and others.

When William Henry Drayton had arrived at the age of eleven years, his father sent him to England in the year 1753, under the care of Charles Pinckney; who, having resigned the office of Chief Justice of the Province, was then going to England with his family: among whom were his two sons, Charles Cotesworth Pinckney, and Thomas Pinckney. With the guidance and protection of this very respectable gentleman, he prosecuted his education at Westminster School in London, until the autumn of 1761; when he was removed to the University of Oxford where, he matriculated on the 10th day of October in Balliol College. He there continued his studies, for near three years; when the call of a parent obliged him to leave his collegiate duties, and to return to Carolina. He did not, however, discontinue the improvements of his mind; but entered upon a course of reading, with great industry; and thereby became well informed in the English, an-

cient and modern histories, the Laws of Nations, and the rights
of his own country. His father being a gentleman of large estate,
and he the eldest son, he had not been brought up to any profession; but his ardent mind, would not permit him to move in a
common sphere: and he therefore turned his attention to law and
politics. In the year 1764, he married Miss Golightly, a young
lady of independent estate; by whom he had two children; a
daughter, and John, the author of this biographical sketch, and
of the following Memoirs.

The proceedings in North America, flowing from British Acts of
Parliament, did not allow Mr. Drayton to continue in domestic
repose; for in the year 1769, under the signature of *Freeman*, he
wrote against the mode of enforcing associations, which he deemed
encroachments on his private rights of freedom. This, involved
him in a political controversy; in which, he and William Wragg,
were opposed by Christopher Gadsden and John M'Kinzie. After
this, he returned to Europe, when, he was introduced at the British
Court of George III; and was noticed by Lord Sandwich and
others of the British nobility. Soon after, he received from
George III, King of Great Britain, on the 27th day of February
1771, an appointment of Privy Counsellor for the Province of
South-Carolina; and on his return to Carolina, he took his seat as
a member of that Council, in Charlestown, on the 3d day of April
1772.

In performing the duties of that station, and in defence of his
country's claims, he frequently was in opposition to the Crown
Officers and Judges, who were members of the Council; and, by
protests which he entered on the Journals against their proceedings, was, with others, the cause of laws passing therein in behalf
of the province, which, otherwise, would have been negatived.
Hence, animosities arose against him at the Council-Board; and
he was watched with a jealous eye, as weakening the pretensions
of the King, and the views of the British Administration. His
standing and abilities at the Board, were nevertheless such, that on
the decease of Judge Murray, he was appointed on the 25th day
of January 1774, by Lieutenant-Governor Bull, an Assistant-Judge
of the province, until his Majesty's pleasure should be known
thereon. In performing the duties of this office, with independ-

ence and zeal, he incurred the ill-will of the Chief Justice and
some of the Assistant-Judges, who had been sent over from England. And the Continental Congress being about to sit at Philadelphia in this year, he wrote and published a pamphlet under his
signature of *Freeman*, which he addressed *To the Deputies of North
America, assembled in the High Court of Congress at Philadelphia.*
" In this, he stated the grievances of America, and drew up a Bill
of American Rights. This, was well received. It substantially
chalked out the line of conduct adopted by Congress, then in session."* It, however, brought upon him an attack from the Chief
Justice and one of the Assistant-Judges, in the Council; by which
the Lieutenant-Governor was obliged to supercede Mr. Drayton,
on the 9th day of December 1774. His public endeavours in behalf of his native country, were not checked by this act of power;
on the contrary, they increased so much, that the Council, some
months after, addressed the Lieutenant-Governor to suspend him
from being a member of his Majesty's Council; and he consequently was suspended by his uncle, Lieutenant-Governor Bull, on
the 1st day of March 1775. The suspension instead of injuring
him, in the opinion of his fellow-citizens, drew towards him their
affection and support; and from that time, he possessed their confidence in a great degree.

When the Council of Safety was originated in 1775, he was
elected one of its members; and he continued being one of that
Board, while that Council existed. He was also appointed Chairman of the Secret Committee of five members; in which capacity
he much promoted the seizure of the provincial arsenal and powder magazines; as well as the seizure of the mail, which had just
arrived in one of the King's Packets from England. He was
elected a member of the Provincial Congress of South-Carolina,
which sat in January 1775; and in the course of that year, was
advanced to the Presidency thereof: continuing in that station,
while the Provincial Congress existed. And in this character, he
issued on the 9th of November 1775, the order from the Provincial
Congress to the garrison at Fort Johnson, to oppose the British
navy. He was, at different times, appointed on important commissions and deputations to the neighboring colonies; and was

---

* Ramsay's History of South-Carolina, published in 1809, vol. 2d, p. 445.

also sent among the disaffected people of the interior, with high
trusts and powers: all of which, he executed with honour to himself, and for the most part, with benefit to his country.

At length, on the formation of a temporary Constitution for
South-Carolina, in March 1776, Mr. Drayton was elected Chief
Justice of the colony; and immediately after, he was chosen one
of the Privy Council: thereby, being more than reinstated in
honour and station, to corresponding offices of State, with those
from which he had been superceded and suspended. The government being soon organized under this Constitution, the Courts
which had been closed for some time, were opened in a solemn
and impressive manner; when on the 23d day of April 1776, in
the presence of the Associate-Justices, he delivered in Court a
Charge to the Grand Jury, replete with patriotism, reasoning, and
learning. He therein expounded to them, the Constitution of the
country, as established by the Provincial Congress on the 26th of
March 1776—he laid before them, the causes of that important
change of our government—compared them, with those which
occasioned the English Revolution of 1688—stated the law resulting from the injuries in each case—and spoke of the late revolution
in South-Carolina: and he declared, that " From such a result of
injuries, from such a conjuncture of circumstances—the law of the
land authorizes me to declare, and it is my duty boldly to declare
the law, that George III, King of Great Britain, has abdicated the
government, and that the throne is thereby vacant: that is, *he has
no authority over us, and we owe no obedience to him.* The British
Ministers, already have presented a Charge of mine to the notice
of the Lords and Commons in parliament; and I am nothing loath
that they take equal resentment against this Charge. For, supported by the fundamental laws of the Constitution; and engaged
as I am in the cause of virtue—I fear no consequences from their
machinations."*

While employed in public duties, he never ceased watching
passing affairs; and whenever he supposed the public weal would

* See 5th page of the Charge, printed in a quarto pamphlet, in the year 1776,
in Charlestown, South-Carolina. Also the London Remembrancer for 1776,
Part II. page 321—330.

be benefited by his writings, he never failed to come forward with them in an able and decided manner. Under such impressions, the Declaration of Lord and General Howe, published at New-York on the 19th of September 1776, as Commissioners for restoring peace to his Majesty's Colonies and Plantations in North America, &c. &c. could not escape his notice : and under the signature of *A Carolinian*, he on the 22d October 1776, answered their Declaration, in a small pamphlet. In this, he pointed out the mischiefs of their proposals, and detected the sophistry of their reasonings. Your Excellencies " *think fit to declare*." (said he,) that you are desirous " of restoring the public tranquillity"— but, is the end you Excellencies aim at, our honour and advantage ? Is it to give a free scope to our natural growth? No! It is to cover us with infamy It is, to chill the sap, and check the luxuriance of our imperial plant. It is, to deprive us of our natural equality with the rest of mankind, by " *establishing*" every State, " *as a part of the British Empire*." In short, your Excellencies invite men of common sense, to exchange an independent station, for a servile and dangerous dependence !

And so, your Excellencies, beside your military commands as Admiral and General, are also, *Commissioners* for *restoring peace*. Is there not some error in the title ? Ought we not instead of ' *peace*' to read *tyranny?* You seem armed at all points for the purpose ; and your very language detects the latent design. But, you are Commissioners; and for the important purpose of " restoring peace," you are honoured with a power—" *to confer :*" and you have condescended to be *mere machines*, through which, as through speaking trumpets, words are to be sounded from America to Britain ! *How much lower is it possible for your Excellencies to degrade yourselves, in the eyes of the world !* " His country, pleased with his zeal and talents, heaped offices upon him."*

On the 15th of October 1776, Mr. Drayton as Chief Justice, attended by the Associate-Justices, again addressed the Grand Jury of Charlestown District. In this Charge, he treated of the

* Ramsay's Hist. of So. Carolina, published in 1809, vol. 2d, page 456.

Rise of the American Empire; and of the conduct which the Grand Jury ought to pursue, for aiding its establishment.*

From this time, Mr. Drayton continued to perform the duties of the various public stations in which he was placed, until the 21st day of October 1777; when, in the presence of the Associate-Justices, he again delivered a lengthy Charge to the Grand Jury, for Charlestown District; part of which, was of a political nature. In this Charge, he treated of the situation of affairs—of the short enlistments, which paralized the operations of the American army† —of Washington, a name which needs no title to adorn it; as being a freeman, above all praise—of his retreat before a superior enemy, through the Jerseys; and his causing the Delaware to bound the enemy's advance—of his summoning General Lee with the corps under his command, to join him; his disobedience thereto, and capture—of Washington's victory at Trenton—of the campaigns of 1776, and 1777. He then turned his attention to the situation of South-Carolina, where the public vigour, was not what it had been; and endeavoured to rouse the public mind, to prepare for the invasions they had a right to expect. We, were the first, he said, in America, who publicly pronounced Lord North's conciliatory motion inadmissible. We, raised the first regular forces on the continent, and for a term of three years. We, first declared the cause of taking up arms. We, originated

---

* This Charge is published at length in the London Remembrancer for 1777, p. 327—342. It was also published in a pamphlet, in Charlestown, So. Ca. in 1766.

"When the Congress began to consider of a Continental army, they were for leaving the army in Massachusetts, as belonging to that Colony, which they were willing to pay—and besides, to raise a Continental one. But the N Delegates said, this army has stood the brunt—you are willing to pay them—why deprive them of rank? Well, they were made continentals. The regulations came on next; the British, were proposed. No, said they, they have signed other articles; and will you impose others upon them? And, this was yielded. The term, was next; the six months the New-Englanders has enlisted for, was thought too short: no, said they, the war will be over in that time—besides, will you make these men serve longer, than they have agreed for? Well, then, they were answered, rescind the resolve for making them continentals. No. And thus it was, that the ruinous policy of short enlistments obtained.— *This from J. Rutledge.*" ☞ *This note, is copied from William Henry Drayton's Manuscript Book.*

the Councils of Safety. We, were among the first, who led the way to independence, by establishing a Constitution of Government. We, were the first, who made a law authorizing the capture of *British* vessels, without distinction. We, alone, *have defeated a British fleet.* We, alone, *have victoriously pierced through and reduced,* a powerful nation of *Indians;* who, urged by *Britain,* had attacked the United States: but, such proceedings, unless supported with propriety, would cover us with infamy. He therefore urged his countrymen, not to trifle with unexampled opportunities, not to be recalled. He said, how many of youth, strength, activity, fortune, learning, sense, and other blessings, had only shown their attachment to America by a momentary vigour, to mark their inconstancy—scrutinizing the conduct of others—good wishes, and inquiring the news of the day? Such men, would be sensible of a disgraceful inferiority, when they heard those American names which the trump of fame now sounds through the world; a blast, that will reach the ears of the latest posterity. To a rich planter he would say, if you will send 20, 30, or 40 labourers to the public works, and *for whom you shall be paid,* you will do an essential service, in a critical time. To another, if you will diligently overlook and push on, the construction of such a battery, or line, you will merit the thanks, of your fellow-citizens. To a third, if instead of hunting, you will ride about your neighbourhood, or a little beyond, and endeavour to instruct those who are ignorant of the importance of the public contest—reclaim the deluded—animate the timid—rouse the languid—and raise a spirit of emulation who shall exert himself most, in the cause of freedom and America; you will deserve the applause of the continent. It was necessary, he said, to speak with boldness, and plainness. In a time like this, language should be as thunder; not as music of the spheres—and, that he should discourse to Grand Jurors of other things, beside their mere duties in a Court of Justice. Hence, on other occasions, he had reasoned on the propriety of our revolution in March 1776—on the legal necessity of American independence—and now, on the situation of affairs. " I do most earnestly recommend, that you urge these topics, when you blend yourselves again among your neighbours. In every station that I have had the honour to fill, *I have counselled the most decisive measures; nor, have I been sparing of my personal assistance, in their execution.* The public service requires an unwearied application, unabating vigour, and a readiness to make the greatest sacrifices   I firmly trust, that we shall act as *men;* and that posterity will have no just cause, to reproach our conduct."*

After this, the Vice-President of the State being absent from Charlestown, and the President being about to leave it for a time, he invested Mr. Drayton with the powers of President during his and the Vice-President's absence from the town, by letters patent under his hand and seal at arms, bearing date the 20th December 1777 : thereby, conferring upon him a trust, which could only be reposed in a tried, and confidential citizen. This power, was vested in the President by the second ordinance passed by the General Assembly of the State, at its first session in April 1776; and the letters patent, were in the following words :

"The Hon. Wm. Henry Drayton, Esq. is hereby invested with the powers of President of this State, during my and the Vice-President's absence from Charlestown; pursuant to the authority given to me, by an ordinance of the General Assembly, in such case made and provided. Witness my hand and seal, at Charlestown, So. Carolina, this 20th December 1777.

" J. RUTLEDGE. (L. s.)"

Early in 1778, Mr. Drayton was elected by the General Assembly of South-Carolina, a Delegate to the Continental Congress; to which he repaired at York-Town in Pennsylvania, in the latter end of March. And he thereby had the honour of taking an active part in the deliberations of that body, against the conciliatory bills of parliament, which had been sent across the Atlantic to Lord and General Howe; and were forthwith transmitted to Congress at York-Town. When they were received, Congress was uninformed of the treaty of alliance between France and America;† but the history of that time declares, with what magnanimity they acted, in repelling the professions contained in those bills; and, in rousing all America, to prepare for resistance. These

---

* See the political part of this Charge, as published in a small octavo pamphlet at Charlestown, So. Carolina, in October 1777.

† Ramsay's United States, vol. II. p. 246.

conciliatory bills, having been passed into acts by the King and Parliament of Great Britain, the Earl of Carlisle, William Eden, and George Johnstone, Esquires, were appointed by the British government, to open a negociation on the subject; and they repaired to Philadelphia, then in the possession of the British troops, for that purpose. They requested General Washington, who then lay at Valley-Forge, on the western side of the River Schuylkill, fifteen miles from Philadelphia, with the American army, to furnish a passport for their Secretary, Doctor Ferguson, with a letter from them to Congress; but this was refused. They then forwarded in the usual channel of communication, a letter addressed " To his Excellency Henry Laurens, the President, and other the Members of Congress;" in which they communicated a copy of their commission, and of the acts of parliament on which it was founded: and they offered to concur in certain arrangements therein contained. Congress gave a decided negative to all their propositions; answering them to that effect, through their President. Mr. Laurens.* Beside this official communication of the Commissioners, Mr. Johnstone, one of them, wrote private letters to Henry Laurens, Joseph Reed, and others; thereby endeavouring to obtain by private correspondence, what had been publicly refused. Congress could not, consistently with national honour, enter into any discussion on these matters; but " some individuals of their body, ably proved the propriety of rejecting them. Among these, Gouverneur Morris, and William Henry Drayton, with great force of argument, and poignancy of wit, justified the decisive measures adopted by their countrymen."† After this, the Continental Congress returned to Philadelphia; when Mr. Drayton put forth, on the 4th September 1778, another publication against the Commissioners, full of argument, ridicule, and point.‡ " This is supposed to be the last offering made by his pen, in favour of America. He was a statesman of great decision and energy—and one of the ablest political writers, Carolina has produced."§

* Ramsay's United States, vol. II. p. 248, 249.

† Ibid. p. 250. Also, the London Remembrancer for 1778, p. 306—310, in which Mr. Drayton's address to the British Commissioners is published at length.

‡ See London Remembrancer for 1778, 1779, p. 55—64.

§ Ramsay's Hist. of So. Carolina, published in 1809, vol. II. p. 456.

During this time, he was sent by Congress on important missions as member of a Committee : one of these was, to General Washington at Valley Forge—the other was, to meet the French Minister, on his arrival in the Delaware River.   The Committee on this last occasion, was composed of Mr. Hancock, Mr. Drayton, and Mr. Duer; who were selected by Congress, for the especial purpose of proceeding to Chester on the Delaware River, to receive Monsieur Gerard, the first Minister Plenipotentiary, whom Louis XVI. King of France sent over to the United States of America.   They accordingly proceeded to that town, on the 12th July 1778; with empty carriages, and a military escort: and returned with his Excellency and suite that day, to Philadelphia; greeted by the salutes of the military, and the applauses of the people.*

* " The Count D'Estaign with his fleet from Toulon, anchored in Delaware Bay, on the 8th of July 1778; having that day driven on shore near Cape Henlopen, the British frigate Mermaid of 28 guns: and finding the enemy had quitted the bay, on the 9th, he sailed in pursuit of them to Sandy-Hook, having taken pilots on board for that purpose.   When the Count sailed from the Bay of Delaware, *La Chimere*, a thirty gun frigate, 12-pounders, with Mons. Gerard on board, sailed up the river, and anchored off Chester; Mr. Hancock, Mr. Drayton, and Mr. Duer, as a committee of Congress, waited on him there, on the 12th July.   They were conveyed on board the frigate, in her barge ; the crew being dressed in a scarlet uniform, with silver lace.   In passing to the frigate, she saluted them with fifteen guns ; and on coming alongside, with three cheers ; the Ambassador, Captain, and other officers, standing at the head of the gangway to receive the Committee, upon their coming on board.   And then passing along the quarter deck to the cabin, they were saluted by the marines, who were drawn up on the occasion.   The Ambassador and the Committee then debarked, under the same salutes; and sat off for Philadelphia, in a coach and four, followed by two post chariots and four; escorted by a party of light-horse.†   They arrived at the head-quarters in the city, about 2 o'clock; where apartments had been provided for the Ambassador: and were received by a battalion under arms, and a salute of fifteen cannon."

† Count Pulaski's.

☞ The above note is taken from my father William Henry Drayton's manuscript book, which he wrote at Philadelphia.   The head-quarters, to which he alludes, were those of General Arnold, on the right side of Market-street, as one passes down to the Delaware River; he, was then military commandant, of Philadelphia.   On this occasion, General Arnold gave the Ambassador and Committee of Congress, a public dinner; attended by a band of military music.   Having gone with my father and the Committee to Chester,

Major General Charles Lee's conduct at the battle of Mon-mouth on the 28th of June 1778, having caused him to be sus-pended from command, by the sentence of a General Court-Mar-tial; and that having been confirmed by the Continental Congress after deliberations, in which Mr. Drayton took a decided part against General Lee; General Lee's mind became much embit-tered against him : and he poured forth his resentments in offen-sive terms, to such members of Congress, as gave him a hearing. Of these conversations, Gouverneur Morris, and Mr. Hutson, two particular friends of Mr. Drayton, gave him notice. Upon which Mr. Drayton wrote to General Lee, stating, that if in his Charge to the Grand Jury at Charlestown, in 1777,* he had misrepre-sented General Lee's conduct immediately preceding his captivity by the enemy, and he had injured General Lee's reputation, and he could be satisfied he had done so—those principles of honour which must make General Lee feel an injury, made him feel even an idea of having done an injury—and impelled him to make reparation, where it was due. This, brought on a correspondence in February 1779, between these two gentlemen, which finally ended in a challenge from General Lee, on the 23d March 1779, through Colonel Oswald; but which Mr. Drayton, through the same conveyance, declined accepting : giving in writing as reasons for so doing, that although custom had sanctioned duelling with the military, it had not done so with the judiciary—and, that such a conduct in a Chief Justice of South-Carolina, as he was, would, in the eyes of the world, appear as a public outrage on government, society, and common decency; and therefore, he could not con-ceive, that he could with the least propriety accept General Lee's *"cordial"* invitation, to meet him, *"armed with pistols and sword."*

and also returned with them, I partook of this dinner. I recollect the occur-rences perfectly, as stated in my father's manuscript; being then a boy, of eleven years of age.   *The Author.*

* That part of the Charge, which related to this matter, was in the following words: " Washington caused the Delaware to bound the enemy's advance. He summoned General Lee with the corps under his command to join him. That veteran disobeying his repeated orders, for which, I presume, rigid inquisition is yet to be made—*loitering*, when he should have *bounded* forwards—he allowed himself to be surprized, and made prisoner (Dec. 13) at a distance from his troops. Washington, in the abyss of his distress, seemed to be abandoned, by his officer next in command."

That in the situation of life, in which he was then placed, he should not sacrifice his public reputation, and outrage his public character, merely to gratify General Lee, in the line of his (General Lee's) profession. That he was charged by the State of South-Carolina, with affairs of high concern; and is sensible, it would but ill accord with his duty to his own reputation, to his constituents in particular, and to the public at large, to enter into a private duel with General Lee: even, if such a conduct by him, would not have thrown disgrace upon Congress; of which body, he was a member. That being under no obligation to do so, he yet assured him, that his first letter to him (General Lee) was written with the most honorable intentions, respecting him; which he was concerned to find, have been entirely misconceived. That he is under no apprehension his conduct, in the present case, would be imputed to a dishonorable principle; because, upon every occasion, he would be found, to possess the manners of a gentleman.

After this, although Mr. Drayton had declined the duel, he did not in the least shrink from any rencontre in the streets of Philadelphia, with General Lee; but walked regularly to Congress, and about the city for many days; armed with his small sword, one of the weapons, which General Lee had designated. But the General did not think proper to meet him in this way—although in his challenge, he wrote Mr. Drayton the quarrel was " *inexpiable.*"

This difference with General Lee is of too trivial a nature, to have been brought into view on the present occasion, had it not been supposed, that to have omitted it, would have been ascribed to some principle, at variance with impartiality. But, as for that reason, it is deemed proper not to omit it; for a better reason, the Author of these Memoirs avails himself of this opportunity to state the above correspondence; which he can always support, from General Lee's own letters and notes to Mr. Drayton, in his possession. And he also thinks it his duty to say, that General Lee's letter of March 15th, 1779, to Mr. Drayton, and which is published in the Memoirs relating to General Lee; although presented to Mr. Drayton by one of General Lee's aids de camp, was never opened or read by him; but was returned to the aid de camp; who said, he did not know what it contained: so, that the scurrility thrown upon Mr. Drayton in that letter, and which the editor of the said Memoirs has given to the world, was lost on that occasion. But still, it is not the said editor's fault, if unfavorable impressions against Mr. Drayton, may not have arisen on the publication of this letter, in his Memoirs—while he ought to have been ashamed, to have suppressed General Lee's challenge afterwards on the 23d March 1779, delivered by Colonel Oswald, and Mr. Drayton's reply in writing of the same date, returned to General Lee, by the same conveyance; which would have afforded a very different inference, than what the editor of those Memoirs has been pleased to draw on the occasion. One thing more, and then both General Lee's affairs, and his admiring editor, shall be left to the opinions which they respectively merit. A part *only*, of the correspondence between Mr. Drayton and General Lee, has been published in the said Memoirs; the rest has been suppressed: for reasons best known to those, who were concerned in such a garbling transaction. And a very unwarrantable liberty has been taken in this dispute between two individuals, to omit, alter, and polish, parts of General Lee's letters to Mr. Drayton; which, otherwise, would not have shown him off in so remarkable a manner for *"poignancy of reply,"* as the above editor thought *"may be worth preserving in these Memoirs."**

* See the said Memoirs, p. 33—*et seq.*

Note. A full statement respecting General Lee's disobedience of General Washington's orders, to march to his assistance, and of his capture in the Jerseys at White's Tavern on Basking Ridge, two miles from his army; has never been fully before the public, until General Wilkinson published his Memoirs in 1816. These go to satisfy any reasonable mind, that General Lee's disobedience of orders was complete; as he had ordered General Sullivan to move with the army towards Pluckamin, which was only twenty-one and a half miles from Princetown, where, an inferior force of the British lay. This was off his route to Alexandria on the Delaware, where, he had been ordered to cross; and directly on that, towards Brunswick and Princetown. And from General Wilkinson's seeing General Lee trace the road from Pluckamin on the map, the morning he was taken prisoner, to Princetown, and other concurring inferences which he thence drew on the spot, General Wilkinson says, "I have strong cause for belief, that the decisive moment had arrived; and that if Lee had not been made a prisoner, he would have attacked the British post at Princetown, the next morning." He farther says, "General Lee merited severe punishment for his neglect of duty, and disobedience of orders: and, he received it, from an unexpected hand. This offence, was well understood by

After this, Mr. Drayton's attentions to his duties in Congress, were arduous and constant; while his hours at home, were devoted to writing, and copying congressional documents. This, induced a sedentary life; leading to the illness, which caused his death. His manners, were elegant, and gentlemanly—his virtues, many—his faults, few. He was a fond, and attentive father, wrapt up in the education of his son—bringing him forward by gradual advances, for a knowledge of public affairs; fondly hoping, that one day, he might be useful to his country. But these hopes were cut short, by his early death; and his son was left at twelve years of age, to struggle through the difficulties and perils of the American Revolution; and to open his way, for support, and preferment, by the energies of his own mind, and the assistances which he drew from an education, much confined by the operations of war.

Such, was Mr. Drayton's useful and honorable career, until September 1779: when, being still a member of Congress, and Chief Justice of South-Carolina, he closed a life at Philadelphia

---

the army; and his misfortune was unpitied by those, who reflected on the cause of it." "I am persuaded, that in the moment of his capture, he meditated a stroke against the enemy; which, in its consequences, would have depressed General Washington, elevated himself, and immediately served the cause of the United States."

General Wilkinson, was then a Major in the army of the United States; and had been dispatched by General Gates to General Washington for orders; and on his way, he called at White's Tavern on Basking Ridge, where General Lee was. He was consequently there, when General Lee was surprized and captured; and by the British not searching the house, he was enabled to make his escape. General Lee was without delay hurried off by the British party, mounted on Major Wilkinson's horse, which, by chance, was ready at the door; the General being bare-headed—in his slippers and blanket-coat—his shirt collar open, &c.

So soon as Lieutenant-Colonel Harcourt, who commanded the British party, retreated with his prize, Major Wilkinson repaired to the stable—mounted the first horse he could find—and rode full speed to General Sullivan; whom he found, *under march* towards Pluckamin. *By which, the disobedience of General Lee*, was completed. And, General Sullivan immediately countermarched, to join General Washington beyond the Delaware.—*See Wilkinson's Memoirs, vol. I. p.* 100—111.

on the third day of that month—which, had been active in defending the liberties of his country: and in which, he had, more than
once, personally risked his life, in her service—wanting at the
time of his death, a few days of being thirty-seven years of age.*

In an account given of him, in a Philadelphia paper of September 31st, 1779, by one, who knew him well, the following
extracted therefrom, will tend to confirm the picture of his life,
which has been drawn. "His family, was always among the
number of the most respectable and opulent, in South-Carolina.
He had taken an early and decisive part, in the present contest;
and been favoured from time to time, by his country, with the
most important and confidential offices. At the time of his death,
he was Chief Justice of that State; and one of its Delegates to
Congress. His literary attainments, acquired by good talents and
an excellent education, are well known here, and in Europe;
where, several of his political papers have been admired and read,
in different languages.

" To speak particularly of his character, would perhaps be improper in a newspaper; which like the grave, generally places
the dead on a level; without respect to the wise man, or the fool—
the saint, or the sinner. Let this subject therefore be reserved
for the pen of some impartial historian; who, when he shall inform posterity, that William Henry Drayton was an honest, independent patriot—and, an upright, candid gentleman—will, at the
same time, communicate facts more than sufficient to establish and
support his title, to that character."

---

* His remains were interred in the Cemetery adjoining to Christ-Church,
Philadelphia.

MEMOIRS

OF THE

AMERICAN REVOLUTION.

———◆———

CHAPTER I.

*A brief view of American affairs, from the year 1753 to
1765.—During this time, Major Washington is sent
by the Lieutenant-Governor of Virginia with remonstrances to the French Commandant; which not being
attended to, troops are raised: and Washington
attacks a French detachment.—The education of
George the III, King of Great Britain is brought into
view; also, the affections of his mind.*

WHEN the French government was promoting its
favourite scheme of colonial aggrandizement, and
with troops, settlements, and military stations, was
forming a belt along the British Provinces in North
America; misunderstandings took place, respecting
lands bordering on the river Ohio. On this subject,
an Express arrived at Charlestown in South-Carolina, on the twelfth day of June 1753, from Robert

Dinwiddie, Lieutenant-Governor of Virginia, to James Glen, Governor of South-Carolina. He brought dispatches from Governor Dinwiddie to Governor Glen; also copies of letters from Governor Clinton of New-York, to Governor Hamilton of Pennsylvania; from Governor Hamilton to Governor Dinwiddie; and several other papers, immediately connected with the matter of correspondence.

By the letter from Governor Dinwiddie Governor Glen was informed, that in the year 1752 he sent Commissioners to the Six United Nations of Indians, and to others in amity bordering on the west of the Virginia settlements; who were charged with presents and a talk, from him as Governor of Virginia. The Indians received the Commissioners at Log-Town,* on the river Ohio: when, after hearing the talk,† and receiving the presents, the Sachems and Chiefs confirmed and ratified the treaty which had been previously made with them at Lancaster in Pennsylvania; also, all former treaties then existing with them. The object of this embassy, was to obtain the assent of these aborigines to the settlement of lands on the Ohio; which the King of England had granted by patent, to a company of gentlemen: some of whom resided in England, and others in North America. And so well were the Commissioners received, that the Sachems and Chiefs acceded to their wishes; and besides granted permission for erecting two forts on the Ohio River, as a protection to those emigrants, who might be induced to commence the settlement of that remote wilderness. When this arrangement was made known, enterprising persons immediately di-

---

* Log-Town, was situated about eighteen miles below where Pittsburg now is; on the western side of the Ohio river.

† Speeches made to Indians on public occasions, are called *talks*.

rected their attention that way; and, when Governor Dinwiddie's letter was written on the 23d of May 1753, one hundred and fifty families had already left the settled part of Virginia, to proceed to these new lands on the Ohio River.

Of this movement, the French in Canada were early apprized; and an expedition was thereupon projected by the Governor of Canada, consisting of regular troops and Indians: whose object was, the destruction of the settlements, and the possession of that territory, for the purposes of France. These forces had no sooner commenced their march, than the Six Nations of Indians dispatched runners with advice of the same to Governor Clinton; who was then at Fort George in the province of New-York. And the exigence was so pressing, that he barely had time to transmit the papers accompanying the information, with a short letter from himself, to Governor Hamilton of Pennsylvania; from which source, they at length reached Governor Glen, through the intervention of Governor Dinwiddie.

The letter of this last Governor mentioned, that conceiving the affair to be of great consequence to all his Majesty's Colonies on this continent, he had consulted his Council; who agreed with him, it was proper the Catawbas, Cherokees, and other friendly Indians, should be advised of the same: and that each Colony should raise a number of men, who might be ready to act, should any emergency require. It likewise mentioned that he had written to the Governor of Pennsylvania, urging him to request Mr. Clinton, Governor of New-York, to send an Express to the Governor of Canada; requiring his reasons for this invasion of his Majesty's territories, in times of profound peace between the two Crowns: and, that so

soon, as he could obtain a proper account of the
French transactions on the Ohio, he should transmit
the same to the ministry at home.*

On the 21st of June 1753, Governor Glen replied
to this letter, stating that on receipt of the dispatches
he had convened his Council; who considered them
with that attention, which was due to every thing
concerning his Majesty's service; and so nearly affecting the peace of a neighbouring province. That as to
the raising a number of men, it would not be adviseable
to promise any great assistance from South-Carolina;
more especially, as the information brought stated,
that a portion of the French force was destined for
the destruction of the Catawba nation; whose sole
dependance was upon the Government of this province. That if the French had succeeded in making
a settlement on the Ohio, he could not be of opinion
that it would be safe for him without special direction
from his Majesty, to take any steps to dislodge them.
And, therefore, with great deference to the Governor
and Council of Virginia, he offered it as his opinion,
that a full representation should be laid before his
Majesty, of the several steps which had been taken by
the Government of Virginia to settle that country;
accompanied with a particular detail of those measures which the French had pursued in opposition
thereto: and, that it would be expedient to wait his
Majesty's pleasure, before any farther steps could warrantably be entered upon.†

On the receipt of this letter, Governor Dinwiddie
wrote to the Board of Trade in England, the situation
of provincial affairs; and more especially, the marching of French regulars and Canadian Indians against

* See Appendix to this Chapter, No. I.   † See Ibid. No. III.

the rising settlements on the Ohio: and, representations from several of the provincial Governors on the same subject, were also laid before his Majesty. After they had been considered, his Majesty George the Second caused instructions to be issued, to Governor Dinwiddie and the other provincial governors, pointing out the line of conduct to be observed on the occasion; and they were transmitted to the Governor of Virginia by a sloop of war despatched for that purpose, which was to wait his orders, for returning to England. Upon her arrival in the Chesapeake, her despatches were forwarded to Governor Dinwiddie: and another Express was sent to Governor Glen, who arrived in Charlestown on the 4th October 1753.

By this Express, letters were received from the Lieutenant-Governor of Virginia;* also, a Circular from the Earl of Holderness, then acting as Secretary of State.‡ In this letter, dated at White-Hall, 23d of August 1753, he informs Governor Glen, that his Majesty having received information of the march of a considerable number of Indians not in alliance with him, supported by some regular European troops, intending as it was supposed, to commit some hostilities on parts of his Majesty's dominions in America; he was directed, to use his utmost diligence to learn, how far the same was well grounded: and that he should be on his guard to resist any such hostile attempts, as might be made within his government. He was farther directed in the King's name, that in case the subjects of any foreign prince or state, should presume to make any encroachment on the limits of his Majesty's dominions, or to erect forts on his Majesty's lands, or commit any other act of hostility, he was immediately to represent the injustice of such proceeding; and to

* See, Appendix, No. IV.   † Ibid, No. V.

require them, forthwith to desist from any such unlawful undertaking.   But, if, notwithstanding such requisition, they should still persist; he was then directed to
draw forth the armed force of his province; and to use
his best endeavours, to repel force by force.

No encroachment being then made by the French,
on the back frontier of South-Carolina, Governor
Glen remained passive, under the directions of the
Circular: but Governor Dinwiddie found himself called
into action by its requisitions, and prepared remonstrances against the encroachments on the Ohio.
When they were ready, he entrusted them to the care
of Major George Washington, then about twenty-one
years old; who, early in November 1753, proceeded
through the wilderness by the way of Log-town, for
the purpose of delivering them to the French Commandant, at whatever place he should find him. Having performed his journey, and delivered his dispatches
to Monsieur Legardeur de St. Pierre, at a fort on
French Creek on the head waters of the Alleghany
river, about fifteen miles from Presque-Isle on lake
Erie, he returned to Virginia in January 1754;*
bringing an unfavourable answer: and the misunderstandings which had commenced, now widened apace.
This state of things, was soon transmitted to England;
and complaints were directed on the subject to the
court at Versailles; but its behaviour evinced, no satisfaction would be given.   On the contrary, preparations were urged with greater activity, for strengthening the French posts in North America; and depreda-
tions and acts of hostility were committed by the
French and their Indians in the disputed territories.
Measures were therefore taken by the provinces im-

* See, Marshall's Life of Washington, vol. 2d, pp. 4 & 5; also, Note I. at the
end of that volume.

mediately concerned, for raising and equipping troops; and, Major George Washington, now promoted to the rank of Lieutenant-Colonel in a Virginian regiment, was sent forward with a part of the same, to carry into effect the instructions which the Governor of Virginia had so received.

In performing this duty, he soon crossed the cordon of mountains which separate the waters flowing east-wardly into the Atlantic Ocean, and westwardly into the Mississippi River; and meeting with a French force a little westward of the Great Meadows, then advancing upon the British settlements, and commanded by M. Jumonville, he attacked and took them prisoners.* Various changes of fortune, soon took place; each nation, charged the other with ambitious views; and as war closely followed this transaction, the affair between Lieutenant-Colonel Washington and Monsieur Jumonville may be considered as its commencement between England and France. It was carried on with much ardour by the belligerent powers; and with enormous expense: while the flame which originated in the wilds of America, spread to the East and the West Indies, to Europe, and to other portions of the globe. At length, peace came forward to the relief of the combatants; by the various provisions resulting from the treaty of Paris in 1763.

The war thus terminated, threw all its honours and advantages into the scale of Great Britain. Her armies had often triumphed, and her fleets had carried victory with her flag. Her reputation, had taken a new flight of greatness. And although her favoured General was prostrated on the plains of Abraham, yet her flag waved on the turrets of Quebec; while

---

* Marshall's Life of Washington, vol. 2d, pages 6 & 7.

her enemies were driven not only from the lands on the Ohio, but from the Atlantic shores of her American provinces. From the frozen shores of Labrador, to the torrid climes of the Gulf of Mexico, her influence was now acknowledged; and her sovereignty extended from the Atlantic Ocean, to the waters of the Mississippi River. Such, were the fruits of this war in North America; whereby, ample satisfaction was obtained for French animosity, and Spanish interposition. For, to the north, Canada was torn away from France; while, to the south, the Floridas were lost to Spain, her ally. With this great extension of dominion in America, prospects were opened of increasing commerce and manufactures; and with them, an increased income to Great Britain, was not overlooked, by those who guided the helm of state.

This peace, however, so advantageously effected against the united power of the house of Bourbon; was not concluded but at great expenditure of the public money and great increase of the public debt. For, at the close of the war in 1763, the public debt of Great Britain was estimated at one hundred and forty-eight millions; seventy-five of which had been contracted during the war. Beside this, the circumstances of the times, and the competition and jealousy of European powers, required a more extensive peace establishment, than what Great Britain had theretofore maintained. And in addition, her new and extensive acquirements in North America, not a little increased the calls upon her treasury, and embarrassed the plans of her administration.—Under these difficulties was conceived, the idea of raising revenue in the British provinces, from taxes to be imposed on them, by the parliament of England. And it was strongly urged by the favourers of this plan, that as the late war was originated for the protection of colonial territory; so, it was but reasonable, they should contribute their proportion, towards defraying the expenses it had occasioned: particularly, as it had terminated so favourably to their interests and safety.   And for promoting this measure Great Britain contended, that her parliament clothed with supreme power, was fully vested with authority to lay taxes on every part of her extended empire.   This doctrine, however plausible it might appear, was not received in the American Colonies without some hesitation; for they had been accustomed to raise taxes, or to grant supplies, only by their Assemblies: and they could not but view with much jealousy, this parliamentary plan of enacting pecuniary laws for them, when they had no representation in that parliament to take care of their interests, or to make known their local claims and necessities.   The more they considered this subject, and reasoned on its principles; the more they believed, the claim of taxation to be unjust: and that taxation and representation were inseparable.   Nor could they suppose, that a nation could be free or happy, when their property might be taken from them by a power, over which they had no control.—By reasonings similar to these, the American mind began to expand; and the situation of the Colonies at the peace of 1763, was contrasted with what it had been in former years: when Spain inclosed them on one side, while France stood ready to attack them on the other.

At that time, the Colonies had many localities which separated them from each other: and it was not the policy of Great Britain, to soften asperities between them.   Wars seldom occurred, in which any great union was expected from them; and the Governors of the Colonies, acted independently of each other.   When particular pressures bore upon any Colony, either from Indians or otherwise; regular

2

troops were dispatched, to meet the emergency: and afterwards, they were withdrawn, leaving the Colony to support her government by her own means, and to provide for the expenses which had been incurred. Hence, few ties of friendship or neighbourhood, were among them; as each was engaged, in promoting her own local interests: and if the citizens of any of the Colonies had the desire and ability of seeing foreign countries, it was not among the neighbouring Colonies they were apt to direct their steps; but to England and Europe, that they bent their course. Virginia and some of the Provinces northward of her, had colleges for the education of their youth: but the Provinces southward of Virginia, had none. Hence, men of fortune in the southern Provinces were obliged to send their sons abroad for a liberal education; and they naturally sent them to Great Britain, as to a mother country, embracing their affections and good wishes: and for whose laws and customs they had not only a respect, but even a fondness for the fashions and manners of her inhabitants. Thus, acquaintances and friendships slowly arose, between the community of the different provinces; and for the same reasons, their strength never approximated to a union, which gave them respect in the eye of the British cabinet. One case arose, where the colonial resources became an object of public attention; when a meeting of the Governors of some of the Colonies was holden at Albany, at the commencement of the war in 1754, respecting the Ohio Lands. On that occasion, the efficiency of a qualified union between the Colonies became so apparent, for the better security of the general safety, as well against Indian savages, as foreign aggressors; that a supervising Council was proposed of members from each Colony, who should, with a Governor-General to be appointed by the Crown, be authorized

to make general laws for the public service; also, to
raise money for special occasions, and to direct the
colonial united strength of force and means on great
public emergences.   And so far was this idea considered feasible; it was believed if this plan were
adopted, the Colonies could have well defended
themselves, not only against the neighbouring Indians;
but against the French and Spaniards, who were
hanging upon each of their wings.   The keen eye of
a British administration, however, soon perceived this
plan must not be permitted: as it would condense into
an empire regions, which a monopolizing policy and
the principle of *divide and govern*, taught them ever to
keep separate, and distinct.   For these reasons, the
plan was immediately negatived by the ministry; and
one, more to serve a turn, than to meet the emergency,
was proposed; of the Governors from time to time,
concerting measures with each other for the public
service, with powers to draw upon the British treasury in the first instance, for erecting fortifications and
maintaining troops; but the same to be ultimately
reimbursed, by a tax to be laid on the Colonies by act
of parliament.*   This was, however, as much disliked
by the colonists, as the first plan had been by the
ministry; and of course, both measures failed.   But
the idea of consolidation once elicited, was never forgotten: and nothing but a suitable occasion was wanting, to bring it into action.

In the mean time, the intercourse of the colonists
with each other, and with the Governors of the Colonies, had in a great degree softened the lines of separation, which had been drawn between them; and

---

* See, London Remembrancer, for 1776, Part I. pages 185, 186, to 191.
Also, Marshall's Life of Washington, vol. I. pages 379 to 382, and note No. VIII.
at the end of that volume   Also, Dr. Franklin's Examination, at the bar of the
British House of Commons, in 1766.

they were more inclined to consider themselves as one
people.   For they had, at times, asssisted each other;
as in the war which had preceded the treaty of
Aix la Chapelle, the northern Colonies had contended
with Canada, and the adjacent possessions of France;
while the southern Colonies had waged hostilities
against Florida and the adjacent dependencies of
Spain.   So, in that which preceded the treaty of Paris
in 1763, the Colonies had been accustomed to give
aids, both of troops and money, to large amounts; and
as well on the plains of Abraham, where victory gave
to George the Second the possession of Quebec; as at
Cuba, where the city of Havana fell under British
dominion, were Colonial troops associated with British
regular forces.*   From this association it followed,
they became accustomed to the use of arms; and
what was of more importance, found they could
stand their shock, as well as the British troops.   For
the most part, however, the eastern Colonies, denominated New-England Governments, acted in concert
with the British forces: and were oftener called upon,
to watch and oppose the designs of the French from
Canada.   Hence, the people of those Colonies were
in close union with each other; as their interests were
nearly the same: and by degrees they ascertained,
their physical strength was imposing.   This, connected
with a spirit of independence, which their fathers had
brought with them from England, gave to the inhabitants of those Colonies a knowledge of arms, and a
spirit intolerant of oppression; which was not so much
the case, of the southern Colonies, whose white

* Dr. Franklin, in his examination at the bar of the British House of Commons, says, " The Colonies raised, paid, and clothed, near twenty five thousand men, during the last war; a number equal to those sent from Britain, and
far beyond their proportion ; they went deeply into debt in doing this ; and all
their taxes and estates are mortgaged, for many years to come, for discharging
that debt."

population was small: and were more removed, from an ambitious enemy. But their inhabitants' ideas of liberty and independence, were equally great: and the removal of hostile neighbours, not a little increased an impatience among them, of being controlled by a parliament, in which they were unrepresented; and which was separated from them, by the vast Atlantic. Such, was the general situation of the British Colonies, at the peace of 1763.—They were, nevertheless, content under British dominion; because, at that time, their liberties and properties were protected; and their agriculture and trade were allowed to flourish: and in return, they willingly afforded such contributions by the votes of their assemblies, as were required for public exigences. The increased power of the British nation, however, could not be satisfied with this: seventy-five millions of debt, had been incurred in prosecuting the war commenced on the Ohio; which, it was supposed, gave a right for proportional reimbursements from the American Colonies; which had incurred a debt by the war, of upwards of two millions. This, with the necessity of devising ways and means for reducing the great national debt, inclined Great Britain to expect more abundant supplies from her Colonies; and to project measures for the readier attainment of them. While the Colonies, more united in strength and informed by greater experience, became impatient of foreign interposition; and naturally repelled pretensions on their rights, which their increasing ideas of freedom taught them, were oppressive and unjust.

Thus stood Great Britain and her Colonies in North America, at the close of the war of 1754; and happy would it have been for George the Third, who after the death of his grandfather, succeeded to the throne, had he ascended it under more favourable auspices.   But the differences which had taken place between his grandfather, George the Second, and his father Frederick, Prince of Wales, and which were unreconciled, even at his father's death;* originated and kept alive, parties and oppositions, which had a fatal tendency in directing the destinies of the nation, at that eventful period. Besides which, his education was by no means such as was expected or hoped for, by his parents: being much influenced, by the views of party, and of tutors directed by court favourites.† Under all these difficulties, it was at least an even chance that he should be misled by the arts of favouritism; which, although hidden from public view, would be perceptible, in the measures advised, as in those pursued. And, notwithstanding informations were forwarded by the Governors of the Colonies, detailing the impatience of the people, and their rising expectations; yet we find they were unattended to, when brought into opposition with the opinions and prejudices of the Earl of Bute, and others; who indulged and supported views of power and prerogative, highly incompatible with the genuine principles of a limited monarchy, and national rights. These views now came forth in avowing the right, the policy, and the necessity, of taxing the Colonies. And for this purpose, and by way of feeling the pulse of the colonists, Lord Grenville,‡ in a series of resolutions, advocated

* See an Account of the Funeral of Frederick, Prince of Wales, in Appendix to this Chapter, No. VI.

† See some Account of Geo. III.'s education, in the Appendix to this Chapter, No. VII.

‡ This scheme, has been generally attributed to Grenville; but he, probably, received instructions on the subject from the Earl of Bute; and, as a financier, completed a plan, which the favourite had previously concerted with those courtiers, who, while they were styled the friends of the King, did not always act, as the friends of the people; though, the true interests of both are undivided.—Coote's Hist. of England, vol. 9, page 306.

the necessity of imposing them. And the only indulgence which America received at his hands, was a year's postponement of passing them into a law; that the expediency of the tax to be levied might be so ascertained, as to prevent the right of imposing it from being controverted. How far this inquiry was pursued or abused, cannot be stated at length, in this summary view of the question. It has, however, been ascertained, that the King and his Council were in full possession of the resolutions and proceedings, which had taken place in the Colonies on that subject; and to them we must look, for such representations to parliament, as the rights of upwards of three millions of people required at their hands.* But, we shall look in vain for such representations; the Colonial complaints were not heard; or, if, heard, they were unattended to. And Lord Grenville's resolutions, eventuated in his long expected bill, for laying a Stamp duty in America.

The Bill met with no opposition in the House of Lords, after it had passed that of the Commons; and,

---

* The following is an estimate of the people in the Colonies, taken by Congress in 1774, from the best calculations:

1. Massachusetts,	- - - -	400,000
2. New-Hampshire,	- - - - -	150,000
3. Rhode-Island,	- - - -	59,678
4. Connecticut,	- - - - -	192,000
5. New-York,	- - - - -	250,000
6. New Jersey,	- - - - -	130,000
7. Pennsylvania, including the lower Counties of Delaware,	- - - - -	350,000
8. Maryland,	- - - - -	320,000
9. Virginia,	- - - - - -	650,000
10. North-Carolina,	- - - -	300,000
11. South Carolina,	- - - -	225,000

Total of the then twelve associated Colonies,   3,026,678

on the twenty-second day of March 1765, it received
the Royal assent.   On that day also, through the destinies of Almighty Providence, the secret foundations
were laid; upon which, the Empire of the United
States of America has since been erected.   And, as if
the British measure of taxation, were eventually to be
covered with confusion, a manifestation of Providence
was evinced, on the person of George the Third; by
commencing about that time, those affections of his
mind* which have since driven him, into confirmed
madness:—closing only, with the termination of his
life.

* Coote's Hist. of England, vol. 9, page 310; also Annual Register for 1765,
page 38.

APPENDIX

CHAPTER I.

THE following papers are copied from the Provincial Privy Council Journals of South-Carolina, for the years 1752 and 1753—pages 475, 482, 499, 645, 644, and 647.

No. I.

Letter from Robert Dinwiddie, Lieutenant-Governor of Virginia, to James Glen, Governor of South-Carolina.

Williamsburgh, Virginia, May 23, 1753.

SIR,

By this Express. I enclose your excellency a copy of several papers, sent me express from Philadelphia; Mr. Hamilton, the Governor's letter to me, as also a copy of Andrew Montour's declaration, on delivering a message from me to the Six United Nations of Indians. As these papers contain affairs of great

3

importance to his Majesty's Colonies, on this continent, I thought it necessary to give you as early intelligence thereof, as possible.

I must observe to you, that last year, I sent commissioners to the Six Nations, and other Indian Nations,
in amity with us and them to the west of this dominion, with an handsome present from his Majesty.
They accordingly met our commissioners at Log-
Town, on the Ohio; where, after delivery of the presents, the sachems and chiefs then present, confirmed
and ratified the treaty of Lancaster. and all our former
treaties with them.   The intention of this treaty, was
to deliver the present; and to obtain their assent, to
settle the lands on the Ohio; which was granted, by
patent from his Majesty, to some gentlemen in London, and in this dominion; which, the Indian Chiefs
then present, immediately agreed to: and further gave
leave to build two forts on the Ohio River.   Agreeably thereto, there are one hundred and fifty families
gone out, to begin the settlement.

By the within papers, you will observe, that the
French from Canada, have marched a large force of
regular troops and Indians; not only, to prevent our
settlement, but to take possession of these lands, and
to build forts on that river.   A step, not precedented
in the time of confirmed peace with Britain and
France, to invade the British territories and lands, that
we have an undoubted right to: not only, as the back
of this dominion, but also by a concession of the native
inhahitants, Proprietors may I say, by a fair purchase; as the agreeing to our settlements, was in consequence of the present given to them.

This affair, I conceive, is of very great consequence
to all his Majesty's Colonies on this continent.   I

immediately called a Council; they all agreed with
me, that it was absolutely necessary to send an Express to you, with a copy of the papers; as also, to
send to the Catawbas, Cherokees, and other Indians
in friendship with us, to put them on their guard for
fear of surprize; which, I am preparing to do. We
are further of opinion, that each Colony should raise
a number of men; which, with the assistance of the
Indians in friendship with us, may be able to prevent
the French settling the lands on the Ohio: and if settled, to dispossess them. As this affair, will require
some time, we thought proper to intimate the same to
you and the other governments, to know your, and
their thoughts therein; and if you are of opinion with
us, we shall be glad to know the number of men that
may be supplied, from your government. For, the
French, possessing the lands of the Ohio, which are so
near our back settlements, will in time affect all our
Colonies; and they are very disagreeable neighbours,
and no doubt in time, will multiply fast. We are also
of opinion, that it would be very agreeable if you possibly could make peace between the Creeks and Cherokees; for the assistance of the Indians, will be of
very essential service. You will further please observe,
that it is of the last consequence, tacitly to allow the
French settlements on the Ohio; as they will continual-
ly harass our back settlements, and also enhance all the
Indian trade, to the great loss and prejudice of Great
Britain. It appears to me, to be an affair that requires
the serious consideration of all the British governments
on the continent. I have wrote to the Governor of
Pennsylvania, to desire Mr. Clinton, Governor of
New-York, to send an Express to the Governor of
Canada, to know his reason for this invasion on his
Majesty of Great Britain's territories, in the time of
profound peace, between the two Crowns: and, so

soon as I can have a proper account of their transactions on the Ohio, I shall transmit the same to the ministry at home: that if they see proper, they may apply to the Crown of France; but at the same time, we should do all in our power to prevent their settlement. Last week, I was informed that the Emperor of the Cherokees, with some of his officers who were here last fall, were intercepted in their return to their own country, by some French Indians. They say, that they scalped the Emperor, and carried the others prisoners to Canada. This, wants confirmation; but Mr. Montour, who I had sent to the Six Nations, says he heard the same at Onandago. I shall be very glad by the return of this Express, that your excellency will please to send me your opinion, on this emergent occasion; and what aid might be expected, from your government: and if it should be thought proper next fall to endeavour to dislodge the French from the Ohio, if they should presume to settle. If you could not engage some of the Creeks and other Indian nations contiguous to you, to assist in this attempt to disappoint their designs; for, I take it to be a great insult on Great Britain, at this time, to make an invasion on our lands. The number of the French forces, are uncertain; some say 6,000; but I cannot think they can exceed 1,000 or 1,200 regular forces, besides their Indians. But, I expect soon to have a more explicit account of their numbers and intentions.

I have been told, that for many years they have been tampering with many of the nations of Indians to the westward of us. The Picts and Twightwees, two powerful nations near Lake Erie, last fall sent me a message of their strong inclination to enter into a strict friendship with Britain. I returned a suitable answer; and desired them to send me some of their chiefs to Winchester, a back town in this dominion, about 200 miles from this; where they should receive a handsome present of small arms, ammunition, &c. to confirm them of our great desire to cultivate a strict friendship with them: which presents are now lying there for them. But, I fear this attempt of the French, will prevent their coming; as they must come by the Log-Town on the Ohio. However, if they can pass them, there is a commissioner with the presents, ready. to receive them.

I could not well abreviate this letter; as I intended to give you as clear a detail of the affair as possible. Please give the messenger all necessary dispatch: with sincere regard, I remain in great truth,

Your excellency's, &c.

ROBERT DINWIDDIE.

No. II.

Letter from James Hamilton, Governor of Pennsylvania, to Robert Dinwiddie, Lieutenant-Governor of Virginia.

Philadelphia, 6th May, 1753.

SIR,

Happening to be from home when your letter of the 3d of October came to hand, I could not return you an answer by the Surveyor-General, as I certainly would have done, had I had the pleasure of seeing him. I concur with you in opinion, that the Indian traders are a very licentious people, and may have been guilty of many bad practices; nor, is it to be much wondered at: since, although we have laws in this government, directing them to give bond, with security for their good behaviour; yet, they constantly neglect to do it. Nor, can the grand juries in those

remote places be prevailed upon, to find bills of indictment against them, though the facts be ever so
clearly proven.

As soon as I received your letter, I forthwith applied myself to inquire after the persons concerned in
the facts mentioned in the affidavit therein enclosed;
but was informed, they were gone to Alleghany; particularly Taff and Cullender: and I believe they are
not yet returned. But, as they may be soon expected,
I have sent copies of the affidavit to the Prothonotary
of Cumberland County, where they reside; with
directions to take their examinations, and send them
to me: and they shall be transmitted to you by first
conveyance, after I shall have received them.   I
heartily offer you my assistance, to bring them and all
evil doers to justice.

Immediately after the receipt of the enclosed letter
from Governor Clinton, on the 4th instant, I dispatched two messengers to Ohio, to make known to
our traders and Indian allies, the intelligence therein
contained. One of them, goes the lower way of
Juniata; by which means the account will be sooner
and more generally spread: and I am in hopes, they
will arrive time enough, to give the traders an opportunity of securing their persons and effects.

I presume, you must have received from Captain
Treul, an account that hostilities have already begun,
by some parties of the Ottaway Indians at Alleghany; and, that some of our traders have been taken,
and murdered: and others, plundered of their goods—
and that a large body of the French and their Indians
was expected at Ohio; with intent, as it is said, to
take possession of the country, and effect the total
expulsion of the English. In which case, the Indians

in our alliance, will be no longer able to maintain their independency; but all must fall, into the hands of the French.   Nor, can the Governors of Virginia, Maryland, and Pennsylvania, expect long to preserve peace, in the parts bordering on these Indian countries.   A most unhappy situation this, both for our Indian allies, and his Majesty's subjects; and a proceeding in direct violation of treaties, subsisting between the Crowns of England and France: by which, a mutual right, to a free and open trade, is firmly and clearly stipulated.

Our assembly being to sit on the 21st of this month, will give me an opportunity of communicating this intelligence to them; and of expressing my own sentiments of the necessity of giving our allies some immediate assistance; and I doubt not you will think something of the same kind ought to be done on the part of your Colony.   In the mean time, I think it necessary, as soon as we are able to establish clear facts, with regard to these proceedings, that the same being duly proved and authenticated, should be transmitted to his Majesty's ministers; in order to enable them to form a true judgement of the conduct of the French, and of its consequences to the independency of the Six Nations, to the right of a free and open trade; and to the safety of the lives and properties of his Majesty's subjects, residing in North America.   I should be well pleased to know, whether it be intended by your Colony to erect any kind of fort on the lands granted to the Ohio Company; and my reason for desiring this information, is, that I have received directions from the Proprietors of Pennsylvania, to enter into any reasonable measures to assist you, in any design of that sort: only, taking your acknowledgement that this settlement, shall not prejudice their right to that country.   And further, that I may assure the settlers, they shall enjoy the lands they bona fide settle, on the common quit-rent. And, in all things to endeavour to maintain a friendly and open correspondence with you; as being a gentleman they have a great regard for. And I the more readily obey their commands, in these several particulars, as they are perfectly agreeable to my own sentiments, and inclinations: being with all imaginable regard

Sir, yours, &c.

JAMES HAMILTON.

No. III.

Letter from James Glen, Governor of South-Carolina, to Robert Dinwiddie, Lieutenant-Governor of Virginia.

South-Carolina, 21st June, 1753.

SIR,

On the 12th of this instant, your Express brought me your letter dated the 23d of May last, enclosing the copy of a letter from Governor Clinton, and of another from Governor Hamilton, with several other copies of papers referred. And as they contain matters of great importance, I without loss of time communicated them to the Council; who considered them with that attention, that is due to every thing, that so greatly concerns his Majesty's service, and the British interest: that may so nearly effect the present peace of a neighbouring province, or by the consequences may disturb the tranquillity of all the Colonies upon the continent. In short, that may involve us in trouble; or have, what the French call, *des suites facheuses*.

The gentlemen of the Council were of opinion, that it would not be adviseable for me to promise any great assistance from this province in its present situation; more especially, as the very persons from whom you have the accounts of the number of the French army, give you also information that a part of them is designed for the utter destruction of the Catawbas: and, as the sole dependance of that little nation is upon this government, it is proper we should endeavour to protect and defend them. Indeed, it is our interest, and absolutely necessary for us to do so. For, if they form a part of our barrier, and if they are cut off, a door will be left open to the French Indians to harass our new settlements, in these our out parts. I am sensible, how greatly it concerns the peace of all his Majesty's Colonies upon this continent, to keep the French at a distance. It not only concerns the peace, but the very being of the province. For, compared with Virginia and some other northern governments, it is but thinly peopled. Our great security is the friendship of the Indian nations; which, I therefore study to cultivate with the greatest care. And, as I find the French spare no pains in stirring up strife, that by constant wars they may weaken one another; I endeavour to heal and reconcile, all their differences.

I have for some time past, taken a good deal of pains, to make a firm peace between the Creeks and Cherokees; and am not without a prospect of success. I am greatly desirous that there should be a peace, between all our Indians, and the Six Nations; and I sent proposals to the northward some time ago, to that purpose. And I hope you and Governor Clinton will strengthen my hands in this good work, if it could be brought about. I could venture to promise a considerable number of Indians, to be employed in defeating any designs of the French for the future; but in their present attempt, they have either succeeded or failed.

4

—If they have succeeded, and made a settlement, with such an army as you have advice of; I cannot be of opinion that it will be safe for me without special direction from his Majesty, to take any steps to dislodge them; or, in other words, to destroy them. And therefore, with great deference to you and the Council of Virginia, I offer it as my opinion, that a full representation should be laid before his Majesty, of the several steps taken by you to settle that country; and a particular detail of the measures the French are pursuing to dispossess you of it, and to settle themselves. And, that we should wait, till his Majesty's pleasure be signified; before we can warrantably proceed any further. But, I think you very justly doubt, the information you have received as to the number of troops. Indians, never see, and seldom, speak of thousands. And from a long, and pretty intimate knowledge of them, I have learned to mistrust their accounts, upon such subjects. Their fears often magnify appearances; and, they are not very scrupulous or exact, in numbers.

I hope, all his Majesty's subjects upon the continent, will make a common cause of it, when any part of them is invaded; but, in the present case, this province is very nearly concerned, *proximus ardet.* For which reason, and for the earnest desire that I know they have of expressing that zeal for his Majesty's service; they will, according to their small ability, exert themselves, like loyal and grateful subjects, in executing his Majesty's commands.

I am, Sir, yours, &c.

JAMES GLEN.

☞ On the 4th October 1753, another Express arrived in Charlestown from Virginia, bringing two letters from Lieutenant-Governor Dinwiddie, and one from the Right Honourable the Earl of Holderness.

No. IV.

Letter from Lieutenant-Governor Dinwiddie, to Governor Glen; and in his absence, to the Commander in Chief, or to the President of the Council of South-Carolina.

Williamsburgh, September 25th, 1753.

SIR,

I received your letter by my former Express.—I then, thought proper to write to the Board of Trade, the situation of our affairs, and the marching of some French regulars with a number of their Indians from Canada; with intention to settle on his Majesty's lands, on the Ohio. The representations from this Continent from the several governors, were laid before his Majesty. He therefore directed, a man of war sloop to be immediately dispatched to me, with several instructions how to conduct myself in the present situation of our affairs, in regard to the designs of the French, and their Indians, attempting to settle the lands, belonging to the Crown of Great Britain. I also, had letters to the several governors on this Continent; with orders to dispatch them as directed; which, is the occasion of this Express to you: and must refer you to the contents of the enclosed letter.

I lately sent a Commissioner, to meet some of the kings and warriors of several tribes of Indians, at the town of Winchester; and there to deliver them a present of guns, powder, &c. from this government. They

met accordingly, and there professed an inviolable
friendship for the King of Great Britain, and all his
Colonies, settled on this Continent.   I directed the
commissioners to ask them to meet me the full moon
next May: and, if they would agree, that some of the
southern Indians should meet at the same time. They
said, they would certainly meet there themselves; and,
would be glad, if the chiefs of the southern Indians
would meet them at the same time; and, that they
would then enter into a strict peace and alliance
among themselves, on this warlike invasion of their
lands, by the French.   And, I am determined if I
have my health, to meet them in person, to deliver the
presents.

   Now sir, I should be glad if you could prevail with
four of the Creek Nation to come to Winchester the
full moon of next May; I shall send a messenger to
the Catawbas and Cherokees, to the same purpose.
As I propose this general meeting for the national service of all his Majesty's Colonies on this continent; I
hope, all particular attachments must subside: and
was willing by this, to acquaint you of my intentions.
The man of war sloop, is to wait my orders.   And as
I think my dispatches will not be ready, till the return
of this Express, if you give him all possible dispatch;
in that case, if you have any commands for Great
Britain, I shall take the proper care of them.   And
am, with great respect,
              Your excellency's, &c.
                    ROBERT DINWIDDIE.

   ☞ Governor Glen was in the back parts of South-
Carolina, when the above letter and papers were received by Edward Fenwicke, President of the Council
of South-Carolina.   They were therefore submitted to

the Council; and by their direction, he acknowledged the receipt of Lord Holderness' Circular; and stated, that some token of friendship and passport, must be sent to the Catawba and Creek Indians from the northern Indians; before, they would send any of their chiefs to the proposed meeting.

No. V.

Letter from the Earl of Holderness, to Governor James Glen, South Carolina.

White-Hall, 23d August 1753.

SIR,

His Majesty, having received information of the march of a considerable number of Indians not in alliance with the King, supported by some regular European troops; intending, (as it is apprehended) to commit some hostilities on parts of his Majesty's dominions in America; I have the King's commands to send you this intelligence. And to direct you, to use your utmost diligence to learn how far the same may be well grounded; and to put you upon your guard, that you may at all events be in a condition to resist any hostile attempts, that may be made, upon any parts of his Majesty's dominions within your government. And, to direct you in the King's name, that in case the subjects of any foreign Prince or State, should presume to make any encroachment on the limits of his Majesty's dominions; or to erect forts on his Majesty's lands, or commit any other act of hostility; you are immediately to represent the injustice of such proceeding: and to require them, forthwith to desist, from any such unlawful undertaking.

But, if notwithstanding your requisition, they should still persist, you are then to draw forth, the armed force of your province, and use your best endeavours to repel force by force. But, as it is his Majesty's determination not to be the aggressor, I have the King's command most strictly to enjoin you, not to make use of the armed force under your direction, excepting within the undoubted limits of his Majesty's dominions.

And whereas, it may be greatly conducive to his Majesty's service, that all his provinces in America should be aiding and assisting each other, in case of any invasion; I have it particularly in charge from his Majesty to acquaint you, that it is his royal will and pleasure, that you should keep an exact correspondence with all his Majesty's Governors on the Continent. And, in case you shall be informed by any of them, of any hostile attempt; you are immediately to assemble the General Assembly, within your government; and lay before them the necessity, of a mutual assistance; and engage them to grant such supplies, as the exigency of affairs may require. I have wrote by this conveyance to all his Majesty's Governors, to the same purpose.

I am your most obedt. hum. servt.

HOLDERNESS.

No. VI.

Frederick, Prince of Wales, died on the 20th of March 1751. The following extracts from the Diary of George Bubb Dodington, *Baron of Melcombe Regis,* published in London in 1785, afford information as to the conduct of George II, on that occasion.

Baron Melcombe states, (page 106) " April 3d. At Council, about the funeral. Ceremonial from the Heralds read—their orders, were to form it on the plan of the Duke of Gloucester's and Prince George's of Denmark. But, they had different orders privately, which, *then*, I did not know. I thought, there was very little ceremony; and therefore said that I supposed, that they had complied with the orders, which their Lordships gave abont the plans, on which this funeral was to be formed. The Lords said, to be sure; and none seemed to have any doubts, or concerned themselves about it; so, I said no more; though I am satisfied, it is far short, of any funeral of any son of a king."

Pages 109, 110, 111, 112. " Lord Limerick consulted with me about walking at the funeral. By the Earl Marshal's order, published in the common newspaper of the day, neither he, as an Irish peer, nor I, as a Privy Counsellor, could walk. He expressed a strong resolution to pay his last duty to his royal friend, if practicable. I begged him to stay, till I could get the ceremonial; he did: and we there found in a note, that we might walk. Which note, published seven or eight hours before the attendance required, was all the notice, that lords, their sons, and privy counsellors had, (except those appointed to particular functions) that they would be admitted to walk.

" At seven o'clock, (April 13) I went according to the order, to the House of Lords. The many slights, that the poor remains of a much loved master and friend had met with, and who was now preparing the last trouble he could give his enemies, sunk me so low.

that for the first hour, I was incapable of making any observation.

" The procession began; and (except the Lords appointed to hold the pall, and attend the chief mourner, and those of his own domestics) when the attendants were called in their ranks, there was not one English Lord, not *one* Bishop; and only one Irish Lord, (*Limerick*) two sons of Dukes, (Earl of Drumlandrig and Lord Robert Bertie) one Baron's son, (Mr. Edgecumbe) and two Privy Counsellors, (Sir John Rushout, and myself,) out of these great bodies, to make a show of duty to a Prince, so great in rank and expectation. While we were in the House of Lords, it rained very hard, as it had done, all the season. When we came into Palace Yard, the way to the Abbey was lined with soldiers; but the managers had not afforded the smallest covering over our heads; but, by good fortune, while we were from under cover, it held up. We went in at the S. E. door and turned short into Henry VII's Chapel. The service was performed, without either anthem or organ.

" The corpse and bowels were removed last to the Prince's lodgings at the House of Lords; the whole Bed-Chamber were ordered to attend them from ten in the morning, till the *enterrement*. There was not the attention, to order the Green Cloth to provide them a bit of bread; and these gentlemen of the first rank and distinction, in discharge of their last sad duty to a loved and a loving master, were forced to bespeak a great cold dinner from a common tavern, in the neighbourhood. At three o'clock indeed, they vouchsafed to think of a dinner, and ordered one—but the disgrace was complete, the tavern dinner was paid for, and given to the poor. The Duke of Somerset was *chief mourner*, notwithstanding *the flourishing state of the Royal family.*"

No. VII.

The education of George III, was not sufficiently attended to, by those, whose duty it was, to have conducted it; hence, in conversations which his mother, the Princess of Wales, had, with Dodington, Baron of Melcombe Regis, in the years 1752, 1753, and 1755, respecting the education and manners of her son George; she said, " that he was very honest, but she wished he was a little more forward, and less childish, at his age. That she really did not well know, what his preceptors taught him: but, to speak freely, she was afraid not much. That they were in the country and followed their diversions, and not much else, that she could discover; but hoped it would be better, when he came to town." On Dodington's suggesting to her, that what he wished the most was, that his Royal Highness should begin to learn the usages and knowledge of the world—be informed of the general frame and nature of the English Government, and Constitution, and of the general course and manner of business,—she said, " that she was of his opinion; and that Stone (one of his preceptors) had told her, that when he talked to the Prince on these subjects, he seemed to give a proper attention, and made proper remarks. As for Lord Harcourt, and the good Bishop, (of Norwich;) she said, she thought he could not learn much from the first; and the latter, though a mighty learned man, did not seem very proper to convey knowledge to children: she did not very well comprehend him herself; his thoughts, seemed to be too many, for his words."

5

"On December 5th, 1752, both of these preceptors resigned; and on the 18th, Lord Waldegrave was declared governor, to the Prince, in Lord Harcourt's room; and the Bishop of Peterborough on the 9th January 1753, in the place of the Bishop of Norwich. Upon this, the Princess told Dodington, that Lord Harcourt had not only behaved very ill to her; but always spoke to the children, of their father, and of his actions, in so disrespectful a manner, as to send them to her, almost ready to cry."—Upon another occasion, in the year 1755, she said, "that George was not a wild, dissipated boy, but goodnatured and cheerful; with a serious cast, upon the whole. (*He was then about seventeen years old.*) That he was not quick; but with those he was acquainted, applicable and intelligent. That his education, had given her much pain; his book learning she was no judge of; though she supposed it small or useless; but she hoped he might have been instructed in the general understanding of things. That she did not know Lord Waldegrave; and as to Mr. Stone, if she were to live forty years in the house with him, she should never be better acquainted with him than she was. That she once desired him to inform the Prince, about the Constitution; but he declined it, to avoid giving jealonsy to the Bishop of Norwich; and that she had mentioned it again, but he still declined it, *as not being his province.*" Upon Dodington asking her what was his (*Stone's*) province? the Princess replied, "that she did not know; unless it was to go before the Prince up stairs—to walk with him sometimes—seldomer to ride with him—and now and then, to dine with him.—And when they did walk together, the Prince generally took that time to think of his own affairs, and to say nothing."—See pages of the Diary, 171, 172, 188, 201, 219, 220, 356, 357.

CHAPTER II.

Measures taken by Massachusetts, respecting the Stamp-Act—Lieutenant-Governor William Bull, his character and conduct—Resolutions of the Commons-House of Assembly—They appoint a Committee to join the approaching Congress at New-York—The Congress meets, performs certain acts, and adjourns The Committee from Congress, report their proceedings—Associations formed, not to import goods from England—The Stamped papers arrive in a sloop of war, in Charles-Town harbour—Proceedings of the citizens thereon—The Judges and Lawyers, hold a meeting, respecting the Stamp-Act—Dougal Campbell, Clerk of the Court of Common Pleas, refuses entering up judgments and issuing process—The Assistant Judges request the Lieutenant-Governor to suspend him; which he declines doing—The Commons-House of Assembly takes up the matter, and sends a message to his Honour, requesting Dougal Campbell's suspension; which the Lieutenant-Governor refuses to order—Upon which the House passes Resolutions, and publishes them—A change of Administration takes place—Parliament takes up the American grievances—Mr. Pitt's conduct, as to the Stamp-Act—Parliament repeals the same; but declares its right to make laws for the Colonies, in all cases whatsoever—Joy of the people, on the repeal of the Stamp-Act—A statue is erected, in honour of Mr. Pitt; and addresses are transmitted to the Throne—

*Acts of Parliament passed, respecting the Customs;
and imposing duties on certain articles, imported into
the American Colonies—American proceedings thereon—John Hancock's sloop Liberty seized—British
troops are ordered from Halifax, to Boston—A non-
importation Agreement, is entered into by the Colonies—Boston Town-Meeting, passes votes respecting
their charter, taxation, and for the meeting of a Provincial Congress or Convention—Proceedings of
Parliament—Earl of Hillsborough appointed a Secretary of State, with a special reference to the American Colonies—Colonel Henry Laurens publishes
against the Court of Admiralty—As William Henry
Drayton does, against the mode of enforcing the
Association—The Commons-House of Assembly remit monies to England, for patriotic purposes; which
leads to a disagreement between that House and the
Provincial Council—Additional Instructions to the
Governor of South-Carolina, respecting the said disagreement—Proceedings of the Commons thereon—
Lord Hillsborough signifies the King's approbation
of the Council's conduct—The Commons petition the
Throne, to withdraw the said Instructions.*

WHILE the Stamp-Act was under consideration in
parliament, the house of representatives of Massachusetts, asserted their sole right to pass laws of taxation.
When therefore the act had passed, they lost no time
in providing against its operations; and so early as the
6th of June 1765, they passed a resolution, which
gave rise to the first American Congress. They fixed
on New-York, as the place of meeting, and the month
of October, as the time for holding the same. They
also transmitted letters to the several Assemblies on the
North American Continent, requesting their concurrence; and inviting them to send Committees, who

should meet theirs in congress at New-York; for the purpose of consulting respecting the acts of parliament laying duties or taxes, on the American Colonies. After this, having obtained a copy of the Stamp-Act, it was publicly burnt; and the vessels in Boston harbour hung their colours half mast high, in deepest mourning: while muffled church bells rang peals of distress, from one township to the other. From the New-England Colonies, the tidings spread through all the towns of the middle and southern Provinces; and similar feelings insinuated themselves, into the hearts of the people.

At this time, Lieutenant-Governor William Bull presided over the Province of South-Carolina. He was a native of the same, was son of the former Lieutenant-Governor, and was descended from one of its most ancient, and respectable families. Having been liberally educated in Great Britain, his mind was informed, respecting the rights of his fellow citizens; as well as the claims of the Sovereign, whose commission he held; and, while he felt the full force of the first, his honour bound him to perform the duties of his station to the last. These, he executed with such kindness and forbearance, as secured to him the public good will; although at the same time, he placed at hazard, the loss of his office, and a separation from a large and valuable estate which he possessed in South-Carolina. His repeated administrations as Lieutenant-Governor, at length closed in a manner, honourable to himself; and, if he could not prevent the scenes which took place, during the latter part of his administration, he at least, was not the public officer, who unreasonably urged them forward. This, will be shown, in various occurrences; wherein, his endeavours were directed to keep affairs quiet between the government and the people, so long, as he possibly could.

Having received the Stamp-Act, the Lieutenant-
Governor manifested a desire of complying with its
requisitions, in causing it to be executed;* but his
powers at that time, were insufficient to effectuate the
same. Encouraged by this weakness, and by the public opinion which was hostile to the act; the members
of Assembly deliberated in what manner they might
most embarrass, and elude its operations.   And, as the
best mode they could devise, they addressed the Lieutenant-Governor on the occasion; requesting to be
informed whether the Stamp-Act, said to have been
passed in parliament, had been transmitted to him;
and if it had, through what channel it had been so
transmitted: and whether he had received it from a
Secretary of State, the Lords of Trade, or from any
other authentic source? These were questions of a
singular nature—however, his Honour, from a desire
to soften as much as possible the fermentation which
existed, answered, he had received it from Thomas
Boone, the Governor of the province.†   The Assembly replied, that while Mr. Boone was out of the
bounds of his government, they could not consider
him in any other light, than as a private gentleman;
and, the act being received through such a channel,
was not sufficiently authentic, to place the Lieutenant-
Governor under the obligation of enforcing it.   He
and his privy council, differed from them in this conclusion; as they said, the channel through which it

* By the LX section of the Stamp-Act, Governors and Commanders in
Chief of the British Colonies, were to be sworn to the due execution of the
same ; for not taking which, or not discharging their duty, in causing the said
act to be executed, they were subjected to heavy penalties, forfeitures, and disabilities.

† Governor Thomas Boone, embarked 11th May 1764, for Great Britain,
with the King's permission ; as mentioned in Lieutenant-Governor Bull's Pro
clamation dated 12th Mc   1764, when he qualified as Lieutenant-Governor,
and assumed the reins of government.—See Council Journal for May 1764.

had been received, was equally authentic with those, by which, many acts of parliament had been received; and to which, the Assembly had, on various occasions, knowingly submitted. The Assembly, however, were not disposed to admit this conclusion; and adhering to the stand they had taken, they passed the following Resolutions: which, being signed by their Speaker Peter Manigault, were ordered to be printed.

" Resolved, that his Majesty's subjects in Carolina, owe the same allegiance to the Crown of Great Britain, that is due from his subjects born there. That his Majesty's liege subjects of this province are entitled to all the inherent rights and liberties of his natural born subjects, within the kingdom of Great Britain. That the inhabitants of this province appear also to be confirmed in all the rights aforementioned, not only by their charter; but, by an act of parliament 13th George II. That it is inseparably essential to the freedom of a people, and the undoubted right of Englishmen, that no taxes be imposed on them, but with their own consent. That the people of this province are not, and from their local circumstances cannot be, represented in the House of Commons in Great Britain; and farther, that in the opinion of this House, the several powers of legislation in America, were constituted in some measure, upon the apprehension of this impracticability. That the only representatives of the people of this province, are persons chosen therein by themselves; and, that no taxes ever have been, or can be, constitutionally imposed on them, but by the legislature of this province. That all supplies to the Crown, being free gifts of the people; it is unreasonable and inconsistent, with the principles and spirit of the British Constitution, for the people of Great Britain to grant to his Majesty, the property of the people of this province. That the act of parlia-

ment entitled 'An act, for granting and applying certain stamp-duties, and other duties, on the British
Colonies and Plantations in America,' &c. by imposing
taxes on the inhabitants of this province; and the said
act, and several other acts, by extending the jurisdiction
of the courts of Admiralty, beyond its ancient limits;
have, a manifest tendency to subvert the rights and
liberties of this province. That the duties imposed
by several late acts of parliament, on the people of
this province, will be extremely burdensome, and grievous; and, from the scarcity of gold and silver, the
payment of them, absolutely impracticable. That, as
the profits of the trade of the people of this province,
ultimately center in Great Britain, to pay for the manufactures which they are obliged to take from thence;
they eventually contribute very largely, to all the supplies granted to the Crown: and besides, as every individual in this province, is as advantageous at least as if
he were in Great Britain, as they pay their full proportion of taxes for the support of his Majesty's government here; (which taxes, are equal or more, in
proportion to our estates, than those paid by our fellow
subjects in Great Britain upon theirs;) it is unreasonable, for them to be called upon to pay any further
part of the charges of government there. That, the
Assemblies of this province, have from time to time,
whenever requisitions have been made to them by his
Majesty, for carrying on military operations, either for
the defence of themselves, or America in general, most
cheerfully and liberally contributed their full proportion of men, and money, for these services. That
though the representatives of the people of this province, had equal assurances and reasons, with those of
the other provinces, to expect a proportional reim-
bursement of those immense charges they had been
at, for his Majesty's service in the late war, out of the
several parliamentary grants for the use of America;

yet, they have obtained only their proportion of the first of those grants, and the small sum of £285 Sterling received since. That notwithstanding, whenever his Majesty's service shall, for the future, require the aids of the inhabitants of this province, and they shall be called upon for this purpose in a constitutional way, it shall be their indispensable duty, most cheerfully and liberally, to grant to his Majesty their proportion, according to their ability, of men and money; for the defence, security, and other public services, of the British American Colonies. That the restrictions on the trade of the people of this province, together with the late duties and taxes imposed on them by act of parliament, must necessarily greatly lessen the consumption of British manufactures, amongst them. That the increase, prosperity. and happiness of the people of this province, depend on the full and free enjoyment of their rights and liberties; and, on an affectionate intercourse with Great Britain. That the readiness of the Colonies to comply with his Majesty's requisitions, as well as their inability to bear any additional taxes beyond what is laid on them by their respective Legislatures, is apparent from several grants of parliament to reimburse them, part of the heavy expenses they were at, in the late war in America. That, it is the right of the British subjects of this province, to petition the King, or either House of Parliament. *Ordered*, that these votes be printed, and made public; that a just sense of the liberty, and the firm sentiments of loyalty of the representatives of the people of this province, may be known to their constituents, and transmitted to posterity."

Having thus expressed their sentiments, the Commons-House of Assembly appointed Thomas Lynch, Christopher Gadsden, and John Rutledge, a Committee, to meet the Committees, from the other provinces.

6

at New-York in October following; for the purposes mentioned in the report of a Committee as agreed to by that house, on Friday, the 26th day of July. The Committee proceeded to New-York, where they arrived on the 15th day of September; and on Monday, the 7th day of October following, the Congress convened, and entered upon the business committed to them; the same being formed of the following Committees, from the Provinces of

Massachusetts-Bay,
Rhode-Island, and Providence Plantations,
Connecticut,
New-York,
New-Jersey,
Pennsylvania,
The Government of the Counties of Newcastle, Kent, and Sussex, on Delaware,
Maryland,
South-Carolina.

To this Congress, the Provinces of New-Hampshire and Georgia sent no Deputies; but forwarded reasons for such omission; which were recorded on the Congressional Minutes. The Provinces of Virginia and North-Carolina, neither sent Deputies, nor any reasons for not doing so.*

During this session, the Congress agreed to fourteen declarations, of their Rights, Liberties, and Grievances;† upon which delarations, they founded a petition to the King,‡ a memorial to the House of Lords,§ and

---

* Ramsay, in his History of the American Revolution published in 1789, vol. I. p. 68, says, " The Assemblies of Virginia, North-Carolina, and Georgia, were prevented by their Governors, from sending a Deputation to this Congress."

† See Appendix to this Chapter, No. I.   ‡ See Appendix, No. II.

§ See Appendix, No. III

a petition to the House of Commons.* The Congress also recommended to the several Colonies, to appoint especial Agents in London, for soliciting relief from present grievances; and that the Assemblies whose Committees were not impowered to sign the ingrossed petitions and memorial, would, with all possible dispatch (if they approved of the applications) do what was necessary therein, and transmit directions to their respective Agents in Great Britain, to unite with the other Agents in support of the same. These things being done, the Congress broke up: and the Committees of each Province returned home; when on the 26th day of November 1765, Mr. Lynch, Mr. Gadsden, and Mr. Rutledge, made their report of the proceedings of the Congress; which were published afterwards, by Order of the Commons-House of Assembly, April 9th, 1766:† and the same being agreed to, Peter Manigault, the Speaker of the Assembly, was directed to sign the petitions and memorial; and the Committee of Correspondence was ordered to transmit the same to the Provincial Agent then in England; directing him to use his utmost endeavours, to obtain success on those applications.

While these matters were carrying on, the stamped papers arrived in the various sea-ports of the Colonies; and greatly excited the feelings of the people. At this time, a sloop of war had arrived in Charlestown harbour with a portion of them, casting anchor under cover of the cannon of Fort Johnson: and a meeting of citizens was effected, to devise means for preventing the landing of the same. The garrison of Fort Johnson, was known to consist only of a Commandant, a

---

* See Appendix to this Chapter, No. IV.

† See Votes of the Commons-House of Assembly of South-Carolina, published by Order of the 9th April 1766.

gunner, and twelve or fourteen privates; and Lloyd, the Commandant, mostly resided in Charlestown: hence, the command and care of the fort, frequently devolved on the gunner. These things being considered, the meeting thought proper to appoint a Committee for farther purposes; and Daniel Cannon, William Williamson, Edward Weyman and others, were nominated members of the same; who. understanding sufficiently the motives of their appointment, and the wishes of the meeting, entered zealously on their duties, respecting the matters they had in charge.

Whether the Government was informed of these measures, is not ascertained; but the public ferment was known to be so great, it was deemed adviseable not to bring the stamped papers up to Charlestown; but to land them at Fort Johnson. The Committee, soon received information of this proceeding; and a private meeting of confidential citizens being called, it was resolved, the Committee be authorized to obtain the stamped paper, so deposited at the fort: and to furnish the means of doing so, that a body of volunteers should be selected and procured by them, with the utmost promptness and secrecy.—Accordingly, about one hundred and fifty volunteers were soon organized and armed, for the purpose; and two nights after, boats being provided at Lamboll's bridge, on the west end of South-Bay, they formed and marched towards that place, for embarkation. From thence, they proceeded in boats across Ashley River; and landed after twelve o'clock at night, on James' Island, between Styles' plantation, and the fort. They then proceeded towards the fort; and halting at a small distance from it, a reconnoitering party was sent forward. This party proceeded to the draw-bridge unnoticed, or challenged by sentries; and finding it down, through the omission of the garrison, they immediately returned and reported the same. The whole body of volunteers then advanced upon the fort; and arriving at the bridge, they crossed it without opposition—pressed through the main gate, which was not secured—and, immediately possessed themselves of the fort. Only one soldier, was found awake; and before he could give the alarm, the remainder of the garrison was secured except Governor Lloyd;* who had not slept there that night. The garrison were then placed under a guard—the bridge was drawn up—and a search commenced, for the obnoxious stamped paper. This, to the great joy of the volunteers, was at length found in one of the rooms of the barracks; and a guard was placed over it. Preparations were then made for maintaining the fort against any attack, which might be made upon it by the sloop of war, when day light should arrive; and for this purpose, the cannon on the platforms were loaded with ball and grape shot; matches, were prepared; and a number of men were stationed at each gun: and a flag showing a blue field with three white crescents, which the volunteers had brought with them for the purpose, was hoisted on the flag staff of the fort. When day light appeared, the crescent banner waved gaily on the wind; and soon attracted the attention of the sloop of war. A boat was then dispatched from her, to ascertain the cause of so unusual a display, and persons were sent from the fort, to meet the boat at the landing place; where, on the landing of the British officer, he inquired the meaning of the flag; on which he was invited into the fort, and was told he would then be informed. At first he appeared doubtful, whether he should proceed; but on being assured protection, and that he would be allowed to return to his boat, he accepted of the invitation.—On his arrival in the fort, he was taken along

---

* The Commander of Fort Johnson, had the title of Governor of the same.

the platforms, where he found each gun manned and loaded, and the fort prepared for action: he also was shown the late garrison under a guard, as prisoners. When the impression had been made upon him, which was intended, he was told it was the fixed determination of the volunteers, to proceed to burn all the stamped paper which they had seized; unless the Commanding Officer would pledge his honour immediately to receive it on board, and forthwith depart with it. It was farther intimated to him, that if the sloop should fire upon the fort, they were resolved to repel force by force: and to these matters an answer was requested from the sloop of war as soon as possible: the officer then took his leave, and returned in the boat. In two hours he returned with the boats of the sloop, saying his commander, would receive the stamped papers, and forthwith depart; when they were delivered to him: and returning with them to the sloop, she weighed anchor in the afternoon, and proceeded to sea.— The object of the expedition being so happily effected, the garrison were released from confinement, and put in possession of the fort; and the volunteers returned with their colours to Charlestown, by the same way, in which they had proceeded; having fulfilled the wishes and expectations of their fellow citizens, without injuring or hurting any person whatsoever.

When it was known in town, that the stamped paper was carried away, an universal joy prevailed; except with those, who were friends to Government. The Lieutenant-Governor was confounded at the boldness of the proceeding; while the leaders of the measure, thinking it best to follow up the blow, were not a little encouraged to offer other obstructions to taxation, in whatever shape it might be presented. Suspicion was still afloat, that some of the stamped paper had been landed in town; and was in the possession of some of

the citizens, as well as of the King's officers. Hence
a tumultuous body of citizens assembled in the evening, and proceeded through various streets, threatening
some public officers and disaffected persons, as they
went along.   Their principal objects, were the houses
of George Saxeby, one of the King's officers, Colonel
Henry Laurens, and Chief Justice Shinner.   Colonel
Laurens, was a gentleman and merchant of great
respectability; and well known, as a warm friend to
American rights: Mr. Shinner was the King's Chief
Justice of the Province.   They first proceeded to Mr.
Saxeby's house in Tradd-street, where, they put him
in no small trepidation, by searching it, and questioning
him respecting stamped papers; but finding none,
they exacted a promise from him that he would not
assist in receiving or distributing the stamps; and
from thence, they proceeded upwards, towards Colonel Laurens'.   When they arrived at that gentleman's
house in Ansonborough, their suspicions were indig-
nantly received by him.   He assured them, he would
not have been concerned, in so odious a measure as
secreting stamped papers; for, he was no friend to
the act of parliament on that head; that he had none
in his house, for which he pledged his word; and he
hoped that would satisfy them; as he was not disposed to permit his house to be searched: but for his
out-buildings, they might search them if they pleased;
and if they wished any refreshment, there were the
keys of his cellars.—Ashamed of having suspected
him in the affair, they gave up the search of his house:
but proceeded to scrutinize the out-buildings without
success: and finally made a direct attack upon his cel-
lar.   In this, their conduct was very reprehensible; and
notwithstanding every endeavour of some respectable
citizens to the contrary, the mob could not be restrained, from wasting much liquor, which they were
unable to enjoy.—From thence, they turned their

course to the Chief Justice's in King-street; whom
they soon roused from his slumbers. Knowing as a
Crown officer he was suspected, he parried their attack by receiving them in the most favourable man-
nor: assuring them, he had nothing to do with the
stamped paper, and that they were welcome to
search every part of his house for it; which they did,
but found nothing. In the mean time, he had large
bowls of punch provided; and at the request of the
populace, he deemed it prudent to drink with them
their favourite toast; which was " *Damnation to the
Stamp-Act;*" after which, the procession moved away,
and fortunately subsided, without any farther interrup-
tion, to peaceable individuals.*

The provisions of the Stamp-Act being highly
penal, as well upon the Judges as the Lawyers, and
all the officers of the Courts, in conducting every matter of legal business; they found themselves reduced
to the necessity of having a meeting, for the purpose
of forming such rules, as might be necessary in carrying the provisions of the act into execution, and for
their own indemnity and regulation. For this purpose they convened, and made some progress in a
work of so novel and delicate a nature; after which,
they adjourned to another day. In the mean time,
news arrived of the tumults and disturbances at Boston, New-York, and other places at the northward, in
opposition to the stamped paper; which had such an
effect, upon the sensibilities of the Members of the
Bench and the Bar, as to postpone indefinitely their
intended meeting, on business so intimately connected,
with the feelings and interests of the community.

* Colonel Daniel Stevens of Charleston, who was one of the volunteers,
politely favoured the author with the above particulars.

At length the first of November arrived; after which time, no business could be legally transacted, unless the papers used in every case were stamped: and as the stamped papers had been sent away, the act could not be complied with—to do business without stamps, was declared to be null and void. This, placed the colonists in a distressing situation; prevented the change of property—and hazarded the security of debts: although at the same time business was done at the Custom-House without stamped papers; and vessels were permitted to enter and depart accordingly. In this emergency, creditors applied to the Attornies at Law, to commence suits against their debtors, and to prevent several of them from departing the province without giving bail; but the Attornies were unable to comply with their wishes, as they could neither purchase nor procure process of the Court for that purpose; although, they had frequently demanded it from Dougal Campbell, Clerk of the same, tendering him at the time his legal fees. But this Officer constantly refused, granting or issuing such process; at one time, saying he had no stamps—at another, that the Chief Justice had taken away the Seal of the Court from his office—at a third time, that he was, by office, named in the Stamp-Act, and made liable to heavy penalties for disobeying its several provisions. At length, on the 13th day of November, the Chief Justice* being alone in the Court of Common Pleas, he declared that no stamped papers could be procured, stopped the business of the Court, and ordered it to be adjourned. After this, the four Assistant Judges† finding by a certificate of the Lieutenant-Governor, under his sign manual and seal at arms, that no stamped papers were to be had, they

* Charles Shinner.

† Robert Pringle, Rawlins Lowndes, Benjamin Smith, and Robert D'Oyley.

7

unanimously ordered (the Chief Justice dissenting) a
Judgment to be entered. agreeably to motion; but
Dougal Campbell, the Clerk, refused to enter the
same, or to issue any process by order of the Court.
On this, the Assistant Judges addressed a letter to
Lieutenant-Governor Bull, stating the circumstances;
and requesting he would suspend Dougal Campbell,
Clerk of the Court of Common Pleas, for not obeying
the Order of the Court, as to entering the Judgment:
but, he declined doing so; and furnished them with
the reasons, which influenced his conduct on the occasion.* These not being satisfactory, the Lieutenant-
Governor's letter, was transferred to the Commons-
House of Assembly; by whom it was referred to their
Committee, which had been appointed to take into
consideration the petition† of the merchants, traders,
freeholders, and other inhabitants of Charlestown,
and the other parts of the province, and to inquire into
the state of the Courts of Justice of the province, and
also to consider whether any, and what, answer should
be returned by the House, to the Lieutenant-Governor's Message of the 22d of March last.

The Committee accordingly took the matter into
consideration, and reported an address to the Lieutenant-Governor in the following words:

" May it please your Honour,

" It manifestly appearing to this House, that
Dougall Campbell, Esquire, Clerk of his Majesty's
Court of Common Pleas of this Province, hath obsti-
nately, contumaciously, and repeatedly, refused to
enter or obey the Orders of the said Court, we have
fully considered his very extraordinary conduct in this

See Appendix to this Chapter, No. V.   † Ibid. No. VI.

respect; and in order to vindicate and support the honour and authority of the said Court, to maintain a due subordination of inferior Officers, and to prevent the ill-consequences which must inevitably ensue from the suffering so dangerous a precedent, of contempt and disobedience, in ministerial Officers, to go unpunished, we find ourselves under the strongest obligations of duty to our Constituents, humbly to represent this matter to your Honour; and to request, that your Honour would be pleased immediately to suspend the said Dougal Campbell from his office, and appoint some proper person in his room, that will not take upon himself to stop the course of Justice, or to judge of, but obey, the orders of the Court, according to the well known duty of such Officer"—which being agreed to by the House, and signed by their Speaker, was on the 24th of April presented to the Lieutenant-Governor in the Council Chamber by the whole House: after which, His Honour delivered an address to the House on the 28th of April, to the following effect:

" Mr. Speaker and Gentlemen,

" I have very maturely considered the subject of your address, and my own power and duty on such occasions.

" By the King's instructions I am commanded, not to displace officers without good and sufficient cause, to be signified in the fullest and most distinct manner, to the Right Honourable the Lords Commissioners for Trade and Plantations; in order to be laid before his Majesty, by the first opportunity after such removal.

" As it is the first principle of Justice, not to condemn any man unheard, Mr. Campbell has been heard

in his defence, against the charge of disobedience to
the Orders of the Assistant Judges; whereby it appears to me, that his said disobedience did not proceed
from any contumacy or want of respect to the authority of the Assistant Judges, but from *his regard* to the
superior authority of an act of parliament.

"And therefore, as, in this case, I do not see good
and sufficient cause, to displace an officer, I shall not
suspend Mr. Campbell.

"I had the less reason to expect this application
from you, *Gentlemen*, as I had very lately before received one to the same purpose, from the Assistant
Judges, to whom I had already given my answer in
writing, with the reasons I have now mentioned,
that it was not in my power to comply with their request.
"WILLIAM BULL."

In reply to this address of the Lieutenant-Governor,
the House of Assembly sent a Message to him on
Tuesday, 29th April, as follows:

"May it please your Honour,

"The great respect we have for your Honour, cannot but induce us to think, that some mistake must
have occasioned so very extraordinary and unexpected
an answer, as that we received yesterday from your
Honour, to the humble address of this House delivered last Friday; relative to the obstinate and contumacious behaviour of the Clerk of the Common Pleas
to that Court; especially, as we perceive your Honour
has in your answer made use of the terms '*Assistant-
Judges*,' which do not carry altogether the same force
and meaning as the word '*Court*' which this House

inserted in their address—and we are sure your Honour cannot but know, that the determination of the majority of the Judges upon the bench, must be, and is always, considered as the determination of the Court, to all intents and purposes, and demands obedience accordingly.

" *We* having been always of opinion, that the Judges in his Majesty's Courts of Justice have, in Court, alone the right to construe the laws, or judge of the possibility or impossibility (according to circumstances) of their being executed, do not understand your Honour when saying ' That Mr. Campbell's disobedience did not proceed from any contumacy, or want of respect to the authority of the Assistant-Judges; but from his regard to the superior authority of an act of parliament.'

" If an obstinate refusal to enter, or obey, the orders of the Court, a fact that neither your address or Mr. Campbell denies, (with regard to himself) is not good and sufficient cause to suspend a ministerial officer of such Court, we are totally at a loss to discover what can be deemed so by your Honour; and we do not know, of any act of parliament whatever, and are very sure your Honour cannot point out a single one, countenancing such a monstrous irregularity, so manifestly subversive of the constitutional liberty of the subject, and introductory of the greatest anarchy and confusion.

" *Our* Journals, from which alone your Honour can have any parliamentary knowledge of our proceedings, take no notice of any application to your Honour, from the Assistant-Judges, relative to Mr. Campbell; and therefore, we cannot see, why your Honour should have had the less reason to have expected one from

from this House: though, had they given your Honour such information, we cannot but think, that would have been a still greater reason for your Honour to have expected an application from us; as we are called together to advise with you, about the weighty and urgent affairs of the province—are the natural guardians of the people's liberties and properties—and could not have passed over such a glaring matter unnoticed—without, a manifest violation of that duty, we owe to our most gracious Sovereign, our Constituents, ourselves, and posterity, in a point of the highest concern.

" We once more humbly entreat your Honour, to reconsider this matter; and not permit a precedent of so dangerous a nature to be established, and pass uncensured."

On the 1st day of May, the Lieutenant-Governor sent the following Message by the Master in Chancery, to the Commons-House of Assembly:

" Mr. Speaker, and Gentlemen,

" That I may show a respectful attention to any application you think proper to make to me, I have, at your desire, very deliberately reconsidered the matter in your late address, with your message relative to my answer thereto.

" As you apprehend there is a distinction between the terms *Authority of the Assistant-Judges* made use of by me, and the word *Court* in your address, I assure you, I had no mental reservation in that expression, or other meaning therein, than what is comprehended in your word *Court*.

" Though it would have been very agreeable to me, to have complied with what so respectable a body as the Assembly of this province, has with repeated earnestness requested; I am to consider, *Gentlemen*, that whenever my conduct in this, or any other matter, shall be questioned by the King, I must stand or fall by the propriety or impropriety of my own judgment. It will be no excuse for me, to have implicitly followed the opinion of the Assembly, if it shall be deemed improper by his Majesty: I therefore acquaint you, that as I cannot see cause to alter it, I still continue of the same opinion I delivered to you last Monday, in the Council Chamber.

"WILLIAM BULL."

The question was now brought to a point, by this Message of Lieutenant-Governor Bull; in which he plainly notified to the Assembly, in what manner *only*, he could co-operate with them in this, *or any other matter*, which might be questioned by the King. And as a last resort, the Commons-House of Assembly passed the following resolutions; and together with a particular account of all their proceedings on the subject, published them on the 7th May 1766, in a pamphlet, under the title of *"Votes of the Commons-House of Assembly of South-Carolina."*

" *Resolved*, that the Court of Common Pleas in this province, has a right to determine all questions of law, arising in causes depending before them; and to make orders for regulating, or concerning, the practice of the said Court; and cannot be controlled, or obstructed, in the making or executing such orders and Judgments, by their Clerk: but that from the nature of his office, he is bound *implicitly* to obey, all their orders and Judgments, in matters within their Jurisdiction.

"Resolved, that *Dougal Campbell*, Clerk of the said Court, by his refusal to enter or obey several of their orders, hath been guilty of a high contempt of, and offered the highest indignity to, the said Court.

"Resolved, that his Honour, the Lieutenant-Governor, ought to have suspended the said Dougal Campbell from his office, for the said contempt, as soon as a regular complaint thereof was made to him.

"Resolved, that the hearing Mr. Campbell's pretended vindication of his said disobedience, before his Majesty's Council, and their taking upon them to acquit him thereof, though declared guilty by the proper Judges, is highly illegal, and unjustifiable; and a precedent of the most dangerous nature, as it tends to destroy all subordination of ministerial officers, and draw the determination of Causes, from the Common Pleas, before the Council, in a summary, ex-parte, and extra-judicial way.

"Resolved, that the said Dougal Campbell, and all persons abetting, countenancing, or supporting him, in his said insult, and contumacy, have therein pursued measures derogatory from his Majesty's authority, delegated to the said Court—destructive to the rights and liberties of the subject—subversive of the laws, their best birth-right and inheritance—and highly injurious to the good people of this province—who, by an illegal and unconstitutional obstruction of the course of Justice, have been deprived of the protection of law, and rendered incapable of pursuing those remedies which it affords, for recovery of their rights, or redress of injuries to their persons and properties.

"Resolved, that it is the indispensable duty of all good subjects to our most gracious Sovereign George

III, and shall be the constant endeavour of this House, to preserve public peace and good order, and a due obedience to the laws. And if, by reason of the said Dougal Campbell's behaviour, the impunity with which it has passed, and the countenance it has received, any disturbance of the public tranquillity had happened, the same would not have been imputable in any degree, to this House; they having used repeated applications, and their best, and well-meant endeavours, to prevail on his Honour. the Lieutenant-Governor, to support and maintain the power of the said Court, by removing a ministerial officer, who presumes to dispute the legality, or disobey the Orders, of Judicial Officers, his superiors. And that as this House did, on this important point, discharge what they conceive to be their duty to the best of Kings, their Constituents, themselves and posterity—those who have failed in such duty, would have been looked upon, as the only occasions of, and answerable for, any ill consequences, that might have ensued therefrom."

These proceedings and Resolutions, together with petitions, papers, and publications, from the different provinces, being forwarded to Great Britain, not a little perplexed the Throne and Parliament. The call, was pressing—the crisis, was eventful;—but the administration which had caused the obnoxious acts, without providing a support to the Governors for enforcing their execution, still existed. The trading and manufacturing parts of the Kingdom, began to feel the interruptions of trade and commerce—a call was made by them upon the justice and forbearance of parliament—and it was so weighty, as to effect a change in the Ministry. This checked in some measure, the influence of the Earl of Bute; and gave

8

assurances of a more temperate consideration of American affairs.

A new Administration being now established, parliament met early in 1766, under happier auspices: all matters of grievance respecting the American provinces were laid before them. In the course of the discussions which took place thereon, Dr. Franklin was examined at the bar of the House of Commons; whose extensive communications on the state of American affairs, not a little contributed to remove prejudices, and spread information throughout that House. It was on this occasion, that Mr. Pitt came forward, as the advocate of American rights. He condemned the proceedings of the late Ministers, respecting them; and contended, the parliament had no authority for taxing the colonists, except for commercial regulations: and if they could be burthened at parliamentary discretion they would be mere slaves. He admitted, however, that for general government and legislation, parliament had a supreme control over them; but he said it ought so to be administered, that fundamental principles, common to both the parent State and the Colonies, should not be violated. As to returns from America, for protection afforded; he judged the profits of the American trade as sufficiently adequate. And deprecating the prosecution of a system, which ultimately would be pernicious to both countries; he advocated an immediate repeal, of the Stamp-Act.

Such were the opinions of this enlightened Statesman; and of many others, both in the House of Commons, and the House of Lords; who advocated the principles, for which he so nobly contended. They, however, did not change the fixed intentions of the Earl of Bute and his Royal Master; but on the contrary, the heart of George III. became callous to all

the persuasions of eloquence; even when displaying
and contending for, the free born rights of his oppressed subjects:—and his weight, and that of his
favourite, Bute, were thrown into the scale of opposition, against repealing the Stamp-Act.   It is true, that
weight did not prevail, and the obnoxious act was
repealed;* but they had sufficient influence to declare
by another act of parliament,† entitled " An Act for
the better securing the Dependency of his Majesty's
Dominions in America upon the Crown and Parliament of Great Britain," the absolute and unlimited
supremacy of the King and parliament, to make laws
for binding the Colonies and people of America in all
cases whatsoever:—and also, "that all resolutions,
votes, orders, and proceedings, in any of the said Colonies or Plantations, whereby the power and authority
of the Parliament of Great Britain, to make laws and
statutes as aforesaid, is denied, or drawn into question,
are, and are hereby declared to be, utterly null and
void, to all intents and purposes whatsoever."   The
act for this purpose, was called the Declaratory Act;
in principle, it was more hostile to American rights,
than the Stamp-Act.   For, it was in direct opposition
to every resolution and act, which had passed in the
Colonies; by which, they had asserted their right of
exemption from all taxes, not imposed by their own
Representatives.

When the news of this repeal arrived in the Colonies, a general joy spread over the land; and the
Courts in South-Carolina resumed their duties, which
had been prevented by the Clerk not issuing process:‡

* In 1766, in the sixth year of George III.'s reign.

† In 1766, immediately after the above act.

‡ The news of the repeal of the Stamp-Act, arrived in Charlestown, South-
Carolina, May 6th, 1766.

while America, recovering her former tranquillity, took
no umbrage at the law for securing her dependence on
Great Britain; rightly conceiving, it could never be
enforced.   For, as to cases of general and Sovereign
Government, she was willing it should be so; and so
far, as the act acknowledged these principles, so far,
she bowed obedient to its control.   In other respects,
the Declaratory Act was viewed with regret, rather
than fear; and the joyful news was notified by bon-
fires, illuminations, ringing of bells, and other demon-
strations of joy.   In these acts of festivity, Carolina
came in for her full share; in addition to which, a
statue of Mr Pitt, in the attitude of haranguing an
audience, was procured from England, at the public
expense; which, for many years thereafter, adorned
the most public place in Charlestown, at the intersection of Broad and Meeting-streets.*   Addresses were

* The Statue, remained at this place, throughout the whole Revolutionary
war, unhurt by any thing, except by a British cannon ball; which during the
seige of Charlestown in 1780, was discharged from a British fort, on James'
Island: which ranging across Ashley River, and along Meeting-street, carried
off Mr. Pitt's right arm, extended as if in the act, of addressing an audience.—
After the peace, of 1783, carriages for the conveyance of persons and goods,
had increased so much in the City of Charleston, as to require the Statue to
be removed, from the intersection of the streets, at so public a thoroughfare;
and Jacob Milligan† with other persons, were employed to effect the same.
This happened, not long after the commencement of the French Revolution.
The persons who were engaged in taking down the Statue, were great sup-
porters of French opinions; and consequently, were the declared enemies of
Mr. Pitt's son; whose great abilities then guided the energies of the British
nation, in the war against France   Through a misguided zeal, the enmity they
avowed against the Son, was extended even to this representation of his Father.
They fixed their ropes around the neck of the Statue, (which was raised on a
high pedestal) for the purpose, as they said, of obtaining a purchase, by which
they might erect the triangle, by whose assistance the Statue was to be raised
from the pedestal: and after having gained this purchase as they called it, and
fixed blocks and tackles to a post at some distance at the side of the street,
they commenced drawing the ropes with all their force.   The event turned
out, as was expected; and of which they had been warned, while in the act of

† This was the same Jacob Milligan, who after the battle of the 28th June, 1776, boarded the
Acteon frigate, while she was on fire.—See Chapter XVI.

also transmitted to the Throne, expressing the public happiness; and commercial intercourse again took place between Great Britain and her American Colonies. This produced, however, but a deceitful calm; as parliament soon after furnished America in general, and Boston in particular, with new causes for other commotions.

For now, (1767) an act of parliament was passed, enabling his Majesty to put the Customs, and other duties in the Colonies, and the execution of the laws there relating to trade, under the management of Commissioners, to be appointed for that purpose, and to be resident therein: as was another act, for more effectually preventing the clandestine running of goods in the Colonies and Plantations, and for granting duties in the Colonies, upon Glass, Red Lead, White Lead, Painters' Colours, Paper, Paste-boards, Mill-boards, Scale-boards, and Tea, imported into them.* These, originated new discontents and commotions, throughout America; resolutions, petitions, memorials, and addresses, against them, following in the train of public measures: and associations for suspending farther importations of British manufactures, until these obnoxious duties, and acts were removed, were again entered into at Boston and other places.

applying the power. For, so soon as the triangle was raised a few degrees high, its weight, and the opposing angle it made to the upright position of the Statue, overcame its fixture; and it was prostrated on the ground By this fall, the head of the Statue was severed from its body; or, was guillotined, as they were pleased to term it; and other parts of the body were mutilated: after which, it was removed to the Orphan-House yard, in Charleston;† where it has since been erected, as well as its injuries would permit.

* By this act, duties were imposed upon *sixty-three* different kinds of paper; and writs of Assistants were authorised to be issued by the Courts in the Colonies to authorise the officers of his Majesty's customs, to enter any house, &c. to search for, and seize prohibited goods.

† Since the peace of 1783, the name of Charlestown, has been altered to that of *Charleston.*

At this time, the heats at Boston might have subsided; had not the Crown Officers there, by endeavouring to show their zeal under the new restrictions
on trade, been the instruments of keeping up the irri-
tability which existed between them and the people.
This town, had arisen to wealth and importance in a
great degree, by carrying on trade to the West Indies,
and the Spanish Colonies on a part of South America;
and this trade, although forbidden by the strict letter
of the British Navigation Act, had nevertheless, under
a liberal construction, been permitted; as it was the
means of introducing specie and bullion, into the American Colonies; enabling the colonists thereby to make
remittances of money to England, in discharge of their
debts.   But the new Commissioners of the Customs,
were not instructed to continue this permission; and
being anxious to evince the utility of their establishment, they kept vigilant eyes over the Boston trade;
and particularly over the vessels, which were owned
in that port.   Under such influences, and a charge of
illicit trade, a seizure took place on the 10th of June
1768, of Mr. Hancock's sloop Liberty.   The cause of
seizure was not of a nature requiring so harsh a measure at that critical period; and Mr. Hancock was one
of the most popular men in Boston: it therefore immediately tended to irritate the people.   The mob
accordingly beat the Collector and the Comptroller of
the Customs; broke the windows of their houses; and
seizing the Collector's boat, they in triumph committed it to the flames.   Upon this, troops were ordered
from Halifax, to support the civil authority at Boston;
or in other words, to enforce the execution of acts of
parliament, which the people of America considered
unjust, and illegal.   On this occasion, another non-
importation agreement was entered into: and the
other Colonies afterwards adopted the measure.   Soon
after this, the Boston Town-Meeting, on the 12th

September 1768, voted, that the levying money within that province by other authority than their General Court of Assembly, was a violation of their Charter. And, as the Governor would not call a General Court, to redress their grievances; the town should choose a certain number of persons; who as a Committee should represent it, in a Congress or Convention, of similar Committees, from the several townships in that province. And hence, we may deduce the origin of Provincial Congresses, or Conventions; which afterwards came into use, throughout the American Colonies.

In December 1768, the Lords came to certain resolutions, touching the proceedings at Boston; which, afterwards received the concurrence of the Commons: and in February 1769, an address of both Houses was presented to the King of England, desiring, that within the Realm, trial might be had of offences done and committed in Massachusetts-Bay, since the 30th December 1767; in pursuance of the statute of 35th Henry VIII. This address, was replied to, by the General Court of Massachusetts, on the 8th July 1769; in which they declared, that all trials for any crime whatever committed in that Colony, ought to be had and conducted in the Courts of the same: and, that the seizing any person residing in that Colony, suspected of any crime whatsoever committed therein, and sending him beyond sea to be tried, was highly derogatory to the rights of British subjects. A deaf ear was, however, turned to these just remonstrances; and a law for that purpose, was passed by King and Parliament. About this time, the increasing importance of American affairs, occasioned the nomination of a third Secretary of State in Great Britain; whose department, had a special reference to the American Colonies: and the Earl of Hillsborough, was appointed thereto. How he executed its functions, in allaying the troubles which were excited; will, in some degree, be shown in these Memoirs, from his official correspondence.

Under the laws respecting Admiralty Jurisdiction, Colonel Henry Laurens of South-Carolina, conceived his rights to have been encroached on, by a decision of the Court of Admiralty; in consequence of which, he published a pamphlet respecting the same: which was answered in another pamphlet, by Sir Egerton Leigh, then presiding as Judge. To this a reply was made by the Colonel; who finally distributed copies of the Correspondence, not only throughout the American Colonies, but to England, and the West Indies. These publications, were not calculated to promote the honour of the Judge; or to sustain his increased Jurisdiction. He of course, lost ground on the occasion; and was soon after under the necessity of resigning his Judgeship, or his Attorney-Generalship; for he held both of these offices: and in each of them, he had been arraigned by Colonel Laurens. In this dilemma, between station and profit, he resigned his Judgeship; and the controversy acting on the public mind, had no little effect in aiding the public sentiment in Carolina, as respected the rights of America. In the following year, (1769) William Henry Drayton, by a series of publications, drew the public attention to the mode of enforcing the Association which had originated at Boston, for suspending the importation of British manufactures, and for other purposes; and which now, by a notification in the public papers, the citizens were called upon to subscribe, *or be considered inimical to American rights.* During the course of his publications, he stated several constitutional and legal objections to the same; in which, he was supported by the pen of William Wragg. On the opposite side of the question, were ranged Christopher Gadsden, and John Mackenzie. These publications being also connected with the passing affairs, afforded subjects of investigation, for inquiry, as to those rights—which were now questioned, by all men of consideration.*

The Commons-House of Assembly of the Province, at length came forward at the close of this year, (8th December 1769,) in support of the Association against the importation of British goods. And so warm were they, in defending the principles by which they acted; that of their own authority, they passed an Order on Jacob Motte, the Public Treasurer, for the sum of £10,500, provincial currency, equal to £1,500 Sterling; to be remitted to Great Britain, " for assisting in the support of the just and constitutional rights and liberties of the people of Great Britain and America."† This sum was accordingly remitted; and was appropriated, in the manner, for which, it was intended. Such was, however, the crisis, at that period, that this measure immediately led to a disagreement with his Majesty's Provincial Council, acting as a branch of the General Assembly; which greatly affected the harmony previously existing between the two Houses: and the disagreement was brought on, in the following manner.

In the month of March 1770, the House of Assembly sent to the Council, (then sitting as a branch of the

* They were republished at London in January 1771, in a small octavo volume, under the title of " The Letters of Freeman," &c.

† See an anonymous pamphlet, supposed to be written by Sir Egerton Leigh, who was a member of the Council of South-Carolina, entitled, " Considerations on certain Political Transactions of the Province of South-Carolina," published in London in 1774, pages 7 and 10, &c.

General Assembly) the annual tax bill, to defray the charges of the Government from the first day of January to the first day of December 1769, both days inclusive; and for other services therein mentioned. And on the second reading thereof, and also of the schedule thereto annexed, the Council discovered the following charge, viz: " To Jacob Motte, Esquire, advanced by him to certain Members of the House, by a Resolution of the House of the eighth December last, £10,500." On which, the Council, by a Message to the Commons-House of Assembly, dated the 5th day of April, 1770, declared, that the grant of the sum aforementioned, " did not appear in any sense, *honourable, fit, or decent:* not fit or honourable, as they conceived the Assembly's jurisdiction was merely local, and for provincial purposes: and not decent, as the grant by the tax bill was expressly declared to be for his Majesty; and yet contained a provision highly affrontive to his Majesty's Government, which they declared to have ever been, in their opinion, gracious, mild, and good, to all his faithful people."—To this Message, the Assembly sent an answer in two days after, " returning, the Council's Message, *for their calm reconsideration:*" which was immediately followed by another from the Council, expressing " that the Assembly's proceedings were neither parliamentary nor proper; and that they were determined to adhere to their former sentiments."—On this, a prorogation took place; and the dispute between the two Houses, remained undecided.

In August following, the Legislature again met; when Lieutenant-Governor Bull, communicated a copy of his Majesty's additional Instruction, bearing date the 14th day of April 1770, which he had lately received. This Instruction recites, That the House of Representatives, or *Lower House* of Assembly in South-Carolina, had lately assumed to themselves a

power of ordering, without the concurrence of the
Governor and Council, the Public Treasurer of the
said province, to issue and advance out of the public
treasury, such sums of money, and for such services,
as they thought fit; and in particular, that the said
Lower House of Assembly did on the 8th day of December last past, make an order on the said Public
Treasurer to advance the sum of £10,500 currency,
out of any money in the Treasury, to be paid into the
hands of Mr. Speaker, Mr. Gadsden, Mr. Rutledge,
Mr. Parsons, Mr. Furguson, Mr. Dart, and Mr. Lynch,
who were to remit the same to Great Britain for the
support of the just and constitutional rights and Liberties of the people of Great Britain and America. It
next states the necessity of putting a stop to such dangerous and unwarrantable practices, and for guarding
for the future against such unconstitutional application
of the King's treasure, cheerfully granted to his Majesty, for the public uses of the province, and for support
of the Government thereof; his Majesty was pleased
to direct the Governor, on pain of removal, not to
give his assent to any bill, that shall be passed by the
Lower House of Assembly, by which, any sum of money shall be appropriated to, or provision made for,
defraying any expense incurred for services or purposes, not immediately arising within, or incidental to,
the said province; unless, upon the King's special requisition; nor, to any bill or bills for granting any sum
to his Majesty, &c. in which bill or bills it shall not be
provided, in express words, that the money so to be
granted, or any part thereof, shall not be issued or
applied to any other services, than those to which it is
by the said bill or bills appropriated; unless, by act,
or ordinance of the General Assembly of the said province.

The Instruction, next forbad the Governor to give his assent to any bill or bills that shall be passed by the Lower House, by which, any sum or sums of money shall be granted to his Majesty, &c. generally, and without appropriation; unless there be a clause inserted, providing, that the said money so to be granted shall remain in the Treasury, subject to such appropriation as shall thereafter be made by act, or ordinance, as aforesaid.

It contained also a provision, that in all future bills, for raising and granting Public Monies, a clause be inserted, subjecting the Public Treasurer, &c. in case he shall issue or pay any such money, otherwise than by express order contained in some act or ordinance of the General Assembly, to a penalty in treble the sum so issued contrary thereto; and declared him or them to be *ipso facto*, incapable of holding, his or their office, or any other office, civil, or military, within the said province.*

When this additional Instruction was known to the Commons-House of Assembly, on the 30th August 1770, that body made another experiment, by sending a like tax-bill and schedule to the Council, containing the same obnoxious item. This was of course, promptly rejected: and the session ended like the preceding one, by a prorogation, to the 16th January 1771. On the 15th February 1771, Lieutenant-Governor Bull communicated to the Council, the following paragraph of a letter he had received the same day, from the Right Honourable the Earl of Hillsborough: " I must not omit to acquaint you, that the becoming manner in which the Council have exerted themselves in

* See the pamphlet attributed to Sir Egerton Leigh, pages 11, 12, and 13.— Also Appendix to this Chapter, No. VII.

support of his Majesty's measures, has not escaped the King's observations. And, I am commanded to signify to you, his Majesty's pleasure, that you should express to them, his Majesty's approbation of their conduct."

Encouraged therefore by the Royal approbation, as well as precluded by the additional Instruction, the executive assent was withholden from money bills, which were in any manner contrary thereto. And the House of Assembly having their reasons, for not giving way; kept up a constant collision, between the two authorities; which proceeded to such a length, that the Assembly even disputed the right of the Council to sit as an Upper House of Assembly. The consequence was, that the tax-bills since August 1770, were rejected by the Council; and not a public debt was provided for, from the commencement of this dispute on the 8th December 1769, until some years afterwards; as shall be farther shown.

In the mean time, the Provincial Agent, Charles Garth, Esquire, was instructed by the Assembly, to apply to the Crown; requesting his Majesty to reconsider the said Instruction, and to withdraw the same. He accordingly presented a petition for that purpose, to the Throne; but, the Instruction was neither reconsidered, nor withdrawn. On the contrary, the Earl of Dartmouth, in the month of June 1773, in a letter to Lieutenant-Governor Bull, relative to the Council having the March before, rejected again the tax-bill, acquainted him; "That, the said proceeding of the Council was considered by the King, as a fresh mark of their zeal and duty; and his Lordship, was further commanded to desire, that his Honour would not fail to signify to the Council, his Majesty's approbation of their conduct."

Such, was the situation, of the two Houses; each, tenacious of what they deemed, their several rights: the Council, supported by the Crown—and the Assembly, by the people. Their ancient Union, was now broken—a coolness intervened—and each House, gave a direction to its actions, as suited the purposes it had in view—or, the events, which were closely following each other, in the destinies of the American Colonies.

APPENDIX

CHAPTER II.

———

No. I.

Declaration of Rights, &c.

WE, the Members of this Congress, sincerely devoted, with the warmest sentiments of affection and duty to his Majesty's person and Government, inviolably attached to the present happy establishment of the Protestant Succession, and with minds deeply impressed by a sense of the present, and impending, misfortunes of the British Colonies on this Continent, having considered, as maturely as time will permit, the circumstances of the said Colonies, esteem it our indispensable duty, to make the following declarations of our opinion, respecting the most essential Rights and Liberties of the colonists, and of the grievances under which they do and must labour, by reason of several late acts of parliament.

1. That his Majesty's subjects in these Colonies, owe the same allegiance to the Crown of Great Britain, that is owing from his subjects born within the Realm, and all due subordination to that august body, the Parliament of Great Britain.

2. That his Majesty's liege subjects in these Colonies, are entitled to all the inherent Rights and Liberties, of his natural born subjects, within the kingdom of Great Britain.

3. That it is inseparably essential to the freedom of a people, and the undoubted right of Englishmen, that no taxes be imposed on them, but by their own consent, given personally, or by their Representatives.

4. That the people of these Colonies are not, and, from their local circumstances, cannot, be represented in the House of Commons in Great Britain.

5. That the only Representatives of the people of these Colonies are, persons chosen therein, by themselves; and, that no taxes ever have been, or can be, constitutionally imposed on them, but by their respective Legislatures.

6. That all supplies to the Crown, being free gifts of the people, it is unreasonable, and inconsistent with the principles and spirit of the British Constitution, for the people of Great Britain to grant to his Majesty, the property of the colonists.

7. That trial by Jury, is the inherent right, of every British subject, in these Colonies.

8. That the late act of parliament, entitled "An Act for granting and applying certain Stamp-Duties, in

the British Colonies and Plantations in America," &c.
by imposing taxes on the inhabitants of these Colonies, and the said act, and several other acts, by extending the jurisdiction of the Courts of Admiralty
beyond its ancient limits, have a manifest tendency to
subvert the Rights and Liberties of the Colonies.

9. That the duties imposed by several late acts of
parliament, from the peculiar circumstances of these
Colonies, will be extremely burthensome and grievous;
and, from the scarcity of specie, the payment of them
absolutely impracticable.

10. That as the profits of the trade of these Colonies, ultimately center in Great Britain, to pay for the
manufactures which they are obliged to take from
thence, they eventually contribute, very largely, to all
supplies granted then to the Crown.

11. That the restrictions imposed by several late
acts of parliament, on the trade of these Colonies, will
render them unable to purchase the manufactures of
Great Britain.

12. That the increase, prosperity, and happiness of
these Colonies, depend on the full and free enjoyment
of their Rights and Liberties, and an intercourse with
Great Britain, mutually affectionate and advantageous.

13. That it is the right of the British subjects, in
these Colonies, to petition the King, or either House
of Parliament.

Lastly. That it is the indispensable duty of these
Colonies, to the best of Sovereigns, to the mother
country, and to themselves, to endeavour, by a loyal
and dutiful address to his Majesty, and humble appli-

cation to both Houses of Parliament, to procure the repeal of the act, " for granting and applying certain Stamp-Duties;" of all clauses of any other acts of parliament, whereby the jurisdiction of the Admiralty is extended as aforesaid; and of the other late acts for the restriction of American commerce.

No. II.

To the *King's* most Excellent *Majesty*.

The Petition of the Freeholders and other Inhabitants of the Massachusetts-Bay, Rhode-Island and Providence Plantations, New-Jersey, Pennsylvania, the Government of the Counties of Newcastle, Kent, and Sussex upon Delaware, provinces of Maryland, and South-Carolina,*

Most humbly showeth,

That the inhabitants of these Colonies, unanimously devoted, with the warmest sentiments of duty and affection, to your Majesty's sacred person and government; inviolably attached to the present happy establishment of the Protestant Succession, in your illustrious house; and deeply sensible of your royal attention to their prosperity and happiness; humbly beg leave to approach the Throne, by representing to your Majesty :

---

* The other provinces represented at the Congress, not having authorized their Committees to sign the petitions and memorial, which were to be sent to England , they were afterwards submitted to their several Assemblies, were signed, and transmitted accordingly.

That these Colonies were originally planted by subjects of the British Crown, who, animated with the spirit of Liberty, encouraged by your Majesty's royal predecessors, and confiding in the public faith for the enjoyment of all the Rights and Liberties essential to freedom, emigrated from their native country, to this Continent, and by their successful perseverance, in the midst of innumerable dangers and difficulties, together with a profusion of their blood and treasure, have happily added these vast, and valuable, dominions, to the empire of Great Britain.

That, for the enjoyment of these Rights and Liberties, several Governments were early formed, in the said Colonies, with full powers of Legislation, agreeably to the principles of the English Constitution.

That, under those Governments, these liberties thus vested in their ancestors, and transmitted to their posterity, have been exercised and enjoyed; and, by the inestimable blessings thereof, under the favour of Almighty God, the inhospitable desarts of America have been converted into flourishing countries; science, humanity, and the knowledge of Divine truths, diffused through remote regions of ignorance, infidelity and barbarism; the number of British subjects wonderfully increased; and the wealth and power of Great Britain proportionably augmented.

That, by means of these settlements, and the unparalleled success of your Majesty's arms, a foundation is now laid, for rendering the British empire the most extensive and powerful of any recorded in history. Our connection with this empire, we esteem our greatest happiness and security; and humbly conceive, it may now be so established, by your Royal wisdom, as to endure to the latest period of time. This, with

most humble submission to your Majesty, we apprehend, will be most effectually accomplished, by fixing
the pillars thereof on liberty and justice; and securing
the inherent rights and liberties of your subjects here,
upon the principles of the English Constitution.

To this constitution these two principles are essential. The right of your faithful subjects freely to
grant, to your Majesty, such aids as are required for
the support of your Government over them, and other
public exigencies; and trials by their peers. By the
one, they are secured from unreasonable impositions;
and by the other, from arbitrary decisions of the Executive power. The continuation of these liberties to
the inhabitants of America, we ardently implore, as
absolutely necessary to unite the several parts of our
wide extended dominions, in that harmony so essential
to the preservation and happiness of the whole. Protected in these liberties, the emoluments Great Britain
receives from us, however great at present, are incon-
siderable, compared with those she has the fairest prospect of acquiring: by this protection, she will, for
ever, secure to herself, the advantage of conveying to
all Europe, the Merchandize, which America fur-
nishes, and of supplying through the same channel,
whatever is wanted from thence.

Here, opens a boundless source of wealth and naval
strength: yet these immense advantages, by the
abridgement of those invaluable rights and liberties,
by which our growth has been nourished, are in danger of being for ever lost, and our subordinate Legisla-
latures, in effect, rendered useless, by the late acts of
parliament, imposing duties and taxes on these Colonies, and extending the jurisdiction of the Courts of
Admiralty here, beyond its ancient limits; *Statutes*,
by which your Majesty's Commons in Great Britain

undertake, absolutely, to dispose of the property of their fellow subjects in America, without their consent, and for the enforcing whereof, they are subjected to the determination of a single judge, in a Court unrestrained by the wise rules of the Common Law, the birth-right of Englishmen, and the safeguard of their persons and properties.

The invaluable rights of taxing ourselves, and trial by our peers, of which we implore your Majesty's protection, are not, we most humbly conceive, unconstitutional; but confirmed by the great charter of English liberty.

On the first of these rights, the honourable the House of Commons found their practice of originating money bills: a *Right*, enjoyed by the Kingdom of Ireland; by the Clergy of England, until relinquished by themselves: a *Right*, in fine, which all your Majesty's English subjects, both within and without the realm, have hitherto enjoyed.

With hearts, therefore, impressed with the most indelible characters of gratitude to your Majesty, and to the memory of the Kings of your illustrious house, whose reigns have been signally distinguished, by their auspicious influence on the prosperity of the British dominions; and convinced, by the most affecting proofs of your Majesty's paternal love to all your people, however distant, and your unceasing and benevolent desires to promote their happiness; we most humbly beseech your Majesty, that you will be graciously pleased to take into your Royal consideration, the distresses of your faithful subjects on this Continent; and to lay the same, before your Majesty's parliament; and to afford them such relief, as, in your Royal wisdom, their unhappy circumstances shall be judged to require.   And your Petitioners, as in duty bound, will ever pray.

No. III.

To the Right Honourable, the Lords, Spiritual, and Temporal, of Great Britain, in Parliament assembled:

The Memorial of the Freeholders and other Inhabitants of the Massachusetts-Bay, Rhode-Island and Providence Plantations, New-Jersey, Pennsylvania, the Government of the Counties of Newcastle, Kent, and Sussex upon Delaware; provinces of Maryland, and South-Carolina,

Most humbly showeth,

That his Majesty's liege subjects in his American Colonies, though they acknowledge a due subordination to that august body the British Parliament, are entitled, in the opinion of your memorialists, to all the inherent rights and liberties of the natives of Great Britain, and have, ever since the settlement of the said Colonies, exercised those rights and liberties, as far as their local circumstances would permit.

That your memorialists humbly conceive, one of the most essential rights of these colonists, which they have ever, till lately, uninterruptedly enjoyed, to be trial by jury.

That your memorialists also humbly conceive, another of these essential rights to be, the exemption from all taxes but such as are imposed on the people by the several legislatures in these Colonies; which right also, they have, till of late, freely enjoyed.

But, your memorialists humbly beg leave to represent, to your Lordships, that the act "for granting certain Stamp-Duties in the British Colonies in America," &c. fills his Majesty's American subjects with the deepest concern, as it tends to deprive them of the two fundamental and invaluable rights and liberties above mentioned; and that several other late acts of parliament, which extend the jurisdiction and powers of Courts of Admiralty in the plantations, beyond their limits in Great Britain, thereby make an unnecessary and unhappy distinction, as to the modes of trial, between us and our fellow subjects there, by whom we have never been excelled in duty, and loyalty, to our Sovereign.

That, from the natural connection between Great Britain and America, (the perpetual continuance of which your memorialists most ardently desire,) they conceive, that nothing can conduce more to the interest of both, than the colonists' free enjoyment of their rights and liberties, and an affectionate intercourse between Great Britain and them.

But, your memorialists (not waving their claim, to these rights, of which, with the most becoming veneration and deference to the wisdom and justice of your Lordships, they apprehend, they cannot reasonably be deprived) humbly represent,

That, from the peculiar circumstances of the Colonies, the duties imposed by the aforesaid act, and several other late acts of parliament, are extremely grievous and burthensome; and the payment of the said duties will, very soon, for want of specie, become absolutely impracticable. And,

That the restrictions on trade, by the said acts, will not only greatly distress the Colonies, but must be extremely detrimental to the trade and true interest of Great Britain.

Your memorialists, therefore, impressed with a just sense of the unfortunate circumstances of the Colonies; the impending destructive consequences which must necessarily ensue, from the execution of these acts; and animated with the warmest sentiments of filial affection for their mother country; most earnestly and humbly entreat, that your Lordships will be pleased to hear their Counsel, in support of this memorial, and take the premises into your most serious consideration: and that your Lordships will also be, thereupon, pleased to pursue such measures, for restoring the just rights and liberties of the Colonies, and preserving them for ever inviolate, for redressing their present, and preventing future grievances, thereby promoting the united interest of Great Britain and America; as to your Lordships, in your great wisdom, shall seem most conducive and effectual, to that important end. And your memorialists, as in duty bound, will ever pray.

No. IV.

To the Honourable the Knights, Citizens, and Burgesses of Great Britain, in Parliament assembled.

The Petition of his Majesty's dutiful and loyal subjects the Freeholders and other Inhabitants of the

Colonies of the Massachusetts-Bay, Rhode-Island and Providence Plantations, New-Jersey, Pennsylvania, the Government of the Counties of Newcastle, Kent and Sussex upon Delaware, Provinces of Maryland, South-Carolina,

Most humbly showeth,

That the several late acts of parliament, imposing divers duties and taxes on the Colonies, and laying the trade and commerce thereof under very burthensome restrictions; *but above all*, the act " for granting and applying certain Stamp-Duties, &c. in America," have filled them with the deepest concern and surprise : and they humbly conceive, the execution of them, will be attended with consequences very injurious to the commercial interest of Great Britain, and her Colonies, and must terminate in the eventual ruin of the latter.

Your petitioners therefore most ardently implore the attention of the honourable House, to the united and dutiful representations of their circumstances, and to their earnest supplications for relief, from those regulations, which have already involved this Continent in anxiety, confusion, and distress.

We most sincerely recognize our allegiance to the Crown, and acknowledge all due submission to the Parliament of Great Britain, and shall always retain the most grateful sense of their assistance and protection.

It is from, and under, the English Constitution, we derive all our civil and religious rights and liberties. We glory in being subjects of the best of Kings, and in having been born under the most perfect form of government: but it is with most ineffable and humilia-

11

ting sorrow, that we find ourselves of late, deprived of
the right of granting our own property for his Majesty's service; to which our lives and fortunes are
entirely devoted, and to which, on his Royal requisitions, we have ever been ready to contribute, to the
utmost of our abilities.

We have also the misfortune to find, that all the
penalties and forfeitures mentioned in the Stamp-Act,
are, at the election of the informer, recoverable in any
Court of Admiralty in America; this, as the newly
erected Court of Admiralty has a general jurisdiction,
over all British America, renders his Majesty's subjects, in these Colonies, liable to be carried, at an
immense expense, from one end of the Continent to
the other.

It gives us also great pain, to see a manifest distinction made therein, between the subjects of our mother country, and those in the Colonies, in that, the
like penalties and forfeitures, recoverable there only in
his Majesty's Courts of record, are made cognizable
here by a Court of Admiralty. By this means we
seem to be, in effect, unhappily deprived of two privileges essential to freedom, and which all Englishmen
have ever considered as their best birth-rights; that of
being free from all taxes, but such as they have consented to in person, or by their representatives; and of
trial by their peers.

Your petitioners further show, that the remote situation, and other circumstances of the Colonies, render
it impracticable, that they should be represented, but
in their respective subordinate Legislatures; and they
humbly conceive, that the parliament adhering strictly
to the principles of the Constitution, have never hitherto taxed any, but those who were actually therein

represented; for this reason, we humbly apprehend, they never have taxed Ireland, or any other of the subjects without the Realm. But were it ever so clear, that the Colonies might, in law, be reasonably deemed to be represented in the honourable House of Commons, yet, we conceive, that very good reasons, from inconvenience, from the principles of true policy, and from the spirit of the British Constitution, may be adduced, to show, that it would be for the real interest of Great Britain, as well as her Colonies, that the late regulations should be rescinded, and the several acts of parliament imposing duties and taxes on the Colonies, and extending the jurisdiction of the Courts of Admiralty here, beyond their ancient limits, should be repealed.

We shall not attempt a minute detail of all the reasons which the wisdom of the honourable House may suggest on this occasion; but would humbly submit the following particulars, to their consideration.

That money is already become very scarce to these Colonies, and is still decreasing, by the necessary exportation of specie from the Continent, for the discharging of debts to British Merchants.

That an immensely heavy debt is yet due from the Colonies, for British manufactures; and that they are still heavily burthened with taxes, to discharge the arrearages due, for aids granted by them in the late war.

That the balance of trade will ever be much against the Colonies, and in favour of Great Britain, whilst we consume her manufactures; the demand for which must ever increase in proportion to the number of inhabitants settled here, with the means of purchasing them: we therefore humbly conceive it to be the interest of Great Britain, to increase, rather than diminish these means; as the profits of all the trade of the Colonies ultimately center there, to pay for her manufactures, as we are not allowed to purchase elsewhere; and by the consumption of which, at the advanced prices the British taxes oblige the makers and venders to set on them, we eventually contribute, very largely, to tke revenue of the Crown.

That from the nature of American business, the multiplicity of suits, and papers used in matters of small value, in a country where freeholds are so minutely divided, and property so frequently transferred, a stamp-duty must ever be very burthensome and unequal.

That it is extremely improbable that the honourable House of Commons should, at all times, be thoroughly acquainted with our condition, and all facts requisite to a just and equal taxation of the Colonies. It is also humbly submitted, whether there be not a material distinction, in reason and sound policy, at least, between the necessary exercise of parliamentary jurisdiction in general acts for the amendment of the Common Law, and the regulation of trade and commerce through the whole empire, and the exercise of that jurisdiction, by imposing taxes on the Colonies.

That the several subordinate provincial Legislatures, have been moulded into forms, as nearly resembling that of the mother country, as by his Majesty's Royal Predecessors was thought convenient: and these Legislatures seem to have been wisely and graciously established, that the subjects in the Colonies might, under the due administration thereof, enjoy the happy fruits of the British Government, which, in their present circumstances, they cannot be so fully and clearly availed of any other way. Under these forms of Government, we and our ancestors have been born or settled, and have had our lives, liberties, and properties protected. The people here, as every where else, retain a great fondness for their old customs and usages; and we trust, that his Majesty's service, and the interest of the nation, so far from being obstructed, have been vastly promoted, by the provincial legislatures.

That we esteem our connection with, and dependance on, Great Britain, as one of our greatest blessing; and apprehend, the latter will appear to be sufficiently secured, when it is considered, that the inhabitants of the Colonies have the most unbounded affection for his Majesty's person, family, and government, as well as for the mother country; and that their subordination to the parliament, is universally acknowledged.

We therefore most humbly entreat, that the honourable House would be pleased to hear our Counsel, in support of this petition, and take our distressed and deplorable case into their serious consideration; and that the acts, and clauses of acts, so grievously restraining our trade and commerce, imposing duties and taxes on our property, and extending the jurisdiction of the Court of Admiralty beyond its ancient limits, may be repealed; or, that the honourable House would otherwise relieve your petitioners, as in your great wisdom and goodness shall seem meet. And your petitioners, as in duty bound, shall ever pray.*

* See Votes of the Commons-House of Assembly of South-Carolina, published by Order of the 9th April 1766, in a folio pamphlet.

No. V.

April 8th, 1766.

Gentlemen,

Your application to me, to suspend Dougal Campbell, Esq. Clerk of the Court of Common Pleas, for not obeying your order in Court, to enter Judgment on the first instant, brings me into a very disagreeable dilemma. I shall, on the one hand, either incur the Royal displeasure, if I should, according to your desire, suspend Mr. Campbell, in case there should not appear to his Majesty a sufficient cause of suspension ; as I am forbid by the King's instruction, to suspend without a sufficient cause, to be immediately transmitted and laid before the King; or, on the other hand, if I should not suspend him, I may appear not to pay that attention to support your authority, and the obedience due to your orders as Judges of the Court, which every motive of esteem for your private characters, and respect for your public stations, would prompt me to show.

In this difficult and delicate situation, it was not prudent for me to rely upon my own judgment, to form my determination thereupon: I therefore referred your application to me, to the consideration of his Majesty's Council, desiring their opinion, whether, in this case, there is sufficient cause for a suspension, according to the King's Instruction.

Before the Council entered upon the matter, the Chief Justice delivered his reasons for his dissent from your order in Court, mentioned in your representa-

tion; which, (he said) were delivered in Court, and
then withdrew.   And Mr. Campbell, by petition,
stated his particular circumstances, and prayed to be
heard before determination, which being agreeable to
equity, was granted: the purport of which declared,
that his refusal to enter your order proceeded solely
from his fear of the penalties of the act, which particularly names his office; he therefore considered himself, and not the Judges, as answerable for his acts
done therein.   And he has made the strongest and
most dutiful professions of respect for your authority
and commands, to which no one can be more ready
to pay all due obedience; and that nothing was more
remote from his thoughts, than the least appearance of
a contumacious disregard to your orders, which, from
his past good behaviour in that office, I am willing to
believe.

His Majesty's Council having maturely weighed the
matter contained in your representation, and the reasons of the Chief Justice's dissent, and those given by
Mr. Campbell, relative thereto, are of opinion, that a
disobedience to the orders of the Court, in a general
sense, is most certainly a sufficient cause for suspension; but, that the present case of Mr. Campbell's, is
attended with such circumstances, as do not subject
him to the charge of disobedience in the general
sense; and therefore, in the present case, there is not
sufficient cause to suspend Mr. Campbell from his
office: especially, as my compliance with your desire,
under such circumstances, must subject me, not only
to the King's displeasure in general, but to the more
severe penalties and disabilities of an act of parliament, as yet of force in this province, which I might,
thereby, be considered as acting repugnant to.

I am sorry, therefore, Gentlemen, that I am to acquaint you, that I cannot comply with your request in this case, tho',

I am, with great truth and regard,

Gentlemen,

Your most obt. humble servt.

WILLIAM BULL.

To the Hon. ROBERT PRINGLE, RAWLINS LOWNDES, BENJAMIN SMITH, DANIEL D'OYLEY, Esqrs. *Assistant-Judges, &c. of South-Carolina.*

No. VI.

To the Honourable Peter Manigault, Esquire, Speaker, and the rest of the Members of the Honourable the Commons-House of Assembly:

The humble Petition of the subscribers, Merchants, Traders, Freeholders, and other Inhabitants of Charles-town, and the other parts of this province,

Showeth,

That since *the first day of November last,* many of your petitioners and numbers of others, have applied to several Attornies of the Court of Common Pleas in this province, to purchase writs to commence actions, and carry on suits therein as usual; and that such Attornies have been, and are ready and willing to comply with such requests, but cannot; being unable to purchase or procure the process of that Court, though they have frequently demanded it from the Clerk of the Pleas, as well as from the Chief Justice: and were.

ready to pay and tender all legal and necessary fees that could be due or demanded, for such process.

That, by reason of the premises, no business has been transacted in the said Court, *since the said first day of November;* to the great loss and detriment of your petitioners and others.

That, the pretence for this refusal of justice, is the want of stamped papers, which it is not the business or duty of suitors to provide; and which cannot be had in this province, as appears by his Honour the Lieutenant-Governor's certificate, under his hand and seal at arms, lodged in the Secretary's office.

That the late resolutions of your honourable House, with regard to the Stamp-Act, and the undoubted rights and liberties of the people of this province, (for which we beg leave to express our gratitude, and return our public thanks) are entirely to the satisfaction, and coincide with the sentiments of your petitioners, for which reason, they think it unnecessary at present, to offer any observations on those points; but they humbly apprehend, it is contrary to the principles of the *British* Constitution, and the express words of the *Great Charter,* so often confirmed, and expressly of force in this province, that justice or right should be deferred or denied; and that your petitioners therefore, cannot, under any pretence, be legally deprived of those remedies, which they are entitled to, for recovery of their rights, and redress of injuries.

That, besides the many other grievances, occasioned by this refusal of justice, these irreparable ones in particular are certain and notorious; that many transitory persons in debt here, have departed the province against the will, and without paying their creditors;

12

others, who want to go, and have debts due to them,
are grievously delayed and detained, being unable to
enforce payment; and numbers, who had, and others,
who have, legal and just demands, will be for ever
barred of recovering the same, by the act of limita-
tions.

That, the same reasons hold for conducting business
in the Courts, as justify the doing of it at the Custom-
House, without stamped papers; nor, can they see
any cause, why the inhabitants of this province, should
be unhappily distinguished in this respect from their
fellow subjects in the other provinces, where stamped
papers are not to be had.

Your Petitioners, therefore, humbly, and earnestly,
intreat your honourable House, as the guardians of
the liberties and privileges of the inhabitants of this
province, to take the premises into your serious consideration, and grant, or procure them, such relief
therein, as you shall think just and necessary.

Elias Vanderhorst	James Sharp	Simon Tufts
John Ward	John Chapman	Daniel Cannon
Brewton & Smith	Woddrop & Cathcart	John Prue
John Paul Grimke	Price, Hest, & Head	John M'Call, jun.
William Logan	Stocker & Jackson	Francis Kinloch
Thomas Smith	William Boone	Melchior Warley
Thomas Hartley	William Lyford	William Trustler
John Neufville	Croft & Dart	Cato Ash
Davies & Wayne	Thomas Boone	Mark Morris
Brian Cape	Edward Lightwood	Braund & Kalteisen
James Poyas	Benfield & Jones	Charles You
John Scott	Downes, Jones & Co.	Charles Odingsell
Tunes Tebout	John Ash	Livingston & Champneys
Godfrey & Gadsden	Atkins & Weston	Frederick Grimke
Andrew Marr	John & Wm. Baker	William Blake
Donald Bruce	James Carsan	John Harvey
Dawson & Dudley	Sheed & White	John Bedon
Edward Jones & Co.	Wm. Bampfield	Samuel Prioleau, jun.
Laurens, Motte & Co.	Inglis, Lloyd & Co.	Peter Bonnetheau

John Wagner	Guerin & Williamson	William Hall
Joseph Creighton	Philip Andebert	Thomas You
William Hopton	Thomas Elliott	Peter Butler
John Packron	Charles Capers	William Holiday
Thomas Mill	Alexander Learmouth	Arthur Downes
Simon Berwick	Thomas Robinson	Darby Pendergrass
Richard Richardson	Joseph Dill	Jonathan Sarrazin
Robert Harvey	Joseph Atkinson	William Gibbes
Jeremiah Theus	Patrick Hinds	Joseph Hutchins
John Wish	Alexander Horn	Benjamin Roberts
Peter Bocquet, jun.	Thomas Pike	James Hogan
Christopher Holson	Thomas Farr	Solomon Legare
John Dodd	Perdriau & Fabre	James Legare
Daniel Legare	Paul Townsend	Christopher Fitzsimons
Timothy Crosby	Philip Tidyman	Edmund Matthews
William Banbury	Rutledge & Lesesne	Robert M·Gillivray
William Savage	John Marley	John Bothwell
Villepontoux & Waring	Edward Martin	Nathaniel Scott
Nowell & Lord	Elfe & Hutchinson	Robert Rutherford

☞ *The two preceding numbers, V & VI, are taken from a folio pamphlet, published by order of the Commons-House of Assembly of South-Carolina, on the 7th May 1766, entitled, " Votes of the Commons-House of Assembly of South-Carolina."*

No. VII.

IN THE COUNCIL CHAMBER.

Wednesday, 15th day of August, 1770.

PRESENT,

His Honour the LIEUTENANT-GOVERNOR,
The Hon. OTHNIEL BEALE, EGERTON LEIGH, JOHN
BURN, THOMAS SKOTTOWE, JOHN STUART, Esqrs.

His Honour the Lieutenant-Governor, communicated to the Board, the following Additional Instruction from his Majesty; which had been transmitted to him by the last Packet, from the Right Honourable the Earl of Hillsborough, one of his Majesty's Principal Secretaries of State:

GEORGE R.
(L. S.)

Additional Instructions to our Trusty and well beloved Charles Greville Montagu, Esquire, commonly called Lord Charles Greville Montague; our Captain General and Governor in Chief of our Province of South-Carolina in America; or, in his absence, to the Lieutenant-Governor, or Commander in Chief, of our said Province or the time being. Given, at our Court of St. James', the 14th day of April 1770, in the tenth year of our reign.

WHEREAS, it hath been represented to us, that our House of Representatives, or Lower House of Assembly of our Province of South-Carolina in America, have lately assumed to themselves, a power of ordering, without the concurrence of our Governor and Council, the Public Treasurer of our said Province to issue and advance out of the public Treasury, such sums of money, and for such services, as they have thought fit; and in particular, that the said Lower-House of Assembly did, on the 8th day of December last past, make an order on the said public Treasurer, to advance the sum of ten thousand five hundred pounds currency, out of any money in the Treasury, to be paid into the hands of Mr. Speaker, Mr. Gadsden, Mr. Rutledge, Mr. Parsons, Mr. Furguson, Mr. Dart, and Mr. Lynch, who were to remit the same to Great Britain, for the support of the just and constitutional Rights and Liberties of the people of Great Britain and America: And whereas, it is highly necessary that the most effectual measures be pursued,

for putting a stop to such dangerous and unwarrantable practices; and for guarding for the future, against
such unconstitutional application of our Treasury,
cheerfully granted to us, by our subjects in our said
Province, and for support of the Government thereof:
It is therefore our will and pleasure, and you are
hereby directed and required, upon pain of our highest
displeasure, and of being forthwith removed from your
Government, not to give your assent to any bill or
bills that shall be passed by our Lower House of Assembly, by which bill or bills, any sum or sums of money whatsoever shall be appropriated to, or provision
made for, defraying any expense incurred for services
or purposes, not immediately arising within, or incidental to, our said province of South-Carolina; unless, upon special requisition from us, our heirs and
successors; nor, to any bill or bills for granting any
sum or sums of money to us, our heirs and successors,
in which bill or bills it shall not be provided, in express
words, that the money so to be granted, or any part
thereof, shall not be issued or applied to any other
services, than those to which it is by the said bill or
bills appropriated; unless, by act, or ordinance of the
General Assembly of the said province. And, it is
our further will and pleasure, and you are hereby
directed and required, upon pain of our highest displeasure, not to give your assent to any bill or bills that
shall be passed by our Lower House of Assembly as
aforesaid, by which, any sum or sums of money whatsoever, shall be granted to us, our heirs and successors, generally, and without appropriation; unless
there be a clause or clauses inserted in the said bill
or bills, declaring and providing, that the said money
so to be granted, shall remain in the Treasury, subject to such appropriation as shall thereafter be made
by act, or ordinance of the General Assembly, and not
otherwise.

And it is our further will and pleasure, that you take especial care, that in all and every bill or bills so to be passed by you aforesaid, for raising and granting public monies, a clause or clauses be inserted therein, subjecting the Public Treasurer, or any other person or persons, to whose custody, public money may be committed, in case he or they shall issue or pay any such money, otherwise than by express order contained in some act or ordinance of the General Assembly, to a penalty in treble the sum so issued contrary thereto; and declaring him or them to be *ipso facto*, incapable of holding the office of Treasurer, or any other office, civil, or military, within our said province. And, it is our further will and pleasure, that this our Additional Instruction to you, be communicated to our Council, and Lower-House of Assembly of our said province of South-Carolina, and entered upon our Council Books.

G. R.

☞ See Council Journal of South-Carolina, for August 1770.

CHAPTER III.

The King relaxes in his measures—Duties repealed, except on Tea—Drawback allowed by Parliament, of duties on the exportation of tea to the American Colonies—And to enable the East-India Company to export Tea, duty free—The Bostonians throw the Tea into the River—Proceedings in South-Carolina, respecting importations of Tea—Committees first called into use—Governor Bull's conduct, respecting the landing of Tea—Prorogues the General Assembly—Meeting of Citizens respecting the Tea, adjourned—General Assembly meets—Governor's Communications—Reply of the Commons—Commons receive advices from their Agent in London, respecting the Complaint they had forwarded to the King, against the Council—Resolutions of the Council thereon—Commons pass a Bill for granting money and raising troops to defend the frontiers, which is rejected by the Council—Commons liquidate the Public Debts—And send a Message to the Governor —Commons issue Certificates of the liquidated debt, which pass as money—General Gage arrives at Boston as Governor and Commander in Chief—The Boston Port-Bill—Petition of Americans in London —Vote of the Boston Town-Meeting—Proceedings of the Honse of Burgesses, in Virginia—Citizens of

Charlestown hold a Meeting—And summon a Gene-
ral Meeting from the Inhabitants of the Colony—
Subscriptions opened to relieve the poor of Boston—
Additional Acts of Parliament arrive.

THE non-importation agreement, and commotions
in the American Colonies, induced the King to relax
his measures; and on the 12th April 1770, the duties
which had been imposed upon Glass, Red-Lead, and
other articles, were repealed; excepting, that which
had been laid, on the importation of Tea. This remained as a test, by which the Colonies might be
tried; as well as a precedent, by which, future taxation might be introduced: and Administration succeeded in their design of dissolving the non-importation agreement. For, although the terms of that
agreement specified, it should continue until the duties
complained of, were all repealed; yet, so much is
interest engrafted in the heart of man, that gain prevailed over public agreements; and the Colonies one
after the other, broke through their resolutions of non-
importation: while the duty of three-pence the pound
on tea, remained to cause other, and more violent convulsions, in America.

In process of time, the article of tea was again
brought into view; and on the 10th of May 1773 an
act of parliament received the Royal sanction, allowing a drawback of duties on the exportation of tea, to
any of the Colonies in America; and to enable the
East-India Company to export tea, duty free;—in
consequence of which, the Company prepared to send
large consignments of the same to the Colonies.
Three ships richly laden with tea, accordingly arrived
in Boston harbour; but they were not suffered to be
unladen. And, as the proper clearances and passes,

could not be procured from the Collector of that port
and the Governor, for the ships to return to England
with their cargoes, they were boarded by citizens from
the town; and three hundred and forty chests of tea
were emptied of their contents; the tea being discharged over the sides of the ships, upon the surrounding waves.

*Not long after this event, Captain Curling, in the
ship London, arrived in the port of Charlestown, on
the 1st December 1773; having on board two hundred and fifty-seven chests of tea, shipped by the East-
India Company; and consigned to certain merchants,
for sale upon commission.—The people, were much
alarmed at this measure; because in their opinions it
tended to impose upon them the duty of that article,
which had not been repealed; and which they conceived to be in violation of American rights.   A general meeting of the Inhabitants of and near Charlestown, was consequently projected; and it accordingly
took place, two days after the arrival of the tea.
Here, the matter underwent some inquiry; and it appeared to be determined, that teas made subject to a
duty by act of parliament, should not be imported.—
Some persons, however, having alleged that what had
been taken as the determination of the Meeting, was
actually against the sense of the majority then present;
the people again convened on the 17th December, for
the purpose of ascertaining, what was the real public
opinion, on a matter of such consequence.   After
much debate, it was carried, " That the tea ought not
to be landed, received, or vended, in this Colony; and
that no teas ought to be imported by any person whatsoever, while the act imposing the unconstitutional

* The manuscript of William Henry Drayton, forms a basis for these Memoirs, from the above arrival of Captain Curling.

duty, remained unrepealed:" and a Committee was
sent to notify this resolution to the Consignees.
When this notification was received, the Consignees
saw the propriety of abiding by the sense of the community thus formally expressed: they agreed, therefore, not to accept of the consignment; and farther,
that they would not interfere in any shape, with 'the
tea.

The affair being so adjusted, a farther day was
appointed for another meeting; that the sense of the
community might be the better collected, as to the
refusal in receiving the tea; and if the same should be
persisted in, that suitable resolutions might be formed
on the subject.—On the point of landing the tea, people were somewhat divided in opinion.   Many friends
to liberty and opposers to the views of Administration,
considered the East-India Company in the light of a
private merchant; and therefore, were of opinion, that
no exception ought to be taken to the landing of their
tea; since, none had been taken to landing consignments of that article, from private merchants in London.   They said, such teas had always been landed,
and had paid the duties here; and that on the very
day, when the first meeting of the people had taken
place on the subject, parcels of tea were landed as
well from Captain Curling's ship, as from two other
vessels, which were the property of private importers;
that the duties had been paid on them,—and they had
even passed by the meeting of the people, in their
conveyance to the respective owners. All this, evinced
a desire of not entering hastily into measures; as the
people wished to act in union on the subject, with the
other Colonies.   And they consequently delayed taking
a more decisive step; as they hoped by gaining a little
time, they would receive accounts from the northern
Colonies on the subject; where, oppressive measures

were urging the people, to successive acts of opposition.—In the mean time, anonymous letters were sent to Captain Curling, threatening to fire his ship, the London; unless, she were moved from the wharf. Others, were sent to the owners of the wharf at which the London lay; threatening to fire it, unless the ship were obliged to quit the wharf: and others were sent to masters of vessels lying near; warning them of their danger, in lying contiguous to a ship, containing so odious a cargo. These letters, excited much alarm to those concerned; and they were forthwith laid before the Lieutenant-Governor. The Collector also, applied to him for protection in the execution of his duty; stating, that in a few days, he should be obliged to seize the teas; unless, before that time, the duties should be paid.

This, was a trying occasion to Lieutenant-Governor Bull. On the one hand, his duty imperiously called on him to support the Collector,* in carrying into execution the act of parliament respecting the duties on tea; while on the other hand, he well knew the hostile opinion of the people, on the subject, and that Administration had furnished him with no means of supporting his authority, but through their intervention. The only thing then which he could do, in this dilemma, was, to convene his Council on the 31st December 1773.† They soon ascertained, nothing could be done efficiently by the Lieutenant-Governor, in aid of the Collector: and the only mode they could devise of assisting him in the performance of his duties, was, that the Sheriff and peace officers, should be notified to be in readiness, to preserve the peace; when the Collector should proceed to seize the tea, and attempt

* Robert Dalway Haliday.

† See Appendix to this Chapter, No. I.

to land it, in pursuance of the provisions of the Revenue laws. The notification, was accordingly issued;
and the Collector at an early hour some days afterwards, seized, and landed the tea, without any opposition; and stored the same, in the vaults under the
Exchange, scarce any persons, being present—as it
was not supposed, the seizure and landing, would
have taken place before noon.

The meeting of the people, respecting the tea, had
been adjourned to the 7th day of January 1774; at
which time, some of the principal opposers to landing
the same, attended. The public mind, however, appeared somewhat cooled; and very few persons, were
at this meeting. It was therefore adjourned, for a
fortnight; in the hope, that the approaching Session of
the General Assembly, might bring many persons to
Charlestown, who could afford aid on the occasion.
The Lieutenant-Governor, however, thought proper
to prorogue the Assembly, to the first of March; and
the people keeping their eyes steady upon Executive
measures, adjourned their meeting likewise to the
third day of the same month.

At length, the General Assembly was allowed to
meet, on the 1st of March 1774; and the Lieutenant-
Governor opened the Session with a speech, laying
the Indian disturbances in Georgia, and his own conduct in the premises, before the Council and the Commons: he also recommended to them, *that such aid
should be given in the case, as the condition and safety
of the province could spare.* To which, the Commons
replied, that nothing on their part, should be wanting
to promote his Majesty's service, or, the safety, honour
and interest, of this Colony.

Before the Commons had decided, however, on suitable measures, respecting the speech which had been delivered, the packet from England brought them dispatches, from their Agent, Charles Garth, relative to the complaint they had sent forward in 1773, against the Council; for their imprisonment of Thomas Powell, the Printer of the South-Carolina Gazette.—This imprisonment was inflicted upon him, by an Order from Sir Egerton Leigh, Baronet, by order of the Council acting as a branch of the Legislature; for publishing without permission, a protest entered on the Journals of the Council, by John Drayton and William Henry Drayton, members of the same; which, by its tendency reflected upon the proceedings of the Council. And under the Habeas Corpus act of Charles II, Powell had been discharged from his confinement by Rawlins Lowndes, Speaker, and George Gabriel Powell, member, of the Commons-House of Assembly; pursuant to an act of Assembly, passed the 12th December 1712; empowering two Justices (*Quorum Unus*) to put in force the Habeas Corpus act to all intents, and purposes, as fully, as the same can be put in execution, in his Majesty's Kingdom of England.—This was immediately resented by the Council, who considered the privileges of the Council, which they called an *Upper-House*, as thereby infringed: and especially, as the said Justices, had judicially declared the Council *to be no Upper-House of Assembly*,* The Council, farther applied to the Commons-House of Assembly, for redress against Mr. Lowndes and Mr. Powell, their members, for the discharge they had given; but the House of Assembly, instead of complying with their requisition, entered into some pointed resolutions; avowed the doctrines, which the Justices had promulgated—returned the

* See the opinion of the Justices, in the Appendix, at the end of this Chapter, No. II.

thanks of the House to them, for the same—requested the Governor to suspend the Members of the Council, who had voted the Commitment—and finally, addressed his Majesty for their removal.—Upon this, the Council finding their Legislative authority and privileges so openly, and directly attacked, lost no time in forwarding an address to the Throne on the subject; and the Assembly nothing backward, also forwarded their complaints to the King, to be presented to his Majesty, by their Agent, Mr. Garth. To this matter then, Mr. Garth's letter referred, which we have shown had been received: and it bore date the 27th December 1773. In this letter, the Agent informed the Assembly, that having notice the Council had sent an address to the King, touching the discharge of the Printer; he had waited upon Lord Dartmouth, to acquaint him with the Orders he had received; and to desire, that the Council's address might not be presented, until he could prepare a petition to the King on the part of the Commons, in pursuance of his instructions from them: so, that the whole affair, might be under consideration, at the same time. That Lord Dartmouth had intimated to him, that if the petition would be formed upon the principle, that the Council was not an *Upper-House,* and *a Branch of the Legislature,* no proceedings would be had upon it; as, his Majesty's Council could not admit, that the established Constitution of the Colony, should be brought into question.—That he had applied to Mr. Dunning, as Counsel; who thought, it would be difficult to maintain, the Council was not an Upper-House; yet, it did not follow, the privilege claimed by them, of committing for contempt, was incidental: and, that he thought the exercise of the power in question, was unwarranted.—The Agent in his letter farther stated, that he had presented a petition to Lord Dartmouth, (of which, he enclosed a copy) to be by him presented

to the King. That, as the petition referred to the
Council Journals, and they were not then arrived; he
had informed Lord Dartmouth, he was ready to proceed, on the discussion of the subject, if he should be
allowed to use as evidence, the Journals of the Council, as printed by authority in the South-Carolina Gazette of the 30th of August 1773; in which, was a
protest signed by John Drayton and William Henry
Drayton, two of the Council: and that proceedings
were stayed, until Administration had given an answer to this point.—By the same Packet, Lord Dartmouth advised the Lieutenant-Governor, that the
King's final determination, on the subject, would be
sent over in the February Packet. But, the matter
was overlooked by the minister, amidst the hurry of
providing measures to operate against transactions,
which were daily arising in America, of far greater
importance.—Mr. Garth's advices, being laid before
the Council; they appointed a Committee to consider
the same. And a report being made thereon, the
Council Resolved, that the petition to the King from
the Commons-House of Assembly, was absurd, false,
unparliamentary, and unconstitutional; and that it
was a scandalous libel, upon the Upper-House of Assembly; tending to destroy the ancient Constitution
of this Government—and in the strongest terms, another Resolution censured Mr. Garth's conduct; in
presenting the petition of the Commons to the King.

Not discouraged by these measures of the Council,
the Commons sent for its consideration a bill, granting
to the King £30,000 provincial currency; and for raising two hundred and ten privates, with their proper officers, for the defence of the frontiers during six months.
But, the Council knowing the Governor could not
pass any money bills contrary to the provisions of the
additional Instruction; and deeming it useless, to pass

a bill which would not receive his assent; rejected the same, on the 22d day of March.

This conduct, afforded new matter for widening the breach between the two Houses; and the Commons were highly irritated at the same. They found, it was in vain to think of sending the Council a tax-bill; as for the same cause, it would assuredly meet with the same fate. They therefore continued steady in their opposition, to the Additional Instruction, attempting to prescribe to them the mode, in which they should be allowed to frame money bills. However, they did not lose sight of the public exigences, because the Council were throwing impediments in the way; for they went seriously to business, and liquidated the public debts, from the year 1769, to 1772 both inclusive. And this they did, with a view of furnishing some relief to the public creditors; who had during all that time, been unpaid. They also on the 24th March came to resolutions, allowing interest upon those debts, to the first of January 1773.

By these resolutions, the Clerk of the Commons-House of Assembly was required to issue to such of the public creditors as should demand the same, certificates for any sums within the amounts of their respective liquidated accounts. In which certificates, was to be stated the sum allowed; and that public provision, would be made for the payment of it: and they were to be countersigned by at least five of a number of their members, appointed for that purpose. The resolutions also held forth indemnification by the House, to the Members and Clerk; for every thing, which they should do, in pursuance of the same.

An act of justice like this to public creditors, who had for years waited a settlement of their claims, to

unsuspecting individuals would have presented to view
nothing more, than an honest, and necessary use, of
legislative power.   But the fact was, the Commons
had now a farther object in view; as they really aimed
at an emission of about £200,000, as a circulating
currency. The necessities of the times, much favoured
this fiscal operation; as there was no prospect when
the public debts would be discharged by a regular tax-
bill; and the Treasury on calling in the public duties,
had well nigh drawn in all the circulating money:
while the sums still remaining in circulation, with the
utmost difficulty kept the commercial wheel in motion.
All these causes combining, placed the Commons in a
situation; that if they could offer the public any thing,
which only bore the appearance of paper money; it
was scarcely possible they could miss their aim of
showing to the Crown, of how little importance the
Additional Instruction was become; and that too, by
a measure the more alarming to the Crown: as
thereby, the Commons of their own authority, created
and issued, what served all the purposes of money.

Having so planned and adjusted, this very important
measure; the Commons by a Message to the Lieutenant-Governor the next day, stated their having finally
arranged the public accounts: and they complained in
severe terms of the Council, for having so long obstructed the passing of tax-bills in the usual way;
also, for their late rejection of the bill for raising the
Rangers: which, left the people on the frontiers exposed to the murders, cruelties, and ravages of barba-
rous Savages.   They informed him, that by such re-
cent conduct of the Council, they were of opinion, it
was unnecessary to prepare a tax-bill.   That should
his Honour be pleased to consider, by what number
and kind of men, a stop had been put to public business for many years in the Colony: they, being per-

sons, most of whom were exclusively supported by the
offices, which they held, and that even, at the will of
the ministry; unconnected also with the Colony,
either by birth, or property: his Honour would have
great reason to admire the loyalty of the people, which
even gross insults, added to the most malignant injuries, had not been able to shake.   That to prevent so
much as they were able, the absolute ruin of many
public creditors, they had ordered certificates of their
liquidated claims, to be issued to each person requiring
them: and they concluded, that as at present, they
could not do any other act, conducing to the public
good; they desired leave, to adjourn to the August ensuing.   The Council, taking up the affair of the Certificates, were fully aware of the consequences, to
which they might lead; but all they could do, was to
pass a Resolution, censuring that measure, as being
unprecedented and unparliamentary; as depending
only, on the faith of one branch of the Legislature.

Matters thus stood, until the 26th day of March;
when Lieutenant-Governor Bull, returned an answer
to the Message from the Commons.   He was silent as
to their complaint against the Council, and the measure of issuing certificates; but, he expressed his concern, that the endeavours of the Commons for the
protection of the frontiers, had proved abortive; and
that the payment of debts due to public creditors, had
not been carried into complete execution.   He also
complied with their wish of adjournment; but, as the
situation of affairs did not render a long recess advisable; he only allowed them to adjourn, to the third day
of May: to which time, the Council also adjourned
themselves.

And now, the Commons in private laboured to bring
to maturity, that measure; to which, their public cha-

racters had given birth. They were aware, its success in a great degree depended upon the mercantile
members of the community; and they consequently
made application to the Chamber of Commerce; who
desired time to consider a propostion of such importance. Meanwhile the public surprize was excited; as
the measure was sudden, and unlooked for:—being
the work of but three, or four days. Its immediate
utility, alone caught the eyes and senses, of the mass
of the people; but, to those who had studied the rise
and fall of nations, and who even now, carried their
views farther, than a mere fiscal operation; it appeared to have an immediate tendency, to diminish the
powers and respectability of the Council; while in
the same degree it increased that of the Commons—
and democratized the public opinion. And they could
not but observe, how nearly the measure approached
that of the Long-Parliament in the year 1642; when
of their own authority, orders were passed for bringing
in money and plate, whose value should be replaced
with 8 per cent. interest; and for which, they engaged
the public faith.—The measure in effect, created and
issued money, without the consent of the Crown;
than which, nothing was more irreconcileable, to the
principles of the British Constitution, or injurious to
the Regal prerogative.

Whatever men thought, of the certificates, the necessity of the times was so urgent, that the Chamber of
Commerce agreed to receive them in payment; and,
they immediately went into general circulation. At
first indeed, they were received under apprehensions,
which rendered each person unwilling to keep them
by him; and caused him to pass them away, as soon
as possible: but afterwards, they settled down in the
public opinion, and became a medium of general convenience. No public creditor refused to receive them

from the Clerk, but Lieutenant-Governor Bull; who thought he owed so much self-denial, to his public station. In all other respects, the most happy effects were produced; and the community was greatly accommodated, by the seasonable relief they afforded.

While the conveniency and policy of issuing the certificates, were daily becoming more visible to the citizens; accounts arrived from England, that on the 7th day of March 1774, Lord North delivered to the House of Commons a Message from the King; accompanied with several papers, relative to the late disturbances of Boston—That he had brought in a bill, to remove the Customs from thence—and, to discontinue the landing and discharging, lading or shipping any goods at that port or harbour. The accounts also advised, that the act was to be enforced by a squadron of men of war, and a body of troops.

Scarce was this news spread abroad, when letters arrived from the popular Committee at Philadelphia advising that General Gage had landed at Castle William, in the Colony of Massachusetts, as Governor; and holding the Chief Command of the British troops in America. A copy of the Boston Port-Bill, which had received the Royal Assent, on the 31st of March, also accompanied the same. While this bill was in the House of Lords, the few Americans who were then in London, (some of them young gentlemen, who had just finished their education, and were about to return to their native country,) by the hands of Lord Shelburne presented a petition to that House; praying, that the bill might not pass into a law; and one was also presented, to the King on the same subject.— And as the bill alluded to, was among the last of the series of those acts of parliament, which produced a crisis; and the petitions, among the last of the remon-

strances against them; it may not be improper, to introduce one of them on the present occasion.

" To the King's most excellent Majesty.

" The Petition of several natives of America, most
humbly showeth:

" That your petitioners, being your Majesty's most
faithful subjects, are obliged to implore, your gracious
interposition, to protect them in the enjoyment of
those privileges, which are the right of all your people.

" Your Majesty's petitioners have already seen with
unspeakable grief, their earnest prayers rejected, and
heavy penalties inflicted, even on the innocent among
their countrymen: to the subversion of every principle
of justice, without their being heard.   By this alarming
procedure, all property was rendered insecure; and
they now see in two bills, (for altering the Government
of Massachusetts-Bay, and the impartial administration of justice there) the intended subversion of the
two other grand objects of civil society and constitutional protection, to wit, *Liberties*, and *Life*.

" Your petitioners most humbly represent to your
Majesty, that to destroy or assume their chartered
rights, without a full and fair hearing, with legal proof
of forfeiture; and the abrogating of their most valuable laws, which had duly received the solemn confirmation of your Majesty's Royal predecessors, and
were thence deemed unchangeable without the consent of the people; is such a proceeding, as renders
the enjoyment of every privilege they possess, uncertain, and precarious.   That an exemption of the Soldiery from being tried in the Massachusetts-Bay for
murder, or other felony, committed upon your Majes

ty's subjects there, is such an encouragement for
licentiousness, and incentive to outrage, as must subject your Majesty's liege people, to continued danger.

"Your petitioners and their Countrymen, have been
ever most zealously attached to your Majesty's person
and family.   It is therefore, with inexpressible afflic-
tion, that they see an attempt, in these proceedings
against them, to change the principle of obedience to
the government, from the love of the subject towards
their Sovereign; founded on the opinion of his wisdom, justice, and benevolence, into the dread of absolute power and laws of extreme rigour, insupportable
to a free people.

"Should the bills above mentioned, receive your
Royal sanction, your Majesty's faithful subjects will
be overwhelmed with grief, and despair.

"It is therefore our earnest prayer, that your Majesty will be graciously pleased to suspend your Royal
Assent, to the said bills."

The petition was signed, by the following thirty
Americans; fifteen of whom, were of South-Carolina.

Stephen Sayre, William Lee, Arthur Lee, Edmond
Jennings, Joshua Johnson, Daniel Bowley, Benjamin
Franklin, Thomas Busten, Edward Bancroft, Thomas
Bromfield, John Boylston, John Ellis, John Williams,
John Allyne, *Ralph Izard*, *William H. Gibbes*, *William
Blake*, *Isaac Motte*, Henry Laurence, *Thomas Pinck-
ney*, *Jacob Read*, *John F. Grimke*, *Philip Neyle*, *Ed-
ward Fenwicke*, *Edward Fenwicke, jun. John Peron-
neau*, *William Middleton*, *William Middleton, jun.
Ralph Izard, jun.* and *William Heyward.**

* Those marked in *Italics*, were from South-Carolina.

The letter from Philadelphia, also enclosed letters from the Committees of other Colonies; animating the Carolinians to adopt the vote of the Town-Meeting at Boston, on the 13th of May.   This celebrated Vote, ought ever to be holden in remembrance by the Sons of America; as from thence proceeded those measures, which made the Colonies united, happy, and free.   It was made at Faneuil Hall, in Boston; and was conceived in the following terms.

"That it is the opinion of this Town, that if the other Colonies come into a joint resolution to stop all importation from Great Britain, and all exportation to Great Britain and every part of the West Indies, untill the act for blocking up this harbour be repealed; the same will prove the salvation of North America, and her liberties.   On the other hand, if they continue the exports and imports, there is high reason to fear, that fraud, power, and the most odious oppression will rise triumphant over right, justice, social happiness, and freedom.   And moreover, that this Vote be forthwith transmitted by the Moderator to all our Sister Colonies, in the name and in behalf of this Town."

On the consideration of this Vote, the Committee of this Colony, conceiving the attack upon Boston, was on all America, answered the Northern Committees, by saying, that it was very sensible of the critical situation of all the provinces; and that in defence of constitutional rights, this Colony would, to the utmost of her abilities, adopt any measure they might enter into for that purpose.—For Boston, was not considered as obnoxious to administration, merely as destroying the tea, and ill-treating Custom-House officers.—For ten years past, the people of that town, had vigilantly traversed all the schemes of Administration; and, their conduct had been a constant source of vexation to the

Ministry, intent upon the taxation of America.—
Hence, the British vengeance against Boston—the
Port-Bill—and the American Resolution of making a
Common Cause with Boston.

The 7th of June now approached, to which time,
the Lieutenant-Governor had farther prorogued the
General Assembly; and the Representatives were determined to act with a proper spirit on their meeting.
They were however, not allowed to convene; and the
General Assembly was farther prorogued, to the second
day of August. This Executive measure, had scarce
taken effect, when letters arrived from Virginia, giving
an account of the conduct of their House of Burgesses,
on the Boston Port-Bill; the dissolution of their General Assembly in consequence of that conduct; and an
association into which, the late Burgesses had entered
after their dissolution.—Great, were the commenda-
tions of the Virginian proceedings; and they gave instant life and motion to the Colonial policy.

A meeting of the Inhabitants of Charlestown, accordingly took place, at a Tavern situated at the north
eastern corner of Broad and Church-streets; a Chairman was chosen, and the advices were laid before
them. They however appeared to be of too serious a
nature, to be acted on, by so hasty a meeting; and on
the 13th of June, they issued summonses, for a general
meeting of the Inhabitants of the Colony, to be holden
in Charlestown, on the 6th day of July. These summonses expressed, that the meeting was " to consider
of the papers, letters, and resolutions, transmitted to
the Committee, from the Northern Colonies; and
also, of such steps as are necessary to be pursued, in
union with all the Inhabitants of all our Sister Colonies, on this Continent; in order to avert the dangers
impending, over American liberties in general, by the

late hostile act of parliament against Boston, and other arbitrary measures of the British Ministry." In this manner, did the Colony first express her sentiments on the Boston Port-Bill. The minds of the people now fermenting, some were for putting all at hazard: while others, were for adopting the Boston Vote at least, and for shutting the Courts of law.

In the mean time, circular letters were dispatched, to the more distant parts of the Province; addressed to such men, as were of principal influence. These letters, stated the subject of the Blockade of Boston; animated an opposition to that measure; and recommended a meeting of the land holders in the different parishes, to elect deputies to represent those parishes, to deliver their sentiments, and to act for them, in the approaching Provincial General Meeting. This was the first attempt, to collect a meeting of the people, on so constitutional a principle:—and, as all new attempts are imperfect, so was this. For the people were at liberty to elect, as many deputies, as they pleased: and in some places ten deputies were chosen; in others, different numbers; while St. Andrew's parish elected none, its white inhabitants being few; and most of them being desirous, of attending the meeting personally. During this time also, subscriptions were opened to relieve the poor of Boston; who had been usually employed in the trade of that town; and on the 29th day of June, 204 barrels of rice were transported over the bar for their support; while the subscription was still promoted, as a source of future supplies.

In this state of things, copies of two other acts which had received the Royal Assent on the 20th of May, arrived from the Northward. One of them, entitled An act for the better regulating the Govern-

15

ment of the Province of Massachusetts-Bay, in a
manner totally changed the Constitution of that Government; which, by the Colony Charter, was extremely favourable to the people. The other, entitled
An act for the impartial administration of Justice, in
the cases of persons questioned for any acts done by
them in the execution of the law; or, for the suppres-
sion of Riots and Tumults, in the province of Massachusetts-Bay.—If we annalize these two acts, we shall
find them to be plainly this.—That whereas by the
Charter Constitution of Massachusetts-Bay, the
Crown had but little power, and the people much: the
one act, took all power out of the hands of the people,
and transferred it the Crown.—The other act, held
out safety to those, who aided and assisted in the support of Revenue laws; and in quelling tumults and
commotions, which might arise in defending American
rights, from British aggression; it also authorized
sending the person indicted to another Colony, or to
Great Britain for trial. In this manner the British
Administration acted; when they had made up their
minds to enforce by the sword, measures which were
untenable by any principle of law, or of Justice. The
acts answered no other purpose, than to increase the
public indignation—to rouse the public opposition—
and to draw the Colonies closer, in the bonds of friendship and assistance—with the suffering, and much
abused town, and Inhabitants, of Boston.

APPENDIX

TO

CHAPTER III.

—◆—

No. I.

At a Council held at his Honour the Lieutenant-Governor's House, Friday the 31st day of December, 1773—

PRESENT,

His Honour Lieutenant-Governor WILLIAM BULL.
The Hon. SIR EGERTON LEIGH, Baronet, JOHN DRAYTON, THOMAS KNOX GORDON, Esqrs.

His Honour, the Lieutenant-Governor, informed the Board, that he had desired to meet them this afternoon, to take their advice upon two letters, which had been laid before him, by Captain Curling, the master of the ship which had brought over the tea belonging to the East-India Company; one of which, was addressed to Captain Curling. And the purport of both of them was, to advise Captain Curling to hawl his ship into the stream; as it was intimated there was a design to do some mischief to her, for bringing over the tea. Captain Curling, and Mr. Lord, the owner of the ship attended; when Captain Curling was asked, if he was apprehensive of any violence being offered; to which he answered, that he was not under apprehensions of personal violence; but, he did not know what might be the consequence, in respect to the ship, if the tea was to be landed: and Mr. Haliday, the Collector, attending, was called in; and asked what he proposed to do, in respect to the tea, in case the duties were not paid, by the persons to whom it was consigned, and whom it was reported had refused to have any thing to do with it? To which he replied, that if the duty was not paid within twenty-one days, after the arrival of the tea, he was required by his Instructions to seize it; and lodge it, in the King's ware house: to secure the payment of the duties. He was then asked, if from appearances he was apprehensive of obstruction in doing his duty, in case the tea was to be seized, and attempted to be landed, to secure the duties? To which, he answered, that although he did not apprehend any danger to his person; from appearances, and the best intelligence he could procure, some disturbances were likely to ensue; in case he was to offer to land the tea. And, he therefore requested, that his Honour, the Lieutenant-Governor, and the Board, would give him such support, as would be necessary to enable him to do his duty. He was thereupon informed, that the Sheriff should receive directions, to assist him with his officers; and to attend to keep the peace, if any tumult should be made, when the tea was to be landed. And his Honour, the Lieutenant-Governor, directed the Clerk, to call on the Sheriff, and to inform him, it was his directions to attend with his officers, upon any information made to him by Mr. Haliday, that he was obstructed in the execution of his office, in attempting to land and store the said tea; and to use every endeavour in in his power, to preserve the public peace on the occasion.

Mr. Bull,* one of the Magistrates for Charlestown also attending, was called in, and examined, as to his opinion on the present occasion; whether any disturbance was probably to be expected, when the tea should be landed? To which, Mr. Bull answered, that he was apprehensive from the present appearances, there would be disturbances; and that he wished, that mischief might not ensue.

The several persons attending being withdrawn, his Honour desired the gentlemen to advise him if they thought any other measures, necessary to be taken on the present occasion? To which they unanimously replied, That they did not apprehend his Honour could, more effectually, endeavour to aid the Collector in the discharge of his duty: but, they were in hopes, the measures already directed, would be effectual on the present occasion.

☞ See Council Journal of South-Carolina, for 1773; pages 8, 9.

Fenwicke Bull.

No. II.

*Opinion pronounced by the Hon. Rawlins Lowndes,
Speaker of the House of Assembly of South-Caroli-
na; when acting as a Magistrate, in the Case of
Powell, the Printer.*

It appears by the Sheriff's Return, of the Habeas
Corpus, that the Prisoner, Thomas Powell, stands
committed by virtue of a warrant, dated August 31st
1773, from Sir Egerton Leigh, President of the Council, said to be by Order of the Upper-House of Assembly.   For, he had acknowledged himself to be the
printer and publisher, of a newspaper called the South-
Carolina Gazette, No. 1966, dated Charlestown,
Monday the 30th day of August 1773; in which paper
is printed, part of the proceedings of that House on
Thursday the 26th day of August last; which, the
House hath resolved, to be a high breach of privilege
and a contempt of the House; and ordering, that the
said Thomas Powell should be therefore committed
to the common gaol of Charlestown, during the pleasure of the House.

I am sorry that this matter hath come before me,
and that I am obliged to decide upon the legality of
the Commitment.   It involves in it, a question of consequence.   If, on the one hand, the Commitment
should be deemed illegal; the Council will so far be
deprived of a power of Commitment, for Breach of
Privilege.   If, on the other hand, the Commitment
should be deemed legal; the prisoner will be restrained of his liberty; which, is one of the greatest
punishments, next to corporal, that can be inflicted on

the subject. I should be extremely sorry, to err either way. I would gladly have declined the task, and I wish from my heart, some able Magistrate had been applied to.

From the rank and station I am in, and from my connection with the Commons-House of Assembly, I may be presumed to be under some bias and prepossession, in favour of that House in its privileges. I confess, I am so;—but, I trust it is no undue bias or prepossession—no propensity, to exclude from any other body of men, or any other part of the community, any rights, privileges, or immunities, whatever, which they may, on a fair inquiry, be found to be entitled to. It was insisted however, that I should grant the Habeas Corpus—that, it was a right:—and, it would very ill have become one, to have been disobedient to so good and salutary a law, although it had not been enforced with such penal sanctions, as it has to secure its execution.

The law of the land provides for the safety of every man's person, his liberty, and his estate. By the great Charter, it is provided, that no freeman shall be taken or imprisoned, but by the lawful judgment of his equals, or, by the law of the land. And many subsequent statutes expressly direct, that no man shall be taken or imprisoned by suggestion or petition to the King, or his Council, unless it be by legal indictment, or the process of the Common Law. By the petition of rights it is enacted, that no freeman shall be imprisoned, or detained, without cause shown; to which, he may answer according to law. And, by the Habeas Corpus Act, of the 31st of Charles II. the methods of obtaining that writ, are pointed out, and enforced. All which statutes, for the security of the liberty of the subject, are expressly of force here; particularly, the

Habeas Corpus Act; which, by an act of Assembly of this province, passed in 1712, is now particularly accommodated to our local circumstances, and some difficulties are removed, which might otherwise have obstructed the execution of that wholesome law. It is in virtue of this provincial law, that we were empowered to issue a writ of Habeas Corpus; which, we did in this case: and by which, we are empowered to take cognizance of the present matter.

It appears then, that no freeman shall be taken or imprisoned, but by the judgment of his peers, or by the law of the land. No judgment of his peers, has been given in the present case against Mr. Powell; for judgment by his peers, means a legal cause of trial by jury. It remains then to be inquired into, whether the law of the land, warrants his commitment, and consequent imprisonment. And whether the cause shown, is sufficient to authorize his detention. Or, whether if his Commitment be legal, he is bailable, or not bailable.

Either House of Parliament, have, from time immemorial, exercised a power of Commitment and imprisonment: and it seems to be a settled point, confirmed by late adjudications, that the Courts of Law, or Judges, will not interfere or intermeddle in any case, so as to discharge a prisoner committed by either House, during the sitting of Parliament—that the Houses are only competent judges of their own privileges; and their determinations, are not to be reviewed or examined by inferior jurisdictions.

The law of Parliament therefore, being a part of the law of the land; commitments in consequence thereof, by either House, are not prohibited by Magna Charta. And, the Judges do now invariably, so far as has fallen within my knowledge, remand the prisoner back to the place of his confinement, without affording him any relief, either by bail, or otherwise.

The law of the land not giving the Council the least colour of right to commit for breach of privilege, or, what they call, contempt of their House; they must found their claim upon the usage, and practice, of the House of Lords in England. It will be necessary therefore, to inquire what affinity or resemblance there is between them, to entitle the Council to a derivative right to the high privilege exercised by the Lords.

The Lords, are a permanent body; inheriting the right of Legislation, independent of the Crown. They are the Hereditary Counsellors to the King, and Guardians to the State. The power of judication resides in them, in the *dernier resort*. They try their own members, on life and death, without being under the obligation of an oath. And all these, and many other high privileges, they inherit from the best of titles; prescription, and usage for time immemorial. Indeed, they are the essence of the Constitution.

Compare the Constitution of the Council, with that of the Lords; and where shall we find cause to infer, that they possess, or ought to possess, the powers of the latter.

The Council, are appointed during the pleasure of the Crown; removable at pleasure: and, may be suspended, by the Governor. They hold their offices, and all the appendages to them at will; and, therefore want that most essential requisite of independency, to constitute them a Branch of the Legislature; or in any respect, to assimilate them to the Lords. Unhappy for the people, it is so; much to be wished, it were

16

not so: and that while they claim the power of the House of Lords, over the person of the subject, the subject had the same degree of security for the due exercise of that power, which he has in the House of Lords. The people, have nothing to fear from the Lords. They, are their Guardians, and a bulwark of defence, against oppression and tyranny. They, are numerous, as well as independent. No private pique, or personal resentment, can influence them. *Here*, the most important concerns of the province, are often, very often, determined at a meeting of three of the Council: very seldom do they exceed four;—and, the object of their case, is more particularly the prerogative.

It is true, the Council do in this, as well as some other provinces, concur in the passing of Provincial laws. This, is in consequence of instructions from the Crown, restraining the Governor from giving his assent to any law, that has not that sanction. And, from this single circumstance it is I apprehend, that the Council have created themselves an Upper-House: and, have assumed that appellation in their intercouse with the Commons-House: although, they are invariably styled by the King's Instructions, and in their Appointment, *The Council*. From this important circumstance also, it is, that they would derive to themselves other powers; incident and indeed indispensably necessary, to the House of Lords; but dangerous and unnecessary to be exercised by the Council. As if a right to advise the Governor to pass or reject a bill, involved in it of consequence, all other privileges belonging to the Upper-House of Parliament.

The freedom and liberty of an English subject, are of so high estimation in the eye of the law; that, to deprive him of them, it is incumbent on those that would do it, to show their right clearly, and incontestably. Loose and vague reasoning, fallacious conclusions, specious inferences, or bold assertions, will not do; the judgment of his peers, or the clear voice of the law of the land, must justify: and nothing else can justify, the commitment or imprisonment, of any free subject whatever.

Upon the most mature consideration, as far as my slender abilities will enable me to judge, I am of opinion, that there is no foundation in law, to warrant the commitment, now under consideration; that it would be dangerous, to countenance such a usurpation of power in the Council; would render the liberty of the subject precarious; and introduce novelty and innovation; destructive of sound law, and every principle of justice.

The Commitment therefore, in my opinion, is to be considered merely as a Commitment of the Privy Council. And in that case, it has no other authority, than if done by a private magistrate. The subject, has his remedy by Habeas Corpus, in either case; and we are to consider, whether the matter charged is an offence at law:—and if an offence, whether it is bailable or not.

And I am of opinion, that it is no offence, at law—that the paper referred to in the Commitment, being a protest from two members of Council, against the proceedings of that Board, in a certain matter depending before the Council; and required by one of the members to be printed by the prisoner; might lawfully, legally, and warrantably be printed by the prisoner, acting only in the way of his profession. The more especially, as it was unaccompanied with any remarks, observations, or additions of his own; but simply and literally as it was received by the prisoner, from one of the members of the Council. And it is not clear to me, that even the House of Lords would include such a paper, under the general idea, of proceedings of their House, for which, they would punish a Printer, who published it. I am therefore, for ordering the prisoner to be released.

CHAPTER IV.

Deputies from Parts of the Colony arrive in Charles-
town—hold a meeting in the Exchange—pass certain
Resolutions—elect five Deputies to a General Con-
gress—A Committee of 99 persons appointed, to act
as a General Committee, until the next General
Meeting—Its powers—Meeting of Deputies dissolv-
ed—General Committee meets, respecting an impor-
tation of Tea—Parliament passes an Act for quar-
tering troops in the Colonies—Also, one extending
the limits of the Government of Quebec, and respect-
ing its Government and the Roman Catholic Reli-
gion—The Commons-House of Assembly meets;
when Col. Powell reports to them, the proceedings of
the late General Meeting, holden at the Exchange—
Resolutions thereon—Message to the Lieutenant-
Governor—Assembly prorogued—Rev. Mr. Bullman
preaches a sermon, which gives offence—He is dis-
missed from his office by the Vestry—Mr. Bullman
departs for England—Deputies from twelve Colo-
nies assemble at Philadelphia—proceed to business
in support of American Rights—Dissolution of Con-
gress—William Henry Drayton, one of the Assistant
Judges, publishes a political pamphlet under the sig-
nature of "Freeman," in favour of American Rights.
Upon which, the Chief Justice and one of the Assist-
ant Judges, petition the Lieutenant-Governor to dis-
miss him from office—Mr. Drayton is superseded—

*Consequences of that measure—Chests of tea, arrive
in the ports of Charlestown and Georgetown; which
are thrown from the vessels into the rivers—The Deputies return from Congress, and are honourably
received—The General Committee pass Resolutions,
for a General Meeting of the Inhabitants of the Colony, by Representation.*

THE sixth day of July now arrived; and Charles-
town was filled with people from the Country.   One
hundred and four Deputies represented all parts of the
Colony, except Grenville County, St. John's Colleton
County, and Christ Church Parish.   These districts
sent no deputies; and in behalf of Charlestown, the
General Committee joined the Deputies, from the
Country.   The Meeting was held under the Exchange, on the 6th of July 1774; and a crowded
Meeting it was.   At nine o'clock in the morning, Col.
George Gabriel Powell took the Chair; and it was
carried the votes should be given by each person present, and not by parishes.   It was also farther determined, that whoever came there, might give his vote.
The business of the day then opened, with reading
the communications from the Northern Colonies.
They then proceeded to consider certain Resolutions,
touching American Rights and grievances.   These
being agreed to, declared, That his Majesty's subjects
in North America owe the same allegiance to the
Crown of Great Britain, as is due from his subjects
born within that Kingdom.   That the King's subjects
in America, are entitled to all the inherent rights and
liberties, enjoyed by natural born subjects within the
Kingdom of Great Britain.   That taxes should not be
imposed on the people, but by their own consent, given
personally; or by their Representatives.   That all
trials, for any crime whatever, committed and done in
the Colony, ought to be had and conducted within the

Colony, according to the fixed and known course of
proceeding. That the statute of 35th Henry VIII,
chap. 2d, entitled " An act for the trial of Treasons
committed out of the King's Dominions," does not,
and cannot, extend to any crimes, committed in any of
his Majesty's American Colonies. That the three
late acts of parliament, relative to Boston, are of the
most alarming nature to all his Majesty's subjects in
America; and although levelled at the people of Boston, they glaringly show, if the Inhabitants of that
town are intimidated into a mean submission to those
acts, the like are designed for all the Colonies; when,
not even the shadow of liberty to his person, or of
security to his property, will be left, to any of his
Majesty's subjects, residing on the American Continent. Wherefore, every justifiable means ought to be
tried, to procure a repeal of those acts, immediately
relative to Boston; and also, of all others affecting
the Constitutional Rights and Liberties of America in
general.

To effect these great points, two measures were
proposed; to adopt the Boston vote, of the 13th of
May—and to send Deputies, to a General Congress.
Upon these subjects, there was great dissimilarity of
opinion. All parties agreed on the proposition, of
sending Deputies; but the Boston Vote, did not meet
so universal a support. This last measure, was therefore first taken up, and considered.

In favour of the Boston Vote, it was urged, that
American lives and property were exposed to be
taken, at the mandate of a British Minister. That
the men, would be exposed to slavery; their wives
and daughters, to the outrages of a soldiery. To
avert these dangers, something vigorous was to be
done; something, that might shake even Majesty itself.

That, a measure of non-exportation, and non-importation, seemed above all others best calculated to force a repeal of the late acts. It was a constitutional measure. For, what power had a right to compel the people to grow, export, and sell commodities of any kind; or, to purchase or import, commodities from any state? That such a measure taking place in America, would ruin the British trade to those dominions; and thereby shake the firmness of Parliament. That should the measure be not adopted, the Colonies by their importations would preserve to the British manufacturers that support, which they had been accustomed to receive from the American trade; whereby, they would be supine, and not join the American demand for a repeal. In addition to this, the remittances from the Colonies, would enable the people of England, to employ those means to assist them in enslaving the Colonies: whereas, being withholden, the national credit of Great Britain would be shaken, and the measures of Administration, be infinitely embarrassed.

To these arguments it was answered, that such a measure ought not to take place, until all others had failed of success; for its operation would be violent, both among ourselves, and the people of England. That, thousands in this Colony, would be ruined by it. That the people of the interior, were averse to so harsh a measure: neither was it certain, whether united America would approve and support it. That nothing less than unanimity among all the Colonies, in executing one general plan of conduct, could affect measures in Great Britain: and as the general opinion, seemed to point to a General Congress; so only, in that Congress, could such a plan of conduct, be formed and agreed upon.

By similar arguments, the matter was warmly contested; when, without forming any determination, the subject was dropped: and the meeting turned their attention to consider the proposal of sending Deputies to the intended Congress. Here, another cause of warm debate arose; as to the number of Deputies, who should be appointed; and the powers, with which they should be invested. And without coming to any conclusion on these points, the meeting adjourned to an hour, in the afternoon.

In the afternoon, the meeting again convened; to determine on the points they were considering: and by a majority of eleven it was carried, that there should be five Deputies; and that they should have unlimited power; but, that these points should still be subject to the vote of the meeting.

On the 7th of July, the meeting was again holden; and the measures of non-exportation, and non-importation were again warmly debated. And it was urged, that before the measure should be adopted, the General Congress ought to send a Deputation with a Petition and Remonstrance to the Throne: and if after that, America remained unredressed; it would be time enough, to break off all commerce with Great Britain. The vote was now taken on the subject, and the proposition of non-exportation, and non-importation was rejected. It was then Resolved, that five Deputies should, by ballot, be elected, on the part and behalf of this Colony; to meet the Deputies of the other Colonies of North America in General Congress, the first Monday in September next, at Philadelphia; or at any other time or place, that may be generally agreed on; with full power and authority in behalf of them, and their constituents, *to concert, agree to, and effectually prosecute, such legal measures; as in the opinion of those Deputies, and of the Deputies of the other Colo-*

17

nies, should be most likely to obtain a repeal of the late acts of parliament, and a redress of American grievances.*

A poll, was now opened, to all persons: and at midnight it appeared, that Henry Middleton, John Rutledge, Thomas Lynch, Christopher Gadsden, and Edward Rutledge, were chosen Deputies, to represent this Colony in General Congress.

During the debate this day, touching the powers of the Deputies; it was strongly contended, their powers should be limited.   To this purpose, among other arguments, it was urged by Mr. Rawlins Lowndes, who was then Speaker of the Commons-House of Assembly, that it was well known, the Northern Colonies in general, totally denied the superintending power of Parliament; a doctrine, which no one here admitted.   And, unless the Deputies from this Colony, appeared in Congress with limited powers; being outnumbered by the Northern Deputies, they, and consequently their constituents, would be bound by votes upon points, which they at present absolutely denied. But, to obviate this danger, the Resolution vesting the Deputies with power, was so worded; that no vote in Congress could bind this Colony, but such as was agreeable to the opinion of our Deputies.   This sentiment from Mr. Lowndes is here brought into view, as being from a gentleman of prudence and consideration; and who at that time, declared the prevailing opinion of the Colony.   It also will serve as a point in public opinion, for tracing the rapidity, with which, the Colony in a few months after, adopted the contrary idea.

* See Journals of the Commons-House of Assembly of South-Carolina, from 2d day of August 1774, to the 15th day of September 1775 inclusive— page 1.

Antecedent to the meeting of the people, the Chamber of Commerce had resolved, not to accede to any measure of non-exportation or non-importation; they therefore dreaded nothing so much, as that such a measure should take place in Congress. Hence, they aimed, that such men should be elected Deputies, as were against the adoption of that measure. They wished, that Mr. Middleton, Mr. Lowndes, Colonel Charles Pinckney, Mr. Brewton, and Mr. John Rutledge, might be chosen. To contribute their endeavours to this end, the merchants assembled; and in a body went to the poll: they also sent for their clerks, to come and vote. The zeal of the merchants in this transaction, blinded their prudence: as they did not observe, that by their appearing in a body, the opposite party would take the alarm: and that by voting for Deputies, they would be bound by the conduct of such, as might be chosen. The meeting accordingly, took the alarm; and many of them ran to all parts of the town, to collect people, and bring them to the poll; in consequence of which, the merchants were defeated; and except two gentlemen, other Deputies than those they supported, were chosen.

On the 8th day of July, the meeting again assembled. They now Resolved, that a Committee of ninety-nine persons be appointed to act as a General Committee; and who should continue in authority until the next General Meeting. This Committee had power to correspond with the Committees of the other Colonies; and to do all other matters and things, necessary for carrying the Resolutions of the General Meeting into execution. A form of words, which virtually vested the Committee with unlimited powers, during their existence. The General Meeting, now proceeded to nominate the members, of the General Committee. They named fifteen Merchants and fifteen Mechanics, to represent Charlestown; and sixty-nine Planters, to represent the other parts of the province. This proceeding, was rather unconstitutional; as the different districts and parishes, did not choose the sixty-nine planters who were to represent them. They however, acquiesced in the nomination; being sensible it proceeded from the best intentions, and the urgency of the occasion.   And now, the General Meeting having sat for three days, and brought those matters to a conclusion, for which they had been convened; Colonel Powell prepared minutes of the proceedings, against a future occasion; and agreeably to the wishes of the General Meeting, dissolved the same.

A calm appearance, now took place in Charlestown; but it was not long, that it remained, in this placid state.   The Collector of the Customs found his duties would compel him to seize three chests of tea, which had been reported at the Custom-House, and had not been landed from on board of the vessel importing it; of which, he acquainted the parties concerned.   The General Committee having received information of this intended step of the Collector, immediately assembled.   In the midst of their consultations, news was brought them, that the teas had been seized, and stored.   In this conjunction, the Committee would not violate the King's authority by forcibly taking from his officer, what he had already received into his possession, on the part of the King; but, they resolved to proceed in this affair, against the master of the vessel, which had imported the tea.

It was soon ascertained, that Captain Maitland's vessel had imported the tea in question.   He had been examined by the late Committee touching the point of his presuming to import that commodity; when he knew, such a conduct was contrary to the sense of this Colony in particular, and of America in general.   And he then assured the Committee that he did not know

any tea was on board his ship, until being at sea he
had leisure to look over his cocketts; and he hoped
the Committee would rest satisfied with his declaration. To this it was replied, that as he had imported
the tea, knowing the resolution of the Colony on that
point, it was expected he would so conduct himself,
that the same should not be landed, or the duty upon
it paid in this Colony. On which, he assured the
Committee, that the tea in question, should neither be
landed, nor should any duties be paid on it here: and
farther, if he could not get rid of the tea any other
way, he would himself throw it into the river, at his
own cost.

The General Committee now determined, that Captain Maitland should be holden to his assurances; and
for that purpose, he was ordered to attend them. He
did so—and the Chairman by order of the Committee
informed him, it was expected he would fulfil the
promises he had made, to the late Committee, by destroying the tea: to obtain which for that purpose
he himself should pay the duties thereon. This, he
accordingly promised to perform; and that he would
burn the tea on the wharf, the next day.

To fulfil this engagement, Captain Maitland applied
to the Collector; and tendered the duty in money, for
the possession of the tea: but the Collector refused to
deliver the same to any other person, than the proprietor, or to his order. While this demand and refusal
took place, between Maitland and the Collector; the
General Committee had assembled, according to adjournment, to witness Maitland's destroying the tea.
But, some members now attending who had not been
present the day before, they endeaved to state the impropriety of the vote which had been passed; and
laboured to rescind it, as touching the tea. It was
now asked, why the property in this article should be

lost to the individual; when the public never dreamed
of annihilating the property of the East-India Company, in their teas?   That this last measure was
thought wise and prudent; and therefore why not
upon an occasion of equal merit, pursue a similar conduct?   That, as the tea in question was obnoxious,
only upon the same principle, with those belonging to
the Company, and was already in the same situation
and custody; common sense dictated, that a similar
fate ought to hang over both. And above all, it should
be remembered, that the tea could not now be obtained, but by violence; which, had hitherto been
avoided; or, by paying a duty; to prevent which being
paid, the General Committee had been expressly convened on the present occasion.   This repsesentation
of the case, brought home to the reflection of the General Committee, the delicate situation in which they
were then placed; and at once they perceived, the
impropriety of the measure; to see which executed,
they were then assembled.   They accordingly voted,
that the tea should remain under the same circumstances as those belonging to the East-India Company; and they adjourned the meeting—mutually
expressing their satisfaction, that the measure which
had been determined on the day before, of having the
tea destroyed; had been so prudently prevented, from
being carried into execution.

   Thus satisfied with their conduct, their minds nevertheless recurred to the person who had placed them in
the dilemma, they had so happily avoided: and the
General Committee considered Maitland, as a man,
who having grossly deceived them, had insulted the
people.   They accordingly denounced him, as being
concerned in shipping, employed in the commerce of
the port of Charlestown; and a Committee was appointed to desire the merchants not to ship or receive
any goods in any bottom, wherein Captain Maitland

was, or should be concerned. This desire, was accordingly signified by a Committee to the merchants; who received it as an order, and complied with its requisitions.

When these transactions became known, the people were much incensed; and in the evening, some hundreds of them proceeded to the wharf. at which Captain Maitland's ship lay. They intended, to have laid hands upon him; and it was impossible to tell, what might have been the consequence, had they found him. Maitland however, having received notice of the intention of the populace, and not being very desirous of receiving the visit, had placed a watch, to apprize him of their approach; and when the mob came to the end of the wharf, and were about entering his ship, he slipped over the opposite side of his vessel into his boat, which he had kept ready there for the occasion; and covered by the obscurity of the night, he proceeded to a British vessel of war, then at anchor in the Roads. He there applied for protection to his person, and vessel; on which, the Commanding officer dispatched two armed barges to her assistance; and about two o'clock in the morning, the crews of the same, removed the vessel from the wharf, and anchored her at a distance in the stream.

About this time, accounts arrived that a fourth act relating to America, had received the Royal Assent, on the third of June. This act, was for the better providing quarters for officers and soldiers in his Majesty's service in North America. Such troops, were in fact, to be billeted upon the American freeholders, without their consent: and was one of the causes applicable to the people of England, which induced the Petition of Rights, in the reign of Charles I. It was also, evidently preparatory, for the arbitrary measures, which British Ministers had then in store, for his Majesty's loyal subjects, in America. Scarcely was this news promulgated, when other advices informed, that on the 22d day of June 1774, an act of parliament had passed, extending the limits of the Government of Quebec; also enabling the Crown by the means of a Provincial Governor, and Legislative Council, called into existence not by election, but by writs of mandamus under the Sovereign's sign manual, to make laws for the province; and establishing therein the Roman Catholic Religion, and the French Canadian law in all civil, and the English Criminal law in all criminal cases; subject nevertheless, to alterations and amendments, by the sovereign legislature of Great Britain.

These acts, sunk deep into the minds of the people; as they saw the Crown now made despotic, and the Romish Church established in a part of America. Men openly said, George III, had broken his coronation oath; as well as the solemn contract, under which, he received his title to the Crown. They said, the Revolution of 1688, was effected, upon a principle of rescuing the English Dominions from the errors, and tyranny, of the Romish Church. That for this effect, William, Prince of Orange, had been placed on the British throne; and after him, the Ancestor, from whom George III. derived his Royal titles: and that he was bound by the same conditions. Under these reflections, the meeting of the General Assembly now approached; and the Representatives with impatience wished for an opportunity of declaring in a legislative manner, their sentiments respecting the late obnoxious acts of parliament.

This opportunity however, was one which they more hoped for, than expected to find; as, the Lieutenant-Governor had repeatedly prorogued them since March last; and they feared he would continue such proceeding: lest, being allowed to convene, the Commons might enter into Resolutions of opposition, to the late conduct of parliament. However, they privately agreed to convene early in the morning of the day, to which they stood prorogued; should they find themselves in a capacity of doing so. For, of late, the Lieutenant-Governor had been accustomed personally to prorogue the General Assembly; instead of doing so by proclamation, as had been usual. They now wished, and thought there was a chance he might continue the same line of conduct: although, from his prudence, experience, and knowledge of the temper of the people, they scarcely had reason to believe, their hopes would be realized.

At length, Tuesday the 2d day of August 1774, arrived; and the Representatives to their great joy and surprize found themselves able to convene, in General Assembly, agreeably to the Lieutenant-Governor's prorogation. In pursuance of their private agreement therefore, they met in the Chamber of the Commons, so early, as at 8 o'clock in the morning; and Messrs. Heyward and Cattell, were ordered to " wait on the Lieutenant-Governor, and acquaint his Honour, that the House has met."—" The said gentlemen being returned, Mr. Heyward reported to the House, that Mr. Cattell and himself had waited on the Lieutenant-Governor with the Message they had in charge; and that his Honour was pleased to say, he would be in the Council Chamber immediately, when he would send a Message to this House."*

Having sent the above message, the Commons-House of Assembly, now availed themselves of the opportunity which offered, previous to the Lieutenant-Governor's arrival, and which they had ardently hoped for; and Colonel Powell, Chairman of the late Gene-

---

See Journals of the Commons-House of Assembly for 1774, page 1.

ral Meeting, requested the attention of the House, to
matters of importance with which he was charged.
The House, being prepared on the occasion, immediately gave leave, in preference to all other business;
and the Colonel acquainted the House—" That during
the recess of this House, namely on the 6th, 7th, and
8th days of July last, at a General Meeting of the
Inhabitants of this Colony, they, having under consideration the acts of parliament lately passed with regard
to the port of Boston, and Colony of Massachusetts-
Bay, as well as other American grievances, had nominated and appointed the honourable Henry Middleton,
John Rutledge, Thomas Lynch, Christopher Gadsden,
and Edward Rutledge, Esquires, Deputies on the part
and behalf of this Colony; to meet the Deputies of
the other Colonies, of North America, in General
Congress, the first Monday in September next, at
Philadelphia; or, at any other time or place, that may
be generally agreed on: there, to consider the acts
lately passed, and bills depending, in parliament with
regard to the port of Boston and Colony of Massachusetts-Bay; which acts and bills, in the precedent
and consequences, affect the whole Continent of America:—also, the grievances under which, America
labours, by reason of the several acts of parliament,
that impose taxes, or duties, for raising a Revenue,
and lay unnecessary restraints and burthens on trade:
and, of the Statutes, Parliamentary Acts, and Royal
Instructions, which make an invidious distinction between his Majesty's subjects in Great Britain, and
America:—with full power and authority to concert,
agree to, and effectually prosecute such legal measures,
as in the opinion of the said Deputies, and of the
Deputies so to be assembled, shall be most likely to
obtain a repeal of the said acts, and a redress of those
grievances.   And thereupon moved, that this House
do resolve to recognize, ratify, and confirm the said
appointment of the Deputies for the puposes aforesaid:

and, that this House, do also resolve, to provide a sum, not exceeding one thousand five hundred pounds Sterling, to defray the expense, which the said Deputies will be at, on the said service.

"Resolved, (*nemine contradicente*) That this House do recognize, ratify, and confirm, the appointment of the said Deputies, for the purposes mentioned in the said motion.

"Resolved, (*nem. con.*) That this House will make provision to pay to any person or persons, who will advance to the said Henry Middleton, John Rutledge, Thomas Lynch, Christopher Gadsden, and Edward Rutledge, Esquires, the sum of one thousand five hundred pounds Sterling, (for the purposes aforesaid;) together with full interest, from the day the said one thousand five hundred pounds Sterling shall be advanced; until it be repaid to the person or persons, advancing the same."

The House also sent the following Message to the Lieutenant-Governor, by Mr. Bee, and Captain Scott:

"May it please your Honour,

"This House, considering the precarious situation of this Colony in regard to Indian affairs, and the necessity there may be for the Inhabitants, of the back parts, to arm themselves for their protection and defence, against that cruel people, in case of a rupture with them; and being informed, that many of the poor settlers are unprovided with arms, and ammunition: do desire your Honour, will be pleased to order, a proper quantity of arms and ammunition, to be distributed to such persons as may be thought to stand most in need of such assistance; such arms and ammunition to be purchased by the Commissary General:

and that this House will make provision, to pay the
expense of the same.

 " By order of the House,
  " RAWLINS LOWNDES, Speaker."

These matters were scarcely performed, and they
were all the business which was done by the House in
the short time in which they acted that morning;
when at half past eight o'clock, a Message was received from Lieutenant-Governor William Bull, by
the Master in Chancery; notifying, that the Lieutenant-Governor was in the Council Chamber, where, he
required the immediate attendance of the House.

" And accordingly, Mr. Speaker, with the House,
went to attend the Lieutenant-Governor, in the Coun-
cil-Chamber; where, his Honour was pleased to prorogue the General Assembly, to Tuesday the 6th day
of September next."*

The convening of the Commons-House of Assembly at so early an hour, was a great surprize upon the
Lieutenant-Governor; as he had no intention, the
Representatives should have had time in that House,
to have entered upon any business. Ten, or eleven
o'clock, were the usual hours, at which the members
assembled upon a meeting after a prorogation; and
the Governor intended, when he should have heard a
few of them, had assembled, to have personally prorogued them, before they could have formed a House.
Indeed, he had given orders to persons to observe and
inform him, when the Representatives should begin to
assemble. They accordingly, did so; but the information was received by him, at so unexpected an hour;
that before his Honour could put on his clothes, repair

* See Journals of the Commons House of Assembly of South-Carolina, from
the 2d day of August 1774, to the 15th day of September 1775, pages 1, 2.

to the Council Chamber, and have the attendance of the Master in Chancery to carry his Message to the Representatives; they had done the business, for which, they had purposely assembled. And so very short a summons, had the Counsellors for so early an attendance; that only one was present at the proroga- tion; and another had barely arrived, when the Lieu- tenant-Governor was departing from the State-House.

Many persons, thought the Lieutenant-Governor connived, at this conduct of the Representatives; but, he certainly was above such an artifice—to his too great attention to a friend, was he indebted, for having been drawn into such a dilemma.   He had often pro- rogued the General Assembly by Proclamation, as all his predecessors had done: of late years, it had been the most usual mode: and it was also, a parliamentary proceeding.   Yet Lieutenant-Governor Bull, allowed Mr. Wragg to pursuade him, that a personal proroga- tion, was a preferable mode: as, being at once, more regular, and more constitutional.   Thus, wtthout the least necessity for such extreme caution, on a point which had never been disputed; and without reflect- ing, that the present, was not a juncture to be scrupu- lous in the exercise of prorogation, which had never been murmured at; the Lieutenant-Governor ran the risk, that the Representatives should enter upon mea- sures, contrary to his inclination, and the views of Ad- ministration.   For, as Lord William Campbell was expected shortly to arrive, as Governor and Com- mander in Chief; Lieutenant-Governor Bull, gene- rously endeavoured to keep affairs as quiet as possible; that his Lordship might enter upon a new administra- tion with every advantage; and without its being burthened by a quarrel with the Representatives, which would have arisen, had they been permitted to have sat and deliberated, upon the late proceedings of parliament.

About this time. the people in this Colony, and particularly in Charlestown, began to assume a tone highly impatient of British arbitrary and unconstitutional measures; and the minds of many were become so irritable, that they were liable by the smallest spark to be kindled into a blaze of civil fury. When therefore, on Sunday the 14th of August 1774, the Rev. John Bullman, Assistant of St. Michael's Church in Charlestown, preached a sermon, in which was an illustration of a pragmatical character; it was supposed to be meant for some persons, who had lately taken a lead against the measures of Government.* With this idea, the greatest part of the congregation took fire; scarcely continuing quiet, during the service. And, as soon as it was over, a report ran through the town, that the preacher had inculcated passive obedience; and had censured the popular proceedings. Against this conduct, exclamations were made in the severest terms; and on the next day, an assemblage of the Vestry took place, who cited Mr. Bullman to produce his late sermon. Upon his entering the Vestry room, he with warmth told the Vestry, that, as he found they desired to see his sermon, he would show them there was nothing offensive in it. But, at the same time he informed them, that he was not to be taught by them, in what manner to compose sermons. Hence, warm words arose on either side: and Mr. Bullman finally left his sermon with them, and departed.

Upon examination of the obnoxious passage, the Vestry did not find any thing so exceptionable, as they afterwards declared, but what might have been passed over; had the Assistant demeaned himself, more respectfully towards them. But, feeling themselves hurt

* See an Extract of the obnoxious part of the sermon, in *Dalcho's Church History*, pages 201, 202, 203.

on this point, they now inveighed, against his intemperate language; as totally unbecoming the gravity, meekness, and charity of the sacerdotal character: a conduct, not to be passed over in silence. Accordingly, they summoned the parishioners to assemble, on business of importance. In the course of the week, the meeting took place at St. Michael's Church; and the Vestry put the question, whether or not they " *approved Mr. Bullman's conduct?*" In vain was it alledged, that the question was not a proper one; for, no person would answer in the affirmative; since all would join in regretting, that the sermon, which had given rise to this uneasiness, had been preached at the present juncture. And while no man could approve of this particular conduct, in the Assistant; all men, could give testimony in approbation of his general character, as a moral man, and an edifying preacher. Sharp altercation now ensued; which caused several mild men, in favour of Mr. Bullman, to quit the meeting. The question, was now again put; with a cry, " *Now we will see, who are enemies to their country:*" and upon the votes being taken it was found, that thirty-three had voted in favour of Mr. Bullman, and forty-two against him. The victory so obtained, was now received as a matter of triumph on the side of the people in favour of the American cause; and it was announced by a shout, in the House of God.* And the Vestry having thus taken, what they deemed the sense of the parish; on the following day, sent Mr. Bullman a written paper, as a dismission from his office of Assistant. This measure, created much uneasiness in Charlestown; and a respectable party, espoused the cause of the Assistant: for, it was their opinion, he had been treated with unreasonable

---

* What then was thought an indecency, has, in the process of time, become common, at public meetings in Churches and places of public worship; as is evinced every fourth of July, throughout the United States—and occasionally, on matters of public consideration

severity, and that the Vestry were not warranted by law, in the conduct which they had pursued.

Upon these grounds, Mr. Bullman's friends evinced a desire of replacing him; as not having been dismissed, with the approbation of the parish. A representation therefore, to take the sense of the parish on the measure, was signed by a large majority of the parishioners, and laid before the Vestry; but, they took no notice of it. Upon this, a memorial was presented to Lieutenant-Governor Bull; praying, that a board of Church Commissioners might be called, to examine into, and decide upon the case. Men's minds, now became variously and violently agitated; each party, espousing their side with peculiar warmth. One, declared the Assistant, should be replaced; the other, that if he were, he should be dragged out of the pulpit; and the affair grew so serious, that if prosecuted, it was feared blows would ensue.

In the mean time, the Commissioners assembled to the number of ten; being all who were then in the province: the other two Commissioners, being Deputies at the General Congress. By law, the surviving original Commissioners were empowered to fill up the vacancies at the Board; and only two of such Commissioners were alive, and present. The whole Board however, joined in supplying the vacancies; and notifications were sent to the new members. The next day, Colonel Charles Pinckney, a new member, attended; but declined taking his seat, because the nomination, in his opinion, was not warranted by law: the same having been made by ten Commissioners, when the law required twelve at the least. The Lieutenant-Governor, although by no means convinced of the solidity of this objection, yet, submitted to his opinion; and without calling in the Counsel, who had been employed to draw the memorial and support the same, his Honour dismissed the Board; as having no power to proceed to business, until the return of the two Commissioners then at Congress. The great distinction, lost sight of in this procedure was this; to fill up the Board, the survivors of the original Commissioners, were fully sufficient: but, no other kind of business could be transacted, unless twelve Commissioners were present.

By one pretext or other, the matter was repeatedly postponed. However, after various meetings and deliberations, the Board of Commissioners were induced to drop the affair; until the defects of their organization should be remedied by an act, which one of the Commissioners promised he would bring, into the General Assembly, at its next meeting. In this manner the affair rested, until the 16th day of February 1775; when leave was given in the Commons-House of Assembly to bring in a bill for amending the act respecting the nominating, and from time to time keeping up, the number of Commissioners, therein mentioned. On the 21st day of February, the bill was accordingly presented by Mr. Lynch; was read the first time, and was ordered for a second reading. On the 22d, the House proceeded to the second reading of the same; but, the amendments and provisions of the bill were so unsatisfactory, and gave rise to so much debate; that on motion, the farther reading of the bill was postponed for six months.* On which, Mr. Bullman took his passage for England; and soon after departed.†

In the meantime, the Deputies from twelve of the Colonies assembled at Philadelphia; chosen and ap-

* See Journals of the Commons-House of Assembly of South-Carolina for 1775, pages 30, 35, 38.

See Dalcho's Church History, page 204.

pointed from New-Hampshire to South-Carolina inclusive, to take into consideration the actual situation
of North America; and the differences subsisting between the Colonies therein, and Great Britain; and the
General Congress was accordingly holden at Carpen-
ter's Hall, in the city of Philadelphia, on the 5th day
of September 1774.*   Peyton Randolph, late Speaker
of the House of Burgesses in Virginia, was unanimously elected President of the Congress; and Charles
Thomson unanimously chosen Secretary.

On the 6th of September, Congress adopted rules in
debating and determining questions.   According to
these, each Colony or Province had one vote.   No
person could speak more than twice on the same point,
without leave.   No question could be determined the
day on which it was agitated and debated, if any
one of the Colonies desired the determination to be
postponed to another day.   The door was to be kept
shut, during the time of business; and the members
to consider themselves under the strongest obligations
of honour, to keep the proceedings secret, until the
majority should direct them to be made public.   At
the same time, a Committee was appointed, to state
the rights of the Colonies in general; the several instances in which those rights had been violated or
infringed; and, the means most proper to be pursued,
for obtaining a restoration of them.   A Committee
was also appointed to examine and report, the several
statutes, which affected the trad and manufactures of
the Colonies.   The Congress was opened by prayer;
a reverential formality that was subsequently observed:
and, by an order of the Directors of the Library Company of Philadelphia, of the 31st of August preceding,
the Delegates were allowed the use of such books of
that institution as they might have occasion for, during

* See Laws of United States, new edition, vol. I. chap. I. page 1.

their sitting. On the 14th of September, Delegates from North-Carolina took their seats. On the 19th of September, it was unanimously resolved, that the Congress request the merchants and others in the several Colonies, not to send to Great Britain any orders for goods; and, to direct the execution of all orders already sent, to be delayed or suspended, until the sense of the Congress, on the means to be taken for the preservation of the liberties of America, should be made public. On the 24th of September, Congress resolved, that the Delegates would confine themselves to the consideration of such rights, as had been infringed by acts of the British parliament, after the year 1763; postponing the farther consideration of the general state of American rights to a future day. On the 27th of September, the Congress unanimously resolved, that from and after the 1st of December 1774, there should be no importation into British America, from Great Britain or Ireland, of any goods, wares, or merchandize, exported therefrom; and, that they should not be used or purchased, if imported after that day. On the 30th of September, it was farther resolved, that from and after the 10th of September 1775, the exportation of all merchandize, and every commodity whatsoever, to Great Britain, Ireland, and the West Indies, ought to cease; unless, the grievances of America, should be redressed before that time. On the 6th of October, it was resolved, to exclude from importation, after the 1st of December following, molasses, coffee, or pimento, from the British plantations, or from Dominica; wines from Madeira, and the Western Islands, and foreign indigo. In consequence of a letter received from the Committee of Correspondence, at Boston, on the 6th of October, Congress on the 7th, resolved to appoint a Committee to prepare a letter to General Gage; representing, that the town of Boston, and province of Massachusetts-Bay, were considered by all America as

suffering in the common cause, for their noble and
spirited opposition to oppressive acts of parliament;
calculated, to deprive the American people of their
most sacred rights and privileges, &c.   On the 8th of
October, it was resolved, that the Congress approve
the opposition of the inhabitants of the Massachusetts-
Bay, to the execution of the obnoxious acts of parliament; and if the same should be attempted to be
carried into execution by force, in such case, all
America ought to support them in their opposition;
and, on the 11th of October, the letter of remonstrance
to General Gage, ordered on the 7th, was brought in
and signed by the President.   On the 11th likewise,
a memorial to the people of British America, stating
the necessity of adhering to the measures of Congress,
and an address to the people of Great Britain, were
unanimously resolved on.   On the 14th of October,
Congress made a declaration, and framed resolves,
relative to the rights and grievances of the Colonies.   On the 20th of October, the non-importation,
non-consumption, and non-exportation agreement,
was adopted, and signed by the Congress.   This
agreement, contained a clause, to discontinue the
slave trade; and a provision, not to import East
India tea, from any part of the world.   In the
article, respecting non-exportations, the sending rice
to Europe, was excepted.   In general, the Association expressed a determination to suppress luxury,
encourage frugality, and promote domestic manufactures: the agreement was dated the 24th of October.
On the 21st, the address to the people of Great Britain was approved; as was the memorial to the inhabitants of the British Colonies, on the same day.
Both these state papers, contain a representation of
the grievances, and a justification of the conduct, of
the Colonies.   It was also determined, that an address
should be prepared, to the people of Quebec, in like
manner; and letters be sent to the Colonies of St.

John's, Nova Scotia, Georgia, and East and West
Florida. On the 22d of October, Peyton Randolph
being unable to attend, on account of indisposition;
Henry Middleton (of South-Carolina) was chosen to
supply his place, as President of Congress. On the
same day, a letter to the Colonies of St. John's, &c.
was reported, approved, and signed: it recommended,
an immediate adoption, of the measures pursued by the
Congress. On the 25th of October, a petition to the
King was adopted, and was ordered to be enclosed in
a letter to the several Colony Agents, in order,
that the same might be, by them presented to his
Majesty; which letter, was approved, and signed, by
the President on the day following. This petition
recited the grievances of the Colonies, and asked for a
redress of them. On the 26th October, the address to
the Inhabitants of Quebec, was adopted and signed.
It set forth, the rights of the British colonists,
breathed a spirit of sympathy in suffering, and invited
a spirit of union in resistance. The Congress, was
then dissolved; having on the 22d of October, passed
a resolution, recommending Delegates to meet at Philadelphia, on the 10th of May 1775.* Such, were
the gradual approaches, which the United States, when
Colonies, made to Independence; and this, is a summary of the principal measures, taken for that effect,
by the first General Congress.

While the Congress was so conducting, the various
matters of consequence it had in charge; William
Henry Drayton, had written and published in South-
Carolina, a political tract, stating the American grievances; and presenting a bill of American rights. The
publication, was signed *Freeman;* and was addressed
to the American Congress at Philadelphia. The act
of parliament commanding Judges to issue writs of

* See Laws of the United States, new edition; vol. I. chap. I. pp. 1, 2

assistance to the Customs, had ever been viewed by the public with abhorrence; and, while the Bench was filled with Assistant-Judges of independence and property in the Colony, serving the public without fee or reward, although such writs had been applied for by the Attorney-General, these Judges upon some pretext or other, evaded giving any determination respecting them. But, when, upon the establishment of Circuit Courts in 1769, salaries were given to the Assistant-Judges; Administration at once caught hold of the opportunity—dismissed the Colony Judges— and sent over from England, men destitute of support in their own country. These Judges, now granted the writs of assistance to the Customs. In showing in this instance, the consequence of having Judges of independence and property, and others who had no support but Royal favour; *Freeman* gave mortal offence to the Judges upon the latter establishment. This was resented by the King's Judges, who fancied themselves pointed at: and Thomas Knox Gordon, the Chief Justice; and Charles Mathews Cosslett, one of the Assistant-Judges, presented a remonstrance to the Lieutenant-Governor, on the 21st September 1774;* complaining of *Freeman's* publication, and charging it to Mr. Drayton; thence submitting to his Honour, whether Mr. Drayton, who then held the appointment of one of the King's Assistant-Judges,† was a fit person, to be continued in the said office.

Lieutenant-Governor Bull, being uncle to Mr. Drayton, from motives of delicacy, would not give any determination thereon; but laid the remonstrance, before his Privy Council; declaring at the same time, he would proceed only by their advice. This dispute,

* See the Council Journal for 1774, page 183.

† See Appendix to this Chapter, No. II.

was carried on before the Lieutenant-Governor by
various pleadings and replications; in which Mr.
Drayton defended his own conduct, and brought into
question the legal abilities of his accusers, as evinced
in their conduct and charges in open court, and in
cases which he specially stated; and in doing so, he
said, that Mr. Lowndes and himself were the only
Judges who had ventured, and with success, to charge
Juries, in contradiction to the rest of the Court: and
that both against Mr. Lowndes and himself, had
judicial vengeance been pointed—that the complaint
against Mr. Lowndes in the year 1771 had been dismissed by the late Governor, with the unanimous consent of the Council: and he trusted, the remonstrance
now against him, would meet a similar fate—he then
declared the Lieutenant-Governor had no jurisdiction
in the case, to hear, judge, and finally determine, that
he was the Author of the publication; and that it was
a libel upon the Judges—as these points, were cognizable only by Juries.* To this, the Judges replied,
after stating new matter of complaint, that the pamphlet published by *Freeman*, was a libel—that Mr.
Drayton wrote it—and that these were points, upon
which his Honour could give judgment.† At this
stage of the dispute, the November Circuits began;
and Mr. Drayton sat out upon that duty; taking the
Northern Circuit to Georgetown, Cheraws and Camden. Mr. Drayton had scarcely left Charlestown,
when Mr. Gregory arrived from England to supercede
him as Judge; and to supply the place of the late
Judge Murray; to whose vacancy, Mr. Drayton had
been commissioned by the Lieutenant-Governor, with
the approbation of his Privy Council.‡ Upon Mr.

* See Council Journal for 1774, page 208.

† Ibid. page 229.

‡ See Appendix, No. II.

Drayton's return from the Circuit, he applied to the
Lieutenant-Governor, requesting the dispute might be
heard and decided on. A Council was accordingly
summoned; but a member was indisposed—and therefore no Council could be formed. The next day was
appointed; but now, the Chief Justice was that morning suddenly taken ill with the gout. It was thence
determined, that the dispute could not now be heard;
as the hearing would be *ex-parte*. As therefore, the
Chief Justice's recovery was uncertain; it was deemed
proper no longer to delay issuing a *supersedeas*, to
Mr. Drayton's commission as Assistant-Justice; since
the King's commission to that office, must have its full
effect. To this determination of the Council, the
Lieutenant-Governor conformed; and the writ of
supersedeas to Mr. Drayton, was immediately (December 9th) signed, and sealed with the seal of the province: it being however understood, it was to be
without prejudice to the dispute; the merits of it being
still to be heard, on some day convenient to both parties.*

After this, inquiries respecting the Chief Justice's
health availed nothing; for, no person saw him, but
one or two of his particular friends. At length, the
duties of his station called him abroad, on the 3d day
of January 1775; when, he appeared in perfect health.
On the next day, Mr. Drayton presented a memorial
to the Lieutenant Governor;† stating the late proceedings between the Judges and himself—that they
were still pending—that, they were to have been
heard on the 9th December last; but, by reason of the
sudden illness of the Chief Justice, the hearing had
been postponed until the Chief Justice should be recovered—that the Chief Justice was now well, and

* See Council Journal for 1774, 1775.

† See Appendix to this Chapter, No. I.

he therefore prayed a day might be appointed for a hearing of the merits of the case. Accordingly, a Council was summoned, for the 6th of January; and the memorial was laid before them. Mr. Drayton, now pressed for a hearing; but the Chief Justice declined it; alledging, that as Mr. Drayton was no longer a Judge, it would be improper and nugatory to deliberate thereon. Upon which, the Council composed of Crown officers, determined, "that there should be no farther consideration upon the transaction had, by this Board upon the said remonstrance; and that the same should be dismissed, without any censure upon any of the parties."* Thus, ended this contest; which was both of a political, and personal nature. But effects followed, which Chief Justice Gordon, and his Assistants, could not relish. For, in a short time afterwards, as shall be shown, the King's Judges were obliged to give way, to others who possessed the confidence of the people. And William Henry Drayton, who had been superseded as a King's Judge, was elevated to the seat of Chief Justice; not of a King's province—but of South-Carolina, one of the United States of America.

The tea which had hitherto arrived, had been deposited in the Collector's stores; but from that time to this, many changes had taken place in the public opinion; and they were more prepared to advocate and support vigorous measures. Seven chests of tea, now arrived in the port of Charlestown, on account of the merchants; and on the 3d day of November 1774, the proprietors by themselves and agents, in the presence of the Committee of Inspection, stove the chests; and from the vessel then riding in the stream of Cooper River, threw all their contents into the same, amidst the acclamations of the people, who crowded the

* See Appendix to this Chapter, No. I.

20

wharves on the occasion. The same conduct, on a similar occasion, was also observed at Georgetown in this Colony.

On the 6th of November, our Delegates arrived from the Continental Congress; and, were respectfully received. And two days after, the General Committee in a body waited on them at the State-House; where, the Delegates acquainted them, with part of the Congressional proceedings. And on the next day, the General Committee honoured the Delegates, with an elegant entertainment.

This had a good effect, in supporting patriotic measures; and in putting down domestic opposition from Crown officers, and other ill-disposed persons. While the Lieutenant-Governor, was obliged to be a silent spectator of measures, which he was unable to prevent: but which, evinced in terms too glaring to be misunderstood, how weakened were his powers; and how strong those of the people, vested in the General Committee, had become. It was now indeed, that body began to feel and know, they in a great degree held the reins of Government. And with a bold and steady hand, they rendered nugatory Gubernatorial writs of election; while in their place, they introduced Resolutions calculated for that purpose.

At this time, the British determinations became more developed; and preventive measures, demanded encreased energy. The General Committee therefore were of opinion, the public union would be strengthened, by having a settled representation from every part of the state; by which, the sentiments of the people would be better known, and established. For this purpose, on the 9th of November, the General Committee issued Resolutions for a General Meeting of the Inhabitants of the Colony, by representation;

in which, the districts and parishes, were described; the time of election, was appointed; and the number of Representatives for each district or parish, was ascertained. The number of Representatives, was then first assumed, not as relating to numbers or property; but as to convenience, and what might be supposed assisting, in disseminating political information among the people. For this purpose, the number thirty, which had been before allowed for Charlestown in nominating members of the General Committee, was now allowed Charlestown, for representatives; ten. representatives, were allowed to each of the four large districts, of Ninety-Six—between Broad and Saluda Rivers—between Broad and Catawba Rivers— and for the Eastward of Watteree River:—and six representatives were allowed, for each of the parishes. From hence, arose the Representatives of the people; and by this mode, the representation was encreased, from forty-eight, which composed the Commons-House of Assembly,* to one hundred and eighty-four members. The Resolutions required the representatives elected, to assemble in Charlestown on the eleventh day of January 1775; they also, expressed the causes of meeting. These were, to receive an account of the proceedings of the late Continental Congress— to elect Delegates for another Congress, to be holden in May ensuing—to elect a new General Committee— and, to establish such regulations, as the urgency of the times might render necessary.

It was at this time, that the popular constitutional line of electing Representatives, was first drawn in South-Carolina; that the minds of the people became better informed, as to the principles of representation; and, the obligations existing, between constituents and representatives. From hence, we may date, the

See Appendix to this Chapter, No. III.

strengthening of the popular branch of our Government: which, advised by able leaders, and supported by its own intrinsic strength, bore down obstacles which were opposed to American rights; and eventually frustrated the views, of a badly advised Monarch, and an arbitrary Administration.

APPENDIX

CHAPTER IV.

———

No. I.

IN THE COUNCIL CHAMBER.

Friday, the 6th day of January 1775.

PRESENT,

His Honour the LIEUTENANT-GOVERNOR.

The Honourable THOMAS SKOTTOWE, JOHN STUART, THOMAS KNOX GORDON, WILLIAM HENRY DRAYTON, THOMAS IRVING, Esquires.

His Honour the Lieutenant-Governor, laid before the Board the following Memorial, from William Henry Drayton, Esquire.

*To the Honourable William Bull, Esquire, Lieuten-
ant-Governor and Commander in Chief, in and over
his Majesty's Colony of South-Carolina.*

The Memorial of William Henry Drayton, Esquire,
humbly represents:

That Thomas Knox Gordon, Esq. and Charles
Mathews Cosslett, Esq. two of his Majesty's Judges
in this Colony, did present unto your Honour a remonstrance, containing charges of a very criminal nature,
against your memorialist: that your memorialist
formed an answer to the said remonstrance, and, that
those Judges made a reply to the said answer: all
which proceedings, are yet pending before your
Honour.

That on the ninth of December last, a hearing was
intended to have been had, upon the said proceedings;
but that by reason of the then sudden indisposition of
the said Thomas Knox Gordon, your Honour did in
Council determine, that a hearing could not then be
had; and that a hearing on the said proceedings should
be postponed, until the said Thomas Knox Gordon,
should be able to attend the hearing on such day to be
appointed, as might be convenient to both parties.

That the said Thomas Knox Gordon, is now so
well recovered, from his late indisposition, that he did
yesterday attend the duty of his office, in his Majesty's
Court of Common Pleas.

Your memorialist therefore most humbly prays your
Honour, that some day may be now appointed for a
hearing upon the said remonstrance, answer, and reply: and your memorialist will ever pray, &c.
                    WILLIAM HENRY DRAYTON.
January 4th, 1775.

Which memorial was read, and Mr. Drayton in his place prayed, that he might either now be heard in farther support of the matter urged in his answer, to the remonstrance of the Chief Justice and Mr. Cosslett; or, that a future day might be appointed for that purpose.

Mr. Chief Justice, thereupon observed, that he conceived any farther deliberation on that matter would be not only improper, but nugatory; as his Majesty by his mandamus had directed Mr. Gregory to be appointed a Judge in the room of the late Mr. Justice Murray; in consequence of which Mr. Drayton had already been superseded from his office of Assistant-Judge: and, that the propriety of his remaining as such, was the sole matter proposed to be submitted to the consideration of his Honour and the Board, by him and Mr. Cosslett in their remonstrance.

And Mr. Chief Justice, and Mr. Drayton, thereupon withdrew.

His Honour, then desired the opinion of the Board, what was proper to be farther done upon the said remonstrance, the answer, and reply thereto.

Who seriatim delivered their unanimous opinion; that as the sole matter submitted by his Honour for their advice was the propriety of Mr. Drayton's being permitted to hold his seat as an Assistant-Judge, if he was the Author of the pamphlet complained of: and, as by his Majesty's appointment of Mr. Gregory, it had become necessary to supersede Mr. Drayton; it would be unnecessary for to investigate whether Mr. Drayton was, or was not, the Author of the pamphlet in question: or, to give it any farther consideration, or any opinion to his Honour thereupon. But, that there should be no farther consideration had by this

Board, upon the said remonstrance; and, that the same should be dismissed without any censure upon any of the parties. And the same is hereby dismissed accordingly.

A true copy.

J. SIMPSON.*

———

No. II.

The full intention of parliament respecting America, became known in South-Carolina by the arrival of the acts, at the same time, when accounts were received that Administration had nominated an Assistant-Judge, regularly bred to the bar, in the room of Mr. Justice Murray deceased; and, a change of conduct taking place in Mr. Drayton at this crisis, some imputed it to disgust, rather than to principle. He was aware of such a construction; but, he was incapable of being intimidated from a system he thought right. The following extract will show, that the appointment of a Judge from England was expected; and therefore, it could have no influence on Mr. Drayton's conduct on the occasion.

" On Tuesday last, a commission passed the great seal of this province,† appointing the Honourable William Henry Drayton, Esquire, to the office of Assistant-Judge, in the room of John Murray, Esquire, deceased. We hear, that when his Honour the Lieutenant-Governor, and his Majesty's Council were in deliberation to nominate a gentleman of a proper rank

* James Simpson was Clerk of the Council.

† See South-Carolina Council Journal, for 1774, page 12.

and character to the office of Assistant-Judge, it was allowed, that no such person at the bar would, for such a consideration, be induced to quit his practice; and, that as no such person of rank and character, would choose to run the risk of being superseded by the appointment of a barrister from England; so, it it would be highly indelicate, to offer the post to any such. The case seemed difficult, yet of necessity a Judge must be appointed. After some time spent, in agitating the subject, Mr. Drayton (being one of the Council) offered his service in that station, *until a barrister should be appointed by the King;* which public spirited behaviour was very readily and unanimously, approved, by the Lieutenant-Governor and Council."—*See General Gazette,* No. 801, January 28, 1774.

No. III.

Members of the Commons-House of Assembly, summoned to meet for the first time, February 23d, 1773; and which was dissolved, in September 1775.

Honourable Rawlins Lowndes, Esq. member for the Parish of St. Bartholomew, *Speaker.*

For the Parish of St. Philip, Charlestown. Christopher Gadsden, Charles Pinckney, Roger Smith.

St. Michael, Charlestown. Miles Brewton, John Edwards, David Deas.

Christ-Church. John Rutledge, Arnoldus Vanderhorst.

St. John, Berkley-County. James Cordes, jun. John Huger, James Ravenell.

St. Andrew.   William Scott, Thomas Bee, William Cattel.

St. George, Dorchester.   David Olyphant, Benjamin Waring.

St. James, Goose-Creek.   John Parker, John Izard, Benjamin Smith.

St. Thomas and St. Denys.   James Akin, Isaac Harleston, John Wigfall.

St. Paul.   Thomas Elliott, Benjamin Elliott, George Haig.

St. Bartholomew.   Rawlins Lowndes, James Parsons, William Skirving, Thomas Osborne.

St. Helena.   Thomas Heyward, jun. Jacob Motte, William Sanders.

St. James, Santee.   Paul Douxsaint, Thomas Horry.

Prince George, Winyaw.   Thomas Lynch, Elias Horry.

Prince Frederick.   Benjamin Farrar, Theodore Gaillard.

St. John, Colleton County. William Gibbes, Charles Cotesworth Pinckney, Thomas Evance.

St. Peter, Purrysburg.   Gideon Dupont, jun.

Prince William.   Isaac Motte, John Ward.

St. Stephen.   John Gaillard.

St. Mark.   Joseph Kershaw.

St. Matthew.   Tacitus Gaillard.

St. David.   George Gabriel Powell.

                    Esquires.

Clerk, Thomas Skottowe.

Clerk-Assistant, Thomas Farr, jun.

Messengers, Edward Weyman, John Calvert.

No. IV.

Members of his Majesty's Council.

The Honourable

The Lieutenant-Governor, John Stuart,
Sir Egerton Leigh, *Bart.* Thomas Knox Gordon,
John Drayton, William Henry Drayton,
Daniel Blake, Barnard Elliott,
John Burn, Thomas Irving,
Thomas Skottowe, Esquires.

Clerk, James Simpson.
Messenger, John Mills.
Door-Keeper, Benjamin Lord.
State-House-Keeper, Mary Pratt.

CHAPTER V.

The British Parliament dissolved, and a new one summoned—Orders of the King in Council—Resolutions of the General Committee—Representatives meet at the Exchange, in Charlestown, and choose a President and Secretary—Adjourn to the State-House—Assume the style of Provincial Congress—They consider the proceedings of the Continental Congress—Privileges granted to the Committees—who are to decide respecting law suits, bail, &c.—A temporary sytem of Government established—Provincial Congress, its continuance; how to be convened on emergencies, after it has been adjourned—General Committee, its Duties—District, and Parochial Committees—Committees of Inspection, their duties—Compensation to be made by Rice Planters, for liberty of exporting their Rice—The five Delegates to Congress re-chosen—The Provincial Congress wait on the Lieutenant-Governor, and present an address—His reply—Provincial Congress pass Resolutions, respecting the use of Arms; and recommend a day of fasting, humiliation, and prayer—Adjourns—General Committee meet—Georgia Proceedings—Resolution of General Committee thereon. Association supported in South-Carolina—Debates in General Committee—The conduct of some persons, begins to attract the attention of the Committee of Inspection.

THESE things were scarcely done, when accounts arrived from England, that the King had suddenly dissolved the parliament, on the 30th of September 1774; and had summoned a new parliament to meet on the 29th of November. General Gage's Express, who sailed in a frigate from Boston on the 5th of September, had landed in England on the 28th of that month: hence, the sudden dissolution of parliament. Upon the arrival of this frigate, no intelligence was allowed to be received from, or private communication to be had with, any person on board: and a strict guard was kept, to prevent the one and the other. On the 24th of October, the frigate was dispatched back to General Gage, with advices, that she should be speedily followed by considerable reinforcements. An order of the King in Council of the 14th of October, for preventing during six months the exportation of any arms and ammunition, demonstrated, that administration considered America as almost on the eve of hostilities; and it was intended if possible, to prevent her from being in a situation of prosecuting them.

The news of such vigorous measures, on the other side of the Atlantic, gave new energy to the proceedings of this Colony: and people began to regret, the late Congress had not acted with more vigour; and that General Gage had not been attacked and overcome in Boston, before the reinforcements could arrive. A proposition had indeed been made by one of our Deputies in Congress, Mr. Gadsden, for that purpose; but it was soon overruled. Not because the people of Massachusetts were not willing, as well as able, to undertake the attack; but because, Congress were of opinion, such a measure would be premature. The loyal Americans, being unwilling to draw the sword against the King; while any other means of obtaining redress remained:—they waited for the last necessity, before they would recur to the appeal of arms.

It was so obvious now, that America had no time to lose, in preparing for defence, that although in the resolutions of the ninth day of November last, for the election of Representatives, it was mentioned the Representatives elect, were to choose a new General Committee; yet on the 8th of December, the General Committee issued another resolution, by which, the Representatives to be elected should " be considered as a General Provincial Committee, so as to act immediately, after the dissolution of the present General Committee;" which, would naturally be dissolved by holding a General Meeting. At the same time, the General Committee issued a resolution of privilege from arrests and civil process; which extended to the people who should be engaged in the election of the Representatives; the Representatives themselves; and the several parochial Committees, to be appointed according to the advice of the late Congress. And on the 12th of December, another resolution was issued, which recited, " that whereas by the late prohibition of exporting arms and ammunition from England, it too clearly appears a design of disarming the people of America, in order the more speedily to dragoon and enslave them;" it was therefore recommended, to all persons, to provide themselves immediately, with at least twelve and a half rounds of powder, with a proportionate quantity of bullets. And these things being done, the year 1774 came to a close; leaving the people of the Colony impatiently expecting the coming of the eleventh day of January; at which time, the meeting of Representatives from all parts, of the province, was to take effect.

This wished for day at length arrived, and the Representatives appeared with great punctuality at the Exchange in Charlestown, agreeably to the resolution of election: eleven only, of the Representatives being absent, owing to double returns, sickness, or accidents.

They immediately organized themselves; choosing Colonel Charles Pinckney to be their President, and Peter Timothy (one of the Representatives) their Secretary. And, they then adjourned, to the Chamber of the Commons-House of Assembly, in the west end of the State-House.

The proceedings of the Continental Congress were now laid before this Assembly; and, as during this session they resolved themselves into a Provincial Congress; we shall hence forward speak of them under this new title.

Our Delegates from Congress being present, the proceedings of that body at Philadelphia were taken into consideration; and many questions were proposed to them relative to various parts of the proceedings; to which, answers and explanations were given by them. One of the most important of these was, why, at a time when a number of gentlemen were sent to Congress, from all parts of America, for the express purpose of considering and stating the American grievances; and for devising the proper means, of redressing them; why, did they limit their reseaches to the year 1763; and not trace back, as could easily have been done, the many aggressions which had been committed by Great Britain upon her infant Colonies; in the jealousies, monopolies, and prohibitions, with which she was so prodigal towards them; for the express purpose, of depressing their population—confining their trade—and crippling their attempts, at even the most domestic and necessary manufactures?* To this it was answered, that our Delegates were willing to have stated all the grievances, as were the

* See, An Appeal from the Judgments of Great Britain, respecting the United States of America, by *Robert Walsh*, jun. published at Philadelphia 1819.—Vol. I. Part I. respecting *Political and Mercantile Jealousy.*

greater part of the other Delegates; but the people of
Virginia would not retrospect farther back, than 1763,
being limited in their powers.   And, although they did
not avow the reason; yet, it was privately declared, it
had been agreed upon at home, not to go beyond that
year: as thereby, the greater odium would be thrown
upon the reign of George III.—which was so fatal to
the peace of America.   The Delegates farther answered, it was then pressed in Congress, that the
other Colonies should, in this measure, act independently of Virginia; but Maryland and North-Carolina
represented, that as their exports were similar to those
of Virginia, so, they could not with any advantage to
the common cause act independently of her; for, their
own commodities would be carried to the Virginian
ports; which, would run away with all their trade.
And, that in this manner, was the measure of stating
all the grievances, defeated.

The articles of association determined upon by
Congress, and recommended to the Provincial Conventions and Congresses to be carried into execution,
now came on to be considered: and the four last
words of the fourth article of that instrument, (" *except
rice to Europe*,") gave room for a long and a violent
debate.   This exception, had created an alarming
disunion, throughout the whole Colony; in consequence of which, the Representatives had met, with
jealous feelings on the subject; as by that article of
the Association, it was contracted, that after the 10th
day of September 1775, America " will not directly or
indirectly export any merchandize or commodity whatsoever, to Great Britain, Ireland, or the West Indies,
except rice to Europe."   This exception had given so
general a disgust, that the whole interior of the province, considered their interests as sacrificed to the
emolument of the rice planters; and, accordingly, a
motion was made and seconded " that the Delegates

to be elected, use their utmost endeavours at the ensuing Congress at Philadelphia, to cause those words to be expunged."

Mr. Gadsden, then rose, and explained to the Congress, what had taken place in the Continental Congress, during the passage of the obnoxious exception. He said, he thought it was his duty to declare, he had not any hand, in causing those words to stand in the instrument of association,—that, they had well nigh occasioned a division in Congress. And, so ill was a proposition of that nature received, that it had occasioned a cessation from business for several days; in order to give our deputies time, to recollect themselves. That when the association was completing, and the members of Congress were signing that instrument, all our Deputies, but himself, withdrew. That he would have been glad of the honour, of signing his name alone; and for doing so, would have trusted to the generosity of his constituents. That, he had offered to do so; and, that Carolina was on the point of being excluded the association, when our Deputies being again summoned by the Secretary, they returned into Congress, yielding up the article of indigo: and, that Congress only for the sake of preserving the union of America, allowed the article rice to be added to the association. That this however, was illy received by the other Colonies: who had thence, become jealous of the rice Colonies: and therefore, it was his opinion, that for the common good, as well as our own honour, we ought to remove this as soon as possible; by having the words " *except rice to Europe*" struck out, of the fourth article of the association.

Mr. John Rutledge now undertook his own defence, and that of his three associates. He said, that at an early period, he and the other Delegates from this Colony had warmly pressed an immediate non-importa-

22

tion, and total non-exportation. That, as a non-exportation to Great Britain and Ireland, was to withhold from thence, the advantages their people might acquire from a receipt of American commodities; so, the end would be more surely effected, by retaining those commodities altogether in America. Such measures however, could not be effected; the Northern Colonies resolving to remit to England, as usual, to pay their debts by the circuitous mode of their flour and fish trade to the rest of Europe. In short, the commodities they usually sent to the mother country were but trifling; and their real trade, would be but little affected by the association. For instance, Philadelphia carried on a trade of export, to the amount of £700,000 Sterling; whereas, scarce £50,000 value of it, went to the market of the mother country. That, as it was evident, those Colonies were less intent to annoy the mother country in the article of trade, than to preserve their own trade: so, he thought it was but justice to his constituents, to preserve to them their trade, as entire as possible. That, as the Northern trade would be but little affected by the association, he saw no reason why ours should be almost ruined; for, nearly all our indigo, and two thirds of our rice, went to the ports of the mother country. That, if we must bear burdens in the cause of America, they ought to be as equally laid as possible. Upon the whole, he said the affair seemed rather like a commercial scheme, among the flour Colonies, to find a better vent for their flour through the British Channel; by preventing, if possible, any rice from being sent to those markets: and, that for his part, he could never consent to our becoming dupes to the people of the north; or, in the least, to yield to their unreasonable expectations. That, as by the association, the rice planters preserved their property; so, it had been the idea of the Delegates at the Congress, that they should make compensation to the indigo planters, who could not send their crops to the mother country. Such a plan, was just, and practicable; and it ought to be the subject of our debate—rather than expunging the means, of exporting a great part of our annual crop; and therewith, supplying ourselves, with those necessaries we might require.

The subject, thus increased, by this new matter of compensation brought into view, the debate became more general; and several members, took parts in the same. Among the principal of these were, John Rutledge, Thomas Lynch, William Henry Drayton, Edward Rutledge, and Mr. Lynch, jun. on one side: on the other, the principal speakers were, Christopher Gadsden, Rawlins Lowndes, and the Reverend Mr. Tennent.

By these latter gentlemen, it was contended, the compensation scheme was impracticable. That if it were to operate in favour of the indigo planter, it should afford in justice also relief to the hemp-grower, the lumber cutter, the corn planter, the makers of pork and butter, &c.; for, why should this benefit be confined to the indigo maker, in exclusion of other classes of citizens, whose commodities were their means of support, and would equally, nay more, be unsaleable by the association? That, as we were all one people; we should all suffer alike; and then, all would struggle through difficulties, which might arise. That union among ourselves, was a *sine qua non;* and this odious distinction had cruelly convulsed the Colony. Besides which, our Northern brethren beheld us with a jealous eye; and, we ought to induce them to look upon us more favourably. For, if blood were to be spilt, in the American cause, theirs would be first shed: while ours, would be running only, in the usual channels.

In reply it was contended by the Delegates, and the first named gentlemen, that a compensation was very practicable, and therefore ought to be proceeded in: and particularly so, as it would render any opposition to the association unnecessary. That we ought not by any measure, to express a public dislike, of any thing the late Congress had done; as, such conduct would be bad policy: on the contrary, we ought to evince the utmost confidence, in their determination, as contributing to the general apparent union;—and at this time, such an appearance alone, was of the utmost importance.

In this manner, the whole day was expended; when, at sunset, a Committee was appointed, to form a plan of compensation; and to report it, on the next morning.

The Committee met in an hour, and sat until twelve o'clock at night; and the next morning at eleven o'clock they brought in their report; the Provincial Congress, having impatiently waited, two hours for them. The first part of the report contained the famous resolve, relating to debt; by which, the Committees, of the several parishes and districts, became Judges and juries; and upon application were to give permission for the bringing, or proceeding on, suits, where the debtors refused to renew their obligations, or to give reasonable security; or where they were justly suspected of intentions to leave the province, or to defraud their creditors; or where there should appear to the majority of such Committee, any other reasonable cause, for granting such permission. That the Congress would indemnify the Committees, in so doing; and that no summons should be issued by any magistrate, in small and mean causes, without the like consent. This part of the report, was immediately agreed to; but all the other parts, were so intricate, and so little satisfactory, that they were rejected; and the Congress resumed the debate, on the four words.

This debate, was now carried on without any cessation, until dark. Great heats prevailed—and the members were on the point of falling into downright uproar and confusion. At length, all parties being wearied out, the question was put by candle-light; and by mere accident at the desire of one among the indigo party, it was put in a manner that lost it. For, instead of voting as usual by acclamation; to save time and mistakes in counting, each man's name was called; and he declared himself *yea,* or *nay,* which was minuted down. By this mode, some were overawed, either by their diffidence, circumstances, or connexions; and to the surprise of the nays, they themselves carried the point by a majority of 12 voices—87 to 75.

The next day, being Sunday, the Congress was opened with the celebration of divine service, by the Rev. Mr. Turquand: after which, a Committee was appointed to adjust some mode of compensation. For, as rice was to be exported, the indigo planters chose to have some mode of compensation, however little satisfactory the same might be; and the other party, sensible the same would never be executed, as either there would not be any occasion for it; or, the hostile situation of affairs would render the compensation a dead letter, very readily agreed to indulge them in the most feasible manner. Upon this, resolutions were passed on the subject; rice being assumed as the basis of valuation, at fifty-five shillings currency the hundred: and as that rose or fell in price, so the other commodities were to rise or fall likewise. Indigo, was valued at 30s. the pound. Hemp, at £8 the hundred weight. Corn, at 12s. 6d. the bushel. Flour,

of the best sort, at £4 10s.; and of the second sort, at
£4, the hundred weight. Lumber, inch pine boards,
per 1000 feet, at £20, in Charlestown; and £15, in
Beaufort and Georgetown; and other plank and
scantling in proportion. Pork, at £13, the barrel.
Butter, at 3s. the pound. Resolutions also were
passed confirming powers, and appointing Committees
to effect the different exchanges of the above commodities, as the conveniences of parties should require;
either in kind, or in money.

It was then resolved, that after the first day of
March next, no lambs or sheep be killed for sale.
Also, that the present representation of this Colony,
shall continue until the next general meeting of the
inhabitants, under the title of the *Provincial Congress*.
That it be adjourned from time to time, by the President. That, it be summoned to convene for dispatch
of business, upon any emergency, by a vote of the
Charlestown General Committee; at which Committee, every member of the Congress who may happen
to be in town, shall attend, and be considered as a
member. That any forty-nine members of the Provincial Congress, be a sufficient number to proceed on
business—and, that any twenty-one members of the
Charlestown Committee assembled, be a sufficient
number, to proceed on business.

The whole proceedings, of the late Congress, were
now approved; and according to order, public thanks
were given by the President to the late Delegates from
this Colony; and a vote of thanks was passed to the
members of the late Congress.

They now proceeded to establish a system of
government, and its subordinate authorities, for the
Colony. What had been called at first the General
Meeting, now assumed the style of *Provincial Con-*

gress, as a Legislature. As such, it was to continue, until there should be a new General Meeting of the people; and in the mean time, it was to be convened when necessary, by a vote of the Charlestown Committee; of which, each member of the Congress being in town, should attend as a member. This body, styled the General Committee, explained the public regulations as Judges; and, caused them to be executed. The immediate representatives of Charlestown, had the cognizance of debts; and out of this body, a Committee of Inspection was formed, to take cognizance of the arrival of vessels and their cargoes; as also, respecting the conduct of people; and to report thereon as occasion might require, to the General Committee, whose directions, they were to obey. The representatives of the parishes and districts respectively, composed their local Committees; and they were also assisted, by Committees of Inspection. The Provincial Congress, made all these appointments in the first instance; and even filled up the double returns of representatives: in order, that no time should be lost in giving a complete appearance to the body politic, and the greatest energy to their operations: but all future vacancies, were to be filled up by the respective districts and parishes, in which they should occur. And by these arrangements, an independent authority virtually arose; while the Royal Government retained little else, than public officers without power; and a show of government, without the means of supporting it.

By the arrangement which had taken place, respecting the compensation rice planters were to make, one third of the crop of rice, or money arising from it, was to be exchanged, for one third of the crop of indigo, hemp, corn, flour, lumber, pork, and butter respectively. Thus, each rice planter was to deliver one third of his crop to particular Committees: and to

receive for it an equal value in any of the other commodities, in turn; as they should have been deposited
for such a purpose. Intricate as such a course of
exchange would be, the mode was adopted; and no
one reflected, that a third of the crop of rice, was
scarcely equal to a third of the crop of indigo alone;
and that of consequence, the various other articles
would not have any fund for exchange, or compensation. One point of considerable consequence at that
crisis, was however gained by the measure; in quiet-
ing the minds of the members and restoring them to
harmony and good will with each other: having, as
they thought, applied the greatest possible relief, to the
mischiefs which had presented themselves. This was
a consummation, of the last necessity; when promptness of action, and union of sentiment, were absolutely necessary, for the public service.

With one mind therefore, they now proceeded to
the election of Delegates to the ensuing Congress at
Philadelphia; and the five late Delegates were re-
chosen. They were elected, without any opposition:
for, as their late proceedings, had been confirmed in
the whole; it was deemed a service to the common
cause, that a confidence should be evinced in their
abilities, and future proceedings. But, had the late
warmly contested question, respecting the exception
of rice, been carried the other way; there was no
doubt, but that no more than three of them at most,
would have been re-elected. The Delegates now
re-elected, were authorized " to represent this Colony
on the 10th of May next, or sooner if necessary, at the
American Congress, to be held at Philadelphia or
elsewhere; with full power to concert, agree upon,
direct and order, such farther measures, as in the
opinion of the said Deputies, and the Delegates of the
other American Colonies to be assembled, shall appear
to be necessary, for the recovery and establishment of

American rights and liberties; and for restoring harmony, between Great Britain and her Colonies."
The Congress farther resolved, that it "will pay the
expenses of the said Deputies, in going to, attending
at, and returning from the said American Congress."

Many other prudent resolves were passed, to preserve good order, and to place the Colony in some
state of defence. And these things being so far dispatched, a Committee was appointed to prepare a
suitable address to the Lieutenant-Governor; and of
whose purport, he was previously informed; so as to
enable him to prepare the answer, he should deem
most proper. On the 17th January 1775, the Provincial Congress waited on his Honour, at his residence
in Broad-street; when, the following address was
presented.

"To the Honourable William Bull, Esquire, Lieuten-
    ant-Governor and Commander in Chief, in, and
    over, his Majesty's Colony of South-Carolina.

"May it please your Honour.

"We, his Majesty's faithful and loyal subjects, the
Representatives of all the good people in this Colony,
now met in Provincial Congress; think ourselves
obliged to address your Honour for redress of a grievance, which threatens destruction to the Constitution,
and ruin to the inhabitants of this Country: we mean,
the long, and still continued disuse of General Assemblies; contrary, not only to every principle of free
government, but, directly against a law of this province.

" To enumerate all the unhappy consequences,
which must follow a denial of the right of the people,
to appear frequently by their Representatives in Gene-

ral Assembly, must be unnecessary. Your Honour, who has, as a private person, enjoyed the blessings of freedom and good government amongst us, can want no information on that head.

" Taxes continuing to be raised and paid, and laws to be executed, against the sense of the people, are but a part of our grievances.

" Mortifying as these considerations are, the causes are more so; being, according to our best information, no other than a refusal of the House of Assembly to obey ministerial mandates, contrary to their consciences, and subversive of the rights of their constituents; and his Majesty's Council, composed chiefly of placemen, paying an implicit and servile obedience to unconstitutional instructions. Such acts, tend immediately, to a total abolition of Assemblies; for if freedom of debate, and a constitutional independence be denied to them, they cannot possibly be useful, probably, they will become dangerous.

" We forbear to trouble your Honour with reasons, in the support of the request which we now, as of right, make, in behalf of all the good subjects of his Majesty in this Colony; that, the holding and sitting of the General Assembly be no longer delayed; but, that it be permitted to sit, for the dispatch of public business, as formerly.

" We pray your Honour to be assured, that by this, our humble address, we do not intend to question his Majesty's prerogative, of calling, proroguing, and dissolving the General Assembly; but only to request, that this power be exercised *for the good of the people.*
" By order of the Provincial Congress.
         " CHARLES PINCKNEY, President.
" In Provincial Congress,   }
   Charlestown, Jan. 17th, 1775." }

To this address, the Lieutenant-Governor replied, in the following terms.

" Gentlemen,

" I know no legal Representatives of the good people of this province, but the Commons-House of Assembly, chosen according to the Election Act, and met in General Assembly. As gentlemen of respectable characters and property in this province, I acquaint you, that the General Assembly stands prorogued to to the 24th instant. I have always endeavoured to make the law of the land my rule of government, in the administration of public affairs; and, I shall not omit observing it, in meeting the General Assembly, according to the prorogation. With whom, I shall, under the guidance of my duty to the King, and zeal for the service of the province, do every thing in my power, that can contribute to the public welfare.

" WILLIAM BULL.

" Charlestown, Jan. 17th, 1775."

When the Provincial Congress returned to their Chamber, they passed resolutions, recommending, that all the inhabitants of the Colony, be attentive in learning the use of arms—and, that their officers train and exercise them, at least once a fortnight. That Friday, 17th of February next, be set apart, as a day of fasting, humiliation, and prayer, before Almighty God; devoutly to petition him to inspire the King with true wisdom, to defend the people of North America, in their just title to freedom; and, to avert from them the impending calamities of civil war. The Congress, then returned thanks, to their President, and Secretary: after which, the Provincial

Congress was adjourned, until it should be convened by the Charlestown General Committee.*

On the 18th January 1775, the Charlestown General Committee met, under the regulations of the late Provincial Congress; and took certain steps for their organization as a body, and for the better carrying into effect, the purposes of their institution. A Congress of Georgia, had been summoned to meet in Savannah about this time, and the result of their deliberations, was impatiently expected. At length their proceedings, and a letter from their Chairman, were laid before the General Committee on the 8th February. It thence appeared, that instead of fully acceding to the general association; the meeting at Savannah, had entered into such resolutions, as were more calculated to elude the penalty, and to contravene the American plan; than to co-operate with it. The General Committee therefore resolved, "that we will have no trade, commerce, dealings, or intercourse with the said Colony of Georgia; *but will hold them as unworthy of the rights of freemen, and as inimical to the liberties of their country.*† Provided, that this resolution, shall not be construed to extend to persons inhabiting this Colony, now having plantations in Georgia; so, as to prevent them from bringing their Crops into this Colony; or, to such persons residing in this Colony, as now have debts due to them; so as to prevent them from receiving payments of such debts there, in money, or in the commodities of that Colony; and having such commodities exported from thence, to Europe."

To the General Meeting of deputies in Savannah, to which we have just referred, the people of St.

---

* See Extracts from the Journals of the Provincial Congress of South-Carolina, printed in 8vo. from page 5, to page 45.

† See 14th article of the Association, in the Appendix, No. I.

John's Parish, in Georgia, in riches at that time, equal to about one third of the whole province, had also sent deputies; but, finding the majority of the deputies, not approbating the continental association in the manner they wished, they did not join them; but returned back to their constituents. And soon after, on the 9th February 1775. they assembled in their own parish; and sent Joseph Wood, Daniel Roberts, and Samuel Stevens, as deputies to the General Committee at Charlestown; praying, to be admitted into our alliance.* On the 24th of February, their deputies had an audience of the General Committee; on which occasion, they were questioned as to various particulars, touching their province. They now declared, there were scarce two thousand fighting men in the whole Colony; of which number, five hundred were in Savannah. After this, the General Committee gave the request of the inhabitants of St. John's parish a full consideration; and it was thence determined, that their case fell under the fourteenth article of the association: and therefore, from us they could not receive the relief they wished. But it was thought, a remedy might be applied by Congress: and they were therefore advised, to transmit a state of their case to the ensuing General Congress. Accordingly, measures were taken by the inhabitants of that parish, for that purpose; and in May 1775, Dr. Lyman Hall, as a Delegate from the parish of St. John in Georgia, was allowed to take his seat in Congress; subject however, to such regulations, as that body should thereafter determine, relative to his rights of voting.

In South-Carolina, the association was punctually complied with; no goods from England, being allowed to be landed; nor, were any other importations, contrary to the provisions of that instrument, permitted.

* See Appendix to this Chapter, No. II.

About this time, the ship Charming Sally had arrived
from Bristol in England, with 3844 bushels of salt,
35 chaldron of coals, and 40,500 tiles: all of which
were (25th February 1775) thrown into Hog-Island
Creek, by the proprietors or their agents; rather than
they would be at the charge and trouble of sending
them back to England, in pursuance of the tenth article of the association.   So also, a cargo of near three
hundred slaves, was sent out of the Colony by the
consignee; as being interdicted by the second article
of the association.   In short, the public regulations
were duly, and patriotically observed.   A case however arose, which called forth the spirit of the people;
and evinced their determination, to support and enforce
the association, in all its various provisions.

A respectable family had been residing in England
for some time, and were returning home; in which
removal, it was expected, the household furniture, and
horses, which had been in use, would also be brought
over.   Some attempts had therefore been made, to
declare the importation of household furniture and
horses, that had been in use, and might be imported
from England, not to be within the meaning of the
tenth article of the association, as relating to *goods* or
merchandize; but, they had been unsuccessful.   At
length, the horses and furniture arriving from thence;
application was made on the 15th day of March, for
their being landed: and after a long contest in a thin
General Committee, of only thirty-three members, the
motion was carried by the voice of the Chairman.—
This permission, occasioned a ferment among the
citizens; and they almost generally exclaimed " *The
Association was broken;*" and that the horses at least,
should not be landed.   Some hundreds, of the inhabitants assembled; and many active and influential
members of the Committee, endeavoured to satisfy
them respecting the vote of permission which had

passed; but in vain.   On the contrary, they continued
in their opposition; and supported it, with a representation signed by a considerable number of persons;
and which was presented to the Chairman of the
General Committee, desiring the Committee would
re-consider their late vote.   In pursuance of this
request, the General Committee was convened, on the
17th day of March 1775; and the room of meeting
was crowded with people.   Edward Rutledge, who
had been one of the most active in the affair, now
commenced censuring the people, in thus questioning
the vote which had been given; but, he was received
with a clamour.   The General Committee, now began to think their authority insulted.   Some members,
accordingly departed in anger—others, became vocife-
rous in rage—and, for a few minutes, all was in confusion.   At length, tranquillity prevailed; the consideration of the subject was postponed, until a more
full Committee could be procured; and the third day
after was appointed, for a final decision.   To procure
the presence of all the members of the Committee,
within reach, was now an object of importance; and
great exertions for that purpose, were made by both
parties.

When the appointed time arrived, the General
Committee convened; and great was the press of
people who attended.   For, the town, was in universal
commotion; and application had even been privately
made, to the incorporated armed companies, to cover
the landing of the horses.   Some individuals of the
companies, agreed to do so; but the majority of them
refused: and the people declared, if the horses were
landed, they would put them to death.   Under these
unpleasant aspects, the debates began; when Mr.
Gadsden moved to reverse the former determination,
relative to landing the horses.   He urged, the vote
had been carried in a thin Committee; that it was

contrary to the association—that it would alarm the Northern Colonies, in a most lively manner—and, that our people were highly dissatisfied with it. And he contended, this last of itself, was a cogent reason to reverse such a determination. The Rev. Mr. Tennent next addressed the Committee, to the same purpose; as did Mr. Rugely: who, in addition urged, that as the horses paid a duty, they ought not to be landed. These gentlemen in speaking, spoke immediately after each other. On the other side, Edward Rutledge, Rawlins Lowndes, Thomas Bee, and Thomas Lynch contended, that the vote of the General Committee ought not to be reversed, but on the contrary, ought to be maintained: otherwise, the Committee would fall into contempt. That the opinions of the General Committee now sitting, ought not to be influenced by the petition; as, the spirit, and not the letter of the association ought to be attended to. That temporising, did not become honest men, and statesmen; who, ought to declare their opinions, according to their consciences. That if we adhered to the letter of the association, no arms or ammunition could be received from England: and, when the letter of the law bore hard against an individual, Lord Chief Justice Hale allowed him to escape by any subterfuge; and, that it was never the idea of Congress to exclude such articles.

William Henry Drayton, was the only person, who rose in reply. He contended, that because an error had been committed, it was no reason it should be continued—that the people thought an error had been committed; and it was our duty, to satisfy our constituents: as we were only servants of the public. That, such conduct was evinced by every day's practice in parliament—therefore, it could not be disgraceful to reverse the vote of the Committee, as on such occasions, parliament had often done so. That our present application to the King, was for such a purpose—and, if we defended ourselves on the principle of falling into contempt; might it not be as reasonable, for the King to retort the same argument upon us? That it was always safer, to follow the letter, than to explore the spirit of a law. That, in the case of the St. John's people of Georgia, we preferred the letter to the spirit of the association; as was evident, by our refusal and advice—then, why not adhere to the letter of that instrument now? That temporizing ever was practised in public affairs, by the most honest men; witness Cato of Utica, in Cæsar's election to the Consulship; and by the best statesmen, witness Cicero's letter to Atticus, relating to a good pilot's shifting his helm, if he could not reach his port by a direct course: witness, the conduct of the Long Parliament—and all history in general. That, to discharge a statesman's conscience, was to aim at the public good; and not be pertinacious, of his own opinion. That, even if there had been an article in the association, that we should not receive arms and ammunition from England; the public necessity would cause it to be a dead letter: as self-preservation, was the first obligation—and *fas est, ab hoste doceri.* He farther contended, that Lord Hale's principle was just, when applied to an individual, in the event of whose case, the public could not be interested; but, it never could be applicable, to such a case as the present, where, the conveniency of the individual, and the national interests of the public, were in direct opposition; and, that he could not hold the understanding of the late General Congress in so trivial a light, as to entertain a thought of looking for the sense, in direct opposition to the words of one of the principal articles of the association.

He farther said, the present case stood divided into two points; the spirit of the regulations, and the union of the people: and, that the latter was infinitely of the

24

greater consequence. That the letter of the association, was clearly in support of the motion; and, in the
present situation of affairs, the spirit of that instrument, was equally in favour of it. That union was
the rock, upon which, the American political edifice
was founded; and, whatever hazards its existence, is
to militate against the ground work of the association.
Hence, it was evident, landing the horses, hazarded
our union: for, the people were in commotion against
it. Upon all public and general questions, the people
ever are in the right: so said Lord Mansfield, in the
House of Commons; and the people now think, the
late vote was wrong. Can it be prudent, to oppose
our constituents? In civil commotions, the common
people ever struck those blows, which were of any
effect. If you retract, there can be no just cause, of
fearing contempt; as it is not reasonable, those should
contemn you, who have ever honoured you; and
whose opinions would be in favour of your retraction.
The Roman Senate, were a wise body; they often
yielded to the people; but, nobody supposed, their
concessions brought them into contempt: and, they
continued illustrious during the existence of the com-
monwealth. Let us imitate on this occosion, so great,
so successful an example; and endeavour by the same
means, to call forth the affections of our fellow citizens; and to bind them to us, by the same ties.

John Rutledge now arose, and endeavoured to take
off the force of the arguments, which had been urged;
but failing in his endeavours, he only added to the
many instances he had previously given, of his ability
as a good speaker. The debate, was then closed:
and the question being put, was carried in the affirmative. It is worthy of remark, that this is the first
instance of a point of importance and controversy,
being carried against those; by whose opinions, the
people had been long governed. And, such was the

powerful effect of habit; that this important question was carried, only by a majority of one voice: 35 against 34.

By this determination, the Continental Association shone out, in all its brilliancy; to the great encouragement of patriotic measures, and the confusion of interested persons: who, anxious about the continuance of trade, allowed private emolument to be more in view, than the public good. Some persons however, could not resist temptation; and from this period, they began to attract the attention of the Committee of Inspection. After this, broad hints of the public opinion, were given; by exposing in the streets, effigies of non-conformists to the general will: and in process of time, reprehensions and punishments of novel natures, were introduced against those, who censured the popular measures; or who contravened regulations, formed for the public safety. Notwithstanding however all these measures of efficiency, and precaution; still a hope was indulged, that this association, like the two former ones, would induce a repeal of the obnoxious acts; and afford quiet, to a disturbed people. But that hope, was fallacious; as the sequel will show. And with the rapid march of revolutionary events, Carolina had to make other provisions, and her citizens to breast other trials—before, the object of her wishes could be obtained; or, her citizens be restored to safety, and repose.

APPENDIX

CHAPTER V.

———

No. I.

The Association.

W E, his Majesty's most loyal subjects, the delegates of the several Colonies of New-Hampshire, Massachusetts-Bay, Rhode-Island, Connecticut, New-York, New-Jersey, Pennsylvania, the three Lower Counties of Newcastle Kent and Sussex on Delaware, Maryland, Virginia, North-Carolina, and South-Carolina, deputed to represent them in a Continental Congress, held in the city of Philadelphia on the fifth day of September 1774, avowing our allegiance to his Majesty; our affection and regard for our fellow subjects in Great Britain and elsewhere; affected with the deepest anxiety, and most alarming apprehensions at those grievances and distresses, with which, his Majesty's American subjects are oppressed; and hav-

ing taken under our most serious deliberation the state
of the whole Continent, find, that the present unhappy
situation of our affairs is occasioned by a ruinous system of Colony-Administration, adopted by the British
Ministry about the year 1763; evidently calculated,
for enslaving these colonies, and with them, the British
Empire.

In prosecution of which system, various acts of
parliament have been passed, for raising a revenue in
America; for depriving the American subjects, in
many instances, of the constitutional trial by jury;
exposing their lives to danger, by directing a new and
illegal trial beyond the seas, for crimes alledged to
have been committed in America; and, in prosecution
of the same system, several late, cruel, and oppressive
acts, have been passed, respecting the town of Boston,
and the Massachusetts-Bay; and also an act, for
extending the province of Quebec, so as to border on
the western frontiers of these Colonies, establishing
an arbitrary government therein, and discouraging the
settlement of British subjects in that wide extended
country. Thus, by the influence of evil principles,
and ancient prejudices, to dispose the inhabitants to
act with hostility against the free Protestant Colonies,
whenever a wicked Ministry shall choose so to direct
them.

To obtain redress of these grievances, which
threaten destruction to the lives, liberty, and property
of his Majesty's subjects in North America, we are of
opinion, that a non-importation, non-consumption, and
non-exportation agreement, faithfully adhered to, will
prove the most speedy, effectual, and peaceable measure; and therefore we do, for ourselves and the inhabitants of the several Colonies, whom we represent,
firmly agree and associate, under the sacred ties of
virtue, honour, and love of our country, as follows:

First. That, from and after the first day of December next, we will not import into British America, from Great Britain or Ireland, any goods, wares, or merchandize whatsoever, or from any other place, any such goods, wares, or merchandize, as shall have been exported from Great Britain or Ireland: nor will we, after that day, import any East-India tea from any part of the world; nor, any molasses, sirups, paneles, coffee or pimento, from the British plantations, or from Dominica; nor wines from Madeira, or the Western Islands; nor foreign indigo.

Second. We will neither import, nor purchase, any slave imported after the first day of December next; after which time, we will wholly discontinue the slave trade; and will neither be concerned in it ourselves, nor will we hire our vessels, nor sell our commodities or manufactures, to those, who are concerned in it.

Third. As a non-consumption agreement, strictly adhered to, will be an effectual security for the observation of the non-importation; we as above, solemnly agree and associate, that, from this day, we will not purchase, or use, any tea, imported on account of the East-India Company, or any on which a duty hath been or shall be paid: and, from and after the first day of March next, we will not purchase or use, any East-India tea whatever: nor will we, nor shall any person for or under us, purchase or use any of those goods, wares, or merchandize, we have agreed not to import, which we shall know, or have cause to suspect, were imported after the first day of December, except, such as come under the rules and regulations, of the tenth article hereafter mentioned.

Fourth. The earnest desire we have, not to injure our fellow subjects in Great Britain, Ireland, or the West Indies, induces us to suspend a non-exportation, until the tenth day of September 1775; at which time, if the said acts and parts of acts of the British Parliament hereinafter mentioned, are not repealed, we will not directly or indirectly, export any merchandize or commodity whatsoever to Great Britain, Ireland, or the West Indies, except rice to Europe.

Fifth. Such as are merchants, and use the British and Irish trade, will give orders, as soon as possible, to their factors, agents, and correspondents, in Great Britain and Ireland, not to ship any goods to them, on any pretence whatsoever; as, they cannot be received in America; and, if any merchant residing in Great Britain or Ireland, shall directly or indirectly ship any goods, wares, or merchandize, for America, in order to break the said non-importation agreement, or in any manner contravene the same, on such unworthy conduct being well attested, it ought to be made public; and, on the same being so done, we will not from thenceforth, have any commercial connexion with such merchant.

Sixth. That such as are owners of vessels, will give positive orders to their captains, or masters, not to receive on board their vessels any goods prohibited by the said non-importation agreement; on pain, of immediate dismission from their service.

Seventh. We will use our utmost endeavours to improve the breed of sheep, and increase their number to the greatest extent; and to that end, we will kill them as sparingly as may be, especially those of the most profitable kind. Nor, will we export any to the West Indies, or elsewhere; and those of us, who are, or may be overstocked with, or can conveniently spare any sheep, will dispose of them to our neighbours, especially to the poorer sort, on moderate terms.

Eighth. We will in our several stations, encourage frugality, economy, and industry; and promote agriculture, arts, and the manufactures of this country, especially that of wool; and, will discountenance and discourage every species of extravagance and dissipation; especially all horse-racing, and all kinds of gaming, cock-fighting, exhibitions of shows, plays, and other expensive diversions and entertainments. And, on the death of any relation or friend, none of us, or any of our families, will go into any further mourning-dress, than a black crape or riband on the arm or hat for gentlemen; and a black riband and necklace for ladies; and, we will discontinue the giving of gloves and scarfs at funerals.

Ninth. Such as are venders of goods or merchandize will not take advantage of the scarcity of goods that may be occasioned by this association; but will sell the same at the rates we have been respectively accustomed to do, for twelve months past. And if any vender of goods or merchandize, shall sell any such goods on higher terms; or, shall in any manner, or by any device whatsoever, violate or depart from this agreement, no person ought, nor will any of us deal with any such person, or his or her factor or agent, at any time thereafter, for any commodity whatever.

Tenth. In case any merchant, trader, or other person, shall import any goods or merchandize, after the first day of December, and before the first day of February next, the same ought forthwith, at the election of the owner, to be either re-shipped, or delivered up to the Committee of the country, or town, wherein they shall be imported; to be stored at the risk of the importer, until the non-importation agreement shall cease, or be sold under the direction of the Committee aforesaid. And in the last mentioned case, the owner or owners of such goods, shall be reimbursed (out of the sales) the first cost and charges; the profit, if any, to be applied towards relieving and employing such poor inhabitants of the town of Boston, as are immediate sufferers by the Boston Port-Bill; and, a particular account of all goods so returned, stored, or sold, to be inserted in the public papers; and, if any goods or merchandizes shall be imported after the said first day of February, the same ought forthwith to be sent back again, without breaking any of the packages thereof.

Eleventh.   That a Committee be chosen in every county, city, or town, by those who are qualified to vote for representatives in the Legislature; whose business it shall be, attentively to observe the conduct of all persons touching this association: and, when it shall be made to appear, to the satisfaction of a majority of any such Committee, that any person within the limits of their appointment has violated this association, that such majority do forthwith cause the truth of the case to be published in the gazette; to the end, that all such foes to the rights of British America, may be publicly known, and universally contemned as the enemies of American liberty; and thenceforth, we respectively break off, all dealings, with him or her.

Twelfth.   That the Committee of Correspondence, in the respective Colonies, do frequently inspect the entries of their Custom-Houses; and inform each other from time to time, of the true state thereof, and of every other material circumstance, that may occur, relative to this association.

Thirteenth.   That all manufactures of this country, be sold at reasonable prices; so, that no undue advantage be taken of a future scarcity of goods.

25

Fourteenth. And we do further agree, and resolve, that we will have no trade, commerce, dealings, or intercourse whatsoever, with any colony or province in North America, which shall not accede to, or which shall hereafter violate this association; but, will hold them as unworthy of the rights of freemen, and inimical to the liberties of their country.

And, we do solemnly bind ourselves, and constituents, under the ties aforesaid, to adhere to this association, until such parts of the several acts of parliament passed since the close of the last war, as impose or continue duties on tea, wine, molasses, sirups, paneles, coffee, sugar, pimento, indigo, foreign paper, glass, and painter's colours, imported into America, and extend the powers of Admiralty Courts beyond their ancient limits, deprive the American subject of trial by jury, authorize the Judge's certificate to indemnify the prosecutor from damages, that he might otherwise be liable to from a trial by his peers, require oppressive security from a claimant of ships or goods seized, before he shall be allowed to defend his property, are repealed. And, until that part of the act of the 12th George III. ch. 24, entitled " An act for the better securing his Majesty's Dock-Yards, Magazines, Ships, Ammunition and Stores," by which, any persons, charged with committing any of the offences therein described in America, may be tried in any shire or county within the realm, is repealed. And, until the four acts passed in the last session of parliament, viz. that for stopping the port, and blocking up the harbour of Boston—that, for altering the charter and government of the Massachusetts-Bay—and that which is entitled " An act, for the better administration of Justice," &c.—and that, for extending the limits of Quebec, &c. are repealed. And we recommend it to the Provincial Conventions, and to the Committees in the respective Colonies, to establish such farther regulations, as they may think proper, for carrying into execution this association.

The foregoing association, being determined upon by the Congress; was ordered to be subscribed by the several members thereof: and thereupon we have hereunto set our respective names accordingly.

In Congress, Philadelphia, October 24th, 1774.

PEYTON RANDOLPH, President.

New-Hampshire. John Sullivan, Nathaniel Folsom.

Massachusetts-Bay. Thomas Cushing, Samuel Adams, John Adams, Robert Treat Paine.

Rhode-Island. Stephen Hopkins, Samuel Ward.

Connecticut. Eliphalet Dyer, Roger Sherman, Silas Deane.

New-York. Isaac Low, John Alsop, John Jay, James Duane, William Floyd, Henry Weisner, S. Boerum, Philip Livingston.

New-Jersey. James Kinsey, William Livingston, Stephen Crane, Richard Smith, John De Hart.

Pennsylvania. Joseph Galloway, John Dickinson, Charles Humphreys, Thomas Mifflin, Edward Biddle, John Morton, George Ross.

Newcastle, &c. Cæsar Rodney, Thomas M'Kean, George Read.

Maryland. Matthew Tilghman, Thomas Johnson, William Paca, Samuel Chase.

Virginia. Richard Henry Lee, George Washington, P. Henry, jun. Richard Bland, Benjamin Harrison, Edmond Pendleton.

North-Carolina. William Hooper, Joseph Hewes, R. Caswell.

South-Carolina. Henry Middleton, Thomas Lynch, Christopher Gadsden, John Rutledge, Edward Rut ledge.

No. II.

On Thursday evening arrived in town, Joseph Wood, Esq. Mr. Daniel Roberts, and Mr. Samuel Stevens, three members of the Committee for the parish of St. John in Georgia; deputed to wait on the General Committee here, with the following letter, and account of the proceedings of the patriotic inhabitants of the said parish, in the present critical situation of American affairs, viz.

At a Meeting held in the Parish of St. John, and Province of Georgia, on the 9th of February 1775; a Letter from this Committee to the Committee of Correspondence in Charlestown, South-Carolina, was agreed on, and written.

It was then moved and agreed, that some person or persons of this Committee, do wait on the Committee in Charlestown, with the said Letter.

Accordingly, Messrs. Daniel Roberts and Samuel Stevens, and Joseph Wood, Esq. were appointed and authorized to present the same; and transact such matters relative thereto, as shall seem prudent and necessary.

Taken from the Minutes, by Order of the Chairman; and certified by

BENJAMIN BAKER, Clerk.

Gentlemen,

We, the Committee of the Parish of St. John, take the earliest opportunity to lay before you, the several steps taken by this Parish, to conform, as near as possible, to the resolutions entered into by the other Provinces, and the measures now adopted, for carrying into execution the Continental Association. As it was particularly recommended to us, we readily embraced those measures, by subscribing an agreement to accede to the general association. on condition "that trade and commerce might be continued to us with the other Provinces," and we should immediately have sent it to you for your approbation, but were delayed by a summons to attend a Provincial Congress at Savannah, the 18th January last, for the purpose, as we understood, of a general association with the other Provinces, and for choosing Delegates to attend at the next Continental Congress, to be held at Philadelphia in May next. We met, at that time and place, and acquainted the Committees of the other parishes then assembled, that the inhabitants of this parish had acceded to the general association on the above mentioned conditions, and earnestly recommended the same to them. They did enter into an association, (a copy of which, we transmit to you) but so different in our opinions from the Continental Association, that it appears to be a contravention of it, and exposes them to the censure of the fourteenth clause of the general association.

First. They have extended the time limited for exportations, beyond what is allowed by the Continental Congress; and thereby indulged a liberty of exportations, to the prejudice of the other provinces.

Secondly. For that, in their limited time of importations, they have, contrary to the Continental Association, extended it in general, to the 15th of March next, for goods to be shipped in England; and for the Indian trade, to a still greater latitude—under the cloak of which, we have reason to believe, may be

introduced a large importation equally adapted to the
Whites, as to the Indians; and, on the whole, such as
we could not, consistent with our own association,
possibly join in.

Had they acceded fully to the general association,
even at so late a time as our Provincial Congress, we
should have had no occasion to trouble you, with this
address: but, as they did not, we now apply to you,
to admit us, the subscribers of this parish, to an alliance with you; requesting, that you will allow trade
and commerce to be continued to us, exclusive (if you
think proper) of this Province in general; the same to
be continued and conducted under such regulations and
restrictions, as shall be consistent with the Continental
Association; and which, on our parts, we engage, with
all possible care, to keep inviolate.

Our being a parish of a non-associated Province,
cannot, we presume, prevent our joining the other
Provinces; as the restriction mentioned in the fourteenth clause of the general association, must, as we
apprehend, be considered as a general rule only, and
respects this Province, considered in a mixed or pro-
miscuous sense: but, as we of this parish, are a body
detached from the rest, by our resolutions and association,* and sufficiently distinct by local situation, large
enough for particular notice, and have been treated as
such by a particular address from the late Continental
Congress, adjoining a sea-port, and in that respect,
capable of conforming to the general association, (if
connected with you,) with the same fidelity as a distant parish of your own Province, therefore we must
be considered, as comprehended within the spirit and

* The number that subscribed the said association, amount to 175 substantial inhabltants, mostly removed from this Colony, with their slaves, to settle
more fertile lands there.

equitable meaning of the Continental Association.—
And we are assured, you will not condemn the innocent with the guilty, especially when a due separation
is made between them.   We now wait your answer;
and, shall be glad of your advice.

Signed by order of the Committee.

LYMAN HALL, Chairman.

Midway, February 9th, 1775.

To the Committee of Correspondence
   in Charlestown, South-Carolina.

———

*Extracts, from the Minutes of the Proceedings of the
Committee of the Parish of St. John, met at Savannah, the 18th day of January* 1775.

Wednesday, January 18th, 1775.

The Committee met, and Doctor Lyman Hall took
the Chair.

The following Message was sent to the Committees
of the several Parishes in Congress sitting:

Gentlemen,

The Committee of the Parish of St. John, present the Committees of the other Parishes with a
copy of the Letter received by them, from the late
Continental Congress; and, agreeably to the advice
therein contained, the inhabitants of the Parish of St.

John have acceded to the general association entered
into, and recommended by the said Continental Congress. They hope, you will adopt the same measures.

Thursday, January 19th, 1775.

The Committee sat until six o'clock in the afternoon,
in expectation that the Committee of the several
Parishes, in Congress sitting, would return an answer
to the Message delivered to them yesterday; which,
not being received, the Committee adjourned.

Friday, January 20th, 1775.

Another Message was sent to the Committees of
the several Parishes in Congress met, in the following
terms:

Gentlemen,

On the first day of your meeting, we presented you
with a Message, acquainting you, that the inhabitants
of the Parish of St. John had acceded to the general
association entered into, and particularly recommended
to them, by the late Continental Congress. We, have
patiently waited your answer; and wish to impute
your silence, rather to inattention, than design. We
now assure you, that if you think proper to enter fully
into the measures of the late Continental Congress,
we will heartily join you, in every thing, that may
tend to inform them.

The Committees of the several Parishes, met in
Congress, sent the following answer thereto.

Gentlemen,

In answer to your Message of this morning, we beg leave to inform you of three determinations, from which, this Congress, we hope, will never recede.

First. That we shall be glad to have the Province upon this occasion, as fully represented as possible; and will therefore cheerfully receive the delegates of St. John's Parish, as a part of us.

Secondly. That we apprehend every delegate here, is accountable to his constituents and his own conscience, for the opinion he gives at this time; and therefore, ought not to let any other man, or set of men, judge for him.

Thirdly. That we trust no member amongst us, has any other object in view, than the public good.

Saturday, January 21st, 1775.

The Committee met, and came to the following resolutions:

Resolved, That the Committees of the several Parishes in Congress now sitting, are not, or cannot be, called a Provincial Congress; as, the greater number of the Parishes in this Province, are not represented therein. They therefore are not bound by the proceedings of the said Committees, although they may arrogate to themselves such a power.

Resolved, That as the Committees of the several Parishes in Congress now sitting, have not fully approved of, and adopted the measures entered into, and recommended by the late Continental Congress; this

26

Committee cannot join them, without violating the general association, which they have already acceded to; and betraying the trust reposed in them, by their constituents.

And then, the Committee adjourned *sine die.*

The above Extracts, taken from the original Minutes by

JOSEPH WOOD, Secretary.

☞ See The South-Carolina Gazette, No. 2032, printed by Peter Timothy, Printer to the Hon. the Commons-House of Assembly, Charlestown, Monday, February 27th, 1775; in which, all the above is published at length.

CHAPTER VI.

*Lieutenant-Governor Bull, commences a series of pro-
rogations of the General Assembly—which, at length
meets; and receives a Speech from the Lieutenant-
Governor—Reply of the Commons—Mr. Lynch presents a copy of the Journals of the Continental
Congress, to the House of Assembly—who consider
the same, and vote thanks to the Congress—The
Speaker, gives the thanks of the House, to our Delegates from Congress—and the House, confirms their
re-election—The Commons, send to the Council, a
bill to prevent counterfeiting the paper money of the
Colonies—Council hesitate thereon—William Henry
Drayton, one of the Council, protests against such
conduct—The Bill passed, being the first Act passed
by the Council, in five years—The Chief Justice
charges Mr. Drayton with publishing against the
King; and frequenting Popular Assemblies—and
moves an Address in Council to the Lieutenant-Governor for his suspension, as a Counsellor—Mr. Drayton is suspended from the office of Counsellor—The
Commons, go in procession to Church—They send a
Bill to the Council reviving and continuing various
Acts; which is passed by the Council—And both
Acts, being ratified by the Lieutenant-Governor, become laws—House of Commons, adjourns—Situation of the public mind—Ministers, lay before Parliament, papers respecting America—Proceedings of
Parliament thereon—Lord North, moves an Address*

to the Throne—Speakers in Parliament, in opposition—Parliament votes an augmentation of troops—Determination of the People—A British Packet, arrives—Conduct, and projects of Lord North—Conduct of the people in Charlestown—Measures taken, for seizing the Military Stores—A Secret Committee, is appointed—who cause the public Arms, and Powder to be seized—The Lieutenant-Governor issues a Proclamation thereon; and sends a Message to the Commons—Conduct of the Commons—A Committee of Intelligence appointed—their duties—Effigies, exposed to public view, and burnt—The Delegates to Congress, propose a question to the Commons-House of Assembly, sitting as a Committee of the whole—and obtain their sentiments thereon—The Commons bring in a Bill, to levy taxes—The Lieutenant-Governor informs them, a new Governor is expected to arrive shortly—and, adjourns them, to the 1st day of June—The Delegates, sail for Philadelphia—News, received from England—A Committee appointed, respecting the Public Security—Civil war, commences in Massachusetts.

THE General Assembly having been prorogued to the 6th day of September 1774, Lieutenant-Governor Bull, commenced a series of prorogations; which, not a little incommoded himself; and unnecessarily drew from their homes, the members of the same.   Taught by the surprise he had received from the Commons-House of Assembly on the second day of August; his arrangements for preventing a sudden meeting of that House were better made; and he was more on the alert, as to his personal movements.   For, no sooner was he now informed by his spies, that Mr. Lowndes, the Speaker, and four of the members, had met in the room of the House of Assembly; than he immediately repaired to the Council Chamber; required their attendance; and forthwith prorogued the General

Assembly, to the 18th day of October. When that day arrived, so soon as the Speaker, and six members had convened, they were prorogued in like manner, to the 22 day of November: and when the 22d day of November came, and the Speaker and five members had convened; they were again treated with this royal mode, of sporting with the rights of the people.

At length, the 24th day of January 1775, arrived; to which day, the General Assembly had been adjourned, from the 22d day of November. And the Lieutenant-Governor being pleased, to permit the meeting of the General Assembly; he received them in the Council Chamber on that day. To the mortification of the Commons, he now informed them, he had nothing in command from the King, to lay before them. That, this was the usual season of the year, for dispatching the public business in General Assembly: and, he therefore recommended the reviving and continuing of such acts, as were expired, or about expiring; which had been found necessary and beneficial, in preserving the good order, and tranquillity, and promoting the prosperity of the Province. He also stated, that the public faith of the Province, was so fundamentally engaged, to maintain several branches of our establishments, which were supported out of the produce of the general duty-law; that he could not admit of the least doubt, of the earliest and strictest attention being paid; to prevent a risk, of any failure therein. And, that he should order the joint Public Treasurers, to lay before them, accounts of the public debts incurred during the last year; for which he hoped they would make effectual provision.

In reply to this speech, the Commons (most part of whom were members of the Provincial Congress) by their address to his Honour, stated, that they were unable to express their surprise and concern, at being informed, he had nothing in command from the King to lay before them—especially, as their Agent had long ago acquainted their Speaker, that the Additional Instruction, which had so often been complained of, had been withheld. in the Instructions made out, to the new appointed Governor.   That this cruel neglect, as well of his Honour, as of this Colony, they could not but consider, as an aggravation of the many oppressive acts of the present Ministry: leaving little hopes, that their deliberations would be of much advantage to the Colony; as, all the former obstructions to public business, seemed to remain in full force. They however assured his Honour, that they were met, with the most sincere and hearty disposition to promote the public good: and consequently, they would take into immediate consideration, what laws ought to be revived and continued; as also, what provision was necessary for discharging the debts, and supporting the public credit.   And, that they would adopt such measures, for those purposes, as appeared to them most effectual and consistent, with the interests of the Colony.

Mr. Lynch, one of the Delegates of the Colony to the Continental Congress, now informed the House, that he had a copy of the Journal of the proceedings of that body, ready to be laid before the Commons.* And, upon the same being laid on the table, Friday the third of February then next ensuing, was appointed for considering them.   It was then resolved by the House, that it entertains, " the most grateful sense of the obligation which all America are under to the several members, of the Continental Congress, which was held at Philadelphia in September last; for the great services which they have done, by the

---

* See a summary of the business done in the Continental Congress, to which these Journals related—*ante*, chap. IV, page 146 to 149.

wise measures concerted and pursued for the relief of the inhabitants of this Continent, from the oppressive plan carried on against them, by the Ministers. And, do return them the thanks of this House, as a testimony of the great respect of the same; and their entire approbation of the proceedings of the said Congress."

It was also resolved, at the same time, that the Speaker (Rawlins Lowndes) do give the thanks of the House, to such of the members of the House, as were appointed in behalf of this Colony, to the late Congress, as they attend in their places; and that to the others, who were not members, the thanks might be conveyed. Accordingly, Thomas Lynch, Christopher Gadsden, and John Rutledge being in their places, the Speaker delivered them the public thanks in the following words:

" Gentlemen,

" The House, reflecting on the signal and very eminent services, which you have rendered to your country in particular, as well as all America in general, in conjunction with the Delegates of the other Colonies met in General Congress, at Philadelphia, in September last, by the wise, judicious, and seasonable plan concerted and adopted, for the defence and maintenance of American rights and liberties; have resolved, to give you the thanks of the House for the same. This testimony of their approbation of your services, is the more honourable to you, as it is founded on the universal sense of the people; whose warmest acknowledgments resound from every quarter of the Colony. You, stood high in the esteem of your country before; and possessed a large share of her confidence; the reward of repeated services. The present instance of your zeal, attachment, and love for her; the sacrifice you made of your ease, your convenience, and your private concerns, when the public voice called you to attend her interest in a distant country; have still endeared you more to her: and established your reputation, upon the firmest foundation. You, have given a sure pledge, that, whenever any future occasion, requires your assistance; no obstacles or difficulties, will make you shrink from the charge. You have the particular happiness, gentlemen, of standing foremost in the rank of patriots; posterity will pay a just tribute to your memories; and, will revere the names of the members of the Continental Congress. And, while they enjoy the rich inheritance and birthrights of English subjects, which your labours and exertions have preserved to them; will look with joy, gratitude and admiration, on the glorious struggle and contest of the present time, from whence, these blessings are derived.

" Permit me, gentlemen, as I am also deeply interested in the issue of these things, to declare to you what warm impulse of gratitude I feel in my heart, for the share I have in those great benefits you have endeavoured to procure and preserve to us: and to assure you, with what pleasure I obey the commands of the House, in giving you the thanks of the House, *as I now do;* for the very singular, eminent, and important services you have rendered to your country, and all America, in conjunction with the Delegates of the other Colonies in General Congress; and, for your diligent attendance on, and faithful discharge of, the great trust, reposed in you by your country."*

After this, the House nominated and appointed the Honourable Henry Middleton, Esquire, Thomas

* See Journals of the Commons-House of Assembly of South-Carolina, from 2d Aug. 1774, to 15th Sept. 1775, from page 2, to page 12, inclusive.

Lynch, Christopher Gadsden, John Rutledge, and Edward Rutledge, Esquires, in behalf of this Colony, to meet the Deputies of the other Colonies in General Congress, at Philadelphia or elsewhere; with full power and authority, to concert, agree to, and effectually prosecute, such measures, as in the opinion of the said Deputies, and of the Deputies so to be assembled, shall be most likely to obtain a redress of the American grievances. It was also farther resolved by the House, that it would provide one thousand five hundred pounds Sterling, to pay the expense of the said Deputies, in going to, attending upon, and returning from the said Congress.*

In the mean time, the Commons sent to the Council, on the 2d day of February, an act which had passed the House, entitled " *An Act to prevent counterfeiting the Paper Money of the other Colonies;*" and this they did, as well with a view of completing the law, as to see if the Council still persevered in their plan, of preventing the passage of any bill to the Governor, until the Commons should have submitted to the Additional Instruction; or, have sent a bill to secure the continuance of the general duty-act; which, unless continued by a new law, would expire at the end of a session.

This experiment, had been made in the year 1773; and the proceedings in Council upon it, drew on the before mentioned commitment of the Printer Powell; under the accusation, by the Council, of a contempt against them. The bill then, was postponed, *sine die;* on which a protest was entered, in the Council Journals by John Drayton, and William Henry Dray-

---

* See Journals of the Commons-House of Assembly of South-Carolina, from 2d August 1774, to Sept. 1775, from page 2, to page 12, inclusive.

ton, two of the Counsellors.* However, an exact
copy of the same bill being now sent to the Council,
they were in a dilemma, whether they should persevere in their old plan, or adopt a new one—and, by
passing the bill, expose themselves to no more difficulties; but throw them upon the Lieutenant-Governor, and hazard the continuance of the general duty-
law. The situation, was a delicate one; and the
Council, endeavoured to proceed warily on the occasion. Hence, when the bill was prepared for being
read the third and last time in the Council. not yet
determined how to act, they postponed the reading to
a certain day; under pretence that a member was
absent. This member, was John Stuart, the Super-
intendent of Indian Affairs; but they took no notice
at other times, of the absence of members, who were
not Crown officers. When the appointed day (Feb.
8th) came, two Crown officers were absent, under
pretence of indisposition; one really was so, but the
other dined abroad, that very day. However, a
motion on the ground of two members being absent
was made, to postpone the bill, to a farther day;
which, after a warm debate was carried in favour of
the postponement. Upon this, William Henry
Drayton, then a member of the Council, entered his
protest;† that it was unreasonable to postpone the
third reading of the bill for the indisposition and absence of two members; who, although Crown officers,
were not expressly required to be present on the occasion; as there was a quorum sufficient for doing business, without them: and the number of members
present, had often transacted business of a similar
nature, in the absence of those gentlemen. That, the
last delay, so far from remedying an impropriety,

* See Council Journals for the early part of 1773

† See Appendix to this Chapter, No. I.

occasioned the absence of two members; perhaps, a perseverance in the measure, would produce the same effect, or one of greater mischief; as three members might be absent; or, the Chief Justice might be suddenly seized with the gout—a complaint with which he had been often very critically seized: and no business of a public nature could be proceeded in.

Here, the matter rested in the Council; but the protest being published in Timothy's paper of the 13th February 1775, brought the matter to a point. The Chief Justice, now felt himself much discomposed by it; and the Superintendant was not insensible of its effects, as he had been the original cause of the protest. The appointed day however, again arrived in the Council, for the third reading of the bill; and one member, was still absent. The matter, was notwithstanding progressed in; and the bill was passed in sullen silence: the Chief Justice, of the old members against it, only saying, he had changed his opinion relative to the bill. And thus, in a space of more than five years, this was the first bill, the Council permitted to be presented to the Lieutenant-Governor.

Upon the conclusion of this transaction, the Chief Justice immediately brought forward a new subject of heat, and controversy. In his place at the Council Board, he made a violent invective against William Henry Drayton then present; charging him, with having made publications against the King. That, even while a Judge, he had delivered charges, stirring up the people to sedition. That, he frequented popular assemblies; where, he loudly inveighed against Government—for all which, he ought to be removed from the Council. And he concluded, by moving an address to the Lieutenant-Governor, for his suspension as a Counsellor; which motion was immediately seconded, by one of the Crown officers. Mr. Drayton

in his place at the board, now replied to what the
Chief Justice had said; urging, that to be obnoxious
to those in Council to whom he found he was, evinced
his attachment to his country; since those very men
who were so against him, were also obnoxious to the
whole people.   That he held it as an honour, those
should desire his suspension, against whom, the Province had publicly complained;* not only to the Lieutenant-Governor, but to the King; desiring, their
removal from the Council.   And, that if he could have
suspected the Commons-House of Assembly, would
so far have countenanced the Council in their claim to
be a branch of the Legislature, as to join them in a
complaint to the Lieutenant-Governor, he would long
ago have impeached the Chief Justice for ignorance,
and incapacity in his office.   Here, Mr. Drayton was
clamorously interrupted—the question was put—and
an address for his suspension was voted.   After having
carried this point, the Chief Justice now presented the
draft of an address, which he had brought with him;
and it so immediately passed, without the alteration of
a single word, that no time was afforded, for drawing
up, and entering a protest.†   However, two days
after, when the address was to be signed by order of
the House, Mr. Drayton made a protest, not only,
against its being signed by the Superintendant as having no precedency in the Council; but also against the
whole matter of the address.‡

The address for suspension, which so attacked the
rights of a Counsellor, and a fellow citizen; was
resolved upon in Council, by *three placemen:* the
whole board at that time being composed of only four

* See *ante,* pages 101, 105, 106.

† See Appendix, No. II.

‡ See Appendix, No. III.

members; Mr. Drayton making the fourth. On the 13th February 1775, it was presented to the Lieutenant-Governor; who, on the same day informed the addressers, that before he took any step in consequence of their address, he desired them to lay before him some of the facts, upon which their complaint was founded: and upon due examination of the same, and of Mr. Drayton's answer, he should take such measures, as were agreeable to justice, and for the service of his Majesty. A Report was now brought forward in Council, charging Mr. Drayton with particular facts, as grounds of suspicion; which, as customary, was carried by a majority of Crown officers, and placemen; to which, however, the only three members of the Council, who were not placemen, and were natives of the Colony, entered a protest, in the proceedings of the Council.* The Report, was then transmitted to the Lieutenant-Governor; and Mr. Drayton answered it, by representing, that if in point of law the Council formed an Upper House of Assembly, he ought not to answer for his conduct charged as in Assembly; and as to other matters, he trusted his conduct would support him in the public opinion; and that the measures which he had been so forced to take, would contribute in some degree, to compose the minds of the people. Upon this, he was formally suspended from the station of Counsellor on the 1st March 1775, by Lieutenant-Governor Bull; who informed him by the same letters of suspension, he should take the earliest opportunity of transmitting to the Lords Commissioners for Trade and Plantations, the Address, and papers relative thereto; in order, that they might be laid before his Majesty, for his Royal consideration.†

* John Drayton, William Henry Drayton, Barnard Elliott; see Appendix, No. IV.

† See Journals of the Commons-House of Assembly of South-Carolina, from 2d Aug. to 15th Sept. 1775; pp. 55, to 66, inclusive. Also, Appendix, No. V.

Thus released, from any farther connexion with the Council, Mr. Drayton spread all these matters before the people; and entered into an examination, whether or not the Council did form an Upper House of Assembly; or whether they were only a mere Privy Council. And in doing so, a new light was cast on this important subject, at a critical time; which had. considerable effects, on the minds of the people, as on the consequences which followed, as well to the King's Council, as to the people in general. The affair did not end here. Mr. Drayton transmitted the whole of the proceedings accompanied by a letter from himself, to Lord Dartmouth: which, left the matter in such a manner with his Lordship, that he might either consider the letter as a justification of Mr. Drayton's conduct; or, as a resignation of his Counsellorship. He went farther; and preferred a memorial on the subject to the Commons-House of Assembly; which was immediately read: and together with the papers connected with it, were referred to a large Committee of grievances; and are upon record, in the Journals of that House.*

While this unpleasant controversy, was going on, the 17th day of February arrived; which had been set apart by the Provincial Congress, as a day of fasting, humiliation, and prayer. And on this occasion, the Commons-House of Assembly with their mace before them, went in procession to St. Philip's Church; where, a pious and excellent sermon was delivered by the Rev. Robert Smith.† And, thence returning to the affairs of the Colony, as the Council had passed one bill, and had thereby yielded the long contest; the Assembly sent them, on the 28th February 1775, a

---

* See Journals of the Commons-House of Assembly of South-Carolina, from 2d Aug. 1774, to Sept. 1775—from page 55 to 68, inclusive.

† See Dalcho's Church History, p. 219, note.

Reviving Bill; by which, among other laws which were revived and continued, the general duty-act was continued for one year only. This law, was also passed by the Council; and on the 3d day of March, they returned it to the Commons-House of Assembly. And, on the 4th day of March, both acts, the one, entitled " An Act to prevent the Counterfeiting the Paper Money of the other Colonies," the other, entitled " An Act to revive and continue for the terms therein limited, several Acts and clauses of Acts of the General Assembly of this Colony," were ratified by the Lieutenant-Governor in the Council Chamber;* and, by so doing, the staff of Government was virtually transferred. For, at the expiration of one year from thence, unless Government gave satisfaction to the people, there would be no fund for the payment of the civil establishment; and, the episcopal Clergy, and all the Crown officers, would be destitute of provision. It was now clearly apparent, that the Council alone had, for so long a space of time, as from the first day of January 1769,† to the 4th day of March 1775, obstructed the passing of any law for the public service: thereby demonstrating, of how dangerous a nature, such an establishment was, to the rights, and liberties of the people. Leave was now given by the House of Assembly, to bring in a bill of a private nature; after which, permission being obtained from the Lieutenant-Governor, the session was closed in a more pleasant manner, than it had been done for some years; and the House was adjourned to Thursday, the 20th day of April.

During these transactions men grew anxious to receive advices from England; and some flattering ones arrived: intimating, that the King had said the

* See Journals of the Commons-House of Assembly for 1775, pages 68, 69

† See Ibid. from 2d Aug. 1774, to 15th Sept. 1775, p. 80.

petition from the Congress " was a decent one;" and
that he would lay it before the parliament. It was
also stated, that the merchants of London and the
trading towns of England, were preparing petitions to
parliament in favour of America; and that Lord
North began to speak in a milder tone, and to exon-
erate himself from blame, should the late parliamentary measures have induced unsuccessful consequences.
The mass of citizens, and men of prudence and
moderation, therefore ardently hoped for a reconciliation, with the mother country; and awaited with the
fondest hopes, and with a well-intentioned allegiance,
manifestations of good intentions from the throne on
that head. At the same time, they were not unmind-
ful of their own affairs. For in pursuance of the late
recommendation of the Provincial Congress, they were
diligently learning the use of arms; and were forming
themselves into volunteer companies; being trained,
and exercised, by their respective officers. A martial
spirit. had gone forth among the people; and Charlestown began to assume military appearances. Such,
was the public situation; when, on the 14th of April,
their prospects were clouded over, by advices; which,
put an end to every hope of accommodation.

For now, news arrived, that on the meeting of
parliament the Ministers had laid before the two
Houses, Extracts of American Correspondence:
among which, were the proceedings of the Continental
and other Provincial Congresses, American papers,
and William Henry Drayton's Charge as one of the
King's Judges to the Grand Jury of Camden, with
their presentments, at the November Session in 1774,
of the Circuit Court, held at that town. All of these
papers, were considered, in a Committee of the whole
House of Commons; but the addresses and petitions
of the merchants of Great Britain in favour of America, although pressed by the minority to be considered

in the same Committee, were referred to another
Committee; sarcastically called the Coventry Committee. The petition from the Continental Congress
to the King, had been laid before parliament; but the
Colonial Agents were refused a hearing by the Commons, in proof of the allegations contained therein.
On the contrary, Administration had exerted themselves, to procure counter petitions, from the trading
towns. And in some degree they succeeded in obtaining petitions, from Birmingham, Leeds, Halifax
and some other places, praying, that the laws respecting America might be enforced. It was also stated,
that on the 2d February, Lord North had brought the
subject to issue; in which, he minutely discussed the
same: describing the characters, and state of each
Province; and, pointing out such, as he declared were
in rebellion. He said that Great Britain containing
eight millions of inhabitants, payed a revenue of ten
millions, beside the expense of collecting, which was
25 shillings per head; while America containing three
millions, only paid £75,000 Sterling; and which, was
not six-pence per head. He stated the supremacy of
parliament over America, and the American measures
of resistance. And, concluded with moving, that " an
address be presented to his Majesty, to thank him for
the information laid before the House; and, that he
would be pleased to take such measures, as might be
suitable to his wisdom, for enforcing the laws against
America; and promising him to support him in a full
and vigorous execution thereof, at the hazard of their
lives, and fortunes."* These measures, amounting to
a declaration of war, were vigorously opposed in parliament, by a virtuous, and an enlightened minority;
during which, some excellent speeches were made by

* See a Resolve of Parliament on this subject, and a letter from Lord
Dartmouth, to Sir James Wright, Governor of Georgia, respecting it, in Appendix to Chap. VIII. No. III.

Lord Chatham, Lord Camden, the Duke of Richmond, the Lord Mayor, Mr. Burke, Col. Barré, and Mr. Fox: and Administration smarted under all the pains, which language could inflict. But, all was of no avail, in favour of the just remonstrances of America. A fatal influence, hung over the King; and by Message to the Commons, he desired an augmentation of his forces. This, was accordingly granted. And regiments of foot and horse, and ships of war, the first ever ordered upon such service, were dispatched across the bosom of the Atlantic Ocean; to scatter the miseries with which they were charged, among a loyal, but highly injured people.

These accounts, announced to America, that her disputes with Great Britain were to be decided by arms. In this light, the people considered it; and with fortitude, indignation, and concern, they appeared to accept the challenge. The prudent and cautious, now admitted our complaints were unattended to; they warmed, with the ardor of their fellow citizens; thought, impelled thought; and action, excited to action; until, wrapped together in one bond of union, their strength was consolidated, and their measures became decided. It was now, the crisis was arriving, which was destined to try men's souls: when nerve, intelligence, and prudence, were necessary for those, whose destinies entrusted them with public affairs. It was now, that the poor looked for consolation to the rich; and the few, animated the efforts of the many. While, in a steady reliance on Divine Providence, they all moved forward, in a firm and determined opposition, to arbitrary sway.

To take measures therefore, for the public defence, the General Committee had met on the 19th April 1775; and, they had scarcely assembled, when they

were informed the British Packet had arrived; and
was come to an anchor. The Committee therefore
adjourned, until the next day; that in the mean time,
the intelligence received by her, might be known, and
digested.

On the next day, the General Committee met
according to adjournment; when the following intelligence was reported by the Secretary. That on the
17th day of February, at a numerous meeting of merchants at the London Tavern, a subscription had been
opened, for the relief of the Americans; and, in less
than half an hour, £15,000 Sterling, was subscribed;
and, that other subscriptions were also opened, for the
same purpose. That on the 18th February, Lord
North had introduced a bill, to prohibit during the
continuance of the combinations and disorders in those
provinces, the four New-England Governments, from
fishing on the banks of Newfoundland; or, to export
to any part of the world, other than to Great Britain,
or some of the British Islands, in the West Indies.
And, that no sort of wines, salt, or any goods or commodities whatsoever, except horses, victuals, and linen
cloth, the produce and manufacture of Ireland, and
goods for the victualling his Majesty's ships, and for
his Majesty's forces and garrisons, or the produce of
the British Islands in the West Indies, should be imported into them upon any pretence whatsoever;
unless, such goods be shipped in Great Britain, and be
carried directly from thence. That on the 20th, Lord
North stated, that the passage in the late address
which had promised the House was ready to consider
and embrace any proposals, if any should be made, to
reconcile the unhappy differences with America, was
of too general a nature—that, it would be proper to
give them some explanation—and, that he had some
propositions to make, which would amount to a precise

definition of them.* That, the exercise of the right of
taxing every part of the British dominions must by no
means be given up. That, he thought it best at the outset, to let them (the Colonies) know, what was expected ; and to learn, whether they meant to dispute the
whole of the British authority, or not. That, the Congress of the Colonies, was an illegal assembly; for, they
were separate states, independent of each other; having
no connection, but, in their relation to Great Britain.
Information was also given, that on the 9th of March,
Lord North, had given notice, he would move for leave
to bring in a bill, in pursuance of his conciliatory plan.
However, notwithstanding this humane intention of
his lordship; the troops which had been ordered, had
not been countermanded, to wait the issue of his conciliatory plan; but, were on the point of embarking for
Boston.

As to Lord North's conciliatory plan, it required no
deep penetration to find out, it was equally wide from
the American idea, of taxation; as, of the power
actually exercised by parliament. The Americans
claimed the right of giving aids upon requisitions, in
such manner as was best suited to their local situa-
tions; and for the current public service. If therefore,
parliament laid taxes on them, incompatible with
these rights, it was nothing more or less, than lying at
the mercy of parliament, as before. Besides this, it
also appeared, the opinion of Administration relating
to the claims of the Provincial Council as an Upper
House, was now utterly irreconcileable with the interests, or the politics of the Colony. These things,
were too obvious, not to be seen at first sight. The
General Committee therefore, did not enter into any

* See a Resolve of parliament in pursuance of these propositions, and a
letter from Lord Dartmouth, pressing them, on Sir James Wright, Governor of
Georgia; in Appendix to Chapter VIII. No. III.

public deliberation, as to these measures, or the conciliatory plan: choosing, to demonstrate their sentiments thereon, by acts, rather than by votes. And, without forming any resolution; it was understood in the General Committee, that the public military stores should be immediately seized into the hands of the people.

To effect this, Colonel Charles Pinckney, the President of the Provincial Congress, in pursuance of a resolution of that Congress of the 16th of January, authorizing him thereto; on the spot appointed a Secret Committee. He first nominated, William Henry Drayton; and asked him, whom he could think of as associates. Upon which, he desired, and the President appointed Arthur Middleton, and Charles Cotesworth Pinckney: and adding, that William Gibbes and Edward Weyman would be proper to be of the Committee, the one having many schooners and stores which might be depended on upon occasion, and the other, being active in confidential services; they also, were appointed. The resolution of the Provincial Congress, which authorized this extraordinary measure, ran in the words following: " Resolved, that a Secret Committee of five proper persons be appointed, by the President of this Congress, to procure and distribute such articles, as the present insecure state of the interior parts of this Colony renders necessary, for the better defence and security of the good people of those parts, *and other necessary purposes*. Resolved, that this Congress will indemnify and support the said Committee, in all their doings, touching the premises." By this authority, the Committee became possessed, of the most important powers; nothing more or less, than an unlimited power, in placing the Colony in a posture of defence. For in those days, terms were used in public resolutions; calculated to bear ample constructions, for the public service.

No sooner was the Secret Committee organized, than without loss of time, they determined, the public gun-powder, and the small arms in the State-House Armoury, should be seized the night after, (Friday, April 21;) and they issued directions accordingly. One party, seized the public powder at the Hobcaw Magazine; and another party, possessed themselves of the powder in the Magazine at Cochran's, on the Neck between Ashley and Cooper Rivers; while a third party, assembled at the State-House in Charlestown at eleven o'clock at night, posting armed sentinels in proper places. On this last occasion, many respectable gentlemen attended; among whom were Colonel Charles Pinckney, President of the Provincial Congress—Col. Henry Laurens, Chairman of the General Committee—Thomas Lynch, one of the Delegates to the Continental Congress—Benjamin Huger, William Bull, and William Henry Drayton, the two last, nephews of the Lieutenant-Governor. The Secret Committee attended, and directed; and Christopher Gadsden attended at the wharf, to receive the powder when it was landed there from the Hobcaw Magazine.

The door of the Armoury in the upper part of the State-House, was now broken open; and, in less than three hours, eight hundred stands of arms, two hundred cutlasses, beside cartouches, flints, and matches, were removed from thence. Of these, the heavy articles were deposited and secreted in the brick cellars of the two brick bildings, at the North-West corner of the State-House; then owned by Mr. Gibbes: and the lighter articles, were carried to the houses of trusty individuals; that at any rate, the Lieutenant-Governor, might not recover the whole of the armament, which had been so taken away. In this affair, the greatest order was observed. No disguises, were used; but the night was chosen for the transaction; as there was no reason for insulting the authority of the Lieutenant-Governor, who was much respected and beloved, by performing it in open day; when the public advantage could be equally promoted, by avoiding such a conduct.

This disappearance of the powder and arms, so immediately following the late advices, which had been received from London; plainly indicated the authority which had taken them, by the daringness and secrecy of the manner, in which it had been conducted. Mrs. Pratt, the keeper of the State-House, was examined as to the matter, by the Lieutenant-Governor; but, although she saw the arms taken away, and the persons who took them, she would not give any information tending to a discovery; even, although threatened with the loss of her place, which, was mostly her support. The Commander of the Town-Watch, who mounted guard every night at the opposite corner of the street, although he saw several persons about the State-House, and knew them, was equally silent. In this perplexity, Lieutenant-Governor Bull convened his Council; and after much consideration respecting what had been done, and what consequences were likely to ensue, both, as to the authority of himself and the Council, and the strengthening of patriotic measures; prudence forbad their doing any thing farther, than to advise the Governor to send a mild message to the Commons-House of Assembly, then sitting, informing them of the event: and which was accordingly sent to them, on the 25th of April 1775, in the following words.

" Mr. Speaker and Gentlemen,

" Mr. Poaug, the Ordnance Store-Keeper, informed me last Saturday morning, that upon examining the public arms and stores in the armoury, about eight hundred stands of arms, two hundred cutlasses, all the cartouch boxes, with some bundles of matches, and some flints, belonging to the public, had been taken out of the State-House the preceding night: and Mr. Cochran, Deputy Powder Receiver, who has the charge of the public Magazine on the town Neck, about four miles from town, informed me, that on his visiting the Magazine last Saturday morning, he found the doors broken open; and that all the gun-powder, about five hundred pounds weight, was carried away, the preceding night, by persons unknown. I have published a proclamation, offering a reward for discovering the persons concerned in such daring acts of violence, against the property, of the public, of this Province.

" I have also been informed, by Mr. Prince, who has charge of the public Magazine at Hobcaw; that it was broken open the beginning of this month, and seventy-five pounds weight of gun-powder then taken out: and, that it was again broken open on the 21st instant, and one thousand and twenty-five pounds of gun-powder, being all that was in the Magazine, was carried away.

" Upon so very extraordinary, and alarming an occasion; it becomes my indispensable duty, to acquaint you therewith, without loss of time; and earnestly to recommend this important matter to your investigation, and most serious consideration.

" WILLIAM BULL.

" April 24th, 1775."

The Assembly, laughed at this act of Government. However, to carry on the farce, it was referred to the Committee who had been appointed to examine the public arms: and Mr. Bee, Dr. Olyphant, Mr. Izard, and Col. Gaillard were added to the Committee. On the 27th of April, Mr. Bee brought in a report to the House on the subject, which being agreed to, was in the following words: " That with all the inquiry your Committee have made, they are not able to obtain any certain intelligence relative to the removal of the public arms, and gun-powder, as mentioned in his Honour's Message; but, think there is reason to suppose, that some of the inhabitants of this Colony, may have been induced to take so extraordinary and uncommon a step, in consequence of the late alarming accounts from Great Britain:" and, a copy of the same, was sent by the House to the Lieutenant-Governor, with the following Message:

" May it please your Honour,

" Your Message dated the 24th instant, which you sent to this House the next day, was referred to a Committee: and their report, as agreed to, by the House, we herewith send you.
    " By order of the House.
            " RAWLINS LOWNDES, Speaker.*

" April 27th, 1775."

After this first efficient act, of the Secret Committee; by which, in hazarding their persons in a treasonable affair, they had proved themselves deserving of the high confidence which had been placed, in their ability, firmness, and patriotism; they privately went

* See Journals of the Commons-House of Assembly of South-Carolina, from 2d August 1774, to 15th Sept. 1775, pages 70, 76.

about, borrowing money for the public service. And
so successful were they on this occasion, that on the
first day of their progress, they procured one thousand
guineas: so ready were the citizens, to meet the call of
their country.

During this time, a report had been made in the
General Committee, on the 26th day of April, that
since the 8th day of March, there had been collected
for the relief of the poor in Boston,

From St. Philip's Parish, £1,400 in cash, and 66
                                        barrels Rice.
      St. Michael's do.   700 in cash, and 14
                                        barrels Rice.
      St. Stephen's do.   600
      St. Paul's   do.   600
                              ————
                             £3,300

All of which, was remitted to Boston. And, on the
same day, a Committee was raised and appointed by
the General Committee, denominated " *The Committee of Intelligence:*" which was particularly charged,
with obtaining and receiving information, both public
and private; and forthwith communicating the same
to the Secret Committee, or the General Committee;
as might be most proper, and advantageous, for the
public service.

With all these occurrences, men's minds had become agitated; and it was deemed proper to bring
forth something, calculated to arrest the public attention; to throw odium on the British Administration;
to put down the Crown officers in the Province; and
to invigorate the ardor of the people. And nothing
was deemed more likely to effect the same, than some
public exhibition, which might speak to the sight and

senses, of the multitude. For this purpose, effigies were brought forward; supposed to be by the authority or connivance, of the Secret Committee. They were executed under the direction of Mr. Poyas, in the Masonic Lodge room, in Lodge-alley; and represented the Pope, Lord Grenville, Lord North, and the Devil. They were placed on the top of a frame, capable of containing one or two persons within it: and the frame was covered over with thick canvass, so that those within, could not be distinguished. In the front of the frame on the top, the Pope was seated in a chair of state, in his pontifical dress; and at a distance immediately behind him, the Devil was placed in a standing position, holding a barbed dart in his right hand; between the Pope and the Devil on each side, Lords Grenville and North were stationed. Thus finished, the frame and effigies were fixed on four wheels; and early in the morning, this uncommon spectacle, was stationed between the Market* and St. Michael's Church in Broad-street, to the gaze of the citizens. Many were the surmises respecting it; but at length by its evolutions, it soon began to explain the purposes, for which it was constructed. For no sooner, did any of the Crown officers, Placemen, Counsellors, or persons known to be disaffected to the common cause pass by, than the Pope immediately bowed with proportioned respect to them; and the Devil at the same moment, striking his dart at the head of the Pope, convulsed the populace, with bursts of laughter. While on the other hand, the immoveable effigies of Lords Grenville and North, appearing like attendants on the Pope, or Criminals; moved the people with sentiments of disgust, and contempt against them and the whole British Administration: for the many oppressive acts, which they had

---

* The Beef Market was then, where the elegant building of the City-Hall is at present.

been instrumental in procuring to be passed, through both Houses of Parliament. In this manner, the machine was exposed; after which it was paraded through the town the whole day, by the mob: and in the evening they carried it beyond the town: where, surrounding it with tar barrels, the whole was committed to the flames. Nor did the idea or influence of the thing, end here—for, boys forsook their customary sports, to make models like it: with which, having amused themselves, and roused their youthful spirits into a detestation of oppression; they also committed them to the flames. And many of those very boys, supported with their services and blood; the rights, and liberties, of their country.

On this occasion, Edward Weyman, a member of the Secret Committee of five, was one of the persons within the machine, who directed the operation of the machinery. And to his knowledge of the men and characters he had to deal with, the public were indebted no doubt, for the significant bows of respect, which the Pope so appropriately paid to all those; who, preferred taxation and royalty, to liberty and social happiness. Mr. Weyman being so engaged in the plot, naturally associates the Secret Committee with him in the scheme: as it has been already stated, that when that Committee was originated, Mr. Weyman was expressly nominated as one of them, *on account of the active and confidential services he could render.*

At this period, most parts of the Continent had raised men; but in this measure, a langour seemed to prevail throughout this Colony. And, as the Delegates were about departing, to meet the Continental Congress at Philadelphia, and the Commons-House of Assembly was fortunately in session; they wished to bring a few particulars before that body, before they should embark for their destined port. For this purpose, on Friday the 28th day of April 1775, Mr. Lynch, one of the Delegates, moved the House, that it resolve itself into a Committee of the whole, to take into consideration the present state of this Colony: which being agreed to, Col. Parsons took the Chair. This they did, in order that the business which they might do in Committee, should not appear upon the Journals of the House: and the doors being shut, this important question was propounded by Mr. Lynch.

" If the Delegates from this Colony, should in General Congress, think it expedient to engage a sum of money, as an aid from this Province to the American association; would the Assembly ratify and raise that quota, which they should engage, for the contribution of this country?"

A conversation, now ensued; some fears and distrusts appearing among the members. Mr. Lowndes in particular, hoped the Delegates would be cautious; as it was yet too early to proceed to extremities; and he thought we had best trust a little to the plans of non-importation, and non-exportation. He said, he did not think the parliament had any right to take money out of the pockets of the colonists; but excepting that particular, he thought parliament had a right to legislate for them, in all national and commercial cases. He however, withdrew his opposition; and, without a question being put, it appeared to be the unanimous agreement of the Committee, that they would fulfil all the engagements the Delegates should make, on the part of this Colony; for promoting the public welfare. After this sentiment of the public will had been obtained; the Speaker resumed the Chair: and Col. Parsons acquainted the House he was directed by the Committee to move, that they

may have leave to sit again. But it does not appear
any leave was granted; for the matter they had in
hand, was already performed. And consequently, no
farther mention was made in the Journals of the
House, of this important transaction.*

   The Assembly now (29th April 1775) ordered, that
Col. Pinckney, Mr. Bee, Mr. Charles Cotesworth
Pinckney, and Mr. Gibbes do prepare and bring in a
bill for raising and granting to his Majesty a sum
sufficient to defray the charges of this Government,
for the last six years past: and on the first day of
May, Mr. Charles Cotesworth Pinckney presented to
the House for that purpose, a Bill for raising and
granting to his Majesty the sum of £——, and applying the sum of £——, being the balance of several
funds in the public Treasury, making together the
sum of £——; to defray the Charges of this Government, from the first day of January 1769, to the thirty-
first day of December 1774, both days inclusive ; and
for other services therein mentioned :† and it was
resolved, that the said bill be read immediately. But,
while the Clerk was reading the bill, the House was
required by the Deputy Secretary, to attend his
Honour the Lieutenant-Governor, in the Council
Chamber. Where, to avoid the disagreeable necessity of rejecting it, as he had received no instruction
from Government to pass it in the usual manner; his
Honour informed the General Assembly, that by the
last advice, he had reason to expect within a fortnight
or three weeks, the arrival of his Excellency the
Right Honourable Lord William Campbell; and he
therefore thought it unnecessary they should continue

* See Journals of the Commons-House of Assembly for April 1775, page 78.

† See Journals of the Commons-House of Assembly of South-Carolina, from
2d Aug. to 15th Sept. 1775, pages 79, 80, 81.

sitting longer at that time. And as he wished, the time which had been employed in preparing the public business, might not be lost, he therefore adjourned the General Assembly to the first day of June, then next ensuing.*

On the 3d day of May 1775, the Delegates sailed for Philadelphia; leaving the public impatiently waiting the determinations of the approaching Continental Congress. And they had scarcely done so, when a private letter arrived from Arthur Lee in London; intimating, that a plan was laid before Administration, for instigating the slaves to insurrection. This, was the more alarming; because, it was already known, they entertained ideas, that the present contest was for obliging us to give them their liberty. To meet therefore, whatever events might arise, the General Committee on the 5th day of May 1775, appointed William Henry Drayton, Barnard Elliott, George Gabriel Powell, William Tennent, Arthur Middleton, Charles Cotesworth Pinckney, William Gibbes, John Huger, Edward Weyman, Thomas Lynch, jun. and Thomas Bee, a Special Committee, to form such plans, as they should think immediately necessary to be carried into execution " for the security of the good people of this Colony;" and, to report to them such things, as should be for the public security. This step was scarcely taken, when on the eighth of May, a vessel arrived from Salem; which place, she had quitted on the 25th day of April. By her, information was brought, that civil war was commenced in Massachusetts-Bay, in a conflict of arms, and a shedding of blood, by British troops at Lexington; on the 19th day of April 1775. It is necessary, here, to pause; as, an era of so great importance, to the future desti-

---

* See Journals of the Commons-House of Assembly of South-Carolina, from 2d Aug. 1774, to 15th Sept. 1775—pages 79, 80, 81.

nies of America, demands our reflection: for it will ever stand enrolled, in the brightest pages of our revolutionary history.*

* See the London Remembrancer for 1775, from page 69, to page 84; giving accounts of the battle of Lexington, with sundry affidavits, respecting the same.

APPENDIX

CHAPTER VI.

———

No. I.

Charlestown, February 13th, 1775.

ON Wednesday the 8th instant, on motion in the Upper-House of Assembly, to discharge a resolution for the then reading a third time, a bill to prevent counterfeiting the paper money of other Colonies, and to appoint Saturday for the reading of the bill; the following Protest was made:

Dissentient.

Because, the reason assigned for postponing the reading of the bill, to wit, the sudden indisposition and absence of two members of Council (who are Crown officers) is by no means, in my opinion, so substantial as to make the measure prudent; especially when we reflect, that by an *express resolution* on the Journal, the bill was appointed to be read on this day. For, although these members are Crown officers, yet their presence is by no means so necessary, as that by reason of their absence we should violate an express resolution; or even postpone reading any bill lying before his Majesty's Council: the number of members present on this occasion, having often transacted business of a similar nature, in the absence of these gentlemen. Indeed, the experience which we have just had, of the consequence of a delay to proceed in the public business; ought to instruct us, to avoid a new delay upon the same principle.

On Friday last, the bill was to have been read; but, because of the absence of one Crown officer, such others as are of his Majesty's Council, caused the reading of the bill to be postponed to this day; a delay, which instead of adding to our number, has diminished it: for, now two Crown officers are absent. In short, so far am I from being of opinion, that the postponing the public business to Saturday; will be of any utility; that on the contrary, to me the measure seems pregnant with mischief. For, if those gentlemen should not be able to attend in Council; and, the Chief Justice should be suddenly indisposed with the gout—a complaint, with which he has been often very critically seized; there would not be any probability of our doing any public business whatever. And even if those gentlemen should recover, yet the Chief Justice might be critically indisposed. And, as the bill has already been postponed, because of the absence of one Crown officer; so, upon the same principle would it be expected, to be again postponed —and probably, continued to be so, *de die in diem.* A procrastination, which in the eye of the public, might appear to be a wanton sporting with their interests—to betray the trust reposed in us by the King—to be detri-

mental to the public service: and contemptuous to the
Representatives of the people.

WILLIAM HENRY DRAYTON.

☞ Last Saturday, a bill " to prevent counterfeiting the Paper Money of other Colonies," passed his
Majesty's Council. It is thought, that its passage was
facilitated by a certain Protest, relative to it, on
Wednesday last. In the year 1773, a similar bill was
delayed in the Council; so, as to be lost by a prorogation. And the circumstances relative to the bill, being
exactly the same now, as they were then; its passage
demonstrates, that the proceedings of the Council, are
not always uniform: or, the effects of judicious deliberation.

[See No. 2030, The South-Carolina Gazette, for Monday, February 13th,
1775; printed by Peter Timothy, Printer to the Honourable the Commons·
House of Assembly.]

———

No. II.

Monday, February 13th.

This day, his Majesty's Council, consisting of three
Placemen, presented the following Address to his
Honour, the Lieutenant-Governor.

South-Carolina:

To the Honourable William Bull, Esq. Lieutenant-
Governor and Commander in Chief, in and over,
his Majesty's said Province.

May it please your Honour,

His Majesty's dutiful and faithful subjects, *The
Council* of this Province met in General Assembly,

with reluctance approach your Honour on a subject
of so disagreeable a nature, as a complaint against one
of their members, the Honourable William Henry
Drayton, Esq.

Although the general tenor of Mr. Drayton's conduct for a *considerable* time past, would not only have
justified, but, seemed to call for, a representation from
this House, to your Honour; yet, anxious to avoid
every measure, which might appear to have a tendency to infringe upon the rights of an individual, or
the privileges of a member, we have hitherto delayed,
to lay before your Honour, our just causes of complaint; and have submitted to many insults and indig-
nities offered to individual members; as well as, out-
rageous breaches of privilege committed against this
House.

But, as we are now thoroughly convinced, that Mr.
Drayton's conduct has been, and still continues, to be
influenced by a determined purpose, as far as in him
lies, not only to destroy all confidence of the people in
this House, and to bring it into contempt, but to subvert the Constitution, and unhinge Government; to be
longer silent would be highly criminal.   And, we
conceive ourselves bound both by principles of duty
and affection, to his Majesty, and justice to ourselves,
humbly to request your Honour will be pleased to
suspend the Honourable William Henry Drayton, Esq.
from being a member of his Majesty's Council in this
Province.
         By order of the House.
                              JOHN STUART.

In the Upper-House of Assembly, }
       11th February 1775.   }

Before signing the above Address, Mr. Drayton claimed leave to enter his Protest against it, which is as follows:

No. III.

Dissentient.

Because, the Hon. John Stuart, Esq. Superintendant of Indian Affairs. being a Counsellor, not vested with the powers of the ancient twelve, ought not to have any precedence among Counsellors, upon that establishment, vested with superior powers; and therefore, ought not, as eldest Counsellor present, to sign any paper in Council: an act, manifesting the possession of superior rank. Mr. Stuart, is incapable as eldest Counsellor, of taking rank as President and Commander in Chief of the Colony; and, in my opinion, this incapability and the appointment to the Council in each Colony in which he is Superintendant, obviously demonstrate, that the appointment was calculated to enable him the better to execute the duties of his office; and not intended to authorize him constantly to interfere, in the merely domestic legislative affairs of any such Colony, in which, the nature of his office, or pleasures, should at any time make his presence necessary, or convenient.

Because, I am of opinion, the Address having a direct *" tendency to infringe upon the rights of an individual,"* and *" the privileges of a member,"* is therefore, arbitrary, unparliamentary, destructive of freedom of speech, derogatory to the ancient dignity of the Council, and a contemptuous insult, to the people of this Colony.

Because, I have just grounds to be assured, the measure will not only *" destroy all confidence of the*

people in this *house, and bring it into contempt;*" (to
effect which, the Address declares I aim with " *a determined purpose;*" and, to prevent which, I even here give
evidence that I aim; although the House have been
losing that confidence, and have been falling into contempt, *in proportion* to the increase of Placemen in it,
and display, of their *dependance* and *abilities,*) but,
that it will otherwise be detrimental to his Majesty's
real service: inasmuch, as the natives of this Colony
will be greatly discouraged from serving his Majesty
and the public in a Council; from which, they would
run the hazard of being suspended, *even by the machinations* of three members who are Placemen.   Indeed,
already are natives almost discouraged from sitting in
Council.   And, this is manifest, when we reflect;
that there are only eight Couusellors, in the Province;
of which number, five are not only Crown officers, but
strangers.

Because, the complaint being only of a general
nature, it is to be presumed, nothing in particular
could be stated; and therefore, in my opinion, the
Address must be considered as of a frivolous nature.

Because, the Address bearing a position inconsistent
with matter of fact; it will reflect the utmost infamy
upon the Chief Justice who introduced it: a load,
which I could wish him to avoid; possessed as I am,
with a zealous inclination to promote his Majesty's
real service; too liable to be impeded by public odium
against *an officer acting under a total loss of reputation.*   The Address asserts, that " *the general tenor of
Mr. Drayton's conduct for a considerable time past;*"
shows that he " *has been, and still continues to be,
influenced, by a determined purpose, as far as in him
lies,*" " to subvert the Constitution " *and unhinge the
Government:*" hence, by not having limited the retrospect, the assertion most strongly insinuates, that my

conduct, has been of such a dangerous tenor, even during several years. But this is an assertion, which not only wantonly, but disrespectfully militates against the truth, *evidenced*, by his Majesty's Royal Sign Manual and Privy Seal, on the 27th day of February 1771; when the King was graciously pleased to declare himself "*well satisfied, with the loyalty, integrity and ability, of our trusty and well beloved William Henry Drayton, Esquire;*" meaning myself: and also, by Royal Letters Patent, under the Great Seal of this Province, so late, as the 25th day of January 1774; declaring, my loyalty, integrity and ability, and constituting me to be one of the Assistant-Judges of this Colony: an office, which I possessed, until the ninth day of December last; when, to make room for a gentleman sent from England, and regularly called to the bar, I was superceded, without the least censure; notwithstanding, a most violent complaint by the Chief Justice to his Honour, the Lieutenant-Governor, against me, touching an anonymous publication, addressed to the late Congress. Which complaint, *notwithstanding my most pressing instances, that it should be brought to issue, was,* on the 6th day of January last, by unanimous advice of a Council composed entirely of Crown officers, "*dismissed without any censure, upon any of the parties.*"

Because, the Address is improper even in its main purpose. For, as it charges me with "a determined purpose, to subvert the Constitution and unhinge Government;" if I am guilty, a suspension is a punishment, by no means adequate to the offence. In my opinion, as the Chief Justice knew *the man* possessed of "a determined purpose," so *criminal and so dangerous,* for him to allow *that man,* to continue uninterrupted by the due course of law, was *to betray the trust reposed in him by the King.* For, the Chief Justice, would have demonstrated his duty to the King, and his own knowledge and abilities as a Judge, had he, *ex officio*, ordered a prosecution to bring me to condign punishment; rather than, by having planned an Address, to *move the extraordinary powers* of Government to inflict a *slight* punishment. The rule, *Nec Deus intersit, nisi dignus vindice nodus*, is as applicable to the political, as it is to the poetical, drama. Upon the whole, but for the reasons assigned, I should have been extremely well pleased with the Address; because, in my opinion, it bears honorable testimony of me. The Placemen in Council declare, that I have "a determined purpose to subvert the Constitution:" *hence*, I am confident, the people will be assured, that I am really defending it with vigour.

WILLIAM HENRY DRAYTON.*

———

The Council sitting as a Branch of the Legislature, being moved to agree with the report of the Committee, respecting the charges which they had made out against William Henry Drayton, a member of the Council; and it being Resolved, that this House do agree to the same; three members of the Council, being natives of South-Carolina, entered the following Protest:

No. IV.

Dissentient.

Because, without particularizing the many objections to which the report in our opinion is justly liable

* See Timothy's South-Carolina Gazette for 1775, No. 2030.

(it being unparliamentary in almost every line:) confining ourselves, to state only two objections; we
deem these to be of such a nature, as even with them
alone, to justify our disagreeing with the report.

In the fourth section there is a culpableness, stated
to be in the assertion "that this House is no Branch
of the Legislature," because "his Majesty hath not
hitherto been pleased to give *any* answer to the address
of this House, dated eleventh of September 1773."
Now as we know this address did most respectfully
and earnestly complain to his Majesty, of what this
House deemed, a most dangerous adjudication, *That
this House was no Upper-House of Assembly and
Branch of the Legislature;* and a most dangerous violation of their privilege by the discharge of a person
committed by their warrant for a contempt; so, we
cannot see any impropriety in the assertion, grounded
upon such a reason. For, we naturally conclude his
Majesty's silence, is out of tenderness to this House;
unwilling to refuse *totidem verbis* what he does not
think proper to grant: thereby, telling us *Le Roy
S'avisera.* The mild mode, in which a British Sovereign refuses those parliamentary applications, which,
in his royal wisdom he deems improper; for had his
Majesty, counselled by the learned Judges, thought this
House an Upper-House of Assembly, and a branch of
the Legislature, we assure ourselves, a Sovereign as
he is, of a "resolution to withstand *every attempt to
weaken* the supreme authority of the Legislature,"
meaning of Great Britain, (a sentiment expressed in
the King's late speech in parliament,) would in the
course of sixteen months not only have displayed his
design, "to withstand every attempt to weaken" the
legal "authority of this Legislature," equally the
object of his royal care; but could have taken such
constitutional measures, as might have tended to preserve to this House, their just rights; and to secure

31

them from being exposed, to a repetition of that
breach of their privilege, of which, they did most
humbly complain; and, against which, they did most
earnestly desire his Majesty's support.

Because, we are so far from thinking the Author of
the " Letter from Freeman of South-Carolina, to the
Deputies of North America," ought to be deemed
unworthy of being continued a member of this House;
that, on the contrary, we are most firmly of opinion,
his dismission must be considered, as a most arbitrary
proceeding—a violation of the constitutional rights of
the people. And, that a seat in this House, upon a
tenure of so arbitrary a nature; cannot be worthy the
attention of an independent American.

JOHN DRAYTON,

WILLIAM HENRY DRAYTON,

BARNARD ELLIOTT.

☞ See Journals of the Commons House of Assembly, of South-Carolina,
from 2d Aug. 1774 to 15th Sept. 1775, pages 60, 61—The above protest was
signed by *all the Carolinians*, who then acted as Counsellors in this Colony.
The other part of the Council, consisted of Thomas Skottowe, *Secretary of the
Province*—Thomas Knox Gordon, *Chief Justice*—William Gregory, *one of the
Assistant Judges*—Thomas Irving, *Receiver General*—John Stuart, *Superintend-
ant of Indian Affairs*—John Burn—and Sir Egerton Leigh, *Baronet, Attorney-
General.*

No. V.

On his Majesty's Service.

To the Honorable William Henry Drayton, Esq.

Charleston, March 1st, 1775.

SIR,

By virtue of the power, with which his Majesty has been pleased to entrust me, I do hereby suspend you from being a member of his Majesty's Council for this Province; until, his Majesty's pleasure shall be known thereupon. And I shall take the earliest opportunity of transmitting to the Lords Commissioners for Trade and Plantations, the Address and papers relative thereto; in order that they may be laid before his Majesty, for his royal consideration.

I am, Sir,

Your most obt. humb. servt.

WILLIAM BULL.*

---

* See Journals of the Commons-House of Assembly of South-Carolina, for 1775, page 66.

CHAPTER VII.

Battle of Lexington—The General Committee summon the Provincial Congress to meet—Barnard Elliott resigns the appointment of Counsellor—The Special Committee prepare a plan for the defence of Charlestown—Proceedings of the General Committee—The Special Committee reports to the General Committee, an association of defence, to be signed by the Inhabitants generally—which, is postponed—An Express arrives, with advices of the Skirmish at Lexington— The route taken, by the Express—Provincial Congress meets—General Committee, reports a plan of measures—The Commons-House of Assembly meets, and proceeds to business—passes some resolutions— and brings in an Ordinance—but, is adjourned by the Lieutenant-Governor—Provincial Congress convenes in the Representatives' Chamber—Col. Charles Pinckney President of the same resigns—Col. Henry Laurens appointed President, in his room—Causes of the Meeting set forth—A Committee of Ways and Means, appointed—The Association recommended by the General Committee, is considered by the Provincial Congress; and, after much opposition, is agreed to, and signed—Provincial Congress, resolve to raise troops—A million of money voted, and Commissioners of a Treasury concluded on—A Council of Safety originated; its members, elected—Their extensive Powers—Non-Subscribers to the Association, made amenable—General Election ordered, for

*a new Provincial Congress—Lord William Camp-
bell, arrives, as Governor of the Province—The
manner of his reception—Anecdote, respecting the
Governor—Provincial Congress, sends an Address
to his Excellency—To which, he replies—His per-
turbation—Officers elected for three Regiments—
Provincial Congress adjourns—Leaving the Government in the hands of the Council of Safety, and
General Committee—The Council of Safety meets,
and elects Henry Laurens, President, and Peter
Timothy, Secretary—It proceeds to issue military
Commissions—gives directions for stamping, and
issuing, money bills—and issues Orders, for recruiting Troops—John Stuart, Superintendant of Indian
Affairs, flies from Charlestown to Savannah in
Georgia—His proceedings there—Advices arrive,
that a vessel with Gun-powder is expected from England, at Savannah, in Georgia—The Secret Committee take measures, for seizing the same—Upon
which, Superintendant Stuart leaves Savannah, and
goes on board a British armed schooner—Friends, to
the American cause, encouraged at Savannah—
Georgia Measures—and assisting the Carolinians in
seizing the Powder—Mr. Drayton, and Mr. Middleton of the Secret Committee, encourage Captains
Barnwell and Joyner, to fit out a schooner, to drive
away the British armed schooner, lying off Tybee—
Arrangements made with the Georgians respecting
the schooner—The British schooner flies, and carries
John Stuart to St. Augustine—News, of the Battle
of Bunker's-Hill—The Powder taken, and divided
between Carolina and Georgia—An Express vessel
arrives in Carolina, for Powder—William Henry
Drayton and Miles Brewton sent to Georgia, to
effect a loan of Powder—They obtain 5000 pounds
of Powder—which is sent by the Express Vessel to
the Carolina Delegates, at Philadelphia—First instance of tarring and feathering in Carolina—A*

General day, of fasting and praying, observed throughout the United Colonies.

THE intelligence of the battle of Lexington, was laid before the General Committee, on the 8th May 1775; and a vote then passed, to summon the Provincial Congress to meet on the first day of June: as the 20th day of June to which it stood summoned to convene, was deemed too distant a period.   For now, that hostilities were actually commenced; immediate and decisive measures were deemed most eligible, for promoting the public welfare.   This, naturally led to the taking of sides; and to the forming, of political opinions: men, could act under cover no longer; and the office of King's Counsellor for the Province, became incompatible, with the duties of a patriot. Under this last influence, Barnard Elliott, now (May 10th) resigned the Royal Mandamus, by which, he had been appointed a Privy Counsellor; and he immediately associated himself with the members of the Special Committee; among whom, he had been lately nominated.

In the mean time, this Committee had taken into consideration, what things were necessary for the public security; and a plan was ready to be reported, of such measures, as they deemed expedient, for the defence of Charlestown and its harbour.   But fearing, if they laid such decisive measures before the General Committee, some timid members, might influence a delay in the execution of them, and thereby the scheme being divulged, might be frustrated; they only reported to the General Committee, that they had an important report to make: but, before they laid it before them, they deemed it necessary, to exact an oath of secrecy, from the members present.

The solemnity of this introduction, was like a stroke of thunder, to several members. They thought that nothing less, than an immediate revolution, was to be ushered in; and, however dangerous it might be to the public safety, procrastination was the line of conduct, which they wished to pursue. For this purpose, these men made a handle of the oath, to prevent their taking it. They did not think they could swear in the dark—they were afraid, this oath would militate against others, which they had taken—and then, they would be guilty of perjury. In vain, were they assured of the contrary; and, that there was nothing more treasonable, in the report to be made; than what, they had already perpetrated. And upon this, the Committee withdrew their report.

On the 10th day of May, the Committee, made another Report to the General Committee: being an association of defence, to be signed by the inhabitants generally. This, was postponed to the next day. On the 11th, the association underwent a long debate of seven hours. At first, the form was objected to; it was couched, in too unlimited terms. And, they did not know, how far they might be extended. At length, they agreed to the form; but insisted, that to sign it immediately would be a premature step. In vain, was it alleged; that an immediate subscription, would be of infinitely good effect: it would be a test, and the means of common defence, against any danger. They still contended, it ought not to be subscribed before the meeting of the Provincial Congress; before, and to whom, it ought to be referred: and whose resolutions thereon, would be binding. Not being able to obtain better terms, the Special Committee were under the necessity of postponing the object of their wishes; and, after this mode, was the matter in contention compromised. It however demonstrated, that nearly one half of the General Committee were so timid, as almost to cause others to despair of the public safety. For, upon the question being put, to recommit the association; it was lost, 25 to 23.— William Henry Drayton, and Rawlins Lowndes, being Tellers. It also afforded the unpleasant evidence; that if a regiment of the King's soldiers should arrive before the sitting of the Provincial Congress; a fatal blow would probably be given, to the popular measures of this Colony.

On this same day (May 11th) an Express arrived from Connecticut, with advices of the battle on the 19th of April last. The expedition with which it was brought, proved the practicability and advantage, of forwarding dispatches, through the intervention of Committees. And, as at the time of writing these memoirs, the time, distance, and route used on the occasion, may be desirable to be known; especially, as the original papers from Committee to Committee, from Connecticut to Charlestown, are in the possession of the writer; it is thought proper to be somewhat particular, in relating the same.

The letter of intelligence, which was transmitted from Committee to Committee, was dated at Wallingford in the Colony of Connecticut, on the 24th day of April 1775; and was written by James Lockwood. The same day, it was received by the Committee at,

New-Haven,	-	-	April 24
Fairfield,	-	-	do. } 1 day.
Nawalk,	-	-	do.
Greenwich,	-	-	25
New-York,	-	-	do.
Elizabeth-Town,	-	-	do. } 1 do.
Woodbridge,	-	-	do.
New-Brunswick,	-	-	do.

Princetown,	-	-	April 26 ⎫	
Trentown,	-	-	do. ⎮	
Philadelphia,	-	-	do. ⎬ 1 day.	
Chester,	-	-	do. ⎮	
New-Castle,	-	-	do. ⎮	
Christeen Bridge,	-	-	do. ⎭	

Head of Elk,   -   -   -   27 ⎱ 1 do.
Baltimore,   -   -   -   do. ⎰

Annapolis,   -   -   -   28 ⎱ 1 do.
Alexandria,   -   -   -   do. ⎰

The route was not regularly kept here : 29   1 do.
  but the Express came to,

Dumfries,   -   -   -   30 ⎱ 1 do.
Fredericksburg,   -   -   -   do. ⎰

King William,   -   -   May 1   1 do.

Surry County,   -   -   2 ⎱ 1 do.
Williamsburgh,   -   -   do. ⎰

Smithfield,   -   -   3 ⎫
Nancimond,   -   -   -   do. ⎬ 1 do.
Chowan,   -   -   -   do. ⎭

Edenton,   -   -   -   4   1 do.

Beaufort County,   -   -   6 ⎫
Bath,   -   -   -   do. ⎬ 1 do.
New Bern,   -   -   do. ⎭

Onslow,   -   -   -   7 ⎱ 1 do.
New River,   -   -   -   do. ⎰

Wilmington,   -   -   -   8 ⎱ 1 do.
Brunswick,   -   -   -   do. ⎰

Carolina Boundary at Little River,   9   1 do.

Waccamaw River,   -   -   10 ⎱ 1 do.
Georgetown,   -   -   do. ⎰

Charlestown,   -   -   -   11   1 do.

——————
17 days.

The Time, in which the route was performed was 17 days; and, as Wallingford is about 100 miles east of New-York, and the route of the Express was by no means direct; the distance travelled over, could not have been less, than one thousand miles.*

* See Copies of the letter of Advice, and of the different Communications from Committee to Committee, in the Appendix at the end of this Chap. No. 1

As the time for the meeting of the Provincial Congress approached, various measures were formed and digested, by the Special Committee; to meet the approaching crisis. They comprehended plans, for blocking up some channels of Charlestown Bar—the equipping some armed vessels, to defend Charlestown harbour—the prohibiting the exportation of corn and rice, for a limited time—the raising and paying, a body of troops—the forming, a general association throughout the Colony. All these important matters, were obstructed by some members of the General Committee; who, were against taking any decisive step. It being however necessary to lay before the Provincial Congress, the causes of their being convened: they were accordingly prepared and digested, by the Special Committee; and the day before the meeting of the Congress, they were agreed to by the General Committee: who ordered them to be laid before the Provincial Congress, by their Chairman.

The Commons-House of Assembly had been adjourned by the Lieutenant-Governor, to the first day of June; and it now met, pursuant to such adjournment. Knowing on how slight a tenure they held their sittings at this time; without even sending a Message to his Honour informing him the House had met, and was ready to receive communications from him; they proceeded to dispatch the public business. For this purpose, some money accounts were agreed to, and ordered to be inserted in the schedule to the tax bill. The Journals of the House on the 23d day of March 1774 were then read; upon which the House came to the following Resolutions:

" Whereas the schedule of the public debts for the year 1774, and for other services therein mentioned have been brought in; twice read, and approved by the House; therefore,

" Resolved, (*nem. con.*) That the Clerk of this
House, do forthwith grant certificates to the several
persons named in the said schedule; who may apply
to him for the same: for any sum or sums not exceeding the amount of their demands; setting forth, that
by accounts audited and allowed by the Commons-
House of Assembly, the said sum or sums appear to
be due to such person, or persons, and that the same
will be provided for by this House.

" Ordered, that before such certificates are delivered
to such persons, the Clerk do fill up, number, and sign
them; and, that they be countersigned by the follow-
ing members of this House, or any five of them, viz:
Mr. Speaker, Col. Pinckney, Mr. Brewton, Mr.
Heyward, Mr. Cattell, Mr. Bee, Mr. Dupont, Mr.
Deas, Mr. Isaac Motte, Mr. Theodore Gaillard, Mr.
Charles Cotesworth Pinckney, Mr. Elias Horry, Mr.
Gibbes, and Mr. Thomas Horry.

" Ordered, that the said members do keep a book;
and that the Clerk do keep another; wherein, shall be
respectively entered, an exact account of the number
of certificates which shall be issued; and the sums
and persons names therein inserted.

" Resolved, that this House, will indemnify the said
members and Clerk, for every thing which they shall
do, in pursuance of the foregoing Resolution and
Orders."

The House was then " moved, for leave to bring in
an Ordinance to prohibit the exportation of rice and
Indian corn, for a limited time," and leave being
given, Mr. Bee presented an Ordinance forthwith for
that purpose; "and for supplying the inhabitants of
this Colony who are in want thereof, at the price and
for the time therein limited;" and the same was

received and read the first time. It was then resolved,
" that the said Ordnance be read a second time immediately." And during the time of reading the Ordinance a second time, the House was summoned to the
Council Chamber by the call of the Lieutenant-
Governor. Upon which, the House attended as summoned: and was immediately adjourned, to the 19th
day of June.

Votes of consequence however had been passed even
in the small portion of a day which the Commons had
employed; and the members did not much lament the
adjournment: as they gave place very opportunely for
the Provincial Congress to convene in their Chamber,
on that very day. And as the members of the House
of Commons were mostly of the Provincial Congress,
it was very easy playing from one hand into another;
and thereby progressing with the public business of the
Colony. This was the last official intercouse, which
Lieutenant-Governor Bull had, with the Commons-
House of Assembly.*

The Provincial Congress having met on the 1st of
June 1775, agreeably to the summonses, which had
been issued; Colonel Charles Pinckney, their President, resigned that office; and Colonel Henry Laurens
the late Chairman of the General Committee, was
chosen in his room. The reasons of their convention
were now laid before them by the President, in the
following manner:

"I. Because the British Troops in the Province
of Massachusetts, did on the 19th of April last, commence a civil war, in America, with force and arms;
seizing and destroying, the property of the people of

---

* See Journals of the Commons-House of Assembly of South-Carolina for
1775, pages 81, 82, 83.

that Colony, and making hostile assaults on their persons: whereby, many of them fell in battle, in defence of the property and liberty of America. A conduct, in the British troops, amounting in effect, to a direct and hostile attack, upon the whole people of this Continent; threatening them, with all the calamities of slavery.

"II. Because, this Colony cannot discharge her duty in defence of American freedom; unless, we are put into a state of security against any immediate attacks by the British arms. This Colony, being in a manner so totally defenceless; that if only a small British military force should arrive; they might easily take post in Charlestown; where, the continuance of the Provincial Congress and General Committee, would thereby become not only dangerous, but impracticable. And, there not being any body of men to enforce the execution of the American Association; there is every probability that in such a situation of affairs, it would be immediately violated. A circumstance, that might be of the most fatal consequence to America.

"III. Because, there are just grounds, to apprehend an insurrection of the slaves, and hostilities from the Indians; instigated, by the tools of a wicked Administration.

"IV. Because, the formidable military and naval forces, lately sent from Great Britain, to reinforce the army in Boston, manifest the accursed design of the British Ministry, to endeavour to quell the American troubles, by the law of arms; and not to quiet them, by the laws of reason and justice. Hence, despairing of a redress of grievances, by dutiful and peaceable applications, long unavailingly presented to his Britannic Majesty; we see no alternative, but, that we submit to abject slavery, or appeal to the Lord of Hosts in defence of the common and unalienable rights, peculiar to Englishmen."

The above reasons appeared so weighty, that no person offered any thing against them; and the Congress proceeded to consider the several objects, recommended by the General Committee. But, before they proceeded to consider them specially, they appointed a Committee of Ways and Means, for placing the Colony in a proper state of defence; and, it was ordered to sit forthwith.

Among the objects recommended by the General Committee, was an association to be entered into by the inhabitants of the Colony; which, having been prepared for the occasion, among the recommendations of the General Committee, was ready to be submitted to the consideration of the Congress. It was accordingly brought before the Provincial Congress, at an early hour; and notwithstanding the urgency of the occasion, much opposition was made to its passage: and, it was even contended, by Mr. Heyward and others, that there was no occasion for an Association. However, its expediency was powerful, and it prevailed: and on the 4th of June 1775, after Divine Service had been performed before the Congress, Henry Laurens, their President, signed the same; after which, the members present, respectively affixed their names to that instrument; "under every tie of religion and honour, and associate as a band in her defence, against every foe." "Solemnly engaging, that whenever our Continental or Provincial Councils shall deem it necessary, we will go forth, and be ready to sacrifice our lives and fortunes, to secure her freedom and safety." "And we will hold all those persons inimical to the liberties of the Colonies, who

shall refuse to subscribe this Association."* A prohibition was also passed, against the exportation of
rice and corn for three months; except the Secret
Committee should have occasion to export rice, for
procuring arms and ammunition.

On the fourth day of the Session, the Provincial
Congress resolved to raise fifteen hundred Infantry,
rank and file, in two regiments; and four hundred and
fifty Horse Rangers, constituting another regiment.
Proper pay, clothing, and provisions were assigned
them; and the troops so to be raised, were to be subjected to military discipline, and the articles of war, in
like manner as the British troops were governed. On
the 14th of June 1775, one million of money was
voted; Commissioners of a Treasury were concluded
on; and a Council of Safety was elected. The
Council of Safety so called into existence, was composed of the following gentlemen. Henry Laurens,
Charles Pinckney, Rawlins Lowndes, Thomas Ferguson, Miles Brewton, Arthur Middleton, Thomas
Heyward, jun. Thomas Bee, John Huger, James
Parsons, William Henry Drayton, Benjamin Elliott,
and William Williamson. As a Council, they were
vested with supreme power over the army, the militia,
and all military affairs; in fact, they were the Executive Power of the Colony. And to them was delegated the authority, of granting commissions, suspending officers, ordering courts-martial, directing, regulating, maintaining and ordering the army, and all
military establishments; and, of drawing on the Treasury, for all purposes of public service.

Matters of important nature, were transacted during
this session of the Provincial Congress. Among

* See Appendix to this Chapter, No. II.

others, the non-subscribers to the Association,* were
made amenable to the General Committee, and by
them punishable, according to *sound policy*. Those,
who violated or refused obedience to the authority of
the Congress, were made amenable, before the
parochial and district Committees; and, upon their
being found guilty, and being contumacious, they were
to be declared inimical to the liberties of America,
and objects for the public resentment. It was also,
resolved that all absentees holding estates in this
Colony, except those who were abroad on account of
their health, and those above 60 years of age, and
under 21, ought forthwith to return: and, that no
persons holding estates in this Colony, ought to withdraw from its service; without giving good and sufficient reasons for their so doing, to the Provincial
Congress: or, during its recess, to the General Committee. A new general election of members of the
Provincial Congress, was then appointed to take
place in the country, on the 7th and 8th days of
August; and in Charlestown on the 28th and 29th
days of the same month: and the Provincial Congress
then sitting, was declared to be expired, on the 6th
day of August: but, the Council of Safety, and all
Committees, were declared to be continued, and to
act, until the meeting of the new Provincial Congress.

The Congress also prepared, an Address and Declaration to Lieutenant-Governor Bull, laying before
him their proceedings and true motives; with the
intention of presenting it to him, just before they broke
up. In the interval, intelligence was received on the
17th June, that the Scorpion, man of war, having on
board his Excellency, Lord William Campbell, appeared on the coast. To avoid any intercourse with
this new Governor, the Address was dispatched by

---

* See the Provincial Association, in the Appendix to this Chapter, No. II.

two members to the Lieutenant-Governor, who was
at his country seat at Accabee, a few miles from
Charlestown.   The deputation, however, did not
arrive at his residence, until he was informed by the
firing of canon, that the Governor had arrived.   The
Lieutenant-Governor therefore declined receiving the
Address, under the plea; that as the Governor was
now in the Colony, he could no longer exercise the
functions of Administration: although, those functions
did not cease if he chose to use them, until the Governor's commission had been read and proclaimed.   It
is believed, however, that his real motive, for not
receiving the Address, was, that he could not with
decency, or propriety receive an Address, which
announced to him, he was despoiled of the powers
and reins of Government; and that the King's Governor was a mere cypher.   Upon this, the Address
was re-arranged; for the purpose of presenting it to
his Excellency, after he should land.

On the 18th day of June 1775, his Excellency
Lord William Campbell, Governor of the Province,
landed in Charlestown, from the Scorpion man of
war.   On this occasion, with the tacit permission of
the Provincial Congress, the militia companies were
drawn up to receive him.   They made no *feu de joie*,
as had ever been usual in such a case; neither was
there the loud and hearty acclamation of citizens,
when his commission as Governor was publicly read
before him, from the portico of the Exchange.
Whatever acclamation was made, was trivial; as the
citizens, for the most part, preserved a sullen silence.
No gentlemen as was customary, awaited his Excellency's landing; or attended his parade, along the
streets—save only, three Placemen Counsellors, including the Chief Justice, Gordon, and Assistant
Judge Gregory; three other Assistant Judges, Savage,
Fewtrell. and Cosslett; the Colonel of the Militia—

33

the Collector, Robert Dalway Haliday—the Clerks of the Council, James Simpson, and Common Pleas, James Trail; and some officers of the Scorpion: the whole of which escort, did not exceed fifteen persons. And, to show farther, with how little pleasure or respect the public received him; the following anecdote, needs only to be related.

At this time, and for some weeks preceding, under the apprehension of an intended insurrection of slaves, as well as to train and accustom the militia of the town to military duty, and subordination to the new authorities; they were required to perform military duty day and night, by companies in rotation. It so happened, that on the day of the Governor's landing, the Artillery Company in course of duty mounted guard; and their field pieces as usual, were placed on the eastern pavement before the State-House in Meeting-street. Just about dusk, his Excellency and his Secretary privately proceeding on foot, wished to take the accommodation of the pavement as they went along; and in doing so, the Governor proposed to go between the guns and the wall But in commencing this passage, he was hailed by the sentinel on duty; who told him he had orders (as usual in such cases) to suffer no person to pass that way. The Secretary, astonished at such a reception, said—it is the Governor. The sentinel replied, I am not to know the Governor. His Excellency then found himself obliged, to quit the pavement: and in doing so, and asking the sentinel his name, he replied, " *Harvey, at your service.*"*

The Provincial Congress, now drawing to a conclusion, a copy of the Address intended to be presented

---

* This anecdote, is recited in the manuscript of William Henry Drayton; but without specifying the name of the sentinel. I have since ascertained, that his name was, Thomas Harvey.

to the Governor, was on the 20th of June sent to his Excellency; with a desire to know, when he would be waited on by the Congress to deliver it in form. He replied, he would acquaint them, the next day. In this interval, his resolution vibrated between a consent, or refusal. However, the next day he sent word, he was ready to receive the Address, either from the Congress, or a Deputation. Upon this answer being reported to the Congress, the following gentlemen were nominated as a Deputation to present the Address: The Hon. William Henry Drayton, the Hon. Captain Barnard Elliott, Col. Charles Pinckney, Col. James Parsons, Col. Isaac Motte, Col. Stephen Bull, Col. William Moultrie, Major Owen Roberts, Captain Thomas Savage, Captain John Huger, and Miles Brewton, Thomas Ferguson, and Gabriel Capers, Esquires. And, on the 21st day of June, they waited on his Excellency with the Congressional Address; when it was presented to him by Mr. Drayton, in the following words:

" *South-Carolina:*

" To his Excellency the Right Honourable Lord William Campbell, Governor and Commander in Chief, over the Province aforesaid.

" The humble Address and Declaration of the Provincial Congress:

" May it please your Excellency,

" We, his Majesty's loyal subjects, the Representatives of the people of this Colony, in Congress assembled, beg leave to disclose to your Excellency, the true causes of our present proceedings, not only, that upon your arrival among us, you may receive no unfavourable impression of our conduct, but that we may stand justified to the world.

"When the ordinary modes of application for redress of grievances, and the usual means of defence against arbitrary impositions have failed, mankind generally have had recourse to those that are extraordinary. Hence, the origin of the Continental Congress; and hence, the present representation of the people in this Colony. It is unnecessary to enumerate the grievances of America—they have been so often represented, that your Excellency cannot be a stranger to them. Let it, therefore, suffice to say, that the hands of his Majesty's Ministers, having long lain heavy—now press us with intolerable weight. We declare, that no love of innovation—no desire of altering the Constitution of Government—no lust of independence, has had the least influence upon our counsels: but alarmed and roused by a long succession of arbitrary proceedings, by wicked Administrations—impressed with the greatest apprehension of instigated insurrections—and deeply affected by the commencement of hostilities by the British troops against this Continent—solely for the preservation and in defence of our lives, liberties, and properties, we have been impelled to associate, and to take up arms.

"We, sincerely deplore those slanderous informations, and wicked counsels, by which his Majesty has been led into measures; which, if persisted in, must inevitably involve America in all the calamities of civil war, and rend the British Empire. We only desire the secure enjoyment of our invaluable rights; and we wish for nothing more ardently, than a speedy reconciliation with our mother country, upon constitutional principles.

" Conscious of the justice of our cause, and the integrity of our views; we readily profess our loyal attachment to our Sovereign, his Crown, and dignity; and trusting the event to Providence, we prefer death to slavery.

" These things, we have thought it our duty to declare; that your Excellency, and, through you, our August Sovereign, our fellow subjects, and the whole world, may clearly understand; that our taking up arms, is the result of a dire necessity, and in compliance with the first law of nature.

" We, entreat and trust, that your Excellency will make such a representation of the state of this Colony, and of our true motives, as to assure his Majesty, that in the midst of all our complicated distresses, he has no subjects in his wide extended dominions, who more sincerely desire to testify their loyalty and affection; or who would be more willing to devote their lives and fortunes in his real service.

By order of the Provincial Congress,
    at Charlestown, June 20th, 1775.

" HENRY LAURENS, *President.*"

To this Address, his Excellency Lord William Campbell, made the following answer:

" Gentlemen,

" I know of no representatives of the people of this province, except those constitutionally convened in the General Assembly; and, am incompetent to judge of the disputes which at present unhappily subsist, between Great Britain, and the American Colonies.

"It is impossible, during the short interval since my arrival, that I should have acquired such a knowledge of the state of the province, as to be at present able to make any representation thereupon to his Majesty. But, you may be assured, no representation shall ever be made by me, but what shall be strictly consistent with truth; and with an earnest endeavour to promote the real happiness and prosperity of the province.

"WILLIAM CAMPBELL."*

Although his Excellency had had twenty-four hours to weigh the contents of the Address before he. received it; yet, in a few hours after, he began to repent he had admitted it. For, the words "*and to take up arms*," and "*our taking up arms*," filled him with serious apprehensions. Indeed, he was so much disturbed by them, that he not only discoursed long that evening on the subject with Mr. Brewton, at whose residence in King-street he stayed, until his own should be ready to receive him; but spurred by his reflections on the occasion, he actually called Mr. Brewton up in the night; to communicate to him his uneasy apprehensions, that those words would cause troops to be immediately sent to this Colony. He thereupon, earnestly entreated Mr. Brewton, to use his best endeavours to cause those obnoxious words, to be erased from the proceedings of the Provincial Congress, and from the address which had been delivered to him; and to substitute some less exceptionable expressions, in their place: saying, that to the secrecy of such transaction, he was willing to be solemnly sworn. Impressed by the Governor's application, and also by his own apprehensions, Mr. Brewton complied with his Excellency's request; and proposed the erasement to three or four members of the Congress: but, it appearing that opposition would arise against such a

---

* See Remembrancer, for 1775, published in London, pages 236, 237.

measure, and thereby the project would become public, he desisted from proceeding farther in a matter, of such tender negociation.

It has been shown, that the Provincial Congress resolved to raise three regiments of troops; two of which were to be infantry, and one of them to be of the nature of mounted infantry or cavalry. And no sooner was this determination known, than a great number of candidates, among whom were many of the first families and fortunes in the Colony, applied for commissions; so great was the military ardor, which the late proceedings had excited. A ballot for officers accordingly took place, soon after the resolution for raising the regiments had passed: when Christopher Gadsden, was elected Colonel—Isaac Huger, Lieutenant-Colonel—and Owen Roberts, Major, of the first regiment; William Moultrie, Colonel—Isaac Motte, Lieutenant-Colonel—and Alexander M'Intosh, Major, of the second regiment; and William Thomson, Lieutenant-Colonel—and James Mayson, Major, of the third regiment. At the same time, the Captains and Subalterns of these regiments were also appointed.* This, took place anterior to the appointment of the Deputation, who presented the Address to Governor Campbell; and is the reason, why so many of that deputation, are named under military titles. This measure, now withdrew from the public Councils many men of respectability, in whom the public confidence was placed; who, by their appointments were called to the active duties of a military life. But, it did not deprive them of their seats in the public Councils: and whenever circumstances permitted, they availed themselves of the privileges of their civil appointments, to support all such public measures, as the American cause required.

See Appendix to this Chapter, No. III.

Although the Congress undertook to raise this body of troops, and to provide for their pay, clothing, and maintenance, and for other contingent charges, to the amount of one million for one year; yet, they prudently avoided laying any tax, or forming any particular fund, for sinking the currency to be issued by their authority.   It was much pressed by some, to lay a tax, and sink a certain proportion of the paper currency, which was to be so issued; but such a proposition was refused.   And in justification of the measure, it was urged that the *Association*, by which, the whole property of the Colony was bound to make good the contracts of the Provincial Congress, was, a sufficient security, that the public would make effectual provision for the public expenses under the authority of the Congress—that a tax ought not to be laid: for, how could the planter procure money, when he could not sell the produce of his estate, because, it could not be exported?   Besides, if a tax should be laid, and from the confusion of the times it was not collected, the paper currency would not only be greatly depreciated; but people, observing the tax for sinking gradually the emission could not be levied, would in all probability be so much alarmed, as that the circulation of the money would be entirely destroyed.   It was therefore holden to be the best policy, in the then situation of affairs, that no tax ought to be laid on the people for sinking the paper currency, during the civil convulsions; and, that so much paper money should be annually emitted, as the public service might require. As to this matter, the Congress contented themselves with passing a resolution, pledging the public faith to make full provision for calling in, and discharging those emissions of money; which were known under the denomination, of certificates of public debt: and which had been legislated on by the Commons-House of Assembly, so far as the reading of the schedule respecting the same the second time in that House, on the 1st day of June 1775. These things being done, the Provincial Congress adjourned itself on the 22d day of June: having previously delegated much of their authority to the Council of Safety, and the General Committee. And it was particularly recommended to the General Committee, to take effectual methods, to have the Association signed throughout the Colony: and to require from the non-subscribers, the reasons of their refusal.

The call of public affairs was so pressing, that before the Provincial Congress had adjourned, the Council of Safety held its first sitting on the 16th of June; when, Henry Laurens was chosen President, and Peter Timothy, Secretary of the same; the latter with a salary of one thousand pounds currency a year. They then proceeded to issue commissions for the army: upon which occasion, some of the members wished to have proper ones issued, under seal. But, by a great majority, the Council would not then hear of any thing looking so independent; for which reason, they only issued certificates, expressing that " *In pursuance of the Resolutions of the Provincial Congress, A. B. is Colonel, &c. of such a Regiment,*" &c. And such certificate was signed, by the members of the Council of Safety then present.* And in this manner, they commissioned all those officers, who had been appointed. Directions were also given by them, for the stamping and issuing of the money bills, which had been voted; and, on the 21st of June they issued orders, to the Colonels of foot, to recruit men, not exceeding fifty in a company; and to the Colonel of horse, not exceeding thirty.†

* See Appendix to this Chapter, No. IV.

† So zealous were the field officers, that recruits were obtained, before the above orders were issued for recruit ng—as, by Captain Mason's orderly book, for the second regiment, it appears, t at on the 20th of June 1775, 7 serjeants,

For a long time, John Stuart, the Superintendant of Indian Affairs, had been suspected of endeavouring to influence the Indians against the American cause.* A person from North-Carolina, had laid before the Committee of Intelligence, some particulars on this subject; which he had collected from the conversation and behaviour of the Catawba Indians, not only in their nation, but from some whom he met loaded with arms, in their return from Charlestown. These particulars, were given by the Committee of Intelligence to Mr. Drayton, as Chairman of the Secret Committee; and he laid them before the Provincial Congress. In addition to this information, the Superintendant suddenly quitted Charlestown, just before the Provincial Congress met on the first of June: and went to Savannah: at which place, an indistinct account of this matter respecting the Catawba Indians reached him. To justify himself in this particular, he wrote a letter to Colonel Howarth in Charlestown, couched in such terms as he thought might have a suitable effect. But this not satisfying his uneasy suspicions, he went to Colonel Mulryne's house at Thunderbolt, some miles below Savannah; and desired that the Colonel would wait on some gentlemen who were in opposition to Government, as it was then called in Georgia, "and beg that they would be so good as to call on the Superintendant at his house, as he wanted to have an opportunity of clearing himself of some aspersions; and likewise to lay before them

3 corporals, and 13 privates, were already recruited for the second regiment— and it is probable, the recruiting of the first regiment, was equally advanced.

* John Stuart, Esq. was sole Agent and Superintendant of his Majesty's Indian Affairs, for the Southern District; comprehending Virginia, North-Carolina, South-Carolina, Georgia, East Florida, and West Florida; in the Privy Councils of all which Provinces, he had a seat, by his Majesty's special writs of *mandamus*, directed respectively to the Governors or Commanders in Chief, of each of those Provinces. Of course, his influence over the Indians was extensive and imposing.

his letters with respect to Indian affairs." Colonel Mulryne accordingly, waited on Joseph Habersham and some other gentlemen who were men of respectability, and friends to the American cause; and they waited on the Superintendant agreeably to invitation, on the 15th day of June 1775. At this conference, the Superintendant was in great agitation of mind; and weakly laid before these gentlemen, his official letter book; in which he expressed himself to Mr. Cameron, his Agent among the Cherokee Indians in this Colony, to the following purport: "I have received information from General Gage, that certain persons at the Northward have been tampering with the Six Nations, and endeavouring to alienate their affections, from his Majesty. I mention this, to caution you against any thing of the kind, with you: and, that you will use your influence to dispose those people, to act in defence of his Majesty and Government, if found necessary." To this, it appeared, Mr. Cameron replied, " That Mr. Stuart's interest with the Indians was much greater; and that he was more beloved by them, than any other man. And that he (Mr. Cameron) had the vanity to think, that he could head any number he thought proper; whenever called upon, in support of his Majesty and Government." The above extracts are taken from a letter written on the 16th June, the day after the conference; by Mr. Joseph Habersham of Georgia, to his friend, Mr. Philotheos Chiffelle of this Colony; and are to be seen in the Appendix of this Chapter:* and Mr. Chiffelle, for the best of reasons, *the service of his country*, delivered it over to the popular public authority. Upon the particulars stated in this letter, Stuart was generally supposed to be guilty. However, before condemnation, it was thought advisable, he should be called upon to make his defence; and for this purpose,

---

* See Appendix, No. V.

the Congress ordered the Committee of Intelligence to write to him on the subject; supposing him to be still in Georgia: but the letter did not reach him, until his arrival in Augustine; from whence he returned an answer, explaining and justifying his conduct as well he could.*

During the time Superintendant Stuart, was at Savannah in Georgia, as above stated, intelligence had been received from a gentleman in Georgia to Captain Thomas Savage, who communicated the same to the public authorities; that a ship with several tons of gun-powder, was expected very shortly to arrive in Savannah. Of this powder, Governor Wright of Georgia, and the Superintendant, had provided a large supply to the Indians; and, as the traders were willing to supply the Indians, if leave could be obtained in England, for the exportation of what was required; the Governor of Georgia had been earnest in his applications to the Ministry on that head; as a great means, of keeping the Savages attached to the British Government. Leave was accordingly granted, by the British Ministry; of which, the Secret Committee of this Colony had notice. The Committee was also farther informed, that Governor Wright intended to lay hands on the powder at its arrival; and seize it for the service of the Crown. The Committee therefore were of opinion, that by getting the powder into their possession, the Governor and Superintendant would lose their influence with the Indians; as they would be unable to perform the engagements, they had made with them: and that in a proportionate degree our influence with them would be strengthened. That, if it were of consequence to Governor Wright, to seize the powder; it was of consequence to us, to prevent such seizure: and, if it were private property,

* See Appendix, No. VI.

we could pay for it.   At any rate, the Carolinians had occasion for it, in defence of their rights and liberties; and if it were property of the Crown, it was expedient to seize that into our own hands; which the King's servants, meant to employ against us.

Under these impressions, the Secret Committee issued a commission to Captains John Barnwell and Joyner of Beaufort, to use all means in their power, to seize the military stores on board the ship, which was so expected from England.   Upon the receipt of the commission and instructions, these two gentlemen, immediately embarked forty men well armed, in two large barges; and proceeding towards the mouth of Savannah River, they encamped on Bloody Point, in South-Carolina; in full view of Tybee Light-House, and of the approach from sea, to the Savannah bar.   A military station being so formed, in the vicinity of the town of Savannah in Georgia; and news also arriving at Savannah, that a large body of regular troops, were immediately to be raised in South-Carolina, threw the friends of Administration in Georgia, into apprehensions for their personal safety.   The report ran, that this party was sent to seize the Governor and the Superintendant.   Consternation seized them; the Governor got some friends to be on the look out, respecting any measures against himself; and without doubt, the report accelerated the departure of the Superintendant, for Augustine: which he successfully effected some little time after.

As it turned out, Captains Barnwell and Joyner with their men, had taken post earlier than was necessary at Bloody-Point: it was however, of considerable advantage to the public affairs.   For, even that small force, had a tendency to overawe the Royal Government in Georgia, particularly at Savannah: and was the means of giving new life and support there, to the friends of America. It was about this time, they formed a Committee—signed an Association—and ordered elections to be holden for delegates to a Congress, to be holden at Savannah, on the 4th day of July. They also, made large collections for the support of the people of Boston—declared, that their Colony should not be an asylum for any person or persons, who from their conduct should be considered, inimical to the common cause of America; or, should have drawn upon themselves, the disapprobation or censure of any of the Colonies.* They also, offered every kind of assistance and support, to Captains Barnwell and Joyner; and told them, if they desired it, they would immediately assist them, in taking the British armed schooner then in the river; and supposed to be waiting the arrival of the vessel from England, with the gun-powder. On this point, the Carolinians took time to consider; and Mr. Drayton and Mr. Middleton, two of the Secret Committee of five, of their own authority sent them private encouragement to fit out a schooner on the occasion, to be used as circumstances might require; and to endeavour to engage the people of Savannah, to join in the enterprize. Soon after, a letter was received by the Secret Committee from Captain Joyner, dated July 1st; stating, that he had engaged a schooner, and she would be ready for sea, in a few days. Arrangements were however made with the Georgians, by which, a junction of Carolinians and Georgians took place; and the schooner was commissioned by the Georgia Congress, then sitting. The British armed schooner was then lying outside of Savannah bar, ready for intercepting the vessel with the gun-powder; but, no sooner did she find the colonial schooner was on the point of coming down to her, than she immediately weighed anchor, and went to sea, with the

M'Call's Hist. of Georgia, vol. 2, page 45.

utmost precipitation. Had there been any longer delay in fitting out the schooner the powder would have been lost For, the schooner had scarcely taken post beyond the bar; when the expected vessel with the gun-powder, appeared in sight. The Carolinians on this occasion were commanded by Captains Barnwell and Joyner; and the Georgians by Captain Brown and Joseph Habersham. The vessel in sight proved to be a ship commanded by Captain Maitland;* and no sooner was the colonial schooner distinguished, than guessing her design, the ship tacked and stood to sea. The schooner however pursued, and brought her to; and with the assistance of the Carolina party and their barges, boarded her, and secured their prize. It was soon ascertained, that the gun-powder on board was private property; upon which, the Carolinians took what was intended for their merchants, and those of Augustine; and the Georgians possessed themselves of what belonged to their people. In this distribution of powder, Carolina obtained about 7,000 pounds, and Georgia about 9,000 pounds, of gunpowder.

During this transaction, which was kept secret, news had arrived from Philadelphia and Rhode-Island, of the battle of Bunker's Hill; that the Continental Congress had appointed General officers to command the American army, George Washington, being Commander in Chief; and, that they had issued two millions of dollars, in paper currency, upon the credit of the United Colonies. An Express vessel had also arrived from Philadelphia, laden with Indian corn as a deception; by which, a letter was brought from our Delegates in Congress, dated July 1st, 1775, and addressed to William Henry Drayton, Arthur Middle-

* Probably, the same Maitland, whose trading to Charlestown, had been interdicted by the General Committee. See *Ante*, pages 132 to 135.

ton, and Charles Cotesworth Pinckney, members of the Secret Committee. In it they stated, that by directions of the Continental Congress, the vessel was sent for gun-powder, for the use of the army then in the field; as from the frequent skirmishes in the vicinity of Boston, the Magazine had become so exhausted, as to make an immediate supply necessary. And the Secret Committee was thereby entreated to purchase all the powder that could be bought; and to dispatch the vessel back with it to Philadelphia, with all possible speed: together with as much as could be spared from the public stock in Carolina. It even implored the sending of damaged powder; and to collect and transmit salt-petre.* The purport of this letter had been kept secret, by the Secret Committee; but, having so happily succeeded in taking the powder from Maitland's ship, the Secret Committee now, July 12th, 1775, communicated the whole of their intelligence to the Council of Safety. They were both pleased, and astonished at the news; pleased, as relating to the seizure of the gun-powder; and astonished, to be informed that the gun-powder at the Northward, was reduced to a very small quantity; when they had supposed their magazines to have been well stored. As the call from the Continental Congress was urgent, it was proposed to make a literary application to Georgia, to assist in a loan of powder. But on farther consideration, it was deemed better, to send a deputation on the occasion: and William Henry Drayton, and Miles Brewton, were nominated for that purpose. These gentlemen, accordingly proceeded to Savannah, and applied to the Provincial Congress on the 15th of July, for a loan of gun-powder, agreeably to their instructions. Their errand being known, it was generally thought it would be fruitless. However, a Committee having been appointed on the application;

* See this Letter in Appendix to this Chapter, No. VII.

they reported, that of 12,700 pounds which they had, they ought to lend only 3,000 pounds; and the Congress were on the point of confirming the report, when the Deputies remonstrated in such terms, that they altered their opinion, and granted 5,000 pounds of powder. The same was in consequence of the grant, immediately delivered to the Deputies; and on the 21st day of July, the Express boat which had so come from Philadelphia for powder, was dispatched by the Secret Committee of South-Carolina, with the 5,000 pounds of gun-powder on board, to the Continental Congress at Philadelphia; and passing through the bar at North Edisto, she commenced her voyage for that destination. She, happily arrived at Philadelphia; and it was by the arrival there of this vessel, with the powder, that the American arms penetrated into Canada, and the seige of Boston was continued.

During the events which took place about this time, and of which mention has been made; it is of some consequence to observe, that in the course of June of this year, Laughlin Martin, and James Dealy, having behaved in a very improper manner respecting the General Committee and their proceedings, as well as respecting the Association; and having threatened Michael Hubart with death, unless he begged their pardon, for having justified the conduct of the Committee; he sent a petition respecting the affair, to the Committee of Correspondence of Charlestown. This Committee immediately transferred it to the Secret Committee of five; who having considered the same, ordered both Martin and Dealey to be tarred and feathered.* The order was promptly put in execution, by suitable agents; and they were both stripped

* The British 47th regiment, under the Command of Lieutenant-Colonel Nesbit, commenced this singular punishment on one of the inhabitants of the town of Billerica, in the State of Massachusetts, on the 8th of March 1775.— See The London Remembrancer, for 1775, page 62.

of their clothes, tarred, feathered, and carted through the streets of Charlestown; affording the first instance of such a spectacle in this Colony. This being done, the Secret Committee sent them on board a ship, ready to sail for England; Laughlin Martin was however, permitted to land again, and was discharged, on expressing his contrition in a public manner: but James Dealy, for an example, was sent away.* These summary measures have been supposed by writers, to have proceeded from the intemperate zeal of the populace; and there can be no doubt, but many of them took their rise from that source. But there can be as little doubt, this first commencement of so ludicrous and disgraceful a punishment, owed its origin in South-Carolina to this very case. And that it was sanctioned and directed by the Secret Committee, is equally clear; as the case is specially noted in the manuscript of William Henry Drayton, who was Chairman of that Committee, as having been done by the sanction of the same; and the original petition of Hubart, with the orders of the Secret Committee thereon, one of them in the known hand writing of the Chairman, Mr. Drayton, is now in the possession of the writer of these Memoirs. We need go no farther for authority to show, what vast power and confidence, were lodged in this Secret Committee of five; and particularly in the abilities, prudence, and enterprize of its leading members, William Henry Drayton, Arthur Middleton, and Charles Cotesworth Pinckney. And had the revolution not taken place, but colonial affairs, had settled down in a rebellion; there can be no doubt, but these distinguished patriots would have been marked out, as early victims to private persecution, and British vengeance. For, the councils of this Committee, were not paralized by timid opposition, as often happened in the Provincial

See the Petition and proceedings in the Appendix to this Chap. No. VIII.

Congress, Council of Safety, and General Committee; it was only necessary, that the emergency should arise calling on the Committee to act—for them to direct the blow: and it often fell, before the cause of it could have been surmised. Hence, the lead and tone, which this Secret Committee gave to the public opinion, and to public operations, was great, and decisive: and they much tended to concentrate the public energies, into a firm and manly opposition.

In pursuance of a recommendation of the Continental Congress, the 20th day of June was appointed for solemn fast and prayer, throughout the associated Colonies. Georgia, observed this day also. And. for the first time, a general fast, and prayer, on the same occasion, was observed through all united America, on the same day.

APPENDIX

TO

CHAPTER VII.

———

No. I.

COPIES of the Letter of Advice, respecting the Battle of Lexington; and, of the different Communications, from Committee to Committee.

Wallingford, Monday Morning, April 24, 1775.

DEAR SIR,

Colonel Wadsworth, was over in this place, most of yesterday; and has ordered twenty men, out of each company in his regiment; some of which, have already set off, and others go this morning. He brings accounts, which come to him authenticated, from Thursday in the afternoon. The King's troops being reinforced a second time, and joined as I suppose, from what I can learn, by the party who were intercepted by Colonel Gardner, were then encamped on Winter Hill; and were surrounded by twenty thousand of our men, who were entrenching. Colonel Gardner's ambush proved fatal to Lord Percy, and another general officer, who were killed on the spot, at the first fire. To counterbalance this good news, the story is, that our first man in command, (who he was I know not,) is also killed. It seems, they they have lost many men, on both sides. Colonel Wadsworth, had the accounts in a letter from Hartford. The country beyond here, are all gone off, and we expect it will be impossible to procure horses for our waggons; as they have or will, in every place employ themselves all their horses. In this place, they send an horse, for every sixth man; and, are pressing them for that purpose. I know of no way, but you must immediately send a couple of stout able horses, who may overtake us at Hartford possibly; where, we must return M. Noy's and Meloy's, if he holds out so far. Remember, the horses must be had, at any rate. I am in the greatest haste, your entire friend and humble servant,

JAMES LOCKWOOD.

N. B. Col. Gardner took nine prisoners; and twelve clubbed their firelocks, and came over to our party. Colonel Gardner's party, consisted of seven hundred, and the Regulars eighteen hundred, instead of twelve hundred, as we heard before. They have sent a vessel up Mystick River, as far as Temple's Farm; which is about half a mile from Winter Hill. These accounts being true, all the King's forces, except four or five hundred, must be encamped on Winter Hill. At the instance of the gentlemen of Fairfield, just departed from hence, this is copied *verbatim*, from the original, to be forwarded to that town.

ISAAC BEARS.

New-Haven, April 24, half past 9 o'clock, forenoon.
PIERPONT EDWARDS.

Fairfield, April 24, 3 o'clock, afternoon. A true copy, as rec'd per Express.

THAD. BURR,
AND'W ROWLAND,
ELIJAH ABEL.

Nawalk, April 24, 7 o'clock, afternoon. A true Copy, as rec'd per Express.

JOHN HAIT, jun.   SAM'L HUTTON,
DAVID WEBB,   DAN'L GRAY,
JONA. WARNING.

Greenwich, April 25, 3 o'clock, morning. The above is forwarded to the Committee of Correspondence, at New-York.

AMOS MEAD.

A true copy, rec'd in *New-York*, 2 o'clock, P. M. Tuesday, April 25, 1775. *

A true copy, rec'd at *Eliz-Town*, 7 o'clock in the evening; Tuesday, 25th April 1775.

JONA. HAMPTON,
Chairman of the Committee;
GEO. ROSS,
JOHN BLANCHARD.

A true copy, rec'd at *Woodbridge*, 10 of the clock, in the evening, Tuesday, April 25, 1775.

NATHANIEL HEARD,   *Three of the*
SAM'L PARKER,   *Committee.*
JONATHAN CLAWSON,

The above rec'd at New-Brunswick, the 25th April 1775, 12 o'clock at night.

WM. OAKE,
JAS. NEILSON,   *Committee.*
AZ. DUNHAM,

A true copy rec'd at Princetown, April 26, 1775, half past 3 o'clock in the morning.

THOMAS WIGGIN,   *Members of*
JONA. BALDWIN,   *Committee.*

The above rec'd at Trenton, on Wednesday morning, about half after 6 o'clock, and forwarded, at 7 o'clock.

SAM'L TUCKER,   *Three of the*
ISAAC SMITH,   *Committee.*
AB'M HUNT,

* No signature appears here for New-York, and it is accounted for in this manner. Mr. Lockwood's Letter, and all the signatures after it down to Baltimore are written in one hand writing on a sheet of paper; hence it is probable the papers with the original subscribers, were withholden at Baltimore, and were copied there on that sheet of paper; in doing which, they omitted inserting the subscribers at New-York. From Baltimore inclusive, the subscribers' names to the papers are in their own hand writing.

Philadelphia, 12 o'clock Wednesday rec'd, and forwarded at the same time by

LAMB. CADWALADER,
WM. BRAADFORD,
THO. PRYOR,
ISAAC MALCHER,
} *Committee for the City of Philadelphia.*

Chester, 4 o'clock, Wednesday, P. M. rec'd, and forwarded by

FRANCIS JOHNSTON,
ISAAC EYRE,
SAML. FAIRLAMB.

New-Castle, 9 o'clock, Wednesday evening, rec'd, and forwarded.

Z. V. LEUVENIGH,
STEPHEN SPENCER.

Wednesday night, Christeen Bridge, 12 o'clock, forwarded to Col. Thomas Couch, Esq. who rec'd it this moment, and he to forward it to Tobias Rudulph, Esq. Head of Elk, in Maryland.

S. PATTERSON.

Night and day to be forwarded.

27th April 1775, half past 4 o'clock, A. M. rec'd, and forwarded to Patrick Hamilton, Esq. in Charlestown by

TOBIAS RUDULPH, and
JOS. GILPIN.

Baltimore, April 27th, 1775, received 10 o'clock, P. M.

JOHN BOYD, *Clerk of Committee.*

A true copy rec'd in Annapolis, Friday, April 28th, 1775, half after 9 o'clock, A. M. and forwarded at 10 per Express.

MAT. TILGHMAN,
CH. CARROLL, of Carrollton,
CHAR. CARROLL,
J. HALL,
THS. JOHNSON, jun.
SAM'L CHASE,
} *Committee of Correspondence for Maryland.*

Friday, *Alexandria*, 8 o'clock, P. M.

We received the enclosed from Annapolis, at 6 o'clock, please forward it to Fredericksburgh. I am for self and the Committee of Correspondence, in this place,

Gentlemen, your hum. servt.

WM. RAMSAY.

To the Committee of Correspondence
     in Dumfries.

Gentlemen,

The enclosed came to hand this morning, about 10 o'clock. In one hour, I hired the bearer to convey it to your place, to the different Committees. For self, and the Committee of Correspondence in this place, I am, Gentlemen, your most obt. hum. servt.   WILLIAM CARR.

Dumfries, April 30, Sunday.
To the Committee of Correspondence at
     Fredericksburgh. By Express.

Fredericksburg, Sunday Evening, half past 4.

Gentlemen,

The enclosed arrived here, about an hour ago, and is forwarded to your Committee by your very hum. servts.

Js. MERCER,
GEO. THORNTON,
MANN PAGE, jun.   }   *Committee.*
HUGH MERCER,

King William, May 1st, 1775.

Gentlemen,

The enclosed arrived here to-day, and is forwarded to your Committee by your most obt. servt.

CARTER BRAXTON.

Surry County, May 2d, 1775.

Gentlemen,

The enclosed arrived here this evening, and is forwarded by your most obt. hum. servt.

ALLEN COCKE.

Williamsburg, 2d May 1775.

Gentlemen,

The enclosed is this moment come to hand, and I forward it to you by Express; with the request, of the Committee of Williamsburg that you will be pleased to forward the papers to the Southward, and disperse the material passages through all your parts. I am very respectfully,

Gentn. yr. mo. ob. Set.

Ro. C. NICHOLAS, Chairman.

Smithfield, May 3d, 1775. 5 o'ck. the morning.

The enclosed arrived here this morning, and is forwarded to your Committee of Correspondence by your humble serts.

ARTH'R SMITH,

NATHANIEL BURUNE.

To the Committee of the County of Nancimond, or any of them. An Express from Boston.

Gentlemen,

The enclosed is this moment come to hand, and we forward it to you by Express, with the request of the Committee of Nancimond, and you will be pleased to forward them to the Southward.

I am, Gent. your mo. ob. sert.

WILLIS RIDDUH,

WILLS CEOWPER.

Nancimond, May 3d, 1775.

To the Committee of Chowan, No. Carolina.

Gentlemen,

The enclosed papers we have just rec'd; and forward them by Express to you. To be sent to the Southward.

We are, Gent. your obt. ser.

THE COMMITTEE OF THE COUNTY OF CHOWAN.

May 3d, 1775.

To the Committee of Correspondence for the town of Edenton. By Express.

Edenton, May 4th, 9 o'ck. 1775.

Gentlemen,

The enclosed is this moment come to hand, and we forward to you by Express, with the request, that you will be pleased to forward the papers to the Committee of Craven County immediately, and disperse the material passages, through all your parts.

We are, Gentlemen,

Your obt. humb. servts.

THO. JONES,   JOS. BLOUNT,
CHAS. BONDFIELD,   Chairman.
JNO. GREEN,   ROBT. HARDY,
WILL'M BENNETT,   ROB. SMITH,
JNO. HAMILTON,   S. DICKINSON.

To the Committee of Beaufort County.

Beaufort County, May 6th, 1775.

Gentlemen,

The enclosed is this moment come to hand, and we forward to you by Express. with the request, that you will forward the different papers to the Southward immediately.

We are, Gentlemen, your obt. hum. serts.

ROGER OSMOND,
WM. BROWN.

To the Committee of Craven County.

Bath, 6th May 1775.

Dr. Sir,

In haste have sent to request you will peruse the enclosed papers; and that you will do, by opening the packet herewith sent, the moment it comes to your house. Get three or four of your Committee to write a line, and send the whole enclosed to the next Southward Committee, with the utmost dispatch. We are, dr. Sir, with regard, your most humb. servts.

WM. BROWN,
ROGER OSMOND.

To Abner Nash, Esq. or either of the Committee
for the County of Craven—Per Express.

New Bern, 6th of May 1775.

Gentlemen,

Th enclosed arrived here about an hour past, and is forwarded immediately to you; and desire you will keep a copy of

James Lockwood's letter.   And send them on as soon as possible to the Wilmington Committee.   We are, Gent. your obt. servts.

SAM. SMITH,   A. NASH.

B. COGDELL,   JOSEPH LEECH,

JOHN GREEN,   JOHN FONVIELLE,

WILLIAM TISDALE, WM. STANLY,

THOMAS M'LIN,   JAMES COOR.

N. B. We have enclosed our last paper, which gives an account of the first beginning of the battle; which please to send to Wilmington, &c. and send all the bundle of papers forward as soon as possible you can.

To the Committee of Onslow County.

Onslow, Sunday Morning, 10 o'ck. *May 7th.*

Gentlemen,

About an hour past, I rec'd the enclosed papers.   Disperse them to your adjoining County.   Keep a copy of James Lockwood's Letter.   And pray write us, what to do. We are for Onslow.

WM. CRAY,   JOS. FRENCH,

SETH WARD,   EDWD. WARD,

ROBERT SNEAD.

Inclosed is the last Gazette for Brunswick.

To the Wilmington and Brunswick Committees.

For Cornelius Harnett, Esq. Colonel John Ash, or any one of the Committee for Wilmington.   Express.

New-River, May 7th, 1775.   Rec'd, and forwarded by

WILLM. CRAY.

Dr. Sir,

I take the liberty to forward by Express, the enclosed papers, which were received at 3 o'clock this afternoon.   If you should be at a loss for a man and horse, the bearer will proceed as far as the Boundary-House.   You'll please direct to Mr. Marion, or any other gentleman to forward the packet immediately to the Southward, with the greatest possible dispatch.   I am with esteem,

Dr. Sir, your most ob. sert.

CORNS. HARNETT.

Wilmington, May 8th. 1775, 4 o'ck afternoon.

P. S. For Godsake send the man on without the least delay; and write to Mr. Marion to forward it by night, and by day.

To Richard Quince, Esq. Brunswick.

Brunswick, May 8th, 1775, 9 o'ck in the evening.
Mr. Isaac Marion,
    Sir,

        I take the liberty to forward by Express, the enclosed papers, which I just rec'd from Wilmington. And I must entreat you, to forward them to your community at George-Town, to be conveyed to Charles-Town, from yours with all speed. Inclosed is the news paper, giving an account of the beginning of the battle; and a letter of what happened after: pray don't neglect a moment in forwarding.

                I am your humb. sert.

                        RICH'D QUINCE.

To Isaac Marion, Esq. at the Boundary.

Dear Sir,

    Tho' I know you stand in no need of being prompted when your country requires your service; yet, I cannot avoid writing to you, to beg you to forward the papers containing such important news. And pray order the Express you send, to ride night and day. I am, dr. Sir, in the greatest haste, your most ob. servt.

                        R. HOWE.

    8th May 1775.
Isaac Marion, Esq. Boundary.

Boundary, May 9th, 1775, *Little River.*
Gentlemen of the Committee,

    I have just now received Express, from the Committees of the Northward Provinces, desiring I would forward the enclosed packet to the Southern Committees. As yours is the nearest, I request for the good of your country, and the welfare of our lives and liberties, and fortunes, you'll not lose a moment's time; but dispatch the same to the Committee of Georgetown: to be forwarded to Charles-Town. In mean time, am Gentn.

            Your oblg. hum. ser. &c.

                    ISAAC MARION.

To Danness Hankins, Josias Allson and Samuel
   Dwight, Esquires, and Messrs. Francis & John
   Allston, Gentlemen of the Committee for
   Little River.

Gentlemen,

The enclosed papers were just now delivered to me, by an Express from Little River. I make not the least doubt, but you will forward them with the utmost dispatch, to the General Committee at Charles-Town. I am Gentn. your very hum. sert.

BENJA. YOUNG.

Wednesday, 1 o'ck 10*th May* 1775.

To Paul Trapier, Esq
    Chairman of the Committee at Georgetown.

Gentn.

We have received your letter, and shall be careful to execute with all the diligence in our power; whatever you have recommended. We send you by Express, a Letter and news paper, with momentous intelligence this instant arrived. We are your humble servants,

PAUL TRAPIER,
S. WRAGG,
P. TRAPIER, jun.
ANTHONY BONNEAU.

½ past 6 Wednesday Evening.
The Committee of Intelligence in Charlestown,
  to the care of the Hon'ble William Henry
  Drayton, Esq. Per Express.

——◆——

No. II.

The Provincial Association.

South-Carolina.

The actual commencement of hostilities against this Continent by the British troops, in the bloody scene on the 19th of April last, near Boston—the increase of arbitrary impositions from a wicked and despotic Ministry—and the dread of insurrections in the Colonies—are causes, sufficient to drive an oppressed people, to the use of arms. We, therefore, the Subscribers, inhabitants of South-Carolina, holding ourselves bound by that most sacred of all obligations, the duty of good citizens towards an injured country, and thoroughly convinced, that, under our present distressed circumstances, we shall be justified before God and man, in resisting force by force—do unite ourselves, under every tie of religion and honour, and associate as a band in her defence, against every foe—hereby, solemnly engaging, that whenever our Continental or Provincial Councils, shall decree it necessary, we will go forth, and be ready to sacrifice our lives and fortunes to secure her freedom and safety. This obligation, to continue in force, until a reconciliation shall take place, between Great Britain and America; upon constitutional principles—an event, which we most ardently desire. And, we will hold all those persons inimical to the liberty of the Colonies, who shall refuse to subscribe this Association.

☞ See The Remembrancer, page 264, published at London for 1775; wherein the above Instrument is published at length.

No. III.

Officers of the first and second regiments of Infantry; and of the regiment of Horse Rangers.

Field Officers of the first Regiment.

Christopher Gadsden, Colonel—Isaac Huger, Lieutenant-Colonel—Owen Roberts, Major.

Field Officers of the second Regiment.

William Moultrie, Colonel—Isaac Motte, Lieutenant-Colonel—Alexander M'Intosh, Major.

Captains of the first and second Regiments.

Charles Cotesworth Pinckney, Barnard Elliott, Francis Marion, William Cattell, Peter Horry, Daniel Horry, Adam M'Donald, Thomas Lynch, William Scot, John Barnwell, Nicholas Eveleigh, James M'Donald, Isaac Harleston, Thomas Pinckney, Francis Huger, William Mason, Edmund Hyrne, Roger Parker Saunders, Charles Motte, Benjamin Cattell.

Field Officers of the Regiment of Rangers.

William Thomson, Lieutenant-Colonel——James Mayson, Major.

Captains of Rangers.

Samuel Wise, Eli Kershaw, Edward Richardson, Ezekiel Polk, Robert Goodwin, Thomas Woodward, John Caldwell, Moses Kirkland, John Purvis.

First Lieutenants in the first and second Regiments.

Anthony Ashby, James Ladson, Richard Singleton, Thomas Elliott, William Olyphant, John Vanderhorst, Robert Armstrong, John Blake, Glen Drayton, Richard Shubrick, Richard Fuller, Thomas Lessesne, Benjamin Dickenson, William Charnock, John Moat, Joseph Joor, James Peronneau, John A. Walter, Thomas Moultrie, Alexander M'Queen.

☞ The Commissions for Second Lieutenants, were given to the Captains of each Company, to fill up with suitable persons.

First Lieutenants of the Regiment of Rangers.

John Lewis P. Imhoff, Charles Heatley, Allen Cameron, Richard Winn, John Donaldson, Hugh Middleton, Lewis Dutarque, Francis Boyakin, Samuel Watson.

☞ It is probable the Commissions for Second Lieutenants in the Rangers, were given to the Captains of each troop, to fill up with suitable persons; as was done with the Captains of the first and second Regiments of Infantry.

☞ Of the above military officers, Christopher Gadsden, William Moultrie, Isaac Huger, and Francis Marion, became General officers, during the American war. And Charles Cotesworth Pinckney and Thomas Pinckney, have since that time served in the armies of the United States of America, as Major Generals.

No. IV.

One of the first Military Commissions, which were issued by the Council of Safety.

South-Carolina.

In pursuance of the resolutions of the Provincial Congress; we do certify, that William Moultrie, Esquire, is Colonel of the Second Regiment, in the

Provincial Congress.   Dated the seventeenth day of June 1775.

William Williamson, James Parsons, Henry Laurens, Thomas Bee, Thomas Heyward, jun. Rawlins Lowndes, William Henry Drayton, Benjamin Elliott, Charles Pinckney, Arthur Middleton, Miles Brewton, Thomas Ferguson.

———◆———

No. V.

A Letter from Joseph Habersham, to Philotheos Chiffelle.

Savannah, Friday, 16th June 1775.

DEAR SIR,

The alarming height to which our disputes with the mother country, has at length arisen, and the many detestable arts that are made use of, by our enemies to involve us in one general scene of distress, are motives sufficient to stimulate every honest man, to use his best endeavours to counteract the wicked designs of our enemies; which, will be a sufficient excuse for my troubling you with this: as, it conveys a piece of intelligence that I think very interesting; and should, when thought proper be made known to the good people of your province, as well as our own.

Mr. John Stuart, who is now at Colonel Mulryne's house at Thunderbolt, desired that the Colonel would wait on some gentlemen, who are in opposition to Government, as it is called here; and beg that they would be so good as to call on the Superintendant at his house yesterday; as he wanted to have an opportunity of clearing himself of some aspersions; and likewise to lay before us his letters with respect to Indian affairs. Accordingly, four or five of us malecontents attended; when Mr. Stuart began with informing us, that he had received letters by the last post, from Charles-Town, which made him very uneasy: as a report had been circulated there, that he had been tampering with certain Indians, at which, he manifested not a little surprise. He showed us the letter he received from Charles-Town, and his answer to Col. Howarth; whom he has desired to make the contents public: and which he means, a justification of his conduct. So far, every thing appeared to me plausible; but unluckily for Mr. Stuart, he produces a number of his letters, to his Deputy, Mr. Cameron, and the answers. In one of which he writes thus: "I have received information from Gen. Gage, that certain persons at the Northward have been tampering with the Six Indian Nations, and endeavouring to alienate their affections, from his Majesty. I mention this, to caution you against any thing of the kind, with you; and, that you will use your influence to dispose those people, to act in defence of his Majesty and Government, if found necessary." Mr. Cameron's answer, was couched nearly in the following words, (I do not differ I am positive as to the substance, tho' I may in some of the words:) " That Mr. Stuart's interest with the Indians was much greater; and that he was more beloved by them, than any other man. And that he (Mr. Cameron) had the vanity to think, that he could head any number he thought proper; whenever called upon, in support of his Majesty and Government."

Now, Sir, I shall leave you to make your own comments on the above; tho' I will acquaint you, with what I said to him on its being read—that we were at no loss to know what was meant by assisting or acting *in defence of his Majesty and Government, if found necessary;* for, as we were not at war with the French or Spaniards, it could not be against them, that they were meant to act. Mr. Cameron further tells Mr. Stuart, that the Traders, must by some means or other, get ammunition among them; or otherwise, they may become troublesome to him, for the want of it. I do not well know, how far I am at liberty to make this public; but, as Mr. Stuart has wrote to Mr. Howarth in order to justify himself, in the eyes of the people of Carolina, I think as a farther justification, he should produce his letters to and from Cameron. Mr. Stuart's letter, that contains the foregoing paragraph, is dated about the middle of January last; and is copied from among a number of others, in a large book, bound in calf.

You may give the Secret Committee intelligence of this; and, if they should think it of sufficient importance to claim a demand from Mr. Stuart, of these letters, and he should then hesitate, and will not grant what they request; and, it should further be thought necessary; I can find four persons, besides myself, to avow what I have said to be true: as, any thing of this kind, should come well authenticated.

We are going on here tolerably well, with respect to our political proceedings; and I hope, soon to convince the world, that Georgia will not take advantage of her sister Colonies, in the present disputes.

I am, dear Sir,
Your most obt. servt.

JOSEPH HABERSHAM.

Philotheos Chiffelle, Esq.

No. VI.

Copy of a letter from the Hon. John Stuart, Esq.
Superintendant of Indian Affairs, to William Henry
Drayton, James Parsons, John Lewis Gervais, Arthur
Middleton, William Tennent, and Thomas Heyward,
jun. Esqrs. Committee of Intelligence at Charlestown.
This letter was published in February 1776; by order
of the Provincial Congress: together with other letters
which had been intercepted on the taking of Moses
Kirkland: and which he was carrying from Augustine
to General Gage—some of which, are also introduced
here.

St. Augustine, 18th July 1775.

Gentlemen,

     I am now to acknowledge the receipt of your
letters of 21st and 29th June, by Express. In the
former, you are pleased to acquaint, by order of the
Provincial Congress, that I stand in a very unfavorable
light with the public; but, you have not thought proper to acquaint me, of what I am accused; and upon
evidence, the public has conceived an unfavorable
opinion of me. You must be conscious of the impropriety of desiring me, to answer in my own vindication, to a charge which is not stated. And here, I
must beg permission to say, that my services to your
Province, have merited very different sentiments, than
you tell me, they entertain of me—and much better
treatment, than I have received.

     I am sorry that it is not in my power to comply with
your requisition, of sending you copies of all my
correspondence on Indian affairs with Administration,

the Commander in Chief of his Majesty's forces, and
my Deputies. But, I hope it will be sufficient to
assure you, most faithfully, that I have always considered myself, to be most effectually discharging my
duty to the King, and fulfilling his intentions; when
employed in securing the friendship and affection of
the Indian nations, to his Majesty's provinces; and, in
preventing, as far as in my power, jealousies arising
from encroachments and mutual violences. And the
long uninterrupted tranquillity which your frontiers
have enjoyed, without any expense to the province,
during the past thirteen years of my Superintendency
evinces, that my endeavours have not been unavailing.
And, this will appear, in a clearer point of view, if you
will contrast the state of Indian affairs, and the expense to the province, during the above period, with
that of the thirteen preceding years. I never have
received any orders from my superiors, which by the
most tortured construction could be interpreted to
spirit up, or employ the Indians to fall upon the frontier inhabitants; or, to take any part in the disputes
between Great Britain, and her Colonies. And I do
not know, that any part of my conduct, through all
the various scenes of my life, can fix upon me the
imputation of cruelty or inhumanity; or, induce a
belief, that I could wantonly use any influence with
Indians, to make them fall upon innocent people.

Yet, such an opinion has been most industriously
propagated; although, it is absolutely impossible, that
it could, or can be supported, by any evidence of the
least credibility. And, I will venture to say, that
every one, and all of you, do, in your consciences
believe, the charge to be false. I therefore think, I
have a right to call upon you, as men of honour, to
efface the impression it has made on the minds of the
people.

With respect to the warm expressions in my letter to Col. Howarth, I cannot help thinking them in some measure justified, by your being authorized by the Congress to tell me, that I stand in a very unfavorable light with the public. What, can have placed me in such an unfavorable light, but calumnious falsehoods, which endangered my life and property? I know not the authors, and shall not repeat illiberal epithets: you know, what are suitable to such characters.

You are pleased to say, that my estate is a security for the good behaviour of the Indians, in the Southern Department. It is disagreeable, that my all should be held by so precarious a tenure as their behaviour; which, in a great measure will depend upon the conduct of the inhabitants of the Provinces: yet, you must allow, that holding my personal safety and life itself on such terms, would be more so. His Majesty's service, will necessarily detain me here some months longer.

My little estate in your province, was purchased under the protection of the laws of my country. I have always considered both life and fortune, as pledged for my dutiful obedience to the King, and the laws. As I am not conscious of having transgressed, I hope for that security to my property, which is inseparable from the idea of a virtuous and well policed community: and, as power is now in your hands, I doubt not, but I shall find this security from your justice.

Your letter of the 29th, renders it necessary for me to tell you; that some time before I left Charlestown, I had received information of a design to seize my person; and in order to give a colour to such a step, a report was industriously propagated, of my having sent to call down the Indians. Immediately after my removal from Charlestown to my plantation on Lady's Island, it was reported, that in consequence of my orders, thirty-four families on the frontiers, had been murdered by the Cherokees. When I was at Georgia, I had information that Captain Joyner and Mr. Barnwell, two members of the Provincial Congress, had returned to Beaufort; where, by most defamatory reports and insinuations, they endeavoured to blacken my character, and render me obnoxious to the people; giving out, that my having called down the Indians, was proven before the Congress—that great quantities of arms and ammunition were shipped, for me to arm the Negroes, and Indians—that, it was now discovered, that I had sold Fort London; and was the instrument of getting the garrison massacred: and Captain Joyner showed at the public musterfield, in St. Helena, printed bills, containing the above, and other false accusations.

From thence, they went to Savannah; and in the night had a meeting with the Committee; of which, Sir James Wright gave me notice early next morning; and advised me to take steps for the security of my person. I accordingly prevailed upon Captain Grant, of the St. John armed schooner, to land me at St. Augustine, where the business of my department called me. But before I embarked, I saw some of the members of the Committee, and read to them some part of my correspondence with my Deputies, which they communicated to you. They candidly told me, that the people were much enraged; and, they could not answer for the safety of my person. I then thought it high time, to provide for my safety; and went on board the St. John armed schooner, at Cockspur.

I have since been informed, that two boats were sent down the river in pursuit of me: and, from the schooner I saw several armed canoes, said to be commanded by Captain Joyner and Mr. Barnwell; who before they left Beaufort, gave out, that they were to receive and conduct me back to Charlestown. The armed schooner however proceeded the next day for this place; where, I landed in a very weak condition; and this, gentlemen, you are pleased to call a precipitate departure—tho' I shall ever consider it, as a most fortunate escape.

I am, Gent'n,

Your most obt. hum. servt.

JOHN STUART.

A true copy from the original.

PETER TIMOTHY,

Secretary to the Congress.

Copy of a Letter from John Stuart, Superintendant, &c. to General Gage.

St. Augustine, 3d October 1775.

SIR,

Last night, I had the honour of receiving your Excellency's letter of the 12th of September; and shall pay *the strictest attention to your commands* contained in it. Nothing in my power, shall be neglected, to *forward the interest of Government,* and *your Excellency's views.*

Since writing my last letter by Col. Kirkland, I have received by the way of Savannah, a copy of a talk from the Cherokees to Mr. Cameron, which I now enclose. It shows their disposition, which I shall by all means cultivate; for which purpose my brother is preparing to set off for the Creek, and afterwards for the Cherokee nation.

It occurs to me, that it will no longer be *good policy* to foment the difference between the Choctaws and Creeks; for, *while they continue at war*, it will be difficult or even impossible, to get *the Creeks to act*, in his Majesty's service; by which, they must expose their women and children, to the attack of their enemies. I shall *impatiently* wait for your Excellency's ideas upon this subject, which I humbly submit; in the mean time, I shall send the necessary instructions throughout the district. I shall immediately take steps to get some Indians here; which will be an acquisition to this place, in its present weak state; and I have been for some time past, using all possible means, of supplying myself with necessaries, for engaging the Indians firmly in his Majesty's interest. I am apprehensive, I shall find difficulty in getting a supply of provisions.

I have the honour of being with the utmost respect, Sir, your Excel. most. obt. and most hum. servt.
JOHN STUART.
To his Excel. Gen. Gage.

Copy of another Letter from John Stuart, to General Gage.

SIR,

Col. Kirkland will acquaint your Excellency, that a great majority of the frontiers, and back inhabitants of Carolina, are attached to, and inclined to support Government. In such circumstances, I conceive, that an *indiscriminate attack, by Indians*, would be contrary to your Excellency's idea; and might do much harm. But I shall dispose them to join in executing *any concerted plan*; and to act with, and assist, their well disposed neighbours.

The Alltachaway Indians, are now here; and I now look *with impatience*, for answers to my dispatches to the different nations, which I have reason to expect every hour.

I have the honour of being, most respectfully, Sir, Your Excellency's most obt. most hum. servt.
JOHN STUART.
3d October 1775.
To his Excellency General Gage.

"The foregoing are printed from copies certified, by *Charles Thompson, Esq.* Secretary to the Continental Congress, to be taken from the original letters.
" PETER TIMOTHY,
" Secretary to the Congress of South-Carolina."

———

No. VII.

Letter written by Henry Middleton, Thomas Lynch, Christopher Gadsden, John Rutledge, and Edward Rutledge, Delegates from South-Carolina to the Continental Congress, to William Henry Drayton, Arthur Middleton, and Charles Cotesworth Pinckney, Members of the Secret Committee at Charlestown.

Philadelphia, July 1st, 1775.
Gentlemen,

By directions of the Continental Congress, we have sent the vessel, by which this goes, to procure from you, a quantity of gun-powder, for the use of the armies actually in the field, for the service of America. The frequent severe skirmishes in the neighbourhood of Boston, have so exhausted their magazines, that an immediate supply, is absolutely necessary.

We entreat you, to purchase all that can be bought in town; and, to dispatch this vessel, with it for this place, as soon as possible; together, with as much as can be spared out of the public stock, without danger to your own safety.

Should there be any damaged powder on hand, please send it also; as, it may be recovered here.

By one of the resolutions enclosed to the General Committee, you'll see, that it is recommended to the Southern Colonies, to secure all the salt-petre that can be got; as well from the stores, as from private persons; which, as you have no powder-mills erected, or persons skilful in making gun-powder, we would advise may be sent to be manufactured here.

Should you be able to send more than four thousand weight of powder, we would wish the overplus might be sent by some other opportunity.

In order to prevent suspicion, we have sent **** bushels of Indian corn in this vessel; which may be exchanged for rice; in which, the casks of powder may be concealed so perhaps, as to prevent suspicion, should she unhappily be unable to avoid being over-taken by a cruiser.

The utmost secresy and dispatch are absolutely necessary.

As large quantities of powder, will be wanted; we strongly recommend, that you continue to import all that you can: and think it probable, that large quanti-ties might be got, from the Government of the

Havana; as we can find no application there, from any of these Colonies.

We are, Gentlemen,

Your most obt. servts.

HENRY MIDDLETON,

THO. LYNCH,

CHRIST. GADSDEN,

J. RUTLEDGE,

E. RUTLEDGE.

——◆——

No. VIII.

The following Petition, was transferred over to the Secret Committee; who acted upon it.

To the Honourable Members of the Committee of Correspondence at Charlestown, the humble petition of Michael Hubart, showeth:

That upon the 2d day of June, your petitioner being in the house of Thomas Nicoll in King-street, a certain James Dealey came in, and told there was good news come to town. Being asked what was it, he answer that a number of arms was sent over to be distributed amongst the Negroes, Roman Catholics, and Indians. Upon which, your petitioner replied, he thought it was very bad news, that Roman Catholics and Savages should be permitted to join and massacre Christians. Upon which, Dealey struck his breast and swore "he was a Roman Catholic, and that he had arms, and would get arms, and use them as he pleased." Your petitioner, went home to his house; and shortly after, came in said Dealey and a certain Laughlin Martin, and A—— Reed.

After sitting down a little, Laughlin Martin arose, and said, " So, Mr. Hubart, you'll not allow Roman Catholics to carry guns." Your petitioner answered, that his circumstances were too small, to forbid any party or sect to carry arms. Martin then damned your petitioner, for a false faced villain; and declared, he would believe Dealey sooner than me; at same time, ordered said Dealey to drag your petitioner out of the house, and pull him to pieces. At the same time standing with a drawn cutteau in his hand, swearing, if he did not, that he (Martin) would have blood himself. Dealey then dragged your petitioner into a shop in front of the house, holding him by the throat, until released by the aforesaid Reed. But, upon being released, said Martin came up with his cutteau drawn, threatening to put your petitioner to immediate death; when your petitioner falling upon his knees, begged his life: your petitioner's wife and children begging at same time, to spare the life of their father and husband. Your petitioner then arose, and went into the next room; but was still followed by Martin, who vowed to God if your petitioner did not beg pardon of Dealey, he would that instant cut off his head. Upon which, your petitioner to save his life, did ask his (Dealey's) pardon.

Martin, then declared he was a Roman Catholic; and vowed to God, to cut off the head of any person, who said, he should not carry arms.

After which, said Martin called for some drink; and drank of it, with Dealey and Reed; and one of his toasts was, " *Damnation to the Committee, and their proceedings.*"

Your petitioner has prosecuted them as law directs. But, as the times appears to be very troublesome, and numbers of enemies both to the Protestant interest.

and the present cause, are lurking amongst us; your
petitioner hopes, that you will inquire into such parts
of the transaction, as concerns the public; and your
petitioner as in duty bound shall ever pray.

MICHAEL HUBART.

SECRET, tar and feather him.*

Passed the Secret Committee, and ordered to be
put in Execution.†

☞ On the back of the Petition, is written in the
real hand writing of William Henry Drayton, the
Chairman of the Secret Committee, the following, viz.

LOCKLIN MARTIN,‡

JAMES DEALEY.§

* This order, is in a disguised hand; supposed to be that of William Henry
Drayton, Chairman of the Secret Committee.

† This certificate, is also in a disguised hand; supposed to be that of Edward
Weyman, one of the members of the Secret Committee.

‡ To land, and be discharged; upon his expressing his contrition in the most
public manner.

§ Send away.

CHAPTER VIII.

The Council of Safety, plans an Expedition for seizing Gun-powder from a vessel off Augustine bar—which succeeds—The Council, direct Major Williamson to enter into a correspondence with Alexander Cameron, Stuart's Deputy for Indian Affairs—The Swallow Packet arrives from England—The Mail is seized—containing letters and Instructions to the Provincial Governors—Letters from Governor Wright of Georgia, to Admiral Graves, and General Gage, are also intercepted—Copies of them sent to Congress, North-Carolina, and Georgia—George Wagner and Felix Long, sent among the Germans in the interior, to remove their misunderstandings, and conciliate their affections—They return unsuccessful—The spirit of disaffection in the interior, increases—Colonel Thomas Fletchall is the leader of the party—some account of him—The Council of Safety, adopt measures respecting him—His letter in reply—The General Committee, cause the Non-Subscribers in Charlestown to the Provincial Association, to appear before them —require their reasons for not subscribing—Twenty-two Non-Subscribers appear, and give their reasons— which are not deemed satisfactory—They are declared inimical to the Liberties of the Colonies—are ordered to surrender their arms—and except Mr. Wragg, are restricted to the limits of Charlestown— Their names are published—The Association is tendered for signature to Lieutenant-Governor William Bull—his conduct thereon—Fort Charlotte on Sa-

vannah River, is taken possession of; containing
arms and powder—Parties, in the Council of Safety
—Dorchester is surveyed, preparatory to making it a
place of arms—Languor of the Council of Safety—
It orders twenty cannon to be mounted—Issues,
Militia Commissions—Orders the cannon platforms
to be repaired—Resolves to arm three schooners—
Major Mayson, with a troop of Rangers under Cap-
tain Moses Kirkland, arrives at Ninety-Six Court-
House with some of the powder and lead, which had
been taken at Fort Charlotte—Captain Kirkland
determines to change sides, and sends an Express to
Col. Fletchall—Kirkland's troop withdraws from
Mayson—Major Robinson, and the Cunningham's,
with a party of men, proceed against Mayson—they
recover the powder and lead—and throw Mayson into
Gaol—Captain Kirkland, joins Fletchall's party—
Conduct of Col. Fletchall, and his men—He corres-
ponds with Governor Campbell, who promises re-
wards; encouraging the disaffection to the American
cause—The Council of Safety send William Henry
Drayton and the Rev. William Tennent, as Commis-
sioners into the disaffected settlements; to explain the
public disputes, and to reconcile the people to the
American cause—Kirkland proceeds to the Governor
in Charlestown; and returns to Fletchall with pa-
pers, and military commissioners—The Commission-
ers, take separate routes, into the disaffected country.

IT has been shown, that a portion of the powder
taken from Captain Maitland's ship, was sent by
South-Carolina to Philadelphia; to be at the disposal
of the Continental Congress. And, that by a due
application of it, the American arms penetrated into
Canada; and the seige of Boston, was continued.

Upon this occasion, the Council of Safety, becoming acquainted with the great scarcity of powder; and

hearing there was a considerable quantity at the Island
of New-Providence; it was moved, and carried in the
Council, but with much difficulty, that an attempt
should be made to seize it.   Every thing being in forwardness for the expedition, the sloop Commerce
belonging to New-York, was taken into service, and
was armed for the occasion; and on the 24th July
1775, Clement Lempriere was appointed and commissioned by the Council to command in the said sloop,
"over all and every person and persons engaged to
embark on board the said sloop, under the authority
of the Council of   afety;" and on the 25th July, he
received his instructions for the enterprize.*   On the
26th, Captain Lempriere sailed over Charlestown bar
in the Commerce; and on the 28th July, he arrived at
Beaufort; where he landed his stores and proceeded
to clean his vessel.   While performing this duty, he
received directions from the Council, to proceed with
all dispatch towards Augustine, and cruize off its bar,
for Captain Lofthouse; who was daily expected from
London, with a large quantity of gun-powder.   In
pursuance of these orders, Captain Lempriere took
his departure in the sloop Commerce from Beaufort,
on the 31st day of July 1775; and going through
Skull-Creek, and the inland passage, he sailed out of
Tybee on the 2d day of August; and on the 7th inst.
at night, he made the Mattanzes, to the southward of
Augustine bar, where he anchored.   On the next
morning, he ran down towards the bar of Augustine;
where, he saw a vessel at anchor: which proved to
be the brigantine Betsey, commanded by Captain
Alvere Lofthouse, from London; and fortunately, the
very vessel, for which his cruize was directed.   On
boarding her, the object of his wishes was obtained;
for, much powder and military stores were on board.
One hundred and eleven barrels, and one half barrel,

See Appendix to this Chapter, No. I

and thirty small kegs, of gun-powder were immediately transshipped from the Betsey, to the Commerce; and this was effected by Captain Lempriere
against the brig armed with two pieces of cannon, and
having on board twelve soldiers from St. Augustine,
besides eight seamen, belonging to the brigantine, the
Captain and two mates, and steward; amounting to
twenty-four in the whole—while Captain Lempriere's
force, was only twenty-one whites, and five blacks.
In the report which was made to the Council by Captain John Hatter, who was one of the party, he says,
" Our situation was such on this occasion, that we
thought it most prudent to bribe the men; which we
did, with one hundred pounds currency; and the Captain accepted a draught for one thousand pounds Sterling, for the powder, drawn on Mr. John Edwards, of
Charlestown.*   And at half past eleven A. M. after
spiking up two pieces of cannon, that were mounted
on board said brigantine, we re-embarked our men, and
made sail."

Pursuing his return voyage from thence, on the 10th
of August, Captain Lempriere made Tybee; and
through Skull-Creek, he arrived at Port Royal: from
whence, an Express was immediately dispatched to
the Council of Safety, in Charlestown; and at three
o'clock P. M. on the same day, the powder was landed
at Beaufort.

On the 15th, an Express came from Charlestown
with accounts, that the armed vessel from Augustine,
was in pursuit of the Commerce; and on the 16th
sundry militia companies of Colonel Bull's regiment,

* Henry Laurens, President of the Council of Safety, had privately furnished Captain Lempriere, with that order, on John Edwards, the Treasurer,
at Charlestown, *as a cloak*, against what might be supposed a robbery, by a
commission under his hand.   Lempriere left this, in the hurry of sailing off
with the powder; as he was pursued from Augustine, by a British armed vessel.

were marched into Beaufort to protect the powder.
On the 17th, a detachment of artillery arrived from
Charlestown; and on the 18th, Capt. William Cattell
with fifty men of regular troops also arrived from
thence, in consequence of orders he had received from
Colonel William Moultrie, on the 14th, for that purpose.*   A small portion of this powder, was left at
Beaufort; and the remainder, amounting to ninety-
one barrels of gun-powder, was put on board of the
vessel Success; which, with a guard on board, proceeded through the inland passage from Beaufort, and
through Wappoo Cut into Ashley River; from whence
she proceeded up Cummings' Creek, landing the
powder at the bluff there, on Harleston's Green, on
the 23d day of August;† to the great honour of those
who had planned and directed the expedition; and of
those patriotic citizens, who had volunteered on the
occasion.   The whole of the powder taken from
Captain Lofthouse by Captain Lempriere, was equal
to about 11,900 pounds weight; which, with 3,074
pounds original acquisition taken from the King's
Magazines in Charlestown and its vicinity, and purchases, and 7,000 pounds taken from Captain Maitland's vessel; amounted in the whole, to 21,974
pounds of gun-powder, with which the Colony was at
this time supplied.   And being so stocked with this
article, the expedition to New-Providence was laid
aside.   We have been thus particular, to bring into
one view, the actual situation of Carolina, as it stood
on the 23d day of August 1775, respecting that article
of the first necessity, gun-powder: when it may be
said, the Colony was in some measure provided with
the means of defence.   And, for the same reason, we
have been obliged to relate, matters which passed in
the month of August; before we had finished with

---

* Moultrie's Memoirs, vol. I. page 86.

† See Appendix, No. II.

those, which happened in June and July. We shall
therefore return to the month of June.

In the latter end of this month, the Council of
Safety turning their attention to Indian affairs, on the
26th day of June 1775, instructed Major Williamson
residing in Ninety-Six District, to lay before Mr.
Alexander Cameron, one of John Stuart, the Superintendant's Agents for Indian Affairs with the Chero-
kees, the late advices from Georgia, relating to Mr.
Stuart and Mr. Cameron: and to endeavour to learn
Mr. Cameron's fixed determination on that subject.
And if it should be in our favour, to assure Mr.
Cameron, " the public will not only, not permit him
to be injured, in case Mr. Stuart should withdraw his
salary; but, will be mindful of his services.   But, if
Major Williamson should " have cause to conclude,
that Mr. Cameron's determination is inimical to this
Colony, the public will support Mr. Williamson in
any steps he shall take, to prevent Mr. Cameron's
executing any plan, that may be calculated to involve
this Colony in distress."*   The Major, upon this
repaired to Keowee, to Mr. Cameron; who had gone
there from Lochaber, his residence in Ninety-Six
District, upon a rumour that he was to be apprehended: and meeting with Mr. Cameron, he delivered
to him, what he had in charge.   Mr. Cameron then
gave the strongest assurances to Major Williamson,
that he never understood Mr. Stuart's letter to him in
February last, or at any other time, to be desiring him
to induce the Cherokee Indians, to fall upon the Province of South-Carolina; but, only to endeavour to
keep the said Indians firmly attached to his Majesty's
Government.   And, if at any future time, he should
receive such orders, he never would be the means of
inducing them to fall upon defenceless women and

children—and believes, before he would execute such
orders, he would resign his office.   He spurned, at
the idea of a bribe.   Major Williamson, then showed
him, the extracts of Mr. Stuart's letters to him, in
January last, with his (Cameron's) answer to Stuart;
upon which he said, that from the whole tenor of Mr.
Stuart's letters to him, he could not construe those
letters in the same manner as the Congress had done;
and, that in writing his answer, he never had any such
thoughts, as leading the Cherokees against the Province of South-Carolina—and God forbid, that he
should be so void of humanity, as to bring the Indians
on this Province.   He farther told Major Williamson,
that he might pledge himself he never would do it.
This discourse, was reduced to writing; and Mr.
Cameron kept a copy of it; the matter being transacted, on the 12th July 1775.*

The Swallow Packet being just arrived from England, William Henry Drayton, Chairman of the Secret
Committee, resolved to seize the mail; and, in his
way to the Post-Office, on the 2d day of July, he met
John Neufville and Thomas Corbet, two members of
the Committee of Intelligence; who were proceeding
thither, on the same errand.   On their arriving at the
Post-Office, then kept by Jervis Henry Stevens, on
the Bay, at the corner of Longitude-alley, as Secretary
to George Roupell, the Deputy Post-Master,† they
demanded the mail which had just arrived in the
packet; to which a peremptory refusal was given.
They then informed Stevens, they would take it by
force, if not speedily delivered—to which he answered,
he should not deliver it.   They then took possession
of it, and carried the public letters to the State-House,
where the Secret Committee was immediately sum-

* Council of Safety's Journal, No. I. page 67.

† See No. VIII. in the Appendix.

moned to meet: and upon examining them, they found
the dispatches, which had been for Lord William
Campbell, Governor of South-Carolina, and John
Stuart, Superintendant of Indian Affairs, had been
already forwarded to them: but their enterprize was
rewarded by obtaining dispatches from the Ministry
to the Southern Governors, regulating their conduct
upon Lord North's conciliatory motion, and to Governor Martin, of North-Carolina, encouraging his
plans of raising the people of the four counties of
Guildford, Dobbs, Rowan, and Surry; whom he had
reported to " *breathe a spirit of loyalty to the King,
and attachment to the authority of Great Britain.*" All
these letters were signed by Lord Dartmouth; five of
which, were for Sir James Wright, Governor of
Georgia; one for the Lieutenant-Governor of South-
Carolina, and one, for Governor Martin, of North-
Carolina. The resolution of parliament also, upon
Lord North's conciliatory motion, was forwarded to
the Governors by Lord Dartmouth in the same packet.
These dispatches, were deemed of so much consequence, that copies of them were immediately forwarded to our Delegates in the Continental Congress,
and to the Committees at Newbern in North-Carolina,
and Savannah in Georgia;* but the originals were
never sent to the Continental Congress, as the public
has been led to believe: for they are now, in the possession of the Author of these Memoirs;† having been
in that of his family, ever since his father, William
Henry Drayton, left South-Carolina, in March 1778,
as a Delegate to the Continental Congress; then sitting at Little York-Town, in the State of Pennsylvania. About the same time the mail was seized, the
Secret Committee were also fortunate in intercepting
two letters from Sir James Wright, Governor of

* See No. VII. in the Appendix.

† See copies of these papers in the Appendix, No. III.

Georgia; each of them dated, 27th day of June 1775; one of them directed to Admiral Graves, and the other to General Gage. They stated, that "the unhappy affair of the 19th of April, and some late occurrences in the neighbouring Province, have at length drawn and forced the people of this Province into the same predicament with others; and, I now expect, as far as they possibly can, they will follow the example of them." And called for support of troops from General Gage, and for sloops of war from Admiral Graves. These letters were withholden, and are now in the possession of the writer of these Memoirs; and others were put in their places; with fac-similes of Governor Wright's signature to them. The one to General Gage stated, that the unhappy affair of the 19th of April, and some late occurrences in Carolina, have occasioned this Province (meaning Georgia) to put on an appearance, which he (the Governor of Georgia) had the pleasure to assure his Excellency is by no means real. And that upon the best information he was fully assured, if any ships or troops should be sent into Georgia, they would not only totally destroy the present favorable appearances; but in all probability would prove destructive to the good of the service. The letter to Admiral Graves told him, he had no occasion for any vessel of war; and referred him to his letter to General Gage of same date, on that head.*

At this time, (July 2d,) from various accounts it appeared the Germans in the interior parts of this Colony, were disaffected to the public measures; and it was thought expedient to send some of their own countrymen among them from Charlestown, who should endeavour to remove their misunderstandings, and conciliate their affections. For this purpose,

* See these letters in Appendix, No. IV.

George Wagner and Felix Long, two of their countrymen, were appointed on the 3d day of July: and they
accordingly proceeded on the objects of their mission.
But, from various causes, they failed of success: and
after a short tour, returned to their homes. It was
now farther ascertained, that the spirit of disaffection
daily spread itself in some back parts of the Colony;
and particularly in the fork between Saluda and
Broad Rivers. In this section of the Colony, Thomas
Fletchall residing at Fair Forest, was Colonel of the
regiment of militia; which, of course, gave him great
influence, in that part of the country: and his conduct
of late had been such, as to give great uneasiness to
the Council of Safety. At length they determined if
it were possible, to induce him to join the common
cause; or, to make known his sentiments, on the situation of affairs. Accordingly, on the 14th of July, a
suitable letter was ordered to be written to him. In
answer to which, by one dated the 24th of the same
month, he complained, that many reports had been
maliciously extended against him, to the General
Committee; which, he could prove to be false. That
upon the desire of Mr. John Caldwell, and John and
James Williams, of the Committee, he called his regiment together, on the 13th instant; when, he proceeded to every company, and caused Major Terry to
read the Provincial Association to them; but, not one
of them signed it; and, he could not compel them.
That the people then agreed, to sign an Association of
their own; and Major Robinson then on the ground
being applied to for that purpose, drew up an Association suitable to their wishes; and which had been
generally signed, from Broad to Savannah Rivers.
He warned them of some of their Highland Gentlemen, as he called some of the interior; who were
aspiring, and fond of commissions: and who, to gain
favour with the gentlemen in town, would say any
thing but the truth. He expressed his concern, that

he was looked upon as an enemy to his country; and
wished the Government might have no greater cause
to complain of some, who were little suspected, than
of him.   But on the main subject, he declared, that he
utterly refused to take up arms against his King; until
it became his duty to do otherwise—and he were convinced of the propriety of the measure.

While these things were transacting, a resolution of
the Provincial Congress, of the 22d day of June 1775,
was brought into action, by the General Committee.
This resolution prescribed, that the General Committee in Charlestown should summon all persons to
appear before them, who refused to sign the Association entered into by the Provincial Congress; and
upon their refusal to associate, or not offering such
reasons in justification of their refusal, as should be
deemed satisfactory; the General Committee were
directed to make such order, *as they should think consistent with sound policy.*   In these times, the patriots
were under the necessity of being cautious, in their
propositions: for, they apprehended, that were they to
attempt a specification of vigorous measures against
non-subscribers, and especially against the King's officers, they would have missed their aim.   It was
therefore their policy, to select terms and phrases, on
these occasions; under which, taking advantage of
events, any vigorous measures might be carried on.
The moderate party were satisfied with the wording
of the resolution; because, they would give an opening for extending mild conduct to non-subscribers;
while the others were better pleased, because under
due construction, whatever they might do in pursuance of the resolution, would be sanctioned under the
meaning of *sound policy.*   Both parties, however,
well understood the views of each other; and each
wished for events, favorable to their separate views.

40

In pursuance of this resolution, the General Committee having had returns of the non-associators in Charlestown, they caused them to appear before them on the 22d day of July: offering each of them the Association for signature, and telling them to use their pleasure, whether to sign or not. And, if they refused to sign, directing them to offer their reasons for so doing.

Twenty-two of these non-associators appeared; refused to sign; and assigned their reasons. The principal of these were, William Wragg—Thomas Knox Gordon, *Chief Justice*—Edward Savage, Charles Mathews Cosslett, John Fewtrell, and William Gregory, *Assistant Judges*—Thomas Skottowe, *one of the Council, and Secretary of the Province*—James Simpson, *Attorney-General*—Mr. Innis, *the Governor's Secretary*—George Roupell, *Deputy Post-Master General for the Southern Department*—Robert Dalway Haliday, *Collector of the port of Charlestown*—Colonel Probart Howarth, *Governor of Fort Johnson*—James Trail, *Clerk of the Court of Common Pleas, in Charlestown*—Richard Lambton, *Deputy Auditor General*—George Milligan, *Chief Surgeon for all his Majesty's forces in this Province*—and John Morris, *Comptroller of the Customs.*

Mr. Wragg assigned as his reasons for not signing the Association, "his gratitude for the honorable notice his Majesty had been pleased to take of him, in appointing him by his Royal Mandamus Chief Justice of the Province; which, although he had declined, he did not consider himself under the less obligations for.*

---

* It appears from the Council Journals of January 1770, that the Earl of Hillsborough was ordered by the King, to repeat the King's offer of the Chief Justiceship; notwithstanding his having declined accepting it, the previous summer. He was also at the same time offered, to be re-appointed to the seat

And in addition thereto, he had a right to exercise his own judgment, in the premises: although in doing so, his sentiments might differ from the general voice." The Chief Justice said, " his allegiance was an insuperable bar: and, that he differed from us in principles." Judge Savage, plead " his duty, and honour;" others spoke of " perjury, perfidy, and their places."

On the 27th July, the General Committee began to consider the reasons of the non-associators. They commenced with Mr. Wragg, who was of very respectable standing in the Colony, being a gentleman of liberal education; much esteemed for his social virtues; and possessing a large and independent fortune: and having considered his reasons, they determined them not satisfactory. On the next day, they deliberated upon what order should be made respecting him, " *consistent with sound policy:*" but after a long and violent debate, all that could be obtained was, that he should take the following oath of neutrality: " I do solemnly swear, upon the Holy Evangelists of Almighty God, that during the present unhappy disputes between Great Britain and America, I will not directly, or indirectly, by word, deed, or writing, attempt to counteract or oppose the proceedings of the people of North-America; and particularly, those of my native country: so, help me God." Mr. Wragg, however, had weighed the cost in his own mind; and determined to persevere, in the resolution he had formed: he thereupon refused to take the oath—was declared inimical to the liberty of the Colonies—was sequestered to confinment at his barony on Ashley River; and finally leaving the Colony with his son, for England, he was shipwrecked and drowned; and his son, barely escaped with his life. Some other

in Council; from which, Governor Lyttleton had suspended him. But, Mr. Wragg declined accepting the one, or the other.

persons of respectability and fortune also, would not
take the oath; and like Mr. Wragg went away; leaving their fortunes to the hazards of a civil war; and
and their claims for indemnity, to the liberality of a
Sovereign, whose allegiance they preferred.

As no better terms could be procured for so respectable a gentleman as Mr. Wragg, all hopes in favour of
other non-associators failed; and on the 31st of July,
the other cases were brought forward before the
General Committee; who determined the reasons
unsatisfactory. And the individuals implicated, not
taking the oath of neutrality, were declared inimical to
the liberties of the Colonies.

At this time, it was strongly contended, it should be
resolved, " that if any person, who refuses to subscribe
the Association, shall depart the Colony without permission from the General Committee, the estate of
such person, shall be forthwith taken into the possession of the General Committee; and, shall be subject
to their order." And " that no intercourse, communication, or dealing, (except for the purposes of procuring
provisions from the public markets, and for transacting
business in public offices) be had, between those persons who have refused, or shall refuse, to subscribe the
Association:" but after every attempt to postpone its
consideration, the vote of the Committee was taken
upon the main question; and the resolution, was finally
rejected.

The non-associators, however, having refused the
oath of neutrality, were ordered to surrender their
arms; and were confined to the limits of Charlestown: and application was made to the Continental
Congress, as to what farther steps should be taken,
against the King's officers. On the 23d of August,
the names of the non-subscribers to the Association,

were ordered to be published; cutting off all intercourse with them, except for provisions in market, or
business in the public offices.   But the King's officers
(Mr. Haliday excepted) eluded the surrender of their
arms, by saying, *"there they were, come and take
them."*   This being reported to the General Committee, on the 1st September, they allowed them one hour
for compliance; which peremptory order, had its effect
—and they surrendered their arms, excepting Mr.
Innis, the Governor's Secretary; who thereupon was
ordered to leave the town, within twenty-four hours;
and not to be seen again in the Colony.   But, on the
Governor's request, he was allowed a respite of four
days.   And in this situation, the non-subscribers remained.

As to Lieutenant-Governor William Bull, some
members of the General Committee were dispatched
to him, with a tender of the Association for signature,
or refusal.   But this respectable gentleman told them,
"that he wished as well to the country as any one;
and both his heart and his hand were with it.   But,
circumstanced as he had been, and still was, even you,
gentlemen, (said he) would look upon me in an odd
light, were I to subscribe an instrument of the kind."
The gentlemen, felt the force of these sentiments,
from a high public officer; whom they had long respected, and esteemed: and in compassion to his situation, they forbore pressing him, any farther on the
subject.

During this time, orders had been issued by the
Council of Safety, on the 26th day of June, to occupy
Fort Charlotte on Savannah River; and on the 12th
of July, Major Mayson, with two troops of the
Rangers, headed by Captains Caldwell and Kirkland,
took possession of the same, without any resistance:
as the few men who garrisoned the fort were often
absent in the daytime; and the Commander of it,

George Whitefield, and his family, were the only persons within.   Among the stores found therein, were two brass field-pieces—fourteen iron cannon, 6, 4, and 2 pounders—1,750 pounds weight of gunpowder—500 pounds more, somewhat damaged—270 iron shot, for cannon—and a quantity of lead.   Major Mayson left Captain Caldwell with his troop of Rangers, to garrison the fort; and, with Captain Moses Kirkland's troop, he proceeded to Ninety-Six Court-House; where, he arrived on the 14th of July; bringing with him 250 pounds weight of powder, and 500 pounds weight of lead.   At this time the patriotic authorities, may be said to have been in possession of all the forts and arsenals in the Colony, except Fort Johnson in Charlestown harbour; and that, was only garrisoned by a few men.

The Council of Safety now turned their thoughts towards placing the sea-coast of the Colony, in a posture of defence; and to procuring additional quantities of ammunition, by purchases from abroad; but bold measures for this service, were much impeded by cautious or timid members of the Council.   At this time, the principal business of the Council went through William Henry Drayton, Arthur Middleton, Colonel Charles Pinckney, and Thomas Ferguson; who promoted every vigorous plan—while Rawlins Lowndes, James Parsons, Miles Brewton, Thomas Heyward, jun. and Thomas Bee, were generally for moderate measures: and, John Huger, Benjamin Elliott. and William Williamson, occasionally joined one side or the other, as matters under consideration, led them to range themselves.   This situation of the Council is here mentioned, as showing that in the best organized bodies, diversities of opinions will prevail: for, it is manifest, that sometimes one party may be too hasty in pressing a measure; while, at another time, the other party, may be too unaccommodating in opposing it. Be this as it may, the object of these Memoirs, is to state things truly as they were, at the times they took place; not as they might have been: or, as persons have been less violent, or waved opposition, during the subsequent course of the American Revolution. Many propositions were now made and plans proposed, for placing Charlestown in a posture of defence; but, from the different modes by which, they were postponed or defeated in the Council, nothing at this time came forth of any efficiency. One thing only, could at this time be carried, in the Council of Safety: and that was done on the 2d day of July: when it was concluded to fortify Dorchester, *as an asylum*, when Charlestown should be lost. A distressing discovery this; that when the Council should have been ardent in preparing for the defence of the Colony; a majority of its members were so influenced by moderation or caution, as to dispair of saving the principal town of the Colony: and were looking towards an asylum, before they had even seen the enemy who was to oppose them! With the view, of making Dorchester a place of arms, it was surveyed, preparatory to fortification; and the plans reported, were approved of by the Council. But, the work went slowly on; except building a magazine for gun-powder, and some other matters of trifling nature. For, as the Council of Safety gradually shook off its apprehensions and cautions; vigorous measures came more into use: and in the same degree, the necessity of fortifying that place, became less evident; and, the inclination to carry the vote of Council on that subject into execution, less strong.

At this period, the languor which possessed the Council of Safety was so apparent, that the General Committee endeavoured to rouse them to greater energies. And after a long debate, in which the question was carried by only 29 to 24, it was resolved by the

General Committee on the 25th of July, and at the very time when they were putting down the King's officers, as non-associators, "to recommend to the Council of Safety, that Charlestown and its harbour, be forthwith put into the best posture of defence." The above recommendation, was accordingly laid before the Council; but they were in no hurry to consider it: as, on the day before, the Council had ordered twenty cannon to be mounted in such manner, as to be ready for being moved to whatever places, the public exigences might require. And this the Council had done, by way of appeasing the incessant calls upon that body, for vigorous measures.

On the 29th of July, the Council of Safety found it expedient to issue militia commissions; as Governor Campbell now required from those who applied for commissions, an oath, not to take up arms against the King. And the Council being now pressed by a motion to place Charlestown and its harbour in the best posture of defence, agreeably to the aforesaid recommendation of the General Committee, they again rejected the motion. But, the opposition relaxed so much, as to agree to place them "*into some posture of defence*," in order to give the town an opportunity, as one of the members in opposition expressly declared, "*to make terms of capitulation, upon an attack.*" The only consequence of this was, an order on the 6th of August, to repair the platforms about the town, "*where necessary.*" However, on the 3d of September, Arthur Middleton, always urging the matter in Council, moved again for making more effectual provision for the defence of Charlestown; but, the consideration of his motion was adjourned to the next day. It was then, at last considered; but, all that the Council would do on the occasion, was to pass a resolve, for arming three schooners in the public service; of which number, only one (*the Defence*) was equipped during this year; and she was not commissioned, until the 13th day of October. Such, was the situation at this time of South-Carolina, along her line of sea-coast; where she was most vulnerable; we will now return to the affairs of the interior.

It has been related, that on the 14th of July, Major Mayson arrived at Ninety-Six Court-House; with a portion of the gun-powder and lead, which he had taken in Fort Charlotte. At this time, Colonel Thomas Fletchall was holding the general muster of his militia regiment at Ford's, on the Enoree River. And Captain Moses Kirkland, who had accompanied Major Mayson with his troop of rangers, to Ninety-Six Court-House, and who had thought himself overlooked by the Provincial Congress in the military appointments; and besides, having an old grudge against Major Mayson, his superior officer, both of whom were rivals for military rank and back-country influence; knowing that Colonel Fletchall had assembled a number of men, and supposing the whole back-country disaffected, resolved to change sides. Under this impression, he dispatched Major Terry, of the militia, who was with him in opinion, to Colonel Fletchall; ardently requesting, that he would send a force, and recover the powder and lead, which had been taken from the King's fort; and was then at Ninety-Six. He, at the same time, assured Fletchall, that the force sent by him to retake the ammunition, should not be opposed: and, that the rangers meant to force him, and every other person in the back-country, to sign the Association. Having expedited these advices, he proceeded to fulfil his part of the profered agreement; and commenced inducing his troop to desert; in which he was so successful, that in a few hours they withdrew to a man.

41

In the mean time, Terry having arrived at Colonel
Fletchall's muster-field at Ford's at the fork of Cedar
Creek and Enoree River, where he continued the
assemblage of his men for three days; and seeing
Fletchall about to tender the Association of the Congress for the signatures of the individuals of his regiment; he concealed his business, until he saw what
turn that affair should take.   And accompanying
Fletchall through the companies, the Association was
tendered under such discouraging expressions, as gave
the people to understand Fletchall's mind on the subject; not a man signing the same.   And passing from
one extreme to another, Fletchall having previously
caused Major Robinson to prepare another association
more suitable to his opinions, and the part he intended
to act in favour of the King, it was offered to the men
for signature, and the people very generally subscribed
it.   Terry seeing the multitude in this disposition,
now communicated his mission from Kirkland to
Fletchall, in presence of Major Robinson and the
Cunninghams; when, Fletchall declined to appear
publicly, in the affair: but the three others declared
they would go, and seize the powder and lead.   At
this, Fletchall showed no disposition to prevent them;
and, they immediately rode off the field, with two
hundred men on horseback.   They arrived at Ninety-
Six Court-House, on the 17th July, about noon; and
had little trouble in possessing themselves of the
ammunition, as Major Mayson had only an officer or
two left with him, beside Captain Kirkland.   Robinson and his party, then committed the Major to the
district gaol; where, having continued some hours,
they admitted him to bail, to answer at the ensuing
Sessions, for having, as they charged, robbed the
King's fort.   In a few days afterwards, Captain Kirkland put the seal to his treachery, in joining Fletchall's
party openly: in addition to which act of perfidy, he

also induced Captain P*** and his troop of the same regiment, to quit the service.

The number of men collected at Fletchall's muster-field, amounting to fifteen hundred at least—the spirit they displayed—the seizure of the powder and lead—the treatment of Major Mayson—and the desertion of Kirkland and P***—encouraged and increased the disaffection of the people, from Broad to Savannah Rivers. The million voted by the Provincial Congress, was an endless theme to harangue upon; for the purpose of stating, that the Congress would ruin them; and, the paper money was cried down as of no value. But, above all, their spirits and cabals were kept up, by correspondences with Lord William Campbell, the Governor, in Charlestown; who, through Colonel Fletchall, commended the loyalty of Robinson and the Cunninghams: promising them rewards, for perseverance in duty. This being circulated, gave these men real consequence among the disaffected; tied them fast to the royal interest, and threw out a lure of recompense to every leader of the party. From this state of things, the most fatal consequences were apprehended; and it was then supposed, that if Lord William Campbell had gone up among the disaffected—had collected Fletchall and his men around him—and had conducted himself with promptness and efficiency—the whole proceedings of the Provincial Congress would have been overthrown. However, for wiser purposes, Providence had not so directed his actions; but left him in Charlestown, to experience the daily loss of his executive powers; and the little consideration in which he was holden, as well by the public authorities, as by the citizens at large.

Accounts of these circumstances, frequently arriving in Charlestown; and through Lord William's plots, affairs becoming more critical every day in the back parts of the Colony; the Council of Safety took into consideration, the urgency of the case, and the necessity which existed, of reconciling the people, to the public measures: but, it was opposed. However, on the 23d day of July 1775, it was resolved, " That the Hon'ble William Henry Drayton, and the Reverend William Tennent be the two gentlemen to make a progress into the back country, to explain to the people, the causes of the present disputes, between Great Britain, and the American Colonies;"* and they were accordingly commissioned on the same day for that purpose: " to go into the interior parts of this Colony at the public expense; there to explain to the people at large, the nature of the unhappy public disputes between Great Britain and the American Colonies—to endeavour to settle all political disputes between the people—to quiet their minds—and to enforce the necessity of a general union, in order to preserve themselves and their children from slavery."† Beside this, they were privately armed with authority, " to call upon all and every officer of the militia and rangers, for assistance, support, and protection" *to act* " *as you shall deem necessary.*"† Colonel Richard Richardson, Joseph Kershaw, and the Reverend Mr. Hart, were desired to accompany them; and to complete the arrangement, the whole militia were ordered to be classed in three divisions; and to hold themselves ready by turns, to march at twelve hours notice.

On Wednesday, the second day of August 1775, the Commissioners, William Henry Drayton and William Tennent, left Charlestown, in prosecution of the duties they had in charge: and proceeding by the way of Monk's Corner, they arrived at the Congaree

* Council of Safety's Journal, No. I. pages 70, 71.

† See Appendix to this Chapter, No. V.

Store,* in the Dutch settlement of Saxegotha, on the Saturday following; in the vicinity of which, a part of the regiment of rangers was encamped, on the western bank of the Six Mile Creek.   On their arrival at that place, they found two gentlemen of the law, prisoners from North-Carolina; who had arrived the evening before: having been sent forward by the Committee of Camden, on charges inimical to the liberties of America.   These gentlemen proceeded in their destination to Charlestown; where they became subjected to the public authorities; and were imprisoned at the public expense, for some months.

As a first step, to the particular object of their progress, they dispatched notices to persons of influence among the Dutch in that settlement; for the purpose of procuring a meeting of the inhabitants at the place of election, which was to be on the day the Commissioners arrived at the Congaree Store.   Not one German, however, appeared there; and only one or two friends of the Association; who had been industrious, to procure a meeting.   By these gentlemen, the Commissioners were informed, their countrymen were against taking up arms, as they imagined, against the King; being apprehensive, in such a case, he would resume the grants which had been given to them of their lands; by which, they would be dispossed of them.   And, they were likewise so possessed with the idea, that the rangers were posted among them, for the purpose of awing them into submission, and forcing their signatures to the Association, that they would not by any arguments, be induced to approach the Commissioners.   Beside this, a report ran among them, the Commissioners had brought orders from the

* The Congaree Store, was situated about 300 hundred yards below the large ditch, which crosses the public road, just below Granby : and lay between the road, and the Congaree River.

Council of Safety, to let the rangers loose upon them,
for the purpose of destroying their properties.   Notwithstanding these difficulties, the Commissioners did
not give up the idea of reasoning with these people;
and for that purpose they prevailed with Colonel William Thompson, who commanded the Orangeburgh
regiment of militia,* to order a muster of two Dutch
companies of his regiment in the neighbourhood, on
the Wednesday following: and, to give greater energy
to his orders, the Commissioners declared, that should
the officers disobey, they should be broken.   This
threat, at that time, was absolutely necessary; as the
Dutch Captains had some little time before, disobeyed
such an order; alledging, that extra musters, were
warranted only, by orders from the Governor.   With
a view also of promoting assemblages of the people;
the Commissioners engaged a Dutch Clergyman, to
perform Divine Service at two different places, on the
Friday and Sunday following.   And to excite the private interests of the Dutchmen, it was made known,
that no non-subscriber in that settlement, should be
allowed to purchase at, or sell to, the Congaree Store,
or Charlestown.

Previous to these meetings, Mr. Tennent performed
Divine Service in the rangers' camp; and afterwards,
Mr. Drayton haranged the rangers, respecting the new
and extraordinary power, by which they had been
raised—the nature of the public disputes, and the
justice of the cause, in which they were engaged—their
duty to their country, their families, and themselves—
and their duty and obligation, to oppose and attack

---

* Although Colonel Thompson had been lately appointed Colonel of the
regiment of rangers, he did not thereby lose his command as Colonel of this
regiment of militia; as it appears, that at this early part of the Revolution, the
custom was so received in Carolina.   At this time, the militia of the province,
consisted of thirteen regiments; one of horse, and twelve of foot.   See Appendix to this Chapter, No. VI.

any British troops, landing in this Colony. Their
honour was also awakened, by contrasting their personal value and importance, with those of British troops
—their complaints respecting provisions were entered
into, and assurances were given, that all which could
be done for them consistent with discipline, and the
situation of affairs, would be attended to. They were
informed, the public could not so much dishonour
them, as to suppose they had enlisted merely for gain:
but that they were persuaded, they acted from nobler
motives. That if they deemed it a hardship, to go in
search of provisions—to do which, they were allowed
extra pay; the Council of Safety was willing to save
them that trouble, by supplying them with provisions
and rations, like the rest of the troops, upon deducting
the extra pay, so allowed them. That, as to their
complaints for the want of tents, they surely, as soldiers were as able to do without them, as the British
troops in America did, during the last war. That, as
they were raised to compete with them in valour;
military pride, called upon them to compete with
them also, in patience, subordination, and the most
perfect obedience to their officers. In addition to this
address, Mr. Tennent added assurances of the value
of Congress' currency; which ill-disposed persons
had endeavoured to depreciate in the opinion of the
soldiers; and he finished by reading and commenting
on the Declaration of the Continental Congress.

The Commissioners, then left the camp, apparently
quiet and satisfied; as the men on being discharged,
expressed their thanks, for the information they had
received. But, about midnight an officer came from
the camp (which was about two or three miles off)
with information, that a dangerous mutiny had broken
out—that command and obedience, no longer existed
—that the men were in uproar, at the idea of deduction
of pay; for they had in some cases been promised by

their officers, provisions above their pay; and that they were determined to quit the camp in the morning, and disband.

After taking the matter into consideration, aided by Colonel Thompson and Captain Kershaw; the Commissioners deemed it most adviseable, to let the matter rest until morning; as thereby, time would intervene for the men to cool; and for the three Captains, and other officers in camp, to sound the men, and know who could be depended upon. This forbearance, had a good effect; as in the morning, the men appeared quiet: and it became evident, the disorder arose from three or four privates of profligate characters; and from the improper conduct, declarations, and conversations, of some of the officers. Captain W———d had incautiously, when enlisting his men, made promises which proved grounds of discontent; and when the Commissioners addressed the rangers in camp, he had the imprudence to attempt to be spokesman, to the Commissioners in the hearing of the men, as to their being found provisions over and above their pay; and Lieutenant D———e also attempted to speak, to the cruelty of keeping men encamped without tents. For this conduct, the Commissioners privately admonished these officers; which they received in a submissive and appropriate manner.

The rangers were then marched from their camp, to the Congaree Store; where Mr. Drayton again harangued them upon the disorders of the last night: attributing it to a few disorderly persons, who, in this first instance of disobedience, would be passed over by their Colonel—in the hope, such lenity would work a reformation in them. The consequences of a mutinous conduct were described: they were told, that if they should prove unworthy of the service; others more worthy, would supply their places—that they ought not to flatter themselves, because some parts of the Colony were disaffected, they might desert, and be in places of security; for, if they did, they would sometimes be off their guard, and then, they would be seized: as a reward would be put upon them, for the purpose of bringing them to punishment. The situation of united America, was also brought to their view; on the side of liberty, were ranged infinite numbers, supported by the best wealth and abilities of the country; while on the side of royalty, only a few disaffected men showed themselves, of little property, and of less knowledge. And it was asked, if among such men as the latter, they could possibly suppose, there was any safety? After this, excepting three men, they were called upon to say what they pleased: and they became well satisfied, and showed the most perfect submission. The three men, were spoken to in private, and were severely reprimanded. In this manner, was the mutiny put down; by the prudent intervention of the Commissioners, at a most critical period. For, had it ended otherwise, their progress would have been much obstructed; and might have been utterly defeated. It gave a trial also, of the prudence and energy of the Commissioners; which, considering the balance of parties in the Council of Safety, was of the utmost consequence. And it led, not only to a continuance of confidence in them, from that body; but actually to the increase of authority to one of the Commissioners, towards the close of the progress, in which, they were so engaged.

Matters being thus composed, and the public arm strengthened at the Congaree Station; the Commissioners thought it might tend to remove the apprehensions of the Dutch settlers, by changing the camp of the Rangers, to some distant place. For this reason, as well as to allow the soldiers to go home, to places of election about to be holden; and to procure necessaries for themselves; and still more, to evince the public confidence in their good behaviour; the camp of the rangers was broken up: and they were sent to their homes for a limited time, under the eyes of their respective officers. A new camp was ordered to be formed at Amelia on the Congaree River; about thirty miles below: where, they were ordered to assemble on the 18th day of August 1775. Major Mayson was also ordered to the same camp, with Captain Purvis' troop: for, owing to some local dissentions at Ninety-Six, his presence was of disservice there, to the public interests.

It was now ascertained, that Captain Moses Kirkland had gone to Charlestown to Governor Campbell: and the Commissioners immediately issued orders, for apprehending him, on his return; hoping to possess themselves thereby, of papers from the Governor. They also advised the Council of his approach; that he might be arrested and punished for his desertion, and disbanding his men. But his good fortune, saved him this time; and he returned full freighted from his Excellency, with commissions, papers, and offers of encouragement, to Colonel Fletchall; and through him, to all the malecontents, in the upper parts of the Colony: and did not a little contribute, as hereafter will be seen, to poison the minds of the people—and so far as in him lay, to defeat the objects of the Commissioners.

With these prospects all before them, and other discouragements which presented themselves, the Commissioners questioned, whether they would be permitted to give public addresses in Fletchall's regimental district: it was, however, not for them to balance whether they should proceed or not; and they accordingly matured their plans, for farther proceedings. In doing this, it was ascertained the public interests required their separation; and, that Mr. Drayton should go up, between Broad and Saluda Rivers; while Mr. Tennent should proceed on the North side of Broad River, between that and the Watteree, as high as Rocky Creek, the upper boundary of Colonel Richardson's regiment. From thence it was agreed, Mr. Tennent was to cross over, and join Mr. Drayton at Fair Forest; where Colonel Fletchall resided.*

* Letter of 7th August 1775, from the Commissioners to the Council of Safety.

APPENDIX

CHAPTER VIII.

———◆———

No. I.

IN THE COUNCIL OF SAFETY.

Thursday 25th July 1775.   The Council met.

PRESENT,

Colonel Henry Laurens, *President.*

Col. Pinckney,	Col. Parsons,
Hon. Mr. Drayton,	Mr. Ferguson,
Mr. Middleton,	Mr. Bee,
Mr. Brewton,	Mr. Williamson,
Mr. Benj. Elliott,	Mr. Heyward,

Hon. Mr. Lowndes.

Resolved, that the following Orders, and Commission, be given to Captain Lempriere :

South-Carolina.

IN THE COUNCIL OF SAFETY.

Charlestown, July 25th, 1775.

To Clement Lempriere, Esq.

THE COUNCIL OF SAFETY, elected and chosen by the Provincial Congress, begun to be holden on the first day of June last, by these Presents testify, that *Clement Lempriere, Esquire,* has been, and is hereby appointed and commissioned to command, in the sloop Commerce, belonging to New-York; and, over all and every person and persons engaged to embark on board the said sloop, on the intended voyage, under the authority of the said Council of Safety. And the said Clement Lempriere, is hereby ordered, to proceed forthwith with all convenient dispatch, to the Island of New-Providence; on that Island to seize, and from that Island to embark on board the said sloop, all such quantity of gun-powder, as he shall find, and be able to take on board, and from the said island: and then, forthwith to return to this Colony; and put into Tucker's Creek, Tucker's Island, North Edisto. And, from thence, to give notice to the said Council of Safety, of his arrival; with all possible dispatch. And, if the said Clement Lempriere, shall not be able to seize any considerable quantity of gun-powder in the Island of New-Providence aforesaid, he shall then proceed to such places, and take such measures to procure gun-powder, as he shall think most proper: and then to proceed to Tucker's Creek aforesaid; and thence, to give due notice as aforesaid. And for so doing, this is your Warrant.

By order of the Council of Safety.

HENRY LAURENS, *President.*

South-Carolina.

Charlestown, July 24th, 1775.

To Clement Lempriere, Esquire.

THE COUNCIL OF SAFETY, elected and chosen by the Provincial Congress, begun to be holden on the first day of June last, by these Presents testify, That Clement Lempriere, Esquire, has been, and is hereby appointed and commissioned, to command the sloop Commerce, belonging to New-York; and over all and every person and persons, engaged to embark on board the said sloop, under the authority of the said Council of Safety. And the said Clement Lempriere is hereby ordered, to proceed to such places, and to take such measures, as he shall think most proper, to procure gun-powder, for the public of this Colony; which, when he shall have procured, he is ordered to convey to this Colony, with all possible dispatch.

It is also hereby declared, that if any commander or officer, under the King's authority, in any degree ill-treat the said Clement Lempriere or any of his company; the King's officers now in our power, shall be treated with equal severity. Of which, all persons are required to take due notice.

Given under the authority, and by order of the Council of Safety.

HENRY LAURENS, *President.*

Ordered, that the foregoing commission be engrossed, sealed, dated, and signed, by the President; and by him delivered sealed up to Captain Lempriere; with orders, not to be opened, until he shall be arrived in sight of the Island of New-Providence.

☞ See Council of Safety's Journal, No. I, pages 78, 79.

No. II.

Captain Hatter's Report to the Council of Safety, of the occurrences which took place on board of the sloop Commerce, Clement Lempriere, Esquire, Commander, in taking the powder from Captain Lofthouse, off Augustine Bar; and of the return voyage to Charlestown with the powder.

1775.

July 24. Our voyage towards New-Orleans commenced.

25. Took on board our stores of provisions, &c.

26. Sailed over the bar, with the wind at N. E. and rain; at 6 P. M. anchored at South Edisto.

27. Fresh gales, with thunder squalls; and a great deal of lightning; weighed, and sailed up Port Royal Creek, where we anchored.

28. It continued to blow hard with rain. We got through Port Royal Creek, and came to at the town; and landed our stores, in order to clean.

29. We hauled on shore, and cleaned; and in the evening, hauled her off again.

30. Took on board our stores, and got ready to sail; fell down the river a little.

31. Sailed from Port Royal, with the wind at South; and turned down to Jenkins' landing.

Aug. 1. Got under way, and turned through Skull Creek, and came to, at Callaboge.

2. Sailed out of Tybee, with the wind at South; turned to windward: at meridian observed in latitude 31 deg. 45 min.

3. Still plying to windward, with the wind at South: latitude observed 31 28.

4. Fine settled weather, wind southerly; beating to windward: latitude observed 31 09.

5. Fresh breeze and thunder squalls; wind southerly: lat. observed 30 51.

Aug. 6. Fine settled weather, with fresh gales: lat. obsd. 29 55.

7. Made the Mattanzes at night; came to under the fort, in seven fathoms water: and rode all night. At 6 A. M. got under way, and run down towards the bar of Augustine; where, we saw a sail at anchor off the bar. We ran down to her, and hailed her; and found her to be the brigantine Betsey, commanded by Captain Alvere Lofthouse, from London. We boarded her with our sloop, and upon strict search, found on board of her a large quantity of gun-powder; of which we took one hundred and eleven barrels, one half barrel, and thirty small kegs. Said vessel had on board of her, twelve soldiers from the shore, eight seamen, the captain, two mates, and steward, which was in number twenty-three men; and our number was twenty-one whites, and five blacks. Our situation was such on this occasion, that we thought it most prudent to bribe the men; which we did with one hundred pounds currency : and the captain accepted a draught for one thousand pounds Sterling for the powder, drawn on Mr. John Edwards, of Charlestown. And at half past 11 A. M. after spiking up two pieces of cannon, that were mounted on board said brigantine, we re-embarked our men, and made sail with a light air at E. N. E. The wind weared to the Northward, at 4 P. M. we passed the River St. John's, and passed a small boat, stretching to the Southward.

8. Turning to the windward with the wind at N. E. squally, with rain: latitude obsd. 31 26.

9. Fresh gales at N. E. plying to windward with all sail set, and a growing sea. Lat. obsd. 31 50.

10. Light breezes of wind, set squaresail and topsail, and made Tybee Tower; and we steered in at it, through Skull Creek, and came to in Port Royal Creek. Lat. ob. 31 50. Got under sail, and at 10 A. M. came to at Port Royal; and dispatched away an Express to Charlestown, and at 3 P. M. we landed the powder.

11. Fine settled weather, with the wind to the Westward.

12. Showery, and thunder squalls—at anchor at Port Royal.

13. Do. weather.

14. Do. weather.

Aug. 15. Showery and thunder squalls. An Express from Charlestown arrived with an account of the Governor's sloop being in pursuit of us.

16. Squally weather, with a great deal of rain. Sundry companies of militia and light infantry, come to town from the different islands, to guard the gunpowder.

17. Ditto weather. Our Express arrived from Charlestown, and brought with him, a detachment of artillery, in order to escort the gunpowder to Charlestown.

18. Received on board of the Success, ninety-one barrels of powder; and got in readiness to sail. At 10 A. M. Captain Cuttell arrived in town with 60 men of the Provincials, and offered to join us to protect the gunpowder, which we accepted of.

19. Got all in readiness to sail, and at meridian we weighed anchor, and sailed through Port Royal Creek; and run down as low as Morgan's Island, when we came to, with our small squadron, consisting of nine sail, and rode all night.

20. At 6 A. M. we got under way, and sailed down towards Otter Island, and fell down to South Edisto inlet, to wait the flood. At 11 A. M. we weighed, and towed up towards Fenwick's Bluff; when we came to, to wait the tide, and water the vessel, in company with the different detachments. At midnight, got under way again, and towed up.

21. Towed up to Block Island, and down to Slan's Bluff, where we waited the tide, and cooked provisions. At 4 P. M. we run down to White Point, and came to, to wait tide to New-Cut.

22. Got under way, and towed up and through New-Cut and down to Wappoo, and there waited tide, to come through. At 4 P. M. we got under way, and run into the Cut, and towed through; and came to anchor in Ashley River, and lay all the night.

23. Got under way, and towed up Cummings' Creek; and at 6 A. M. we came to the bluff, where we landed ninety-one barrels of gunpowder.

JOHN HATTER.*

* From documents of the Council of Safety.

No. III.

Copies of Letters and Papers from the Earl of Dartmouth to the different Governors of Provinces; brought over from Falmouth in the Swallow Packet, and seized in the Post-Office of Charlestown.

(CIRCULAR PRIVATE.)

Duplicate.   *Whitehall, March 3d,* 1775.
  SIR,

It is fit that I should acquaint you, that the Resolution of the House of Commons which accompanies my separate dispatch, passed in the Committee by a majority of 274 to 88; and was received and agreed to, by the House, without a division. And indeed, the great majorities which have appeared in both Houses, upon every question that has been proposed for maintaining the supremacy of parliament, is such an evidence of the general sense of the nation upon that subject, as must show how little ground there has been for those assurances which have been artfully held out to the Americans of support here, in the dangerous conduct they have adopted; and convince them that there neither can, nor will be any the least relaxation, from those measures, which that conduct has made indispensably necessary, for reducing the Colonies to the constitutional authority of parliament.

    I am, Sir, your most obt. humble servt.

                DARTMOUTH.

His Honour the Lieutenant-Governor of
   South-Carolina, Charlestown.

Resolved, That when the Governor, Council, and Assembly, or General Court of any of his Majesty's Provinces, or Colonies in America, shall propose to make provision according to the condition, circumstances, and situation, of such Province or Colony, for contributing their proportion to the common defence; (such proportion to be raised under the authority of the General Court, or General Assembly of such Province or Colony, and disposable by parliament;) and, shall engage to make provision also, for the support of the Civil Government, and the administration of justice, in such Province or Colony; it will be proper, if such proposal shall be approved by his Majesty, and the two Houses of Parliament, and for so long as such provision shall be made accordingly, to forbear, in respect to such Province or Colony, to levy any duty, tax, or assessment; except, only, such duties, as it may be expedient to continue to levy, or to impose, for the regulation of commerce; the net produce of the duties last mentioned, to be carried to the account of such Province or Colony respectively.*

A Duplicate, Circular Private, similar to the one preceding—to the Governor of Georgia.

—

(No. 19.)
Duplicate.   *Whitehall*, 3d March 1775.
Sir,

I have received your letters of the 19th and 20th of December; the latter numbered 35: and have laid them before the King. But having nothing in command from his Majesty thereupon, I have only to lament, that his Majesty's subjects in Georgia, who have hitherto in general shown so great respect for the mother country, and loyalty to the King, should have at length manifested a disposition to adopt the sentiments, and follow the ill example of their neighbours. But, I trust, that the measures I have taken for your support, and the zeal and alacrity of the King's officers, and of those gentlemen who you say, stand forth in the maintenance of the public peace, will have the effect to prevent the sons of liberty, as they are called, from committing themselves in any act of violence.

I find by a letter from Mr. Cooper to Mr. Pownall, that the Lords of the Treasury, have had under their consideration the proposition which you transmitted some years ago, in the shape of

* See proceedings of the Continental Congress respecting this Resolution, in the proceedings of the Congress at the latter part of Chapter XII, for the month of July 1775.

a bill for better collecting his Majesty's quit rents ; they seem however to be of opinion, that the provisions of an act of the province of North-Carolina, for the same purpose which they have had before them, are better calculated to answer the object in view, than the bill you recommended ; and principally, because, it enacts, that no patent, deed, or conveyance of land shall be held valid, unless enrolled in the manner the act directs—whereas, in your bill, the enrolment is enforced merely by penalty. I therefore think fit, to send you a copy of the North-Carolina act; that by comparing the two together, you may be enabled to frame and pass such a law, as shall correspond with the sentiments of that board.

     I am, Sir, your most obt. hum. servt.

DARTMOUTH.

Sir James Wright, Baronet, Georgia.

—

(CIRCULAR PRIVATE.)

Duplicate.   *Whitehall, 3d March* 1775.
    SIR,

     My separate dispatch of this day's date, enclosing a Resolution of the House of Commons, may be ostensibly of use, in case the General Assembly should think fit, to take up the consideration of that resolution. But, it is fit, I should observe to you, that it is not his Majesty's intention, for very obvious reasons, that you should officially communicate it to them. At the same time, as I think it cannot fail to be an object of discussion in the Assembly, I must add, that the King considers that the good effect of it, will, in a great measure depend, upon your ability and address, in a proper explanation of it, to those, whose situation and connexions may enable them to give facility to the measures it points to. And, his Majesty has no doubt, that you will exert every endeavour to induce such a compliance, on the part of the Assembly, as may correspond with his Majesty's ideas of their justice, and his earnest wishes to see a happy restoration of the public tranquillity.

     I am, Sir, your most obt. hum. servt.

DARTMOUTH.

The Governor of Georgia.

(CIRCULAR.)

Separate Duplicate.

Whitehall, March 3d, 1775.

SIR,

You will have seen in the King's answer to the joint address of both Houses of Parliament, on the 7th of February, (which address and answer have already been transmitted to you,) how much attention his Majesty was graciously pleased to give to the assurance held out in that address, of the readiness of parliament to afford every just and reasonable indulgence to the Colonies, whenever they should make a proper application on the ground of any real grievance, they might have to complain of; and, therefore, I have the less occasion now to enlarge upon the satisfaction it hath given his Majesty, to see that address followed by the enclosed resolution of the House of Commons: which, whatever may be the effect of it, (I trust a happy one) will for ever remain an evidence of their justice and moderation; and manifest the temper which has accompanied their deliberations upon that question: which has been the source of so much disquit to his Majesty's subjects in America; and the pretence, for acts of such criminal disorder and disobedience.

His Majesty, ardently wishing to see a reconciliation of the unhappy differences, which have produced those disorders, by every means through which it may be obtained, without prejudice to the just authority of parliament; which his Majesty will never suffer to be violated; approves the resolution of his faithful Commons; and commands me to transmit it to you, not doubting that this happy disposition to comply with every just and reasonable wish of the King's subjects in America, will meet with such a return of duty and affection, on their part, as will lead to a happy issue of the present disputes, and to a re-establishment, of the public tranquillity on those grounds of equity, justice, and moderation, which this resolution holds forth.

The King has the greater satisfaction in this resolution, and the greater confidence in the good effects of it, from having seen, that amidst all the intemperance, into which a people jealous of their liberties have been unfortunately misled, they have nevertheless avowed the justice, the equity, and the propriety of subjects of the same state, contributing according to their abilities and situation to the public burthens; and I think I am warranted in saying, that this resolution holds no proposition beyond it.

I am unwilling to suppose, that any of the King's subjects, in the Colonies, can have so far forgot the benefits they have received from the parent state, as not to acknowledge, that it is to her support, held forth at the expense of her blood and treasuse, that they principally owe that security, which hath raised them to their present state of opulence and importance. In this situation, therefore, justice requires that they should in return contribute according to their respective abilities, to the common defence; and their own welfare and interest demand that their civil establishment should be supported, with a becoming dignity.

It has therefore been the case, and I am persuaded it is the firm determination of parliament, to see that both these ends are answered; and their wisdom and moderation have suggested the propriety of leaving to each Colony, to judge of the ways and means, of making due provision for these purposes; reserving to themselves the power of approving or disapproving, what shall be offered.

The resolution, neither points out what the civil establishment should be; nor demands any specific sum in aid of the public burthens. In both these respects, it leaves full scope for that justice and liberality, which may be expected from Colonies, that under all their prejudices, have never been wanting in expressions of an affectionate attachment to the mother country; and a zealous regard for the general welfare of the British empire. And therefore, the King trusts that the provision they will engage to make, for the support of civil government, will be adequate to the rank and station of every necessary officer; and, that the sum to be given in contribution, to the common defence, will be offered on such terms, and proposed in such a way, as to increase or diminish according as the public burthens of this kingdom are from time to time augmented or reduced; in so far, as those burthens consist of taxes and duties, which are not a security for the national debt. By such a mode of distribution the Colonies will have full security that they can never be required to tax themselves, without parliament's taxing the subjects of this kingdom, in a far greater pro-

portion.   And, there can be no doubt, that any proposition of this
nature, made by any of the Colonies, and accompanied with such
a state of their faculties and abilities as may evince the equity of
the proposal, will be received with every possible indulgence:
Provided, it be at the same time unaccompanied with any declarations, and unmixed with any claims, which will make it impossible
for the King, consistent with his own dignity, or for parliament
consistent with their constitutional rights, to receive it.   But, I will
not suppose, that any of the Colonies will, after this example of the
temper and moderation of parliament, adopt such a conduct; on
the contrary, I will cherish the pleasing hope, that the public peace
will be restored; and that the Colonies forgetting all other trivial
and groundless complaints, which ill-humour hath produced, will
enter into the consideration of the resolution of the House of
Commons, with that calmness and deliberation, which the importance of it demands; and with that good will and inclination to a
reconciliation, which are due to the candor and justice with which
parliament has taken up this business, and at once declared to the
Colonies, what will be ultimately expected from them.

I have already said, that the King entirely approves the resolution of the House of Commons; and his Majesty commands me
to say, that a compliance therewith, by the General Assembly of
Georgia, will be most graciously considered by his Majesty, not
only, as a testimony of their reverence for parliament, but also as
a mark of their duty and attachment to their Sovereign; who has
no object nearer to his heart, than the peace and prosperity of his
subjects in every part of his dominions.   At the same time, his
Majesty considers himself as bound by every tie, to exert those
means, the constitution has placed in his hands, for preserving that
constitution entire; and to resist, with firmness every attempt, to
violate the rights of parliament, to distress and obstruct the lawful
commerce of his subjects, and to encourage in the Colonies ideas
of independence, inconsistent with their connexion with this
kingdom.

I am, Sir, your most obt. hum. servt.

DARTMOUTH.

Governor of Georgia.

(No. 20.)

Whitehall, 3d May 1775.

SIR,

    I have received your letters numbered from 35 to 41, and have laid them before the King.

The grounds upon which masters of ships, who were midshipmen and acted as master's mates on board the fleet in the last war, claim each 2,000 acres of land, in virtue of the royal proclamation refers to facts, of which I have no official information. Whenever the Lords of the Admiralty shall, upon a proper application to them, by those claimants, certify the facts on which they state their claims, I will not fail to receive his Majesty's pleasure upon their case; in the mean time, the matter must rest upon the opinion, I think very properly adopted by yourself and the Council.

I have already so repeatedly expressed to you my sentiments of the present disorders in America, and the sense I have of your meritorious conduct, in the prudent and proper measures you have pursued, for preventing as far as you are able, the contagion from spreading itself through the province of Georgia; that I have nothing to add on that subject, but to express my wishes that the steps I have taken for your support, will encourage the friends of Government to resist the violences that are threatened, and preserve the public peace, in all events.

    I am, Sir, your most obt. hum. servt.

                 DARTMOUTH.

Sir James Wright, Baronet.

(No. 16.)

Whitehall, May 3d, 1775.

SIR,

    Your letters of the 26th of January and 1oth of March, Nos. 27 and 28, the latter of which I received only yesterday, contain matter of very great importance.

The addresses from the four counties of Guildford, Dobbs, Rowan and Surry, breathe a spirit of loyalty to the King, and

attachment to the authority of Great Britain, which cannot be too
much encouraged; and it will be necessary that you lose no time,
in acquainting the inhabitants of those counties, that these testi-
monies of their duty, and affection, have been most graciously
received by his Majesty. That his Majesty will not fail to afford
them those marks of his royal favour, which such a meritorious
conduct appears to deserve; and, that as soon as the necessary
forms will admit, his Majesty's clemency towards the insurgents in
1770, will be extended in a proclamation, of general pardon to all
except Horman Husbands. In the mean time, it is his Majesty's
pleasure, that you do pursue every step that may improve so
favorable a symptom in the present state of general frenzy, and
perhaps you will not find it difficult, through the channel of some
respectable persons in those counties, to procure proper associations
of the people, in support of the Government. Such a measure,
cannot fail to cast a damp upon the machinations of faction, and
disconcert any desperate measure, they may have in contempla-
tion.

I hope, we may yet avoid, the fatal necessity of drawing the
sword; but it is prudent to provide, as far as we are able, against
every possible mischief; and therefore, you will do well, to consider
in time, whether it may not be practicable in such an event, to
embody and lead forth, in support of Government, such of the men
in those counties, as are able to bear arms. If matters should
come to this issue, it is the King's pleasure, that you hold out to
gentlemen of interest and leading amongst them, assurances of his
Majesty's favour in granting them such commissions, as shall be
suitable to their rank and station; and every other encouragement
and advantage allowed to any other troops, in his Majesty's service, as far as is consistent, with the established rules of the army.

I confess to you, Sir, that this appears to me to be a matter of
so much importance, that I cannot too earnestly recommend it to
your attention; and that no time may be lost, in case of absolute
necessity. I have received his Majesty's commands, to write to
General Gage, to apprize him of this favorable circumstance; and
to instruct him, that he do, upon application from you, send some
able and discreet officer, to you, in order to concert the means of
carrying so essential a service into effect; and if necessary to lead

the people forth, against any rebellious attempts, to disturb the public peace.

There are several other matters in your letters, which will require consideration, and instruction ; but, as the mail for Charlestown will be made up to-night, I can only for the present add; that
I am, Sir, your most obt. hum. servt.
DARTMOUTH.

His Excel. Gov. Martin, North-Carolina.

◆

No. IV.

Savannah in Georgia, the 27th of June 1775.

SIR,

I had the honour to write to your Excellency, of the 7th inst. enclosed to Lieutenant-Governor Colden, which I hope you have received. And last night I received a letter from Lord William Campbell, acquainting me, that he is going to send the Scorpion with letters to your Excellency, and which opportunity, I now embrace ; and hope some method may be fallen upon that we may receive frequent information of the state of things your way; as it has the greatest effect and influence on the conduct of the people in these provinces, and may contribute much to his Majesty's service.

The unhappy affair of the 19th of April, and some late occurrences in the neighbouring province, have at length drawn and forced the people of this province into the same predicament with others. And I now expect, that as far as they possibly can, they will follow the example of them. And I see no probability of any tolerable quietude, unless the prudence and moderation of the Continental Congress, should lay a foundation for it. Your Excellency's order to Major Furlong, I have not yet forwarded; indeed, I have neither vessels, nor money, to pay the expense of sending for them, and as things are circumstanced at present. It is the opinion of the gentlemen of the Council, that such a number

might only inflame the whole province, and be liable to insults, if
not *worse.* For, we have no fort, of defence, for them to be in, or
retire to: and they could neither awe or prevent any attempts
against them. This number a year ago, might have been of great
use, or if things take a favorable turn may, but not just now. And
it is our opinion, that not less than five times that number, could
answer any effectual purpose. And therefore, I do not mean to
forward it yet. But, if your Excellency could for this length, and
authorize me to draw for the expense of putting up a temporary
fort, I think matters would soon wear a different aspect here.
But without, neither law or government, can be supported. And
I have neither men or money. And the Governors had much
better be in England, than remain in America. And have the
mortification to see, *their* powers executed by committees and
mobs. And I am really amazed, that these Southern provinces
should be left in the situation they are, and the Governors and
King's officers and friends to Government, naked and exposed to
the resentment of an enraged people. Stuart has been obliged to
take sanctuary in St. Augustine. I shall hope for a full and clear
answer from your Excellency, that I may know better how to
conduct myself. And have the honour to be with respect and
esteem,

Your Excel. most obt. and most hum. servt.

JAMES WRIGHT.

To his Excel. General Gage.

☞ The above Letter, was withdrawn from the
envelope, and the following was substituted in its
place, and forwarded, by the Secret Committee.

Savannah in Georgia, 27*th June* 1775.

SIR,

The unhappy affair of the 19th of April, and some late occurrences in
Carolina, have occasioned this province, to put on an appearance, which I
have the pleasure to assure your Excellency, is by no means real; and I am
happy, that I can with equal confidence assure you, that there is nothing really
formidable in the proceedings or designs of our neighbours of South-Carolina,
notwithstanding the late address of their Congress to Lord William Campbell;
who being but just arrived, and as your Excellency knows but unexperienced
in affairs of Government, may think them very serious, and express his apprehensions to you on the subject. However unwilling I write this, yet the good
of his Majesty's service, compels me to make this intimation to your Excel

lency, least you should otherwise be disposed to believe, that affairs are in extremity in these Colonies, and act accordingly.

My private intercourse is so extensive in these Colonies, and I am so well informed of the private sentiments of their leading men, that I assure you no danger is to be apprehended from their designs. And their measures I am convinced will quickly change, provided they are left to do it in their own way. And upon the best information, joined to certain knowledge of men and matters in Carolina and Georgia, I am fully assured, that if any ships or troops were to be sent into these parts, they would not only totally destroy the present favorable appearances; but in all probability would prove destructive to the good of the service. Upon these ideas, I have regulated my conduct; and I have not as yet even dreamed of applying to Major Furlong; and I firmly believe, that I shall have no occasion to do it.

I sincerely wish your Excellency success in your undertakings; and I have the honour to be, with perfect esteem,

Your Excel. most obt. and most hum. servt.

☞ A fac-simile signature of   JAMES WRIGHT,   was affixed to this letter by the Secret Committee; and an impression of his seal having been taken in clay, the new envelope carried the resemblance of Sir James Wright's seal.*

To his Excel. General Gage.

———

Savannah in Georgia, the 27th of June 1775.

SIR,

Some time ago, I had the honour to receive a letter from the Earl of Dartmouth, dated the 1st of February last, wherein he wrote me, that an order was gone from the Admiralty to you, Sir, to send me one of your cruisers; but, none is yet arrived—nor have I heard any thing of it since. And I am now to acquaint you, that four or five boats, from the South-Carolina side, of our inlet, have been here for ten or twelve days past, full of armed men —it is said near one hundred. We expect a vessel from London every day, with a considerable quantity of gun-powder on board—

* It is said, this forged letter was received by General Gage; and was in a great measure the reason, why troops and vessels were not forwarded at that time, to Georgia—and that upon Governor Wright's meeting General Gage afterwards in London, he asked the General, why he had not assisted him with troops as he had written to him for? When General Gage replied, you wrote me quite the contrary, as I can prove by your own letter in my possession— and upon Governor Wright's inspection of the same, the letter as coming from him, turned out to be a counterfeit!

and *report says*, that these people mean to take it out, and carry it away : and it is not in my power to prevent it. And thus you see, Sir, that our port may, and in short is, blocked up by our neighbours, and that they have it in their power to plunder any thing, that arrives here, and do just what they please. I hope, therefore, that you will be kind enough to give such immediate assistance, as may be in your power, to prevent such insults, and attempts, as I have mentioned.

Pardon me, Sir, for saying, that an armed schooner will be of little use : or any thing less, than a sloop of war of some force— and which, from Lord Dartmouth's letter, I have been long expecting, and impatiently looking out for.

I doubt not, but the situation we are in, will strike you in such a light; that you will see the propriety, of immediate assistance.

Another matter seems to be also necessary for his Majesty's service ; viz. frequent accounts from yourself, and General Gage, with respect to the state of affairs, your way—as, I find it has the greatest influence on the conduct and proceedings of the people here. And I have no way by which, this can be done, unless you are pleased to send it, by some of his Majesty's vessels under your command. I have the honour to be, with perfect esteem,

Sir, your most ob. and most hum. servt.

JAMES WRIGHT

Admiral Graves.

☞ The above Letter, was withdrawn from the envelope, and the following was substituted in its place, by the Secret Committee, and forwarded.

Savannah in Georgia, the 27th June 1775.

SIR,

Some time ago, I had the honour to receive a letter from the Earl of Dartmouth, dated the 1st February last, wherein he wrote to me, that an order was gone from the Admiralty to you, Sir, to send me one of your cruisers. It gives me the highest pleasure so acquaint you, that I now have not any occasion for any vessel of war, and I am clearly of opinion, that his Majesty's service will be better promoted by the absence than the presence of vessels of war in this port. On this subject of military forces, being at present sent to this part of the continent, I have written fully to the General, and I beg leave to refer you, Sir, to that letter, which is of equal date with this.

As I am persuaded it will be for the benefit of the service.that the Southern Governors should have early information of important transactions in your part of the continent, I doubt not, but that if you, Sir, shall be of the same opinion, you will send such by some advice boat. And if such vessel proceeds to Charlestown, my packet may there be sent on shore, and it will reach me, by a secure land conveyance by Express from the Post-Office.

Perhaps Captain Tollemache may give you, Sir, some little alarm about two or three canoes from South-Carolina in this river; waiting, as report says, to take some gun-powder from on board a vessel daily expected to arrive here. But, I acquaint you, Sir, that they are sent upon a smuggling party of goods, into their own Colony, by private directions of their Committee. They mean to procure some gun-powder, and I shall not be displeased if under the appearance of some violence they purchase such an article—as, it is intended to make good the contract made by Mr. Stuart and myself, with the Indians, both Creeks and Cherokees; the latter of whom, will be more convenient for the Carolinians, than the people of Georgia to supply. I have the honour to be, with perfect esteem,

Sir, your most humb. and most obt. servt.

☞ A fac-simile signature of   JAMES WRIGHT,   was affixed to this letter, by the Secret Committee.

Admiral Graves.

☞ The two original letters of Sir James Wright, as well as the copies of the substituted letters, are in the possession of the writer of these Memoirs.

No. V.

Saturday, 23d July 1775

PRESENT,

Colonel Henry Laurens, *President.*

Mr. Ferguson,   Mr. Brewton,
Mr. Middleton,   Mr. Bee,
Hon. Mr. Lowndes,   Capt. Benj. Elliott,
Hon. Mr. Drayton,   Mr. Heyward,
Col. Pinckney,   Col. Parsons.

On motion, Resolved, That the Honble. William Henry Drayton, and the Reverend William Tennent, be the two gentlemen to make a progress into the back country, to explain to the people the causes of the present disputes, between Great Britain and the American Colonies.

Resolved, That the following commissions and powers, be given to the Honble. William Henry Drayton, and the Rev. William Tennent:

South-Carolina:

IN THE COUNCIL OF SAFETY.

July 23d, 1775.

THE COUNCIL OF SAFETY, elected and chosen by the Provincial Congress, begun to be holden the first day of June last; by these Presents, testify, that they have nominated, appointed and commissioned the Honble. William Henry Drayton, and the Reverend William Tennent, to go into the interior parts of this Colony, at the public expense; there, to explain to the people at large, the nature of the unhappy public disputes between Great Britain, and the American Colonies—to endeavour to settle all political disputes between the people—to quiet their minds, and to enforce the necessity of a general union, in order to preserve themselves and their children from slavery. And that the said William Henry Drayton, and William Tennent, may proceed in this business with safety and advantage to the public; all the friends of the Liberties of America, are hereby requested to afford them every necessary aid, assistance, and protection.

By order of the Council of Safety.

HENRY LAURENS, *President.*

South-Carolina:

IN THE COUNCIL OF SAFETY.

Charlestown, 23d July 1775.

GENTLEMEN,

In order to give you every necessary and proper support and protection in your progress into the country, in execution of our commissions of this date, you are hereby authorized, to call upon all and every officer of the militia and rangers, for assistance, support, and protection; and they and each of them, are hereby ordered, to furnish such assistance, support, and protection, as you shall deem necessary.

By order of the Council of Safety.

HENRY LAURENS, *President.*

To the Hon. W. H. Drayton, Rev.
Wm. Tennent, Commissioners, &c.

☞ See Journal of the Council of Safety, No. I. pages 70, 71.

———

No. VI.

Provincial Militia in the early part of 1775, consisting of thirteen Regiments, viz.

Regt. of Horse—William Moultrie, Colonel.

Twelve Regiments of Foot, viz.

1. *Charlestown*—Charles Pinckney, Colonel— Lieutenant-Colonel, James Parsons—Major, Wm. Savage.
   Artillery Company—Owen Roberts, Captain.
2. *Berkley County*—Richard Singleton, Colonel—Lieutenant-Colonel, George Paddon Bond—Major, Stephen Miller.

3. *Granville County*—Stephen Bull, of Sheldon, Colonel—Lieutenant-Colonel, Benjamin Garden—Major, John Lewis Bourquin.
4. *Craven County*—Job Rothmahler, Colonel—Lieutenant-Colonel, Daniel Horry.
5. *Colleton County*—Joseph Glover, Colonel—Lieutenant-Colonel, Samuel Elliott—Major, James Laroche.
6. *Orangeburgh*—William Thomson, Colonel—Lieutenant-Colonel, Christopher Rowe—Major, Lewis Colson.
7. *Cheraws*—George Gabriel Powell, Colonel—Lieutenant-Colonel, Charles Augustus Steward—Major, Abraham Buckholts
8. *Ninety-Six*—John Savage, Colonel—Lieutenant-Colonel, James Mayson—Major, Andrew Williamson.
9. *Camden*—Richard Richardson, Colonel—Lieutenant-Colonel, James M'Girth—Major, Samuel Cantey.
10. *Forks of Saluda*—Robert Starke, Colonel—Lieutenant-Colonel, Moses Kirkland—Major, —— Tyrrel.
11. *Upper Saluda*—Thomas Fletchall, Colonel—Lieutenant-Colonel, John Lisle—Major, John Caldwell.
12. *New Acquisition*—Thomas Neel, Colonel—Lieutenant-Colonel, —— —— —Major, Joseph Robinson.

———

Forts and Garrisons.

Governor of Fort Johnson—Colonel Probart Howarth.
Commander of Fort Charlotte—George Whitefield.
Ordnance-Keeper, and Barrack-Master of Charlestown—John Poaug.
Surgeon, for the Garrisons in the Province—George Milligan.
Commander of Broughton's Bastion, Charlestown—William Henry Drayton.
Commander of Lyttleton's Bastion, Charlestown—Edward Savage.

No. VII.

*To the Delegates in the Continental Congress at Phi-
ladelphia, from South-Carolina.*

Charlestown, July 4th, 1775.

Gentlemen,

The enclosed, are a copy and extracts of letters which fell into the hands of the Secret Committee, who laid them before the Council of Safety. They are thought to be of so great importance, that the Council have desired the Committee of Intelligence to transmit them to you, not only by sea, but through Committee Conveyance, by land. They seem to give some light into the real intentions of Administration; and thereby, you may in some degree, be enabled to guard against their machinations. We have also transmitted proper copies of them, to North-Carolina and Georgia; and we have desired the former Colony, to forward to you, our duplicate of this packet.

We also enclose to you, some copies of our circular letter, to the Committees of this Colony.

This day, the Provincial Congress of Georgia is to sit in Savannah—it is thought, that they will make ample amends for their past conduct—indeed, we think there is no room to doubt of it.

Our own affairs, continue in a good posture. The regiment of Horse, is nearly completed; and the regiments of Infantry are in great forwardness. At present, between 200 and 300 garrison the Barracks; and we mean immediately to establish a fortified Post at Dorchester.   The Council of Safety on Thursday, will go there, to reconnoitre the situation.   This letter comes forwarded by Committee Conveyance from North-Carolina; and is a duplicate of the original, which we have sent by a pilot-boat.

—

To the Committee at Newbern, North-Carolina.

GENTLEMEN,

The enclosed are a copy and extracts of letters, which falling into the hands of our Secret Committee, were laid before the Council of Safety.   By desire of the Council, we transmit them to you; as well to enable you, to counteract your Governor, as to manifest how dangerous he is, to the liberties of America. You see, he means, and is ordered, to arm one part of your people against the other.   We trust, that you will, on this occasion, act with due vigour and policy, in your endeavours to defeat so diabolical a design.

The Council of Safety, most seriously recommend, that you so manage the communication, of this important letter, as to confine it if possible only among the friends of American rights:—as it might be of the most pernicious consequence, if your Governor, or his emissaries, or the disaffected counties, or people at large, should obtain any particular knowledge of it.

We transmit to you, copies of our circular letter —which, if you think proper, may be reprinted:— and, we also transmit to you, a letter to our Delegates, at Philadelphia, which we beg you will forward to them, from one Committee to another.

—

To the Committee at Savannah, Georgia.

GENTLEMEN,

The enclosed are extracts of letters, and an original, which having fallen into the hands of our Secret Committee, and being by them laid before the Council of Safety, the Council have desired the Committee of Intelligence to transmit them to you. Your Chief Justice seems to hold a very criminal correspondence, and to show a disposition no less inimical to the liberties of America.

We also recommend in the most pressing manner, that you keep a watchful eye upon *every motion*, that your Governor *can* make. We enclose to you, copies of our circular letter; and we hope, this dispatch will arrive in due time, to be laid before your Provincial Congress; of whose proceedings, we have the highest expectation.

No. VIII.

Charleston, 22d August 1820.

DEAR SIR,

In compliance with your wishes, to be informed from me, what took place in the Post-Office, when your father, William Henry Drayton, John Neufville, and Thomas Corbet, Esquires, seized the King's Mail, which had just arrived from England, in the Swallow Packet; I have the pleasure to send you, the following account, so far, as I can recollect.

It was about the beginning of July 1775, when those gentlemen came to the office, and demanded the mail. I kept the Post-Office, as Mr. George Roupell, the Post-Master's Deputy: I was then about twenty-five years of age. Upon their arrival at the Post-Office, which was then kept on the Bay, at the corner of Longitude-alley, they demanded the mail which had just arrived from Falmouth in the Swallow Packet, Captain William Copeland; to which, I gave a peremptory refusal. They answered, they would break open the door, and take it by force, if it was not instantly delivered: and came from the window in the street, into the house, for the purpose of forcing open the door. Being then alone in the office, assorting the letters, and late in the evening—the door, but a slight one—and fearing the confusion the breaking it open might cause; as well as exposing the letters and papers of the Office unnecessarily—I did open the door, and admit those gentlemen. They selected all the public documents, and took them away—(I afterwards learnt to the Secret Committee.) The Letters for Lord William Campbell had just before they came, been delivered to his Secretary, Captain Innis; and which, Lord William had received. I immediately informed the Deputy Post-Master-General, George Roupell, Esquire, of the transaction, who, of course, was not well pleased with the conduct of those gentlemen.

This is all I can recollect of this transaction; it being so many years past.

With great respect, I remain,

Dear Sir, respectfully yours,

J. H. STEVENS.

The Hon. Judge Drayton.

CHAPTER IX.

*The Commissioners, William Henry Drayton and
William Tennent, visit certain meetings of people,
and deliver addresses—They recommend measures to
the Council of Safety—Mr. Drayton, accompanied
by Joseph Kershaw of Camden, crosses Saluda River,
and enters the Dutch-Fork—Addresses the Germans
—M'Laurin and Summers influence them against
signing the Association—Mr. Drayton proceeds from
thence, and delivers addresses at other meetings, with
better success—Cunningham and Brown attend a
meeting, and oppose the endeavours of the commissioner—Some account of Brown—The commissioner
alters the time of election at some places—His conduct approved by the Council—The commissioners
form a junction at Fair-Forest, the residence of Col.
Thomas Fletchall—where, they meet Cunningham,
Brown, and Robinson—They endeavour to persuade
Fletchall in favour of American measures—At their
request, he orders a regimental muster—which, Cunningham, Brown, and Robinson, much disapprove—
Brown insults the commissioners—They organize
companies of Volunteers—and recommend to the
Council, that no more goods be allowed to be brought
up to M'Laurin's store—Account of what passed at
Fletchall's—Directions sent to the commanding officer at Fort Charlotte, to be on his guard against surprize—Major Williamson ordered to throw a reinforcement into it—The Frontier towards N. Carolina,
formed into Volunteer companies—Cameron's dupli-*

city—Mr. Drayton sends a Talk to the Cherokee Indians; and invites some of their warriors to a meeting—writes to the Council for presents for them, and Instructions—He recommends vigorous measures, and the seizure of disaffected leaders; without which, an insurrection will ensue—Mr. Tennent's progress, between Broad and Watteree Rivers—The commissioners arrive at Ford's muster-field on the Enoree River; at which place, Col. Fletchall's regiment was to assemble—few men, appear—Kirkland's behaviour—would assault Mr. Drayton—but is prevented by the people—Brown's conduct—The commissioners, meet with little success at the muster-field —and direct their course, towards Savannah River— They arrive at Snow-Hill, and address the people— Mr. Tennent proceeds to the Long-Cane Settlement —where, he gives addresses, and encourages the Volunteer companies—Mr. Drayton turns his attention to the people of Augusta, Snow-Hill, and the Ridge—He receives accounts of an intended insurrection, with the view of attacking Fort Charlotte and Augusta—He sends an Express to Mr. Tennent, who returns to Snow-Hill; and proceeds from thence down Savannah River, towards Charlestown—Mr. Drayton puts forth a Declaration; after which, he takes the field with four swivels, and some militia; and marches for Ninety-Six Court-House—Kirkland makes offers to him, of surrender, which are refused —Kirkland flies to Governor Campbell, in Charlestown—Description of affairs in the Long-Cane Settlement—Three Volunteer companies formed there— Cunningham and Brown collect men—Mr. Drayton arrives at Ninety-Six Court-House—Detaches a party, to surprize Robert Cunningham at O'Neel's Mill—Col. Fletchall approaches—Mr. Drayton prepares to oppose, his crossing Saluda River—sends dispatches to the Council—and, advances his camp, towards the Insurgents—upon which, Col. Fletchall

*moves his camp, nearer Saluda River—Mr. Drayton
issues another Declaration—which. is read in
Fletchall's camp—Mr. Drayton's powers for conduct-
ing this enterprise, considered—A conference takes
place between the Leaders of the contending parties
—A treaty of pacification made—Armies on both
sides discharged—Mr. Drayton proceeds to the Con-
garee Store—where, he meets the Cherokee Chiefs—
Gives them a Talk and presents—Strength of the
Cherokee Nation—Mr. Drayton writes to Alexander
Cameron, and obtains a reply—after which, Mr.
Drayton returns to Charlestown.*

ON the 8th of August, the Commissioners, William
Henry Drayton and William Tennent, crossed the
Congaree River, at the Ferry just above the Congaree
Store, and proceeded some miles to an election. To
the people collected on this occasion, both of the
Commissioners spoke much at length; and they were
so fortunate as not only to give desirable information
to the audience, but to convert some, who had attended
with mischievous purposes; and who, cheerfully
signed the Association. And when the election was
over, the people formed themselves into Volunteer
Companies.

On the 9th of August, they also attended one of the
German musters, which had been ordered by Colonel
Thomson; and the Dutch audience, were so warmed
by the addresses which were delivered, as to induce
several of them to shed tears. Their hearts at this
time, became expanded; and at the conclusion of the
meeting, all of them except fifteen persons signed the
Association; and those fifteen mildly requested they
might have until Friday, to consider of the business,
when they would meet Mr. Drayton, at the place of
Divince Service. The election which had been post-

46

poned by the Commissioners, now took place at the close of this meeting, after the people had been informed of the nature of the dispute with Great Britain; it was conducted, with decorum and satisfaction, and with a view to the public interests.

It having been suggested by the Committee at the Congarees, to the Council of Safety, that Dutch waggoners carrying to Charlestown certificates of their having signed the Association, would tend to influence the interested views of the Dutch settlers, and draw them more easily into the Association; the Council of Safety wrote to that Committee, approving of the measure. But a sly Dutchman, who lived in the Dutch Fork, replied, "that waggoners might easily sell their loads in Charlestown, without any danger of inquiries about certificates." This, being reported to Mr. Drayton, by the Committee of the Congarees, he on the 9th of August wrote to the Council of Safety on the subject; earnestly recommending, that a constant guard of regular troops should be stationed at the town-gate; who should inspect, and inquire of, all waggoners from the Congarees, the fork between Broad and Saluda Rivers, commonly called the Dutch Fork, and Fair-Forest, for certificates of their having associated. And upon their non-production, that they should cause the waggoners to return with their waggon and contents. And he concluded that letter, with this remark: " as I know such a conduct will have great influence, in those parts; I shall give the inhabitants to understand, that such a regulation will take place."*

On the 11th of August, Mr. Drayton, attended by Mr. Joseph Kershaw, of Camden, left the Congaree

* Mr. Drayton's letter to the Council of Safety, dated at the Congarees, 9th August 1775.

Store, and proceeded to a Dutch Church, about ten miles higher up Saluda River. At this place he gave a discourse to the congregation, consisting entirely of Germans; in which, he "thought it prudent to mix many texts of Scripture, showing, that our breaking off all trade and communication with non-subscribers was not any force put upon them." They were otherwise influenced, however, than the former Dutch audience: and only one of them signed the Association. It appeared this conduct of theirs was brought about, through the intrigues of some non-subscribers, who were at the last meeting; and who, on this occasion, not only kept back this Dutch congregation from signing the Association; but actually prevented the fifteen from signing it, who at the last meeting, had requested to be allowed until this day, to make up their minds, and who had attended here for that purpose. Upon this Mr. Drayton thought proper to call to his aid other arguments, than those of patriotism; as he found, these did not go sufficiently home, to the Dutch sensibilities; and he now declared, that no miller who was a subscriber, should grind wheat or corn for any one, who was a non-subscriber. For, as he had failed in drawing on their patriotism, he now trusted to this measure to bring their interests into requisition. This, gave an immediate shock; and excited a general alarm among the Dutch settlers: and they were thereby brought more to reason, as their interests were more closely affected by it. From this place, the progress was continued across Saluda, into the Dutch Fork, to the house and store of Mr. M'Laurin;* where, a meeting of Germans was to assemble: and they were there, addressed on the occa-

---

* M'Laurin's store was situated in the Dutch Fork, at a place he called Spring-Hill; fifteen miles from Saluda River, on the road from thence to Kennedy's Ford on the Enoree River, by the Long-Lane, commonly called the Charlestown Road, on the West side of Broad River—and three miles distant from that river.

sion. But, no arguments could persuade them;
neither was one subscriber to the Association procured: for M'Laurin threw a damp on the people, as
did other disaffected persons, who were present. John
Adam Summers, then a lieutenant in that militia regiment, and Mr. Newffer, men of influence thereabouts,
were also at the meeting; but although Summers had
been induced by the Council of Safety to sign the
Association in Charlestown, and told them "*he will
at any time assemble the people for the purpose;*"* he
nevertheless proved himself a false brother on this
occasion, by keeping at a distance: and by having
reproached Jonas Beard as having been the cause of
his subscribing the Assocation in Charlestown.†
"Newffer, had the day before gathered about one
hundred people together, and was in a fair way of
procuring a numerous subscription; but M'Laurin
hearing of the meeting, and posting to it, soon put a
stop, only by his presence, to the business. Ten, had
subscribed; but, after his appearance, not one person
added his name."† So decided a bearing on the
principles of the Dutch Settlers, by a few influential,
and in general illiterate persons, was very discouraging; and led to much reflection, in the mind of the
Commissioner. However, although the treatment he
received whispered him to desist; yet his duty urged
him forward, to greater trials, and personal dangers.

On Sunday, therefore, (August 13) he proceeded to
another place of Divine Worship, for the purpose of
addressing the congregation after service; but, when
he had nearly arrived at the place, information was
received that Summers would not be there; having
gone to another place of worship. Mr. Drayton now

---

* Letter from Arthur Middleton, member of the Council of Safety, of the
4th August 1775, to Wm. Hy. Drayton, by order of the Council of Safety.

† Wm. Hy. Drayton's letter of 16th August 1775, to the Council of Safety

reflected, that as Summers was a leading man in that settlement, and by his absence manifested his dislike to the object of the progress; and most of his audience the day before, had come from this part of the Fork, he might as well save himself the mortification of speaking to a people, who being ill-advised and obstinate, would not hear.   Mr. Kershaw was also of the same opinion; and, that an attempt, at that time, to shake their opinions, or to remove their scruples, would be useless against the influences which evidently held them in check.   For these reasons, Mr. Drayton, in his letter to the Council of Safety of the 16th of August, says, " we made the best of our way, from this stiff-necked generation:" after which, they arrived at King's Creek, near the lower part of Enoree River.

The settlement in the vicinity of this place, promised better success; it began from the division line between Orangeburgh and Ninety-Six Districts, to Henrick's mill on the Enoree, ten miles above King's Creek.   On the fifteenth of August, a *large gathering*, as it was called in these parts, took place at King's Creek; when, Mr. Drayton delivered a discourse, which was received with apparent satisfaction: and the people expressed a pleasure, and readiness, to sign the Association.   But at this moment, a man came forward, saying Cunningham was at hand; and he hoped the people would first hear, what he had to say. This, brought every thing to a pause—the multitude now indulging the idea, of having the subject argued on both sides: and thus the Commissioner was unexpectedly arrayed as a public disputer, in spite of himself.   It was no time, however, to shrink from the controversy; and Mr. Drayton determined forthwith, to follow Cunningham in all his windings, and misleadings, with which he might endeavour to warp the opinions of the people.   The report ran, that Cun-

ningham had brought a proclamation from the King,
showing the fallacy of the American proceedings.
Upon Cunningham's arrival, he and his company,
were invited to dine with the Commissioner at a dinner which he had ordered; and after it was over, Mr.
Drayton took Cunningham aside, and spoke to him
seriously and politely, respecting the business in hand;
but it did not alter the purpose, for which Cunningham
had arrived.

The people were therefore collected, to receive
what communications should be made; when Cunningham, and Thomas Brown, a Scotchman,* who
had been tarred and feathered at Augusta in Georgia,
took out Dalrymple's Address from the people of
England, to the people of America; and which, they

---

* "A similar circumstance occurred soon after in Augusta, by order of the
Parish Committee of that place. *Thomas Brown*, and William Thompson, had
expressed their enmity to the American cause; accompanied by toasts at a
dinner, ridiculing their procedure. A party pursued them to New-Richmond,
in South-Carolina. Thompson escaped, but Brown was brought back; and
after undergoing a trial before the Committee, was sentenced to be tarred and
feathered, and publicly exposed in a cart; to be drawn three miles, or, until
he was willing to confess his error, and take an oath, that he would thereafter
give his aid and assistance to the cause of freedom."—*M'Call's Hist of Georgia*,
vol. 2d, page 46.

"*Keowee, 16th August* 1775.

"Dear Andrew,

"Mr. Thompson arrived here about ten days ago, round about by Colonel
Fletchall's, and the heads of Saluda; after his miraculous escape from the party
of Liberty Boys, under the command of the heroic Patriot Captain Hamilton
of Augusta. He has been, and is still very ill with a fever, since his arrival: I
believe owing to fatigue, and uneasiness of mind. I am extremely sorry for
Mr. Brown, and poor Donald; and Mr. Thompson informs me, that you were
both obliged to push, the same day that he and Mr. Brown were attacked."—
*Extract from a letter written by Alexander Cameron, one of John Stuart's Deputies
in the Cherokee Nation, to Andrew M'Lean, Esq. intercepted by William Henry
Drayton, during his progress in the Back Country.*—In a postscript to this letter,
the following was written "If the Butcher *Malborrow* has a mind to show his
war exploits, let him come up with a party to the Green Corn dance, which
will be in a few days at Sinicca."

had received from Lord William Campbell, the Governor of Carolina. Brown, performed the part of Orator on this occasion; and read the Address aloud, from beginning to end. In answering the Address, Mr. Drayton applied ridicule, where he thought it would have effect; at which, the people laughed heartily; and Cunningham and Brown had not one word to say in reply. After this, the people were satisfied; and according to their mode of expression, they said Cunningham was beaten off the field. And so he was, in fact: for highly mortified, he and his worthy companion of tar and feather memory,—stole away.

The day of election for Representatives to the Provincial Congress, now arriving; the people in this part of the Fork, assembled on the occasion: but, a letter from Cunningham, Kirkland, and others arriving, the election was quashed: and, the people departed. The Commissioner, however, gave notice, that there would yet be an election, at which he would attend; and he afterwards directed the same should take place on the 23d of August: he also appointed an election to take place in the lower part of the Fork, on the 24th. He was induced to these measures, as deeming them the most prudent modes of composing the minds of the people; and as bringing them as nearly as could be, within the resolution of the Provincial Congress on the subject: for which reasons, he thought himself authorized to order these elections.* And his conduct in the premises, was not only approved by the Council of Safety; as expressed to him, by their letters of the 11th and 13th; but they also directed him to appoint elections for those places, where none had been holden.

* Mr. Drayton's letter to the Council of Safety, dated King's Creek, near Enoree, Aug. 16th, 1775.

On Thursday the 17th of August, Mr. Drayton and Mr. Kershaw, arrived at Colonel Fletchall's residence at Fair-Forest; where, they found Thomas Brown, Cunningham, and Robinson, who had arrived the evening before; as had also, Mr. Tennent and Colonel Richardson. The Heads of Parties as they then stood, were now convened; and, for the first time, they had all met together, since the Commissioners had commenced their progress. Mr. Tennent in his letter to the Council of Safety of the 20th August says, "We have at length visited the great and mighty nabob, Fletchall. We found him surrounded by his court, viz. Cunningham, Brown, and Robinson; who watch all his motions; and, have him under great command. We soon found, the unchangeable malignity of their minds; and the inexpressible pains they were at, to blind the people, and fill them with bitterness against *the Gentlemen,* as they are called. Gen. Gage's pamphlet, is raging through the District, and greedily read. The leaders have taken the same methods with the Romish Church, to keep the people ignorant; and in general, they firmly believe that no man, that comes from below—and that no paper printed there—can speak the truth. This was necessary, in order to prevent any thing we can say, from taking place. We soon found, that reasoning was vain, with those who were fixed by royal emoluments."* This letter shows in a new light, the state of things in the interior: and is the first of the Rev. William Tennent's letters during the progress, which has come to the hands of the writer of these Memoirs. It is to be regretted, that his letters had not been more; or if they were, that they have not been found among those papers, which form the basis of the present Chapter: by reason of which, Mr. Tennent's progress between the Broad and Watteree Rivers, has not been

See Appendix to this Chapter, No. I.

brought into that public consideration; to which, no
doubt his valuable services in that tour, justly entitled
him.   However, the rough manuscript of William
Henry Drayton mentions, that Mr. Tennent and himself, had very good success; and especially so, as they
quitted the Dutch Settlements.   And Mr. Tennent in
his letter above mentioned, states that he had formed
one, and was then forming another troop of Volunteer
Horse Rangers; who were then hemming in the
Dissidents on that side of the progress.   Indeed, he
appears to have been indefatigable in executing the
duties he had in charge, as particularly evinced by the
closing of his letter; in which he says, " I have forsook my chaise, and ride on horseback from day to
day, meeting people."

On the 21st of August, Mr. Drayton wrote a letter
from Lawson's Fork, to the Council of Safety; giving
the particulars of what passed, while the Commissioners remained at Col. Fletchall's.   In that letter,
he acknowledged the receipt of letters from the
Council of the 11th and 13th insts.: and returns them
thanks, for the approbation of his conduct in general;
as well as for their approbation of his postponing the
election at Saxe-Gotha, and their authorizing him to
appoint elections for those places, where none had
been holden.   He therein assured the Council, " that
unless our friends in the country find, that the non-
subscribers are debarred all communication with
Charlestown, and all trade with the country stores,
they will be much chagrined; and bad consequences
may ensue.   In particular, I most earnestly recommend, that no more goods be allowed to be sent up, to
M'Laurin's store.   His partner in town, is one
M'Curry, or Curry,—some such name.   This man,
has signed the Association: and under this sanction,
he means to supply M'Laurin's; by which means, the
Dutch will be encouraged to persevere in their obsti-

nacy. And I beg leave to caution you, even against
M'Laurin's signing the Association, if he should think
proper to do so to procure goods; for, the Dutch
agree, if there should be a necessity, that he should
be allowed to subscribe, and then, they would be
supplied as usual, without their acceding to the Association.

" The commissions for the Volunteer Companies
are not come to hand; but I suppose they are with
Col. Thompson; who, in all probability will continue
in his new camp, until my arrival there. I reached
Col. Fletchall's last Thursday morning, before breakfast; and Mr. Tennent and myself after breakfast,
engaged him in a private conversation, during near
three hours. We endeavoured to explain every thing
to him. We pressed them upon him; and endeavoured to show him, that we had a confidence in him.
We humoured him. We laughed with him. Then
we recurred to argument, remonstrances, and entrea-
ties, to join his country, and all America. All that we
could get from him was this: ' *He would never take
up arms against his King, or his countrymen; and,
that the proceedings of the Congress at Philadelphia,
were impolitic, disrespectful, and irritating to the King.*'
We charged him, with having written to the Governor; and with having received an answer: he confessed both. We named the day, (the Sunday preceding,) he received the answer: he allowed it. We
named the method, by which he received it, concealed
in a cane; he appeared confounded: but after a pause,
he attempted to laugh off this last particular. Robinson brought up this letter; and Fletchall would not
show it to us. Robinson declares, he has brought up
a commission to raise men for the King; and he even
had the imprudence to say before me, that he should
raise men for the defence of his person, since many
people had threatened him. I answered, surely the

civil power, would not allow him to go about with armed men, to the terror of the King's subjects. He replied, why did not the civil power prevent the Congress from having armed men; and, surely, he would have armed men so long, as they had any. This man's looks, are utterly against him; much venom appears in Cunningham's countenance, and conversation. Neither of these men, say much; but Brown* is the spokesman; and his bitterness and violence, is intolerable. He has in various ways insulted us, during our twenty-four hours stay at Fletchall's; as if he wanted to provoke me to violence. At length, he went so far, as to tell me, he believed we did not mean well to the King; and, that our professions, were nothing but a cloak. At this provocation, after many others, I almost lost my caution; but thank God, I did not even appear to do so: in a very firm tone, I severely checked him; the Colonel, bid him go to bed. Before this happened, we had engaged the Colonel in the private conversation, to call out his regiment as on the 23d instant; upon our return to the house, where this Brown, Cunningham, and Robinson were, he mentioned what he had promised. All three of them, were open mouthed against the measure; and Mr. Tennent and myself, had much to do, to keep the Colonel to his promise. This meeting of the regiment, will be at the time and place of election, at Ford's; and, I am not without some apprehensions, that some violence will then be used against us. I enclose a letter from Mr. Tennent to me, the day we parted at the Colonel's. And, besides this; it is my firm belief, that Brown, Cunningham, and Robinson, will do every thing in their power, to bring things to extremities: for, they are clearly of opinion, they can beat the whole Colony. These men, manage Fletchall as they please; when, they have him to themselves.

_____

The same who was tarred and feathered at Augusta

Indeed, he is so fixed, and has made so many declarations; that I firmly think, his pride and false sense of honour, will never allow him to appear to think as we do; even, if these men were not about him. Mr. Kershaw told me, he knew the man; and, that no confidence was to be placed in him.

"Things wearing so unfavorable an appearance, Colonel Richardson, Mr. Kershaw, Mr. Tennent and myself, unanimously thought it absolutely expedient, to direct Captain P—— to raise an additional troop of Rangers immediately, to lie on the back of these people. And Mr. Tennent and myself have given directions accordingly: not doubting, but that the necessity of the case, will induce you to approve the measure. Captain P—— came to us, appeared much concerned for his past conduct; attributing it to a mistake, touching the station of the Rangers; which, he had thought, had been by the Congress fixed to the back country and frontiers. He has been since, active in our favour, and is a person of influence in his part of the country, on the back of Fletchall—his brother, is a man of great influence in Mecklinburgh; and ready to march to our assistance when called upon: and already, Fletchall looked upon Captain P——, as an acquisition to his party. Hence, to bind Captain P——'s brother, and all the friends of both to us; to quash Fletchall's expectation from the Captain; and, to have a troop of Rangers on the back of Fletchall's people to watch their motions; we all thought it absolutely necessary to direct the raising of this *additional troop; as we* apprehended you would consider Captain P——'s letter and conduct, as a resignation of his commission: and that you had already disposed of it.

" In consequence of the affidavit taken by Captain P——,* I have dispatched an express to the Commanding officer at Fort Charlotte, and directions to Major Williamson, to throw into the fort, a reinforcement of thirty militia; to be continued there, by proper relieves, during one month.   In which time, I make no doubt, the whole Colony, will be in a state of perfect security against internal commotion.   The garrison there, will now consist of seventy odd men.   I have also given Major Williamson directions, to hold the militia in readiness, to march in case of any commotion.

" I had this day a meeting with the people in this frontier.   Many present, were of the other party; but

---

* " Appeared personally before me Zachariah Bell and swore, that walking near the house of Colonel Fletchall, he heard one of six or seven men in a group say ; that a person (whose name he did not hear) was to go, within ten days, to seize upon powder ; the Deponent could not hear the name of the place.   At which, another answered, that he (the first speaker) had better not go ; for, if he did, with double the number of men, they might expect to be killed, and not succeed.   Sworn before me, this 18th day of August 1776, on the road near Fair-Forest.

" E—— P——, jun."

This affidavit, was enclosed to Mr. Drayton, in a letter from Mr. Tennent, of the following purport.

" DEAR SIR,

" Coming to the knowledge of the above, and no longer doubting of the infernal design to take Fort Charlotte, by the Governor's order, and to open a dismal campaign in this quarter, by this means; I send this express: that you may advertize the Fort, and throw as many men into it as possible, and disappoint them.   I have put things together, and am no longer at a loss, as to the design to embody men; as an asylum for all the tories, and that shortly.   And am yours,

" WM. TENNENT.

" P. S. From a question asked me by the Colonel, I suspect some harsh design : be upon your guard.

" To the Hon. Wm. Henry Drayton,
         at Mr. Muckelwaines."

I have the pleasure to acquaint pou, that these became
voluntary converts. Every person received satisfaction, and departed with pleasure. I finished the day,
with a barbequed beef. I have so ordered matters
here, that this whole frontier, will be formed into
Volunteer companies; but, as they are at present,
under Fletchall's command, they insist upon being
formed into a regiment, independent of him; and I
flatter myself, you will think this method of weakening Fletchall, to be consistent with sound policy.
These people, are active and spirited; they are staunch
in our favour; are capable of forming a good barrier
against the Indians; and, of being a severe check upon
Fletchall's people on whom they border, if they
should think of quitting their habitations under the
banners of Fletchall, or his companions. For these
reasons, and to enable them to act with vigour, I shall
take the liberty to supply them with a small quantity
of ammunition; for, now they have not one ounce:
when, they shall be formed into regular companies.
Several companies will be formed, by this day week.

"I enclose to you, an affidavit, by which you will
see, there is no dependance on Cameron. I have sent
up a short talk to the Cherokees, inviting them to
come down to me within twelve days to Amelia. Mr.
Pearis, has undertaken to conduct six of their head
men to me; and I should be glad, within the time
mentioned, to receive from you £70, or £80 worth of
shirts, watch-coats, blankets, linen, strouds, and
paints: and your instructions, if you choose I should
say any thing in particular to them. On Wednesday,
I shall with Mr. Tennent, Mr. Hart, and Mr. Reise,
attend the election and review of Fletchall's regiment,
at Ford's, at the mouth of Cedar Creek upon Enoree.
You will see the place, in the small map. What the
event will be, I am at a loss to say. I do not expect,
any success. I apprehend some insults. I may be

mistaken, in both opinions. Within twelve days, I
purpose to be, at Colonel Thompson's camp; where, I
think it will be adviseable that I should remain, till I
shall see every spark of insurrection extinguished:
but, in regard to this, I shall regulate myself by your
orders on the subject; which, I hope to receive, by
the time I arrive at the camp. If Kirkland shall be
seized, without doubt a commotion will follow; and,
if he goes off with impunity and without question, it
will be fatal to the discipline of the army—especially,
the Rangers. But this is not all. Vigorous measures
are absolutely necessary. If, a dozen persons, are
allowed to be at large; our progress, has been in vain
—and, we shall be involved in a civil war, in spite of
our teeth. In giving you this information, I tell a
melancholy truth; but, I do my duty. If certain persons should be secured, some commotion in all probability will follow; but, I am so well acquainted with
the situation of the disaffected parts of the country;
and with such parts, as may be brought against them,
that I am under no apprehensions, for the consequences: provided, prompt and vigorous measures,
attend every appearance of insurrection.

"I would beg leave to observe, that as this business
is of the highest importance; so, your orders on the
subject should be clear and general, to vest proper
authority, to take such measures, as may tend to suppress this threatening insurrection; that will assuredly
break out, by delay; and come upon us, unexpectedly."

"Perhaps, my being arrived at the camp, in my
return home, may be construed an expiration of the
powers vested in Mr. Tennent and myself; and his
return to Charlestown, may work an annihilation of
powers, to be exercised by us together. For, as our
continuance in the country, will be of but little benefit

in the Dutch Settlements, and the disaffected quarters, while under the influence of Fletchall's people; so, I make no doubt, but that Mr. Tennent, will choose to return to town; sensible, that his presence in the country will not be of any advantage, in the way of expounding our political texts to the people.

"I have the honour, to lay all things, fully before you, that, you may regulate yourselves thereupon; and send orders to me at Amelia; by which, I shall either remain with the camp—or, return to Charlestown. But, I pray you to be expeditious; for, a delay on your parts, will allow the enemy, to recover many of our converts; and, I know they are active, malicious, and bent upon mischief.

"Mr. Tennent and Col. Richardson, were successful in their journey, beyond Broad River. Mr. Tennent, is now in Neel's quarters;* where, they are very hearty in our cause. Mr. Kershaw and Col. Richardson, took their leave of us, when we quitted Fletchall: being sensible, they could not in those parts, be of any assistance to us. They, have been very diligent."

Such, was the situation of public affairs, on the 21st August 1775, in all that portion of country, which spreads from the Wateree and Catawba Rivers, westwardly, to Savannah River; and extends northwardly, from Saluda River, up to the Cherokee nation, and the boundary between North and South-Carolina. And Mr. Drayton's letter to the Council of Safety has been introduced nearly at length, to show the various emergencies which he and Mr. Tennent had to meet, on an occasion like this; and with what ability and foresight, he spread forth impending dangers to the

---

* Thomas Neel, Colonel of the Regiment of militia, in the New Acquisition.

Council, while, he proposed means of preventing their mischievous effects. Nor, had he any time to lose. For, on the very day, on which he wrote the above letter, Major Andrew Williamson found it necessary to forward dispatches from White-Hall, the place of his residence, to Captain John Caldwell of the Rangers, commanding at Fort Charlotte; by which he informed him, some of the disaffected people about Stephens' Creek, were going to attack Augusta; and that he should be on his guard as to the defence of that fort; as in such attempt, they would have the fort also in their view.

The Commissioners in the course of their progress met again on the 23d August, at Ford's on the Enoree; where Colonel Fletchall, Kirkland, the Cunninghams, and Brown, had also arrived: and by the contrivances of the heads of the party, very few persons had assembled. At this place one thousand men generally meet, at regimental musters; and, when Fletchall's Association, of which mention has been made, was signed at this musterfield, fifteen hundred men were present. At this time, however, there were not more than two hundred and fifty persons; and many of those, were friends to the American cause, who had come there, from distant homes. And so little care did the disaffected leaders take to beguile the reason why so many men stayed away, that Captain Cunningham, informed the Commissioners himself, he had told his men, " that if they were satisfied with their present opinions there was no occasion for them to come to hear the *addresses.*" Other Captains told their men " the Colonel left it to them, to come or not as they pleased; and if they stayed away, he would not be angry with them." It will, however, be better to give an account of this meeting, in the language of the Commissioners themselves, as expressed in their joint letter from Ford's, on the 24th of August, to the Council of Safety.

48

" The most perfect good order prevailed with the
people, who heard us with much attention.   But
Kirkland treated the Congress, the Committee, the
Council, and ourselves, with the highest insolence.
Nay, he was on the point of assaulting Mr. Drayton;
and, in all prbability would have done it, which would
have brought on bloodshed;* but that the pressure of
the people about Mr. Drayton, gave him to understand, that an attack made by him, would be premature.   Imagine every indecency of language, every
misrepresentation, every ungenerous and unjust charge
against the American politics, that could alarm the
people, and give them an evil impression of our designs against their liberties, and the rights of Great
Britain—imagine all you can, on these points; and,
you will not exceed, what we heard, as well from
Kirkland, as from Brown.   Our indignation was
painful—for, we were obliged to conceal it: and, our
situation was as disagreeable, as you can well conceive.   Brown, loudly declared, that when the King's
troops arrived, he would join them against us; and,
he hoped, every other person in these parts, would do
the same.

" We have the pleasure, however, to inform you,
that the Address from the people of England, to the
people of America, appears to have lost its credit.
Brown read it—but, he had but few hearers: we, did
not think it worth our while, to attend to it; or, say
one word in answer to it.

" We waited so long, for the assembling of the people; and, the discourses and pamphlet took up so

* On this progress, Mr. Drayton always had about his person, a dirk and a
pair of pocket pistols; for the defence of his life—and for protecting himself
from insult.

much time, that no election could be held.   This day fortnight, is appointed for the holding of it.

" Kirkland and the Cunninghams, appeared here with arms, sword and pistol.   Their intention did not appear good; and the very small audience clearly manifests, that the sentiments of the party, continue inimical.   However, we have acquired several of Fletchall's Captains.

" There was a subscription of the Association; about seventy names: but, most of these persons had already signed: and now again signed, in order to give a good example.   We shall be at Ninety-Six Court-House, on Sunday; and, from thence, we shall shape our course to Amelia."

The Commissioners now turned their backs on Colonel Fletchall, and his party; and proceeded towards Savannah River, on their way to Ninety-Six Court-House: and from thence, they passed on, to Mr. Hammond's residence *Snow Hill*, nearly opposite to Augusta.   At this place, the Commissioners gave addresses to a numerous meeting; and Mr. Tennent then went on a progress into the Long-Cane Settlement: while, Mr. Drayton turned his attention to the people of Augusta, and those in the neighbourhood of Snow Hill, and the Ridge; at which last place, a meeting of inhabitants was shortly to assemble.

By various accounts which Mr. Drayton received on the 29th of August and the day following, the fact appeared established; that Kirkland had actually taken up arms, for the purpose of attacking Fort Charlotte, and Augusta: and, that the King's men, as they were called, were to meet on the 29th inst. at a place about twenty miles above Snow Hill.   This put an end to the progress: and Mr. Drayton sent an express to Mr. Tennent, advising him of the existing circumstances; which caused him to retrace his steps down Savannah River. The intended meeting, accordingly took place; after which, these King's men seaparated during the night; having agreed, to meet again in two or three days with arms and provisions, in order to march upon Fort Charlotte and Augusta: and Cunningham and Brown were to be of the party.

In this situation of affairs, Mr. Drayton in his letter of the 30th of Aug. 1775, dated at Mr. Hammond's near Augusta, and directed to the Council of Safety, says, " by virtue of your letter of the eleventh instant, I have ordered out three companies near this place to assemble immediately; and who will be joined by one hundred men from Augusta. I have ordered Major Williamson to march with three hundred men, to Harlen's Ford on Savannah River, about thirty miles above this place. I have also ordered Colonel Thompson to march his Rangers, and as near three hundred militia as he can, to take post at the Ridge; and Colonel Richardson with three hundred men, to take post near the mouth of the Enoree, to be a check on Fletchall's people, in case they should show any intention of assisting Kirkland. I beg leave to recommend, that a proper quantity of powder and ball, be sent to Colonel Richardson, so that he may be enabled to supply Colonel Neel's regiment.

" I have not been honoured with any letters from you, but those of the 11th and 13th instants. However, as soon as Kirkland's party shall take the field, I shall hold myself fully authorized by your letter of the eleventh, and the necessity of affairs, to proceed to every extremity, that may have a tendency to suppress those men, who oppose the authority of Congress."

Having taken these measures, Mr. Drayton now prepared to support the cause, in which he was engaged, by other means than discourses: but, before he resorted to the. *ultima ratio*, he caused the following Declaration to be published by the sheriff of Ninety-Six Dictrict.

" *South-Carolina, Ninety-Six District.*

" By the Honourable William Henry Drayton, Esquire.

" Whereas by commission from the Honourable the Council of Safety, for this Colony, dated the 23d day of July last, I am upon a progress through the country, ' to explain to the people at large the nature of the unhappy disputes between Great Britain and the American Colonies; to endeavour to settle all political disputes with the people; to quiet their minds; and to enforce the necessity of a general union, in order to preserve themselves and their children from slavery:' And whereas the progress having been continued almost through the Colony, with success to the state, satisfaction to the people, and, upon the most perfect principles, tending to promote peace and good order; for the purposes of the progress aforesaid, I did appoint, that a meeting of the people should be held, on Friday next, the first day of September, at the Ridge in the district aforesaid: But whereas, one Moses Kirkland having, without lawful authority, assembled men in arms, in the district aforesaid, it is but too evident, that, to his treachery against this Colony, he means to add crimes of a deeper dye, and, by force of arms, to violate the public peace: wherefore, it is become inexpedient, that the intended meeting of the people should be held as aforesaid; lest the meeting should furnish occasion for civil bloodshed, which it is our purpose to avoid, as long as may be possible:

" And whereas, by the arts, frauds, and misrepresentations of the said Moses Kirkland, some weak and
ignorant people have been led into measures of so
criminal a nature, as, if persisted in, must inevitably
involve them in destruction—from motives of humanity, I therefore do hereby recommend to all such persons, that they forthwith desist from following the
counsels of the said Moses Kirkland in points tending
to sedition and hostility; and I do hereby notify, that
all such persons as, without lawful authority, shall
assemble in arms, in company with, or by instigation
of, the said Moses Kirkland, will be deemed public
enemies, to be suppressed by the sword.

" Given under my hand, at Snow Hill, in the district aforesaid, this 30th of August 1775.
       " WILLIAM HENRY DRAYTON."

These prompt and decided measures, the knowledge of which was industriously circulated, confounded Kirkland, and paralized his exertions.   The
intended meeting with provisions and arms was dropped; and he dispatched his brother to Mr. Drayton,
with offers of surrender, on promise of pardon.   But
Mr. Drayton well knowing his demerits, demanded
his surrender at discretion; and his heart thereupon
failing him, he thought only of escape.   In devising
the means of doing so, he lurked about for some days;
after which, with two trusty friends he fled in disguise
to Charlestown; from whence, he was privately sent
on board the sloop of war Tamer, by the directions of
Governor Campbell.

When Mr. Drayton put forth this declaration, Mr.
Tennent was in Long-Cane Settlement; where, he
was diffusing political and moral information with
that zeal and address, which had marked his conduct,
throughout the progress of the Commissioners.   And

the following letter from him to the Council of Safety, dated "Long-Cane, 1st September 1775," will picture the situation of that part of the Colony, through which to Fort Charlotte, Kirkland's first movements would have taken place, at the eventful period; at which, we are about to arrive. "This comes by Captain George Reid's waggon from the Long-Canes, where I am at present. I parted from Mr. Drayton on Monday morning; he steered his course to Augusta, and thence designed for the camp at Amelia. I thought it necessary to visit the settlements, on this side of Saluda. Met a large congregation yesterday, and found the people divided in their sentiment. Spoke at least two hours to them, to good effect. The prevailing party here, is for American measures, by the agency of some of our worthy members; but, they need confirmation. I have therefore appointed three meetings, at which, I expect to see the greater number of the disaffected. I shall then cross over into Fletchall's regiment, once more, to be at an election appointed at Ford's, on Enoree; where, we expect great opposition, if not violence, from Cunningham's party. Brown will bring them to blood, if he can, but I still hope, it may be prevented. I consider myself, as running great risks; but, think it my duty.

"Our visit, has given their party a great shock—divided their friends—and strengthened our interest much. One of their chiefs confessed to me, at Little River; that he brought up the thanks of the Governor to Mr. Cunningham, for what he had done, and is doing. The Governor's intrigue here, is as evident as the light of the sun. The evidences of their design by the Indians, is no doubt clear to the Council from the papers sent down already.

"The inhabitants here, are in great terror, as far as they have heard of their danger; and that because

they have no ammunition. The leaders have frequently dropped in company, that they intend to form
a camp. I am sure, they will find a smaller number
ready to befriend them, than they imagine: but, their
dependance, is upon the savages to join their army;
and that the rest of the inhabitants will be forced to
join them, to save their families from a massacre. I
am taking proper measures in this district, to prevent
the horrible conspiracy. Three volunteer companies
are formed—one under Major Terry, who now seems
animated in the cause—another, under Captain Pickins*—a third, under Captain James M'Call. More
of the like kind, is going on as fast as may be. The
great difficulty, is the want of ammunition. They
evidently have a design upon Fort Charlotte; and, our
friends cannot collect to defend it, unless they are supplied. I have therefore, promised them a supply. If
you, therefore, gentlemen, think it proper, it will be of
the greatest utility to send up 100, or 150 pounds
weight of powder, and some lead by the bearer Samuel
Reed; who will effectually secrete it, until delivered
safe into the hands of the volunteer companies; to be
subject to the order of the Council, in case it is not
used for the defence of the Colony. It will be effectually secured, and a small delay, may be greatly dangerous. The same measure will be necessary, on the
other side Broad River.

"I could wish, that Virginia might be alarmed and
ready: and, that a categorical answer might be demanded of the Cherokees, before the time of danger.
The Creeks are in some danger, from one Thompson,
an emissary, now among them. I shall visit Fort

---

* This appears to be the first commencement of the honourable military
career which this gentleman ran, during the American Revolutionary war. As
Col. Pickins, he commanded the militia at the battle of the Cowpens; and a
part of the militia at the battle of Eutaws: which ended highly honourable to
the American arms.

Charlotte before I return; and hope to let you hear more particularly on these subjects, next week."

In consequence, however, of the express Mr. Drayton sent to Mr. Tennent from Snow Hill, he did not proceed to Fort Charlotte as he proposed. But he dispatched orders to Captain Caldwell commanding there, to erect platforms for fighting the cannon, as expeditiously as possible; and to mount two of the best four-pounders, on high wheels, for field use. He was directed to be careful who entered the fort; and to advance centinels and patrols. In addition to this, the standing Indian corn around the fort was ordered to be cleared away, to some distance; and what was left, was to be bladed and topped; so, as not to afford cover to an enemy. In case of the approach of enemies, alarm cannon were ordered to be fired towards the settlements, as a signal to the volunteer companies, to commence their march, and be in readiness. Capt. Caldwell was farther ordered by Mr. Tennent, to issue 150 pounds weight of gun-powder, and lead in proportion, to the Captains of the volunteer companies; who had associated, for the security of that part of the district: and to send away his troop horses to safe pasturage, at a distance, where they might be commanded again, within a day and a half, that men might not be hazarded as a grass guard for them; and be more ready to defend the fort. Having done these things, Mr. Tennent retrogaded towards Snow Hill; but Mr. Drayton having marched from thence, Mr. Tennent proceeded down Savannah River towards Charlestown.

Notwithstanding Kirkland's flight, his principal coadjutors, Cunningham and Brown, proceeded in collecting men. And affidavits taken before Colonel Hammond, were transmitted to the Council of Safety, stating, that men were assembled in arms by Kirkland

—that their objects were Augusta and Fort Charlotte
—that Kirkland kept armed men about him—and,
that he endeavoured to extend the opposition against
the Congress.

To counteract all these projects of the malecontents,
Mr. Drayton on the 6th day of September in the evening, commenced his march for Ninety-Six Court-
House, with one hundred and twenty men, and four
swivels: his intention being with the Rangers and
militia when assembled at the Court-House, to march
into Fletchall's quarters, and compel a surrender of the
principal opposers.   His arrival at Ninety-Six on the
8th, brought the first news of his having marched;
and he immediately dispatched a party, to surprize
Robert Cunningham: but he had quitted his residence
the day before.   However, some of his papers were
taken possession of; particularly, two letters from
Colonel Fletchall.

On the 10th of September advice was received, that
a party of the malecontents, were collecting at
O'Neel's Mill; when one hundred men were sent off,
to disperse them.   In their march they received information apparently plausible, that Colonel Fletchall
had joined the party at O'Neel's, with a large body of
men; and that he contemplated attacking the troops at
Ninety-Six Court-House, about two o'clock in the
morning.   At this time, Mr. Drayton's whole force,
including those who had been detatched to O'Neel's
Mill, consisted only, of eighty-four volunteers from
Georgia, and one hundred and forty-one Carolina
militia; amounting in the whole, to two hundred and
twenty-five men, including officers.   In this emergency, a consultation was holden with the principal officers, Major Mayson, Major Williamson, and
Captain Hammond.   A choice of three propositions
was presented, for consideration.   To retreat towards

Colonel Thompson and his Rangers, then at the Ridge—to defend Ninety-Six—or, to march and ambuscade the enemy. As to the first, it was considered, that if it placed a small force out of the reach of one greatly superior; the retreat of that small force would dishearten the people, and encourage the malecontents. The second was difficult; for the Court-House at Ninety-Six, was not musket proof; and the brick gaol, was unequal to contain a third of the troops. As to the third proposition, it was concluded, that the malecontents coming to surprize, would not expect to be surprized on their march in the night; during which, they would be in confused order: and that if pressed on the occasion, a general rout would probably ensue. This last measure, was consequently adopted; and orders were issued, for carrying it immediately into execution.

For this purpose, the four swivels were planted in the four windows of the gaol, so as to command every front of approach; and a suitable number of men were posted in it, with ammunition, and a supply of water. Nothing could force this post, but its being fired by the roof; which was shingled. One hundred men, were then advanced in ambush to the Island-ford, six miles from the Court-House; and where, the malecontents must pass, in approaching to it—and one hundred men were posted, about midway, between the Island-ford, and Ninety-Six Court-House. All this was done, by 10 o'clock that night; and Mr. Drayton, with Major Williamson, proceeded to view, the disposition which had been so directed. When they arrived at the Island-ford, the disposition of the troops there under Major Mayson was altered in such manner, as to deliver a diagonal fire upon Fletchall's party, as they crossed Saluda River. After which, in good order, they waited their approach, until half past two in the morning; when Mr. Drayton received certain accounts, the alarm was false; for, only Cunningham was at O'Neel's with about one hundred men. However, to leave every thing safe, the advance under Major Mayson, was continued until daylight; and Mr. Drayton and Major Williamson returned to Ninety-Six, between three and four o'clock in the morning with the rest of the troops: during all which time, the men behaved with the most perfect obedience; and demonstrated a determination of doing their duty.

The day after this event, Mr Drayton addressed a letter on the 11th September from Head-Quarters at Ninety-Six, to the Council of Safety; giving a detailed account of these transactions. In which he mentions that "Fletchall, Brown and Cunningham have been, since the first alarm that I wrote you of, and still are, endeavouring to assemble men. As they have yet no force embodied, it is plain their influence is declining; and, that their people are terrified. And this last, I assure you, is a fact: as they never dreamed we would take the field. They thought, their boast of four thousand men, would ensure their security against us. And, I have well-grounded information, that the assemblage they are now endeavouring to make, is with a view to make terms of accommodation, so as they may be quiet, (that is, for the present; while the Governor cannot assist them, *as he tells them,*) and trade to Charlestown: rather, than with any design of fighting."

On the 17th of September Mr. Drayton addressed another letter to the Council of Safety; in which he recommends to them, not to distribute any powder in the Dutch Fork, or Ninety-Six District. He therein stated, that the hundred men which Cunningham had with him at O'Neel's mill, were but the first of a large party which had been summoned to rendezvous there.

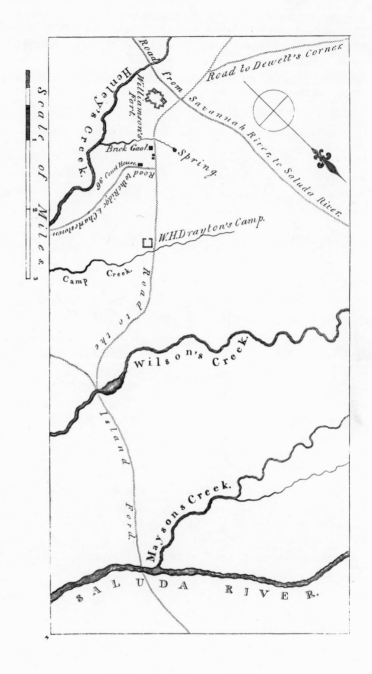

about ten miles over Saluda: and that Col. Thompson with his Rangers, and a few militia had joined him, at Ninety-Six Court-House. In two days after, Mr. Drayton was joined by a considerable number of Major Williamson's regiment of militia. In the mean time, Colonel Fletchall had arrived at O'Neel's mill; and his men, were increasing fast in numbers. At this time, Mr. Drayton marched from Ninety-Six Court-House; and formed a camp in advance of that place, about three quarters of a mile; upon which, Fletchall moved his camp to within four miles of Saluda River; so, that the opposing parties, were within ten miles of each other, being separated by the river Saluda. At this time, Fletchall's men amounted to upwards of twelve hundred; while Mr. Drayton's hardly reached one thousand. However, they were in good spirits, had been kept under due subordination, and were desirous of being led against the malecon-tents. Had this measure been then entered into, many lives would have been lost: as the minds of Fletchall's people, were not then turned towards any other mea-sure, than opposition to the patriots, or their submis-sion or dispersion. Mr. Drayton, however, found, that he could perfectly rely upon the officers and men, who were embodied with him; and as they had been trained to good order in camp, and were well supplied with provisions, he had reason to believe, he could keep them together, so long, as the occasion might require: particularly, as Fletchall's men being under little command, and having no regular supplies, would probably not keep long together; and that having their greatest influx of strength, impatience and dis-content might produce a re-action and decrease.

With the perfect approbation of Colonel Thompson, Major Williamson, and Captain Hammond, Mr. Drayton for the above considerations, determined to continue encamped; and to watch Fletchall's mo-

tions: and with this view, he put every thing in practice, to persuade Fletchall, he would persevere in this
plan.   Among other devices, he sent a letter directed
to Col. Richardson, written for deception; in order,
that it might be intercepted.   These had an effect, in
weakening the impulse of the insurgents; and led to
farther delays: during which time, Mr. Drayton's
forces were increasing, by the coming in of militia.
At length, in order still farther to amuse and gain
time, while the army was increasing—to shake the
belief of the malecontents, mischievously raised against
the public intentions—to point out to them, that their
safety was to be found only, by being peaceable at
home—and, to threaten the utmost rigour to such as
continued in arms—Mr. Drayton put forth another
Declaration on the 13th of September, and which,
being sent to Fletchall's camp, was there publicly
read.   This instrument, was in the following words:

" *South-Carolina.*

"By the Hon. William Henry Drayton, Esquire.

" A DECLARATION.

" Whereas, the liberties of America, being treache-
rously and cruelly violated by an abandoned Administration in Great Britain, surrounding the Throne, and
deceiving Majesty for their own corrupt purposes;
thirteen American Colonies, including New-Hampshire to the North, and Georgia to the South, virtu-
ously, glorously, and thanks to the Lord of Hosts,
successfully, are confederated at the hazard of their
lives and fortunes, to wrest from the hands of traitors,
those invaluables, which they had ravished from them,
and which, the Americans have in vain, endeavoured
to recover, by every peaceable mode of application :

" And whereas, the tools of Administration have encouraged certain inhabitants of this Colony, to attempt, by every practicable measure, to oppose and to counteract, the virtuous efforts of America; these inhabitants, men of low degree among us, though of eminence in this new country; men, totally illiterate, though of common natural parts; men, endeavouring in this calamitous time, to rise in the world, by misleading their honest neighbours; men, who are by his Excellency the Governor, promised to be amply rewarded, for such an infamous conduct; *these men,* knowingly deceiving their neighbours, and wickedly selling their country, have practised every art, fraud, and misrepresentation to raise in this Colony an opposition to the voice of America.   To oppose this hellish plan, the honourable the Council of Safety for this Colony, commissioned the Reverend William Tennent and myself, to make a progress through the disturbed parts of this Colony; 'to explain to the people at large, the nature of the unhappy disputes, between Great Britain and the American Colonies.' Thousands heard, and believed us; they owned their full conviction; they expressed their concern, that they had been misled; and they most sincerely acceded to the Association, formed by the authority of our late Congress.   Such a proceeding, did not accord with the designs of these men, betrayers of their country; or the wishes of his Excellency the Governor, *who, by letters instigated them to strengthen their party.*   To prevent a farther defection, the leaders of the party resolved, by the din of arms, to drown the voice of reason.   For such an infernal purpose, by the instigation of Moses Kirkland, on or about the 29th of August last, men did assemble in arms, and with hostile intentions.   My immediately assembling, and marching with a part of the militia; caused these men, to disperse.   But now, other leaders of the same malignant party, correspondents of his Excellency the

Governor, have assembled men in arms, on the North side of Saluda River; who are now actually encamped *at a charge and expense, which his Excellency the Governor has promised to pay;* and these men, threaten to attack the troops under my orders. Wherefore, to prevent the effusion of civil bloodshed, I think it my duty to issue this Declaration; in order, *that I may leave no moderate step untried,* to recover a few of our unhappy countrymen from those delusions, by which, they have been drawn on, to lift their arms against their injured country, gloriously struggling to enjoy the rights of mankind.

" And whereas, his Excellency the Governor, has issued private directions, that all magistrates and militia officers, be required to take the oaths of allegiance, under the penalty of dismission from their several stations; I do hereby declare, that in point of law his Excellency has no authority to make such requisition from persons, *who have already sworn according to law,* when they were invested in offices civil and military: and, that it is not only highly unbecoming in his Majesty's representative to threaten his Majesty's subjects, in order to induce them to do things, *not warranted in law;* but, such a conduct, is of a most destructive tendency, to the good of the King's real service; inasmuch, as it tends to convince the people, that his Majesty's servants in high trust in America, as well as in Britain, *equally conspire,* to act without authority in law, to the destruction of their just rights and privileges.

" And whereas, the leaders of our unhappy and deceived countrymen, now assembled in arms against the liberties of America, have drawn them into this dangerous, and disgraceful situation, by filling their minds with fears and apprehensions, that their lives and properties are in danger from the designs of Congress, the honourable the Council of Safety, the General Committee, and the troops under my orders; because, they our said countrymen, have not acceded to our Association: wherefore, to remove all such ill-founded apprehensions, in the name of, and by the authority vested in me, by the honourable the Council of Safety, I solemnly declare, that all such apprehensions, are actually groundless. And I also declare, in the name of the Council of Safety, that our said unhappy and deceived countrymen, may in perfect safety of their lives, persons, and properties, repair to, and continue to dwell and abide at home, so long, as they shall choose to behave peaceably. We shudder even at the idea of distressing them, in any shape: we abhor the idea of compelling any person to associate with us; we only with sorrow declare, that any person who will not associate with, and aid and comfort us, in this arduous struggle for our liberties, cannot by us be considered as friendly to us: and therefore, that we cannot aid and comfort such person, by holding that intercourse and communication with such person, as is usually held between friends.

" And thus, having in the name of this Colony, declared the terms, upon which peace and safety may be had and enjoyed, by our unfortunate countrymen as aforesaid; it is my duty also to declare, that I shall march, and attack, as public enemies, all and every person in arms, or to be in arms, in this part of the Colony, in opposition to the measures of Congress; and having, with the utmost patience, and industry, gently endeavoured to persuade men to a peaceable conduct; I now, shall with equal patience and industry, prosecute military measures with the utmost vigour: and, I make no doubt, but that with the assistance of the Almighty, witness of our endeavours to avert the calamities of war, we shall speedily obtain

50

the wish of every virtuous American—peace, safety, and security to our rights.

> " Given under my hand, this 13th day of September, at the Camp, near Ninety-Six.
> "WILLIAM HENRY DRAYTON."

An official declaration like this, formally promulged, and backed by the support of a large body of troops, some of whom were Provincials; the whole well supplied, with the munitions of war ; made an impression upon the malecontents, and brought them to a pause. Hence, after consultation, they sent a deputation to the camp near Ninety-Six Court-House, to confer with Mr. Drayton: after which, Colonel Fletchall, and other malecontent leaders, arrived in his camp; with full powers to treat of, and conclude terms of pacification.   Before, however, we treat of this matter, and the terms which were obtained; it is necessary, we should understand with some precision, how far, Mr. Drayton was actually authorized by the Council of Safety, to act on so important an occasion.

When Mr. Drayton and Mr. Tennent commenced their progress from Charlestown, the powers, which had been given to them by the Council of Safety,* were of very general nature; as the obstacles which might arise on that progress, could not be so easily foreseen: and therefore, could not be so specially guarded against.   Mr. Drayton, however, being a member of the Council of Safety, well knew the principles of action of that body; and the manner in which his measures were likely to be supported by their votes.   He also knew, the commissions and instructions which he and Mr. Tennent had received,

* See Appendix to Chapter VIII. No. V.

were intended for their protection on the progress, and to frustrate any measures tending to insurrection; rather than, to authorize their taking such vigorous measures, as might lead to one. Beside which, the powers given them, by the Council of Safety, as expressed in their commissions, were jointly, and not severally. When, therefore, matters assumed such an aspect, as to threaten great commotions; Mr. Drayton perceived difficulties would occur, as well respecting the continuance of his authority, as the extent of it, in calling out the militia and Rangers; especially, if Mr. Tennent should have occasion to return to Charlestown: unless, some farther provision should be made in that respect, by some expression of opinion by the Council of Safety.

To obviate these difficulties, as well as to satisfy the scruples of his own mind, about assuming more authority than that with which he might really be invested; in the lengthy communication which he addressed to the Council from Lawson's Fork on the 21st of August, he touched on this subject: therein, stating, that he thought it adviseable after the progress should be finished, he ought to remain at Colonel Thomson's camp at Amelia, until he should see every spark of insurrection extinguished. He informed them therein, that if a dozen persons who were leaders and active characters, were to be allowed to continue at large, the progress of himself and Mr. Tennent, would have been in vain; and a civil war, would certainly be the consequence. That to be sure, an apprehension of such persons, would excite an insurrection of the disaffected people; but, nothing was to be feared from it, if met with prompt and vigorous measures. That, perhaps, his being arrived at Thomson's camp, on his return towards Charlestown, might be construed as an end of the powers, which had been given for the progress; or, Mr. Tennent's return to Charlestown, might have the same effect: on all which points, he requested the Council to instruct him clearly, and fully.

Upon an alarm from Georgia, that Kirkland was going against Augusta, the Council of Safety wrote Mr. Drayton, on the 11th of August, that on such an occasion, *they were perfectly satisfied he would leave nothing undone, that should appear to be necessary.* And it was by virtue of this letter, that he had collected an army against Kirkland, when he attempted about the end of August to proceed against Augusta. After Mr. Drayton had taken this decided and vigourous measure, partly on the above implied authority, and partly on his own responsibility, he received a letter from the Council of Safety, dated the 31st day of August, stating, " that they viewed with horror the spectacle of a civil war, and were not ashamed to own, that they could not hastily determine, upon measures which at first sight may promise to avert the calamity; but, which for aught they knew, might rush them upon the very danger, which they would wish to avoid. If," (said they,) " the removal of twelve active mischievous men, will really quash the growing opposition, that work may be easily accomplished; but, may not our enemy prove an hydra, and start twice as many heads to bring on their four thousand adherents, with fury, to rescue their first leaders, or to revenge their cause?" However, all things being considered, the Council in the same letter said that " from that confidence which they reposed in his wisdom and prudence, as well as from their certainty of his zeal for the welfare of this Colony—assuring themselves also, that he would premeditate every important step, and weigh probable consequences—they resolved, not only to vest in him, as they thereby did, all the powers and authorities, which were contained in their commissions to him, and the Reverend Mr. Tennent

jointly: but also, to enlarge those powers, by authorizing him, to put a stop to the proceedings of such evil-
minded persons, be they who they may, as are, or
shall be known, to be active in creating divisions
among the people, in order to disturb and destroy, that
harmony and unanimity, which is essential to the
cause of liberty and America, at this critical juncture:
and for more effectually enabling him to accomplish
that good and desireable end, he is thereby required
and empowered, to take every decisive step, and to use
every vigorous measure, which he may, or shall, deem
proper to promote the public service.   For which,
that should be his warrant." But when they heard
that Mr. Drayton was embodying troops against Kirkland, on the 5th of September, and, that the crisis had
arrived which required energy, they wrote to him,
" that they were not under the least doubt, of his
ability to defeat any plots, which Kirkland may have
concerted against Fort Charlotte or Augusta; and
since he had thus seriously entered upon a contest with
him, it became absolutely necessary to subdue him;
or, drive him out of the country. But they strongly
recommended to him, to discharge the militia, as soon
as he could possibly do it with safety; as such additional expense, would be very heavy on the treasury."

By these different communications from the Council
of Safety, Mr. Drayton now became sufficiently
authorized, to meet the business he had in hand; but,
while he found himself invested with powers; he was
sensible, of the responsible situation in which he was
placed. He was fully apprized by Mr. Arthur Middleton, one of the members of the Council of Safety,
and his confidential friend, of all the debates which
took place at that board, when the subject of increasing his powers was under consideration. He was
informed by Mr. Middleton, that the powers granted
him on the 31st of August, had been much debated in

the Council; and had been carried only *four* to *three;* which last, expatiated upon the " Danger of creating a civil war—young man—hot—rash—may raise the people, and set them to cutting one another's throats— decisive step, and vigourous measures, meant too much." In fine, Mr. Middleton informed Mr. Drayton, that two of the affirmatives were on the point of retracting; and that although he wished him to act with vigour for the public good, yet for his own sake " he could not but request him, to act with caution;" and for the public sake " to hurry down: as the Council were doing nothing, but repairing two or three bastions, to amuse the people."

Mr. Drayton well considered all these particulars. He said he was vested with full powers, but they had been acquired by a bare majority; who repented, almost as soon as they had consented. Any ill consequence, from any unforeseen accident—any check to his inferior army, who were strangers to him, and almost to each other—and a part of whom, were but lately disaffected—might be productive of the most dangerous consequences; all of which would be attributed to his (Mr. Drayton's) youth,* heat, and rashness. On the other hand, he considered, that if he could induce the enemy to enter into a pacification; expressly disavowing an intention of joining the King, or aiding his forces, or of designs inimical to the American proceedings; thereby contracting, that as they never did mean to aid or assist, or to join the British troops against the Congress, they never would do so directly or indirectly: and that if any of those described in the pacification, should by discourse reflect upon, or condemn, or by any conduct oppose the proceedings of the Congress—upon application they should be delivered up within a specified time; or

* Mr. Drayton was near thirty-three years of age, at this period.

afterwards should be liable, to be apprehended and proceeded against by the authority of Congress: Mr. Drayton thought, such terms signed and executed by themselves, would overthrow Governor Campbell's assurances to the King, that they were in opposition to the Congress; and, that the people were widely divided. It was also, his opinion, that such terms would create disunion among the chiefs: as those who were parties to and signed the pacification, would be obliged to support their own acts, against the clamours of those, who might think them too humiliating. Hence, the party being divided, the common people would be confused in their opinions; and would withdraw their confidence from their leaders, so thwarting and abusing each other: and thereby, the party would moulder away, and insensibly fall into the public measures. For these reasons, Mr. Drayton thought, he ought to grant Fletchall and his party, a neutrality; well knowing, that provided they only remained quiet, the public did not need their assistance.

This determination being formed, Mr. Drayton proceeded to carry his plan into execution with Colonel Fletchall, and the other leaders, who had arrived at his camp. And, a conference with them, eventuated in a treaty between the parties, which produced a pacification: and was respectively signed at Mr. Drayton's camp near Ninety-Six Court-House, on the sixteenth day of September 1775; the same being in the following words:

" *South-Carolina.*

" WHEREAS misunderstandings but too often precipitate men and friends into quarrels and bloodshed, which, but for such misunderstandings never could have happened: and whereas the present unhappy

disputes between Great Britain and North America
have unhappily occasioned uneasinesses between a
part of the people living between Broad and Saluda
Rivers and other adjacent parts, and the other inhabitants of the Colony aforesaid, from misunderstandings as aforesaid: inasmuch, as the said part of the
people as aforesaid, having tender consciences, declined to accede to the Association signed in Congress on
the fourth of June last; and the said other inhabitants,
thereby thinking, that the said declining to accede,
proceeded from principles and designs, in them the
said part of the people, inimical to the proceedings and
designs of the said other inhabitants; and that they,
the said part of the people, did mean to aid, assist, and
join, the British troops, if any should arrive in the
Colony aforesaid, during the present unhappy disputes
as aforesaid:

" And whereas, *these are all misunderstandings;*
and it being the sincere wish and desire of all parts of
the Colony, to live in peace and friendship with each
other; wherefore, for the clearing up the said misunderstandings, and for the manifestation of the wish
and desire aforesaid, Colonel Thomas Fletchall, Captain John Ford, Captain Thomas Greer, Captain Evan
M'Laurin, the Reverend Philip Mulkey, Mr. Robert
Merrick, and Captain Benjamin Wofford, Deputies
for, and sent by, the part of the people aforesaid, have
repaired to the camp of the Honourable William
Henry Drayton, Esquire, acting under the authority of
the Council of Safety for this Colony. And, for the
purposes aforesaid, it is hereby contracted, agreed, and
declared, by the Honourable William Henry Drayton,
in pursuance of powers vested in him by the Honourable the Council of Safety as aforesaid, on the one
part; and the Deputies aforesaid, in pursuance of
powers vested in them by the said part of the people,
on the other part:

" 1st. That the said declining of the part of the people aforesaid, to accede as aforesaid, did not proceed from any *ill,* or *even unfriendly principle or design*, in them the said part of the people, to or against the principles or designs of the Congress of this Colony, or authorities derived from that body; but proceeded only from a desire to abide in their usual peace, and tranquillity.

" 2d. That the said part of the people, *never did mean* to aid, assist, or join the British troops as aforesaid; and hereby it is declared, that if at any time during the present unhappy disputes between Great Britain and North America, any British troops shall or may arrive in this Colony, the Deputies aforesaid for themselves and the part of the people aforesaid, by whom, they the said Deputies are authorized, and whom they do represent, declare, that if any British troops as aforesaid, shall arrive as aforesaid, they the said Deputies and the part of the people aforesaid, shall not, *and will not, give, yield, or afford, directly or indirectly* to, or for, the use, advantage, or comfort, of the said British troops, or any part of them, *any aid*, or *assistance whatsoever;* or hold with them the said troops, or any part of them, any *communication*, or *correspondence.*

" 3d. That if at any time during the unhappy disputes as aforesaid, any person or persons of the part of the people aforesaid, shall by discourses or words reflect upon, censure, or condemn; or by any conduct oppose the proceedings of the Congress of this Colony, or authorities derived from them; the said Congress, the Council of Safety, or General Committee as the case may be, shall, without being deemed to give umbrage to the part of the people aforesaid, send to any of the Deputies aforesaid to make requisition that

51

any and every such person or persons as aforesaid, offending in any of the premises aforesaid against the proceedings of the Congress or authorities aforesaid, may and shall be delivered up to the authority of the Congress, or the tribunals under that authority, to be questioned and tried, and proceeded against, according to the mode of proceedings by authority of Congress; and if such person or persons as aforesaid be not delivered up as aforesaid, within fourteen days after requisition as aforesaid, then in such case, the Congress, or Council of Safety, or General Committee, may and shall be at liberty to use every means, to apprehend any, and every such person or persons as last aforesaid; and question, try, and proceed against as aforesaid, every such person or persons as aforesaid.

" 4th. That if any person or persons, who has or have signed, or shall sign the Association aforesaid, shall, without authority of Congress, molest any person or persons of the part of the people aforesaid; in such case, application shall be made to the said Congress, or Council of Safety, or General Committee, in order that such person or persons so molesting, be punished for, and restrained from, molesting as aforesaid.

" And it is hereby declared, that all and every person of the part of the people as aforesaid, not offending in, or against, any of the premises aforesaid, shall and may continue to dwell and remain at home as usual, safe in their lives, persons, and properties: such, being no more than what has been, and is the aim, intention, and inclination of the Congress of this Colony, and the authorities under that body. All persons, who shall not consider themselves as bound by this treaty, must abide by the consequences.

Done at the Camp, near Ninety-Six, this 16th day of September 1775.

	Signed,	Wm. Hy. Drayton,
Witness.		Tho. Fletchall,
Wm. Thomson,		John Ford,
Ely Kershaw,		Tho. Greer,
Francis Salvador.		Evan M Laurin,
		Benj. Wofford."

These things being done, Mr. Drayton on the 17th of September wrote a letter to the Council of Safety informing them of his proceedings; and transmitting therewith the original declaration and treaty, (*now in the possession of the writer of these Memoirs,*) and sundry other papers respecting the business, which he had in hand. In this letter to the Council of Safety, Mr. Drayton expressed his sentiments in the following manner: " But after all, I assure you our situation is utterly precarious while the Governor is at liberty. He animates these men: he tempts them: and although they are now recovered, yet their fidelity is precarious, if he is at liberty to jogg them again, and lay new toils for them. Gentlemen, allow me in the strongest terms to recommend, that you make hostages of the Governor and the officers. To do this, is not more dangerous to us, than what we have done. It will secure our safety; which otherwise, will be in danger. I would also recommend, that the trade with the country be opened; it, will give infinite satisfaction; it, will convince every person of the rectitude of our designs; it, will obliterate a distinction, which, now if permitted to remain will give Fletchall's people room to sell their patriotism, &c. to King's troops, and thus renew a communication: and indeed, if we will not trade with them, we cannot in conscience blame them for trading with those, who will trade with them. And this seems to correspond with the spirit of the resolution of the General Committee, August 23d, '*but also to give such assurances.*' &c. I am clearly of opinion, that upon the instrument of the 16th of September, such a relaxation might be grounded; I am persuaded, it will be attended with the most salutary consequences: and therefore, I do most heartily recommend, that it may be done. But above all things, I think it is my duty most strongly to represent, *that the Governor should be taken into custody.*

" I beg leave also to represent, that the declaration of the 13th and the instrument of the 16th instant, be not only printed generally in the gazettes, and in sheets to be immediately (by the Committee of Intelligence) circulated throughout the Colony, to give general notification thereof, which is greedily desired; and to prevent erroneous copies; but, that they be published in England for this reason—they will show, that no part of the people of this Colony are *even unfriendly* to the designs of Congress—that none of the people will encourage any person *even by word* to condemn our proceedings—that all offenders, shall be delivered up to punishment—that no part of the people will even hold communication with the King's troops. All this, will be in direct contradiction, to the Governor's representation of the meritorious conduct and zeal of Fletchall's people, for the King's service. And, for all this to appear, is of infinite importance; and infinitely preferable to our having put a part of those people to the sword; which, would not only have lain the foundation for lasting animosities; but would convince Administration, that the Governor's representations were true, that there was a strong party here against the Congress; all which, would invite them to send a strong body of troops here; and that very early."

The same was received by the Council in Charlestown on the 24th day of September; and on the 27th of the same month, Colonel Henry Laurens, the President of the Council of Safety, by order of the Council, wrote to Mr. Drayton, that, " On Sunday last, we received your letter of the 17th, together with the sundry papers, which you refer to; and if Captain Wilson is detained one day more, we will send by him the declaration and treaty, to be printed in London; but, shall defer a publication here, until we have an opportunity of considering the propriety of such a measure in your presence; which we suppose, will happen in the course of a few days."* It was in this manner, the public authorities at that time endeavoured to counteract in Great Britain, and with the Ministry, the official dispatches of Lord William Campbell, the Governor of South-Carolina; and with this view, the above declaration and treaty, were directed to be published in London; that, the Ministry might see upon what little grounds they had to rely, respecting information and assurances, from the Provincial Governor of South-Carolina.

After this treaty was executed, by which, the peace and harmony of the upper country was in a great measure restored, and settled, on a just and honorable basis; Colonel Fletchall and the rest of the Deputies, returned to their camp beyond Saluda River; where, the treaty which had been executed, was published and made known. Upon this, the principal associates who had remained in camp, disclaimed the pacification in great wrath; while those who had signed the treaty and their friends, maintained its propriety, and happy tendency. Hence, the consequence resulted, which Mr. Drayton had foreseen, *that they would be divided among themselves;* and the greater

---

* See this letter in Appendix to this Chapter, No. III.

part of the people, rejoiced in the event. The whole
camp, therefore, excepting Robert Cunningham and
about sixty of his followers, broke up immediately;
each man returning to his own home. Robert Cunningham and his sixty men, remained on the ground
some hours; but he was obliged to submit to the necessity of the case; and retired, declaring he was not
included in the treaty. When Mr. Drayton was informed of his conduct, he wrote him a letter on the
21st of September, with a view of drawing from him
an explicit declaration, which might authorize an
apprehension of his person according to the treaty;
and on the 6th of October he answered it, disclaiming
the pacification.*

These affairs being so adjusted, and Mr. Drayton
having no farther call for military support; on the
18th day of September, he discharged the troops
under his command, with thanks; the army then
being one thousand one hundred strong. And Major
Williamson was ordered to transmit suitable returns to
the Council of Safety, of the militia and volunteers
who served on the occasion; also a general return of
rations, monies disbursed, and necessaries found, for
the use of the army; which was done by Major Williamson under date of the 16th of October following.
And it is but justice to those patriotic troops, who had
come forth at their country's call, to say, that during
the whole time this army lay encamped near Ninety-
Six Court-House, they were patient under all the
difficulties and deprivations they experienced. During
the most of this time, their huts and dwellings were
penetrated by heavy rains; but discontent was not
seen among them; for, satisfied with the cause in
which they were engaged, and with the leaders who
commanded them, they submitted to such military

* See these letters in Appendix to this Chapter, No. IV.

regulations as the occasion required: in the camp, good order was observed; and without it, the advanced posts were duly and regularly stationed, and relieved.

The progress being now closed, in a different manner, to what many had supposed it would have been; Mr. Drayton proceeded from the camp to the Congaree Store, where the Good Warrior and other head men of the Cherokee Nation were in waiting for him, by his invitation. He there met them, on the 25th day of September; and explained to them in a talk* adapted to the occasion, the nature of the dispute between Great Britain and America; exhorting them to hold fast the chain of peace and friendship, with the people of this Colony; and assuring them, they should receive such supplies of ammunition and other articles, both for trade and comfort, as could be spared them by the Provincial Congress, or Council of Safety. He also made them presents, suitable to the occasion; after which, they took their leaves and returned home; apparently satisfied with their reception, and the information as to the cause of dispute between Great Britain and America, which they had received. These Indians were brought down from the nation by Richard Pearis, at the special desire of Mr. Drayton; and by a list furnished Mr. Drayton by Mr. Pearis it appears, the Cherokee Nation at that time, was composed of forty-three towns: nine of which, were Lower Towns—twenty-four of the Middle Settlements and Vallies—and ten, of the Overhill Settlements. And he calculated that the Lower Towns, could bring 356 warriors into the field—the Middle Settlements and Vallies, 908—and the Overhills, 757: amounting in the whole to 2021 warriors.† This account of Mr. Pearis', is supposed to be tolera-

---

ably correct; as it very much agrees both in numbers and names, with one to the same purport, furnished Lieutenant-Governor Bull in 1741, by the white Indian trader, James Maxwell; who had been sent to the nation by the Lieutenant-Governor.   Mr. Maxwell says, " In the Cherokee Nation, I find there is forty-seven towns; and from the best information I could get from the traders,

There is about 2,000 Gunmen.

And about   1,000 Boys, from the years of 12 to 15.

At least   4,000 Women—also abundance of children.

Total number 7,000 of the nation in 1741.*

Not to leave any thing undone, however, which his powers authorized him to perform, Mr. Drayton while at the Congaree Store, wrote on the 26th of September to Mr. Alexander Cameron, Deputy Superintendant in the Cherokee Nation, requesting him in the name of the Colony, to remove from the Cherokees, to whom he had retreated from Lochaber, his plantation on Little River in the Long-Cane Settlement: and holding out to him as examples for doing so, the retreat of his Excellency Lord William Campbell, Governor of the Province, and of his principal, the Honorable John Stuart, Superintendant of Indian Affairs.   To this letter Mr. Cameron, on the 16th of October replied, declaring that the chiefs of the Colony " can be under no apprehension of danger from him, or his connection with the Indians; if they were at liberty to enjoy peace and tranquillity where they were."   But, he nevertheless declared, that he must implicitly observe the direction and orders of his superiors; and could not recede from his post, without

* See South-Carolina Council *Indian Book*, vol. 9. page 64, where the names of the towns are also to be seen.

first obtaining their leave.   And as to "the great men (his Excellency Lord William Campbell, and the Hon. John Stuart, Esq.) whom you are pleased to mention to me, Sir, for the rule of my conduct; they, were very differently situated.   They were stationed among the most strenuous of the people, in the present quarrel; where they could not officiate any part of their duty, without censure; and run perhaps the risk of their lives to no end."   The above mentioned letter to Mr. Cameron, appears to have been the last official act, which Mr. Drayton thought existing circumstances required him to perform, in the continuance of his progress: after which, he hastened to Charlestown, to which Mr. Middleton and Mr. Timothy had urged his speedy return; for the purpose of giving his assistance in the council, to those important measures, which former procrastination, and existing necessity, now rendered absolutely necessary for the public security and welfare.*

* See Appendix, No. VII.

52

APPENDIX

CHAPTER IX.

———◆———

No. I.

To the Honorable Henry Laurens, Esq.

DEAR SIR,

WE expect to write you a public letter next Wednesday, but opportunity offering I must inform you, that after visiting the upper part of Col. Richardson's regiment, and the High Dutch in the Fork between Broad and Saluda Rivers, the former with great success, the latter with very little, we have at length visited the great and mighty nabob Fletchall. We found him surrounded by his court, viz. Cunningham, Brown, and Robinson, who watch all his motions, and have him under great command. We soon found the unchangeable malignity of their minds, and the inexpressible pains they are at, to blind the people, and fill them with bitterness against the Gentlemen, as they are called.

General Gage's pamphlet is raging through the District, and greedily read. The leaders have taken the same methods with the Romish Church, to keep the people ignorant; and in general they firmly believe that no man that comes from below, and that no paper printed there, can speak the truth. This was necessary in order to prevent any thing we can say, from taking place. We soon found that reasoning was vain with those, who were fixed by Royal emoluments; but perceiving that Fletchall affected to play between, we let him know that we had discovered things, which he thought were a profound secret; and surprized him much. He confessed receiving a letter from the Governor, within five days last; and offered to swear, there was no harm in it: and that he would not take arms against the country. But we surprized him into a promise to assemble the regiment, next Wednesday, which highly affronted Cunningham and the rest of the Upper House; some of whom treated us with insolence upon it. We expect to meet the regiment accordingly, and many of our friends whom I have advertised of it, will be there; some having intimated a design, to put some trick upon us.

In the mean time, Mr. Drayton has gone up to his iron works, and to the people about Lawson's Fork; where, he will do something. I turned my course into the New Acquisition, where I am to have a meeting from day to day, in Col. Neel's regiment; I think I shall fix this District, in the right cause. I discovered on my way a scheme to surprize Fort Charlotte, and take all the powder and arms away; took an affidavit of it, and sent it express to Mr. Drayton; so, hope it will be prevented. The Governor has undoubtedly given orders for it; and they are privately enlisting volunteers to the service. I shall this morning privately obtain affidavits to prove, that Major Robinson, has attempted to enlist many in the King's name; assuring them, that he had a number of commissions in his pocket, which should be distributed to the most worthy: and that they should have King's pay, after ten days. He is just returned, and it is known that he met the Governor at Dorchester. They think that they are nearly ripe, to show themselves; and make no scruple to threaten the whole province with devastation in a short time.

They say, that Cameron is among the Over-hill Cherokees, and will soon join them with three thousand gunmen. I have just heard, that the Lower Towns will not join them; but confess, that the Over-hill Indians are preparing to fight for the King. In short, your friends in town are preparing a great dish of blood for you; and expect soon, by their army not only to have an asylum to fly to, but to bear down all before them. This both you and I have prophesied many times; but a lethiferous slumber seems to have sealed the eyes of some of our brethren. Robinson assures the people here, that a great multitude in town of those who have signed the Association, are in the scheme, and will join them upon notice.

I am now convinced, that a certain affidavit which some have so much despised, is with a small exception true in every particular. There is here, all the appearance of an hellish plot; and the friends of America have no ammunition, and may be surprized without remedy: I wish the Council would think of this. We have greatly weakened, and expect more to weaken them; but, to overset the plan immediately, is impossible. I have formed one, and am forming in this district another troop, of volunteer Horse Rangers; who are as good as sworn to the Council of

Safety, when they enlist. We are hemming in the Dissidents on all sides, as much as possible; but their leaders seem determined if possible to bring the people to draw blood, before they have time to be enlightened. I have forsook my chaise, and ride on horseback from day to day, meeting people.

And in great haste, am, dear Sir,

Your most obt. servt.

WM. TENNENT.

Bullock's Creek, 20th Aug. 1775.

P. S. If you don't keep a look out, these people and the Savages will receive ammunition by waggons from town, or from Dorchester, from on board the fleet: they have no doubt of a supply.

—◆—

No. II.

South-Carolina, Ninety-Six District:

This day, personally appeared before me, Jonathan Clark, resident upon the banks of Saluda River, in the Cherokee country, who being duly sworn sayeth, that on or about the thirteenth instant, being in the Cherokee country aforesaid, he saw and conversed with John Garwick, an intimate friend and countryman of Alexander Cameron, Deputy Superintendant among the Cherokee Indians, touching the danger of the Cherokees commencing hostilities; that if there was any danger, he the said Jonathan might remove in time to a place of security: and that he spoke on this subject to the said John, because of his close connection with the said Alexander, and thereby of his, the said John's, ability to give information touching that subject.

That on this subject, the said John answered, that he, Jonathan, need not be under any apprehensions of danger, until such time as there should be some disturbances below, in the country, between the King's army and the Colonists: and, that then it would be high time for him, the said Jonathan, to take care of himself, and remove from the frontiers. Also, the said John continued his discourse and said, that about three weeks then last past, the said Alexander had held a meeting with the Cherokee Indians; at which, about four hundred of them were assembled; when he, the said John, heard the said Alexander tell the said Indians, that the people of America had used the King very ill; and had killed a considerable number of his army: and that the King was to send out more soldiers to suppress them. That the Indians ought not to turn against their father, meaning the King; but that they should join his army, against the people of America. That to this the Indians replied, they could not fight, for they had not any gun-powder; and the said Alexander returned, that should be no obstacle, for he would take care to supply them. The said John also further said, that the said Alexander did all he could to influence the said Indians to join the King's forces against the people of Carolina; and who could blame him for doing so, since he, the said Alexander, was in the King's service. Also, that in conclusion, about forty of the said Indians turning their backs to the said Alexander, discharged their guns; and then the whole assembly sat up the war-whoop; which he, the said John, said, was as a signal that they, the said Indians approved the discourse of the said Alexander, and agreed to what he had said. And further this deponent saith not.

JONATHAN CLARK.

Sworn and signed before me, this 21st day of August 1775.

Wm. Hy. Drayton, *Quorum Unus.*

South-Carolina, Ninety-Six District:

This day personally appeared before me James Wood, John Wood, Moses Wood, and John Prince, of the District aforesaid, who being severally sworn according to law, say, that they know the above-mentioned Jonathan Clark, believe him to be an honest man, and worthy of credit; and that they do not know any thing to the prejudice of his reputation. And further, the said deponents say not.

JAMES WOOD,
JOHN WOOD,
MOSES WOOD,
JOHN PRINCE.

Sworn and signed before me, this 21st day of August 1775.

Wm. Hy. Drayton, *Quorum Unus.*

—◆—

No. III.

Letter from Colonel Henry Laurens, President of the Council of Safety, to William Henry Drayton.

Charlestown, 27th September 1775.

Sir,

On Sunday last we received your letter of the 17th, together with the sundry papers which you refer to; and if Captain Wilson is detained one day more, we will send by him the declaration and treaty, to be printed in London;* but, shall defer a publication here, until we have an opportunity of considering the propriety of such a measure in your presence; which we suppose, will happen in the course of a few days.

The intelligence from the Cherokees received in Mr. Wilkinson's letter, is very alarming; we hope you have sent away the Good Warrior and his fellow travellers in good humour; and that they will influence their countrymen to remain quiet, and give us time to discover the perpetrators of the murder, intimated by Mr. Wilkinson—in the mean time, we trust that you have taken proper measures, for that purpose.

Le Despencer Packet arrived here from Falmouth, with advices from London to the 3d August. Accounts in brief are, that Administration were sending more troops and ships to America; determined to persevere in the execution of their plan. General Gage in his account of the Bunker Hill affair on the 17th June, transmitted to Lord Dartmouth, owns about 1056 of the King's troops killed and wounded: and his number of officers rather exceeds our early advices. We have heard nothing since the first of August, from our Delegates.

By order of the Council of Safety.

HENRY LAURENS, *President.*

The Hon. Wm. Hy. Drayton, Esq.
at the Camp, Ninety-Six.

---

* The Declaration and Treaty were published afterwards in London. See The London Remembrancer for 1776, Part I. pages 112 to 116.

No. IV.

Letter from William Henry Drayton to Robert Cun-
ningham.

SIR,

My only intention in coming into the country
was, to promote peace, and to ascertain whether there
were any people possessed of a disposition to run
counter to, and to oppose the efforts of America; and
to lift their arms against their country, their old acquaintances, and their friends and relations, in order to
assist British troops if any should arrive here.

It was therefore with the highest pleasure that on
the sixteenth instant, I, together with Col. Fletchall
and other gentlemen signed an instrument of writing,
fully clearing up all the particulars above mentioned.
As I cherish the best opinion of the honour of Colonel
Fletchall and the gentlemen who signed after him; so,
I persuade myself they will do all in their power to ex-
cute what they have contracted, as I shall do on my
part.

But, it was with concern that I have heard, that
you do not hold yourself as included in the above instrument of writing, and that you will not be bound
by it. I am sincerely inclined to believe, that these
are not your sentiments; I do most heartily wish, that
it will turn out the information is erroneous. I therefore, Sir, entreat, that you will as soon as may be,
favour me with an answer to this letter; assuring me
that you hold yourself as included in the above instrument of writing. Such a conduct in you, would give
me particular pleasure. But, that I may be under no
mistake, I am sorry to be under a necessity of saying,

53

that unless I shall be favoured by you as above, common sense will dictate to me, that you do not hold yourself as included in the above instrument of writing.   I am, Sir, your most obt. servt.
              WILLIAM HENRY DRAYTON.
Ninety-Six, Sept. 21st, 1775.

P. S. Mr. James Williams will convey to me, any letter you may think proper to favour me with.
To Robert Cunningham, Esq.

Answer to the foregoing letter, from Captain Robert Cunningham.

Sir,
        This day I received your letter dated the 21st of last month, desiring to know whether I considered myself as bound by the peace you made with Colonel Fletchall and the other gentlemen from our camp. I think, Sir, at this time the question is rather unfair; however, as it always was my determination not to deceive either party, I must confess I do not hold with that peace.   At the same time, as fond of peace as any man; but, upon honorable terms.   But, according to my principles, that peace is false and disgraceful from beginning to ending.   It appears to me, Sir, you had all the bargain making to yourself; and if that was the case, I expected you would acted with more honour, than taken the advantage of men (as I believe) half scared out of their senses, at the sight of liberty caps, and sound of cannon; as seeing and hearing, has generally more influence on some men, than reason.
        I am, Sir, your most hum. servt.
              ROBT. CUNNINGHAM.

Page's Creek, Oct. 6th, 1775.

The Hon. William Henry Drayton, Esq.
Per Mr. James Williams.

No. V.

*A TALK from the Honorable William Henry Dray-
ton, Esq. one of the beloved men of South-Carolina,
to the beloved men, Head Men, and Warriors of the
Cherokee Nation, at the Congarees, Sept. 25, 1775.*

Friends, and Brother Warriors,—I take you by the
hand, in witness, of the peace and friendship which
has so long subsisted between your brothers the White
People of this country, and you and your people—and,
I hold your hand fast, in testimony, that your brothers
the white people wish, that our peace and friendship
with you and your people may continue.

I sent a talk to you in your nation, to desire that
you would come to see me at the Congarees, in order
that we might talk together face to face. When I
sent to you, I thought to have been here, before you
could have arrived; but, some of our people did not
understand the things, about which I intend to speak
to you; and to explain which to them I came into the
country; my stay among those people was therefore
longer, than I expected. This being the case, I make
no doubt but that you will readily excuse my absence,
which I assure you, was as disagreeable to myself, as
it could possibly be to you.

I sent to you, to come to me, that I might explain to
you, the causes of the unhappy quarrel between a part
of the people in Great Britain, and your brothers the
white people living in America. Also, that I might
tell you, why our people have put on their Shot
pouches, and hold their Rifles in their hands.

The causes of this unhappy quarrel are very plain,
as you will see as I go on with my talk; but, in order

that you may see them, and understand them, clearly, I must first talk of the time before any of our white people came to this country, and, what was then done.

Before our forefathers left England, they made an agreement with the Great King; that when they came to America, they and their children after them, should then continue to have and enjoy the same rights and privileges, that the people of England, who you know were their own brothers, did actually enjoy. And, to this agreement, the Great King put his hand and seal; and declared, that all the Great Kings after him, should be bound by the agreement he had made.

Now, in consequence of this agreement, your brothers the white people in America say, the money they have in their pockets is their own; and the Great King has no right whatsoever to send or to order any officers to take this money or any part of it out of our pockets, or to make any laws to bind us, but by our own consent, given by our wise men whom we ourselves elect and appoint to make laws for us. And we say so, for this plain and good reason; because, the Great King has no right to send any officers to take any money out of the pockets of our brothers the people of England, or to bind them by any laws, but by their own consent given by their wise men, whom they themselves elect and appoint to make laws for them. For, as this is the right and priviledge of our brothers in England, so, this agreement declares we have the same right and priviledge.

But, notwithstanding these things, the men about the Great King, have persuaded him, that he and the men in England whom we never elected and appointed to make laws for us, have a right to take our money, out of our pockets without our consent, and to make laws to drag us away from our own country,

across the Great Water; and all this, without asking
us any thing about the matter, and violently against
our consent and good liking. And, unjust and wicked
as all this is, yet this is not the worst part of their
usage to us. They have by other laws broken our
agreement in whatever particular part they pleased;
and these men about the Great King, have so teazed
and persuaded him, that the Great King and the men
in England, whom as I told you before, we never appointed to make laws for us, have made one law,
which says, the Great King and those men, have a
right to bind us by laws of their making, in all cases
whatsoever: which is as much as to say, they have a
right to treat us and every thing belonging to us, just as
they please. And this you know is as much as to say,
they have a right to take all our money, all our lands,
all our cattle and horses and such things; and not only
all such things, but our wives and children, in order to
make servants of them; and, beside all these things,
to put us in strong-houses,* and to put us to death,
whenever they please.

Friends and Brother Warriors,—is it not now as
plain as the sight at the end of your rifles, that these
laws and proceedings are like so many hatchets, chop-
ping our agreement to pieces? Are not these, unjust
things? Enough, to make us put on our shot pouches
—and especially, when we find, that our brothers over
the Great Water, will not only not hearken to the
many good talks which we have sent them about these
matters; but have really sent over people to take the
hatchet up against us.

Oh, my *Brother Warriors*, it is a lamentable thing,
that our brothers beyond the Great Water, should use
us in this cruel manner. If they use us, their own

* Among Indians, *strong-houses*, mean Prisons

flesh and blood, in this unjust way, what must you
expect—you, who are Red People—you, whom they
never saw—you, whom they know only, by the hearing of the ear—you, who have fine lands? You see,
by their treatment to us, that agreements even under
hand and seal go as nothing with them. Think of
these things, my friends, and reflect upon them, day
and night.

Having told you, that the men about the Great King
persuaded him, that he and the men in England have
a right to take our money out of our pockets, without
our consent; I must now tell you the contrivances
they have fallen upon to take this money, whether we
will or not. In order to take this money from us,
they have ordered that we must pay a duty upon this
and that thing, that we are accustomed to purchase;
which is as much as to say, that upon those things we
purchase, we must pay to the Great King against our
consent, a sum of money above the real value of those
things. And in particular, they ordered that if we
drink tea, we must pay so much money to the Great
King. I must tell you, this tea is somewhat like your
Black-Drink. But, as we know, that this order is
contrary to our agreement; and also, as we know the
evil consequences of our paying this money; so, your
brothers the white people in America have resolved
that they will not pay it. And, therefore, the men
about the Great King have persuaded him to send soldiers to Boston, and we are told some are coming here,
to force the people here to give their money without
their consent; and thereby to give up their rights and
privileges, which are mentioned in the agreement.

Some foolish people, say it is better to pay this
money for the tea, than to go to war about it. But I
tell you, it is not about this money alone that we
quarrel; for the money itself, we do not regard as two

corn stalks: but, we are afraid bad consequences will
follow, if we pay the money; as I will show you directly.

We find that the men in England talk among themselves, that they intend to make us in America pay to
them, a great sum of money every year. The way
they intend to raise this money, is as I have told you
already, by making us pay a duty upon this and that
thing, that we are accustomed to purchase. Now,
this duty upon tea, brings in but a very small part of
that great sum of money they want to make us pay to
them; and therefore, we refuse to pay this money for
the tea; lest if we paid it, they would be encouraged
to go on time after time, to lay duties upon a great
many other things, which we are accustomed to purchase; in order, that they may at last get from us, that
great sum of money which they want, and which perhaps, is all we have. By which means, as your brothers the white people will be obliged to give more
money than usual, for those blankets, strouds, checks,
linens, guns, powder, paint, and rum with which you
are supplied; so, if money is thus taken out of our
pockets without our consent, and against our agreement, it is plain and certain, that you and your people
must pay two and three deer skins for those goods,
which you used to purchase of the traders for one
deer skin. And thus you see, that we do not quarrel
only upon our own account; but that we have put on
our shot pouches, not only to preserve our money, but
also, to preserve your deer skins.

Friends and Brother Warriors, I have now told you
the causes of our unhappy quarrel with the men over
the Great Water. I hope your eyes are now opened,
and that you see plainly, that your interest is as much
concerned in this quarrel, as our interest. And that
you also see, that we have put on our shot pouches,

and have taken up our rifles, only, to defend our rights and privileges according to the agreement; and by so doing, to defend your deer skins against those, who wish to rob you of them.

Therefore, as your people and our people, were born upon, and live in, the same land—as we are old acquaintances, and have thereby contracted a regard for each other—as our interest in this quarrel, is the same; for the men over the Great Water cannot take our money against our consent, without taking your deer skins also—as you see, that no agreement is kept with us, so you cannot expect to be better treated by men, who want all that you and ourselves have—I say, as all these things show you, that if we are hurt, you must be hurt also—if we lose, you must lose also —so, I tell you in time, that you and ourselves ought to join together, in order to save all of us from being hurt, or from losing, or from falling. Let us, there-fore, exert ourselves, you at your end of the chain of peace, and we at our end: in order, that we may keep this chain bright and shining. So, shall we act to each other like brothers—so, shall we be able to sup-port and assist each other, against our common ene-mies—so, shall we be able, to stand together in perfect safety, against those evil men; who in the end mean to ruin you, as well as ourselves who are their own flesh and blood.

I am informed, that you have been told, that your brothers the white people in Charlestown, used you ill, when t ey seized some ammunition which your traders intended to have sent you. It is true, my friends, that we did seize this ammunition; and I tell you, that your brothers the white people seized it with great concern; because, they knew their seizing it would in some degree distress you. But I tell you also, the men about the Great King, are the only per-

sons to be blamed in this affair; for, as we found that
these men persuaded the Great King to send soldiers
against us, and to stop all kinds of ammunition from
coming to us as usual, in order that we should not be
able to defend ourselves; so, these men about the
Great King, by this proceeding compelled us to seize
such ammunition for our defence, as came among us
by accident: and accordingly, we greedily seized the
ammunition that was intended for your hunting, in
order, to have in our hands the means of defending
our lives, our money, and your deer skins, as I told
you before, against our oppressors. And this behaviour of ours, was so natural and just, that we knew
that when we came to talk to you on the matter, you
would think we did nothing but what was just—and,
what you would have done, had you been in our situation. However, the ammunition that was seized,
was intended to be sold to you; but, to show you that
we regard you as brothers, we intend to make you a
present of some. We wish, we were able to give you
as much as your occasions require: but, as the Great
King has so ordered it, that we cannot get much for
ourselves, and as we expect to fight our enemies;
therefore, we cannot afford to give you much of what
we have. I know your good sense will inform you,
that this is perfectly reasonable: and, that we ought
not to give away so much ammunition, as would leave
us, and you also, exposed to enemies, *who*, as I told
you before, *cannot hurt us, without hurting you also.*

It is a concern to us when we reflect, that the present quarrel occasions a scarcity of goods in your nation. But goods are scarce with us also; and we
submit to this inconvenience cheerfully, rather than
purchase those goods; which if we did purchase, would
strengthen the hands of our oppressors against us.
We hope, our example will encourage you, to suffer
this scarcity as patiently as we do. When the public

54

peace shall be restored, by our rights and privileges being restored to us; and when we can purchase goods without any risk of paying for them more, than they are worth, by paying duties upon them contrary to our consent, contrary to our agreement, and contrary to our, and to your interest; then, will you and your children after you, be plentifully supplied again, as usual. In the mean time, we advise you to be patient; and to show you, that we look upon you as brothers; and that we will give you all the friendly aid, assistance, and supplies in our power—I say, as a token of this, I take the coat off my own back, and I give it to you. For my part, in this unhappy time, I will be content to wear an Osnaburg split-shirt.*

I hear that one of your people has lately been killed, and that two others were at the same time wounded, by some of the white people on the ceded lands in Georgia. I feel great grief at this news. Mr. Wilkinson is just come from Essenecca, and has brought me a talk from the Warriors and Head Men, who were nine days ago assembled at that town in council upon the occasion of this bad news. In this talk, the Warrior Sawney says, he and the other Warriors remember, that in the last treaty of peace it was agreed, that if any white man should be killed by their people, the perpetrators of the murder should be put to death; and that the same satisfaction should be given by the white people, in case one of your people should be murdered by ours. Sawney also says, that the War-

* *Split-shirts*, were worn very much by the people of the upper country at that time. They were ornamentally made, and were *split*, or *open before;* hence their name: and were worn in summer as coats are, over other dress. Mr. Drayton thought proper to adapt his dress to the customs of the people he was among; and when he finished his progress and returned to Charlestown, he wore his split-shirt at particular times; which introduced it in some measure in the lower parts of the colony, at a time, when merchandize was scarce, and economy desirable.

riors and beloved men will wait to see if this will be
complied with or not; and in the mean time they will
not think of resentment, or of saying any thing to
lessen our friendship. The Warrior Chenesto, also
sends a good talk, and says he does not desire to break
the line of friendship, which the beloved men who are
dead and gone, drew between us. These talks sound
well in my ears; and in return to these good talks, I
tell you, that this matter shall with all possible speed
be inquired into; and, if the white people have done
wrong, and, without provocation, have killed your
countryman, you may be assured that those white people who were concerned in such a wicked and black
affair, shall be punished; and thereby, your people
will have satisfaction according to the treaty. I desire
you will tell the relations of the poor man who has
been killed, how much I am concerned at their loss.
I am told that he has left a widow, and children: I
give these presents, and I desire you will carry them
to the unfortunate widow; in order to show her, that
all the white people in this country pity her misfortune.

Friends and Brother Warriors,—this talk I give to
you, as a talk of peace and friendship—as a talk to
open your eyes—and as a good talk, from all the beloved men and white people of this country, to you
and your beloved men, and all the red men of your
nation. I give you this talk, as so much oil to keep
the chain of peace and friendship between us bright,
and shining, like the sun. And, as in the corn-plant-
ing season, the sun warms the earth, and makes the
corn to sprout and to grow for the good of the people;
so, I hope this talk will warm your hearts; and make
thoughts of friendship and good will sprout and grow
in you and your people, for the mutual good of our
people, and of your nation.

No. VI.

A List of the Names, and Numbers of Towns; also, the Number of Men in the Cherokee Nation: as furnished William Henry Drayton in 1775, by Richard Pearis.

LOWER TOWNS.		Men.	MIDDLE SETTLEMENTS AND VALLIES.		Men.	OVER-HILLS.		Men.
Estatoe,	-	40	Little Highwassy,		12	Chilkowee,	-	120
Qualache,	-	30	Chaneusay,	-	50	Settaco,	-	160
Toxaway,	-	51	Cutolope,	-	12	Chota,	-	100
Sugar-Town,	-	29	Kewone,	-	30	Island,	-	200
Socauny,	-	26	Nottelly,	-	25	Toco,	-	40
Esseneca,	-	80	Little Tellico,	-	12	Tuskege,	-	12
Cheowee,	-	29	Noewee,	-	50	Mouth of the River,		40
Tugelow,	-	30	Temotly,	-	50	Nachy Creek,	-	15
Little Chota,	-	41	Burning-Town,	-	30	Tellico,	-	30
		——	Little Chota,	-	60	Highwassy,	-	40
		356	Nacutche,	-	30			——
		——	Callugojoy,	-	10			757
			Cewecutrie,		10			——
			Cheowee,	-	15			
			Fork of River,		12			
			Cowee,	-	100			
			Joree,	-	50			
			Wottogo,	-	40			
			Nucesy,	-	60			
			Noewee,	-	60			
			Cheowee,	-	100			
			Cannowca,	-	15			
			Econewrighty,		45			
					——			
			Middle Settlements and Vallies,		908			
			Lower Towns,	- -	356			
			Over-Hills,	- - -	757			
					——			
			Total, Cherokee Men,	-	2021			
					——			

☞ In the above list, some towns appear to be twice or thrice mentioned; but as it was copied from the original document, no attempts have been made to reconcile any irregularities. The same observation will apply, as to the numbers of men.

No. VII.

Letter from Henry Laurens, President of the Council of Safety, to William Henry Drayton.

Charlestown, 21st September 1775.

SIR,

We refer to our last, dated the 15th, by your messenger from Ninety-Six, which we hope has reached you; and that you are now on your way to meet those Indians, who, led by Captain Pearis, came from the Cherokees at your command: and who have, in the utmost anxiety and impatience, been many days waiting for you.

We have several copies of intercepted letters from the Superintendant, at St. Augustine, to his Agents in the nation; they look so much like design to amuse us, that we hold it unnecessary to trouble you with them: but, since you have entered upon that branch, a caution against every stratagem may not be unnecessary. Pearis applies for a commission, to the Good Warrior; if one is granted, it must be special: and you will be the best judge of the necessary terms—we have therefore, referred him to you.

Col. Wofford has likewise applied for commissions, in order to erect a whole regiment in the Colony's service, from Fletchall's District. For that purpose, we send you thirty-four, signed by us; and blanks left, for you to fill up. You will keep a copy of the names of officers, &c. as formerly directed.

We are called together, by an alarming account, which threatens the destruction of this town by three frigates and a bomb ketch; we hope it may prove a groundless report: but, it becomes us to act instantly, as if it was real. We shall be glad to hear, that you have established peace and quietness on our backs; and of your outset for Charlestown, as soon as possible after, as you please.

By order of the Council.

HENRY LAURENS, *President.*

The Hon. William Henry Drayton, Esq.
Head-Quarters, Ninety-Six.

END OF VOL. I.